THE NATIONALISTS OF NORTHERN IRELAND

For my parents,
Kathleen and Des,
and in memory of my grandmother,
Mary Delia Staunton

Enda Staunton

The Nationalists of Northern Ireland 1918-1973

the columba press

First published in 2001 by
the columba press
55A Spruce Avenue, Stillorgan Industrial Park,
Blackrock, Co Dublin

Cover by Bill Bolger
Origination by The Columba Press
Printed in Ireland by ColourBooks Ltd, Dublin

ISBN 1 85607 328 9

Contents

Acknowledgements

It would not be possible for me to list all of those who helped bring this project to conclusion, but it behoves me to attempt to include as many as possible. Firstly I want to thank the supervisor of my doctoral thesis, Professor Paul Bew, for his helpfulness and support throughout. The staff at all of the following locations deserve the highest praise: In Dublin, the National Archives and National Library, the UCD, Trinity and Department of Defence archives and the Franciscan Archive, Killiney; in Belfast, the Public Records Office, the Central and Linenhall Libraries, Queen's University and the University of Ulster; in Armagh, Marlene at Ara Coeli, and David Sheehy at the Dublin Diocesan Archive.

This work would not have been possible without privileged access to private papers. I would like to express my gratitude to the donor of the Cahir Healy papers for allowing me to peruse the entire collection, and to the donor of the J. H. Collins and the Fred Crawford Papers for permitting similar access. I cannot say enough in this regard about the kindness and helpfulness of the family of the late Eddie McAteer MP in Derry city, who facilitated me in every way in examining their father's papers and clarifying matters for me about his life and work. I wish to offer a sincere and heartfelt thanks to Eddie's sons Fergus, Sean, Hugh and Brian, and his daughters Gráinne and Síle, not least for the excellent photographic collection which they put at my disposal and which now graces this book. On the subject of photographs, thanks are also due to Noreen Cunningham at Newry Museum for permission to reproduce illustrations from its developing collection, to Armagh Museum for similar permission, to Dr Patricia McClean and Dr Vivienne Pollock at the Ulster Museum, Belfast, and to the National Photographic Archive, Temple Bar, Dublin.

A special thank you to all of those who, in the course of discussion or correspondence with me, helped broaden my understanding, often offering guidance as to source material. These include James Kelly, the veteran Belfast journalist, Andrew Boyd, Barry and Brenda Bruton, the late Jack Macgougan and Paddy Devlin, Patrick Marrinan, Richard MacAuley, Phelim Campbell, Claire Fitzpatrick, Jack Myers and 'Sean Fox', Jack Mulvenna and Mícheál Ó Cuinneagáin. Thanks also to Michael and to Yvonne Murphy in Belfast's two main libraries.

The task of typing the various thesis drafts was a difficult one for which I am indebted to Pamela, Regina, Gerry, Marita Jaschob and the late Betty Donnelly. Subsequent work was done for me by Deirdre and Madeleine to whom I am also extremely grateful. A particular debt of gratitude is due to Grace O'Malley for her meticulous and painstaking retyping of the entire recast manuscript into book form.

Last, but not least, I wish to record my debt to my family, both to my sisters Ethna and Evelyn and to my parents, to whom it is fitting that I dedicate this book.

Introduction

The two centuries following the plantation of Ulster had confirmed the position of the Roman Catholic population as the poorest economic group in the province.[1] The hemmed in situation of northern Catholics, the weakness of their middle class and the consequently disproportionate clerical influence left them strongly insulated from trends in the rest of Ireland.[2] The O'Connellite era had strengthened the role of the Catholic clergy as the community elite and correspondingly weakened the influence of Ribbonism – a hangover from the agrarianism and communalism of the 1700s with echoes of the dispossessions of the century before.

By the 1850s a pattern had clearly established itself across rural Ulster whereby Catholics, both those qualified to vote and the unfranchised majority, joined forces with Presbyterians to support Liberal candidates against their Episcopalian Tory rivals.

The Fenian movement in the 1860s had little impact there, despite displays of sympathy for the later Amnesty movement, and the Home Government Association developing in its wake signally failed in Ulster to match its electoral development in the remainder of the country. When the 1880 general election established the hegemony of the new Home Rule organisation in the other three provinces, in the north it resulted in the return of only two MPs.

Within the next half decade the picture changed dramatically under the impact of a Land League struggle linked to the Home Rule movement and the increasing defection of Roman Catholic clergy from a liberalism they perceived as unreliable on the education question. Gradually the Catholic/Presbyterian/liberal alliance began to fracture, the gap widening in direct proportion to the advance of the Home Rule movement in the province following its 1883 decision to extend its organisation there.

In the space of two years the intercommunal co-operation

which characterised the early phase of Michael Davitt's Land
League in the region had become merely a memory, the elections of 1885 and 1886 confirming for all times the replacement
of the Liberal Party by the National League in Catholic Ulster
and the increasingly dominant role of clergy in the new order.[3]
Politics in the north were cast in the denominational mould
which has characterised them ever since. Nowhere was this divide more pronounced than in the city which had come to dominate the province, Belfast. From a backwater bypassed by the
main routes southwards in the 1730s, its record since had been
one of growth, modestly at first in the late eighteenth century
and then spectacularly throughout the nineteen hundreds as
part of Britain's Industrial Revolution. Labour flooded into this
economic powerhouse from its rural hinterland and farther
afield. By the 1850s its population had topped the 100,000 mark,
an increase of more than fivefold. Forty years later, with more
than a quarter of a million inhabitants, it had outstripped Dublin
as the country's most populous city. The Catholic presence within
this metropolis had undergone a parallel expansion. A little over
1,000 strong in the 1780s, it had increased to more than 4,000
during the early 1800s, surging in the succeeding decades to a
peak of almost 85,000 by the start of the new century. From the
1820s onwards a pattern had been established within this community of enclave existence, clerical leadership and friction with
the Protestant majority erupting into savage sectarian rioting in
every decade from the 1830s onwards. Not surprisingly it was
there that the alliance with non-Catholic liberalism first began to
fracture. Whereas in 1841, at the laying of the foundation stone
for St Malachy's church, the liberal Protestants of Belfast had
been the subject of a toast for their contribution, by the 1860s
Bishop Patrick Dorrian was complaining of 'too much
Presbyterianism' as he moved to stifle manifestations of independence within his flock. In 1877 disillusionment with liberalism's record on the educational question led him to throw his
weight behind the conservative candidate, Lord Castlereagh, in
a by-election. When Parnell decided to bring Ulster within the
fold of the new movement, Catholic West Belfast proved receptive, the Home Ruler, Thomas Sexton, gaining a seat in 1886 having
been defeated by fewer than forty votes the previous year.[4]

The death of Parnell and the defeat of his followers left mainstream nationalism top-heavy with Catholic Church personnel,

a feature most profoundly marked in Ulster. A survey of the 139 northern branches of the Irish National Foresters (the benefit society most closely linked to the Home Rule Party) listed 123 of them as 'under clerical control'.[5] Not surprisingly Parnellism was unable to put down roots in nationalist Ulster and with the defection of T. M. Healy, the deposed leader's most vituperative enemy, from the official movement, the support of at least two northern bishops – McKenna of Clogher and Henry of Down and Connor – went with him in support of his clericalist project. This latter individual through his Catholic Representation Association (CRA), formed in 1896 for the protection and advancement of Catholic interests, congregational and general, mobilised the better-off Belfast nationalists and successfully kept the Home Rule Party at bay in the city. Though his control seemed unshakeable, events in the wider society were running against him. In 1900 the sundered Irish Parliamentary Party had reunited with hierarchical approval, opening the way for the rise in Catholic Belfast of the man who was to dominate its life through many vicissitudes for more than three decades.

Joe Devlin was born in Hamill Street near the city centre, the son of a cab driver. Despite little formal education he had perfected his writing and debating skills to become by his mid-twenties a leading figure in the political life of his community. In the late 1890s he had broken from the CRA and aligned himself with the emergent national movement, gaining election as Home Rule MP for North Kilkenny in 1902. In Belfast infighting continued between his party and Henry's organisation, ending with the latter's defeat and the dissolution of the CRA. Devlin's election as Home Rule MP for West Belfast in 1906 crowned his role as the city's nationalist supremo and symbolised the new dispensation.[6] Devlin's support was a coat of many political colours and the catch all nature of his approach reflected this. His largely working class electorate he satisfied with a welfarist programme which championed progressive legislation. The Vintners Association and other conservative proprietors, the backbone of his organisation as they had earlier been of Henry's, could rest assured that his demands went no further than this and were counterbalanced by a passionate hostility to both socialism and a commitment to Ireland's place as a self governing entity within the British empire. The Devlinite party organ, the *Northern Star*, right wing, sectarian and pro-business in tone, provided succour to nationalists of this stamp. Nothing better epitomised the contradictions in Devlin's outlook than his response to the 1907 dock strike in the city. Having stayed aloof from the crisis for more than two months he appeared on a platform in support of the strikers only when the deployment of British troops, following a police mutiny, enabled him to address the issue in national rather than class terms. Later, when passions had cooled (his intervention having further inflamed them), he dissociated himself from the strikes organiser James Larkin and condemned his politics.[7]

With Devlin's dominion came a new image role for a secret organisation of which he had long been a member, a body which the Fenian John O Leary had described as 'having nothing in common with the republican movement but illegality'. This was the Ancient Order of Hibernians, a Catholic defence group with origins traceable to the seventeenth century. Often dismissed as the mirror image of the Orange Order, it was sectarian, conservative and oath-bound in character. Repudiated by the Catholic Church for this latter feature, it was, in 1892, placed under a ban of the Holy Office. The previous year the Dublin Castle authorities had pooh-poohed this (largely Parnellite) body as 'scarcely worth considering' but added the important caveat that 'in the hands of clever and designing leaders' it 'might even become dangerous'. Such a man had now appeared on the scene in a city where the Order had traditionally been weakest. The change in its image and its fortunes were not long in coming. In July1905, when Devlin took over as National President of its Irish section (the American one had split from it earlier), he purged it of republican sympathisers (the American section has ever since acted as a magnet for them), and inaugurated a new constitution.[8] That same year, thanks to the good offices of his friend Cardinal O'Donnell, the papal condemnation was lifted and the organisation never looked back. Registered as a Friendly Society it became an arm of the Home Rule movement so widespread in Ulster as to be almost synonymous with it. As the figures show, the organisation enjoyed a strength in that province unrivalled in any other part of Ireland: in 1911 there were 85 divisions of the AOH in Tyrone, 72 in Donegal, 51 in Derry, 50 in Down, 35 in Antrim, 44 in Fermanagh, 39 in Armagh, 24 in Cavan and 23 in Monaghan. By contrast, in the neighbouring province of Connacht, Leitrim had 38, Roscommon 15, Sligo 4, Mayo 3 and Galway 2.[9]

Militant republicanism remained a tender plant in the north and was to become even weaker in the aftermath of the Parnellite split in which it championed the deposed 'Chief'. A police report of January 1891 recorded the Irish Republican Brotherhood as 'almost non-existent' in counties Antrim, Donegal, Down and Tyrone, 'very disorganised' in counties Armagh, Derry, Fermanagh and Louth, 'practically dead' in Armagh and 'showing no signs of life' in Fermanagh. Even the southern part of County Down and the Armagh borderlands, 'long a stronghold of Ribbonism' and anti-state activity, had changed considerably. In particular a notorious government show trial of 1883 on the charge of 'Treason Felony' (later to achieve infamy as the Crossmaglen Conspiracy Case) had 'greatly alarmed' the 'secret society men of the county' as the convictions resulted from one of their number breaking the region's code of silence and turning Queen's evidence.[10]

With the dawn of the new century, the separatist tradition underwent a revival of sorts through the formation of the literary, semi-political and patriotic Dungannon Clubs by Sean McDermott, a native of Leitrim. Named after the 1782 Dungannon Volunteer Convention, they had little impact outside of County Tyrone. McDermott had been inducted into the IRB by Denis McCullough of Belfast, a rising star in the organisation who had earlier sworn in the Quaker, Bulmer Hobson.

Those three, together with Patrick McCartan, founder of a Dungannon Club in his native Carrickmore, became the leading lights of republicanism in the province. As Arthur Griffith's Sinn Féin movement developed between 1905 and 1908, these clubs were subsumed into it, Hobson becoming Vice-President of the movement in 1907.[11] Because the Griffith movement advocated a dual monarchy on the Hungarian model and proposed protectionist measures to develop Irish trade and industry, the gap was not great between it and the radical wing of the IPP at Westminister, to which Devlin belonged. Recognising this, the latter wrote to John Dillon shortly before Christmas 1907 suggesting the 'making of a strong appeal to the Sinn Féin crowd to come into the movement' as their presence there would bring it 'added strength and power' and their ideals stood a greater chance of being realised inside rather than outside the IPP. The only point on which they differed, 'the retention of the Irish members at Westminster', might be waived, provided that 'the party members would pledge themselves to devote themselves during the parliamentary recess – to all the practical objects contained in the Sinn Féin programme'. It was Devlin's opinion that the Sinn Féiners should be met in every way possible.[12] He also sounded out this idea through John D. Nugent, the National Secretary of the AOH, who promised him an article on the subject in the Order's journal, *The Hibernian*.

Although Dillon shared the same populist wing of the party as Devlin, the proposal does not seem to have won his approval and nothing further was heard of it. The IPP, riding high as a government in waiting, could afford to ignore rivals. The 1912 introduction of the Third Home Rule Bill, no longer subject to the House of Lords veto was the party's finest hour, but as in 1886 and 1893 unionist opposition mounted.

While the Bill was going through its committee stage at Westminster, mass expulsions of Catholics from the Belfast shipyards took place against the backdrop of 12 July celebrations. On the streets loyalism mobilised. An Ulster Solemn League and Covenant was signed by over 200,000 people on 28 September. Four days previously a Provisional Government had been formed by the Ulster Unionist Council with Carson, Craig and Lord Londonderry among its executive members. Fortified by the support of Bonar Law and the conservatives at Westminster, the 'government' organised the importation of arms at Larne, an action paralleled on the nationalist side two months later. Militarisation had been introduced into Irish politics. Something else had been introduced earlier, first in a speech by Thomas Agar-Roberts during the Second Reading of the Home Rule Bill, the idea of Partition. In March 1914, with the need to placate 'Ulster' high on their agenda, Lloyd George and Birrell, Chief Secretary for Ireland, met Devlin, Dillon and Redmond and secured an agreement to a temporary three year exclusion within days of Devlin having brought the nationalists to an acceptance of the scheme after a turbulent meeting in St Mary's Hall, Belfast. Birrell was telling Redmond that the exclusion period would be extended to six years.[13] The position of the party was being undermined by the very people it had attempted to accommodate.

The outbreak of war in August 1914 was providential from the point of view of Britain's Ulster policy. A Home Rule Act was placed on the statute books with a Suspensory provision postponing its implementation until the war was over, agreement not having been reached on Ulster at the Buckingham Palace Conference. Encouraged by Redmond and other IPP leaders, Catholic Ireland flocked to the colours. Nowhere in nationalist Ulster was recruitment for the Imperial cause more enthusiastic than in Belfast; to James Connolly's daughter, Nora, it seemed from the forest of Union Jacks on the Falls Road that the area had been magically transplanted to the Shankill. By contrast, those nationalist areas west of the Bann were to be among the least fertile ground in Ireland for army enlistments.[14]

That northern republicans were able to make such little contribution as they did to the Easter Rising 1916 was in itself remarkable. In the white heat of war fever in 1914, the numbers of the Irish Volunteers (who had broken from John Redmond's National Volunteers on the war issue) shrunk dramatically. The 4,000 under McCullough's command in Belfast in September collapsed to 2,099 within the month. In Derry a complement of 2,000 was reduced to 40. A recruitment drive by Ernest Blythe and the work of Pat McCartan in Tyrone was all that enabled them to field a force when the moment finally arrived.

The strategy envisaged was that the north would act in support of the Rising in Connacht. McCullough from Belfast with 150 men, Joe O'Doherty from Derry with his detachment and McCartan from Tyrone with several hundred were to converge on Belcoo, County Fermanagh and march to 'the line of the Shannon'.[15] The reality was to fall far short of these expectations.

When news came through of the capture in County Kerry of Sir Roger Casement and the failure of his attempt to import German arms, McCullough's men returned to Belfast; confronted with the failure of the Belfast contingent to arrive, the Tyrone men went home. 'We have failed in Tyrone,' McCartan wrote, 'but it is not the fault of Tyrone but the fault of Dublin.' O'Doherty's Derry unit did not mobilise.

The executions of the Rising's leaders increased nationalist feeling throughout Ireland to a point where Home Rule was back again on the agenda. And the 1914 problem of Ulster's special position returned with it. This time the number of counties to be 'temporarily excluded' had increased from four to six. While some Home Rulers were prepared to admit privately, as T. P. O'Connor did to John Dillon on 17 October, that 'no settlement' was possible 'in any period which we can see clearly ahead which does not involve the Partition of Ulster', yet even he told Redmond that Lloyd George's proposal of county option 'could not be publicly embraced'.[16]

In June Redmond had failed to get the approval of the northern bishops for the proposals, O'Connor noting that they remained 'solidly and implacably hostile'.[17] Nevertheless, Devlin recommended acceptance to the National Directory of the UIL as offering 'under present circumstances' 'the best means of carrying on the fight for a united self-governing Ireland'.[18]

Though he had told Dillon in 1913 that 'the exclusion of even one county for 12 minutes would not find half a dozen hands raised in its favour', he was the prime mover behind the decision of the conference of 770 delegates in St Mary's Hall on 23 June 1916 to endorse the proposals with only 265 dissenters. This 'Black Friday' meeting split northern nationalism along east/west lines, Antrim and Down voting overwhelmingly in favour, and over two thirds of the Armagh delegation supporting it. By contrast, Derry county opposed by a one vote majority and Fermanagh and Tyrone repudiated the package by a margin of almost two to one. Devlin had told Dillon in early June that 'outside Belfast' the terms were rejected with contempt'. The result was a tribute to his leadership, influence and charisma when so much clerical feeling was running in the opposite direction. Dillon, writing afterwards of Devlin's 'great triumph', added ominously that 'the priests' were 'working hard in Tyrone, Fermanagh, Armagh and Derry'. That September Bishop McHugh openly aligned himself with the 'Irish Nation League'[19] recently formed in the west of the province by disaffected nationalists, many of them lawyers, some of them like George Murnaghan, former Healyites. Murnaghan had been one of Devlin's strongest opponents at the St Mary's Hall meeting. As one republican writer later recalled, 'It was presently described as a place where some should suffer for a time before they enter the republican movement. It became merged in the more advanced movement very soon.'[20]

The 'more advanced movement' won a series of by-election victories in southern Ireland throughout 1917. The first halt to their triumphal progress was in the South Armagh constituency in January 1918, a county where the Sinn Féin presence was described as 'negligible'.

Sinn Féin, while hampered by the lack of an organisation in the constituency, was aided considerably by the support of the

Frontier Sentinel newspaper, the local branch of the Omagh based North West Publishing Company chain whose proprietor, Michael Lynch, had thrown his weight behind the new movement. It was typical of the new party's clericalist character that the Sinn Féin manifesto, published in full in the paper's edition of 26 January, stressed that Patrick Donnelly, the Home Rule candidate, had 'voted against the bishops on Black Friday'.[21] The paper then went on citing dubious evidence to present the Home Rulers as less reliable Catholics. 'The vast bulk of Irish clergy, from the most eminent Jesuit to the humblest curate, recognise the only hope of Ireland's solution lies in Sinn Féin' the manifesto concluded, quoting from Bishops O'Dwyer, Walsh, Fogarty, as well as Cardinal Logue and the Australian, Bishop Daniel Mannix. It is unclear whether or not the nationalist won solely as a result of votes from the unionist camp which declined to run a candidate, but the interpretation is at least tenable. In the final shake-up Donnelly had 2,324 votes to McCartan's 1,305.[22]

Sinn Féin's organisation work began immediately in the constituency after the defeat, under the guidance of Frank Aiken. Its failure in a second northern by-election in East Tyrone showed the distance it still had to travel in a constituency whose new Hibernian representative had opposed his party at the St Mary's Hall meeting and which Sinn Féin had at first not intended to contest. All was to change when, at the end of the year, marked by further blunders on its part, all redounding to Sinn Féin's advantage, the British government dissolved parliament and called a general election.

The election, which was to result in Lloyd George getting the overall majority he had hoped for, took place with a United Kingdom electorate enlarged from 8,357 to 21,392,322. For the first time non-owner occupiers and women (over thirty years of age) were enfranchised. Other developments were the holding of the poll on a single day and the placing of responsibility for registration in the hands of the County Clerk.[23] Sinn Féin's fortunes in Ulster looked considerably brighter at that point than at any time previously.

Whereas in the aftermath of the South Armagh by-election that January, John Dillon could confidently predict that Sinn Féin would not win a single seat in Ulster and de Valera could dismiss the northern Catholics as 'a people in whom the melt has been broken',[24] events later in the year combined to alter the picture. The impact of the conscription crisis and the 'German plot' roundup, the failure of the Lloyd George convention, coupled with an increased organisational drive by Sinn Féin in the province as the fall-out continued from the 1916 St Mary's Hall meeting, all shifted the balance towards the new movement. Nowhere was this more evident than in those western areas likely to be the chief victims in any partitionist settlement. By midsummer 1918 the police for Tyrone could report that the Sinn Féin party there was in the ascendant.[25] In Derry City a similar situation was recorded and more dramatic evidence of it was supplied. Sinn Féiners had begun collecting funds in October of that year and taken their own 'plebiscite' of over 10,000 citizens to signal that their position in the city would prevail. Before a nationalist candidate had even entered the field, Sinn Féin in the city had ruled out any compromise with him. Their message there and elsewhere was simple,[26] they stood on the high ground of an undefined 'Irish Republic' repudiating attendance at a Westminster parliament which had proven its perfidy by introducing the threats of conscription and partition, having promised nationalists that neither would be imposed. These twin issues, abstentionism and separation, were what distinguished them from the Home Rule Party, Any putative differences, which were later alleged on the question of armed opposition, did not figure in the election rhetoric.

PART ONE

1918-1922
'The greatest and last of all calamities'

'I felt it all during the controversy about partition, and indeed it strongly influenced my action two years ago, that in the absence of any agreement about the six counties a parliament would be set up in Ulster and I consider that would be the greatest and last of all calamities.'
Joe Devlin MP to Bishop O'Donnell
2 April 1920

CHAPTER 1

The 1918 election and its aftermath

As the countdown to the 1918 general election entered its final stage the intensity of the conflict between both schools of nationalism in the north-east threatened to drown out the wider conflict with the forces of unionism and allow otherwise winnable seats go by default. As early as 24 October it was reported that the Lord Mayor of Dublin had been approached by northern bishops and asked if anything could be done 'to obviate three cornered contests in northern constituencies'.[1]

Bishop McHugh of Derry had been a prime mover in this regard, advising the Sinn Féin candidate. By mid-November as electioneering gathered force he was writing to the *Freeman's Journal* appealing for 'national unity' in the eight affected constituencies. His suggestion was a conference, to be presided over by the Bishop of Clogher, in which each constituency would be represented by two priests chosen by their fellow priests and two representatives from the IPP and Sinn Féin respectively.[2] Six days later, McHugh was again forced to write to the *Freeman's Journal*, this time to deprecate the suggestion emanating from the Sinn Féin Standing Committee meeting of 19 November, that matters be decided by a plebiscite in each constituency. McHugh proposed instead that a candidate make: 'a written pledge of support for unrestricted Irish self determination at the Peace Conference,' promised by Woodrow Wilson, the US President, to decide the shape of the post-war world.[3]

Each member would be guided by a committee elected in the constituency on the basis of this pledge. This proposal might have provided common ground for both parties. Not only was Sinn Féin committed to an appeal to the conference but the Wilson doctrine, of self-determination for peoples within an overall League of Nations, held some attraction for Home Rulers as the achievement of the wartime sacrifice. The 14 November edition of *The Freeman* had on its front page a portrait of Wilson,

18

his 14 points framed by a triumphal arch on which the heads of the six allied kings were festooned with laurels.[4]

In an oracular reply to McHugh on 25th November, Sinn Féin approved the plan 'in as much as the Lord Bishop accepted as proper the proposal to decide by a plebiscite'.[5] Pressure continued from the hierarchy for a division of the seats. The leading Tyrone Sinn Féiner, George Murnaghan, told the Standing Committee on 28 November that they were 'ruined' if Dillon accepted the proposal and they did not.[6]

Since Murnaghan could assert, with justification, that four of the seven northern bishops were on the side of Sinn Féin,[7] (a claim quite tenable in the light of their record over the previous four years), his view prevailed over that of Piaras Béaslaí who stated that such a division would lose them the 'support of every decent man in Ireland'. On Murnaghan's suggestion, East Donegal, South Armagh, East Down, East Donegal, should go to the Irish Parliamentary Party, with North West and North East Tyrone and South Fermanagh going to Sinn Féin, He did not see this as the basis for the negotiations desired by the hierarchy. His alternative was that the Lord Mayor of Dublin be informed that Sinn Féin would not go into the proposed conference, opting instead for a meeting on the 30th of local bodies to decide the question. Michael Collins proposed that it be held in Dungannon, the venue suggested in Bishop McHugh's earlier proposal. This conference at which Eoin McNeill, Seán T. O'Kelly and Piaras Béaslaí represented the executive, came out in favour of the earlier 'division by plebiscite' idea. The suggestion was put into practice at the chapel gates in North Fermanagh the following day, the IPP losing by 1,711 votes. However, North Fermanagh was not one of the affected constituencies. Their fate was to be thrashed out over the next two days at the Mansion House in Dublin by McNeill and Dillon at a conference presided over by the city's Lord Mayor.

Dillon, who had toyed with the idea of an arbitration conference for the whole country which Sinn Féin would not accept, only reluctantly entered those talks after receiving a letter from Devlin, on 29 November, conveying in stark terms the embattled position of the party within the province:[8]

I wired you last night when I saw the Bishop's letter in the *Evening Telegraph* and I thought it would be well to know my views before making any declarations. The judgement I formed and what I stated in the telegram was based upon my instinct at the moment, but having considered the thing since, I am firmer than ever that the proposal ought to be accepted. If we reject it there is no doubt whatever about it from all the information I have gathered, that Harbinson's and Donnelly's seats will be lost and that North Tyrone will either go to Sinn Féin or to the Tories. I am quite certain we will not win a single seat in the north except West Belfast. In addition to that the refusal will damage us considerably in other constituencies in Ireland.

The acceptance of the pact would strengthen them, he told Dillon, giving them at least ten seats in Ulster with which they could form 'the nucleus of a small but effective party'. For these same reasons he felt Sinn Féin would not accept it. 'I cannot', he stated in conclusion, 'agree with this cry of no compromise. Even here among my own friends there is great feeling against the view I hold, but I do not mind as I think it is the only possible way to save the situation.'

Sinn Féin's assessment of how the political land lay was not fundamentally different. On 28 November O'Mara, the Sinn Féin Director of Elections, had told the standing committee that East Donegal, Falls and South Armagh would be lost. Of these three constituencies the first was within the pro-Home Rule Bishop of Raphoe's sphere of influence; the second was the stronghold of Joe Devlin; and the third the scene of Sinn Féin's electoral defeat in January. Only this last constituency was among the seats under discussion. In all likelihood Sinn Féin underestimated its chances of success there. As results showed, the party had undergone considerable expansion in the constituency over the previous two years, particularly since its by-election defeat.

In December 1916 two Sinn Féin had only two clubs in all of County Armagh. By February 1918 there were 15.[9] That December the number had risen to 26 with one company of the Volunteers also formed. GAA clubs in the county were reportedly split into Sinn Féin and AOH factions.[10] Most telling of all were the comments in a letter to Dillon on 29 November from P. Donnelly, the solicitor elected the previous January.

On the last occasion there were a number of factors at work which cannot be used this time and, from a unionist point of view, the situation is changed. (The unionists had voted for him in the previous election).

There are a considerable number of youth who have got the vote this time and who had not the last time. I have gone carefully into the figures and I find the youthful SF votes outnumber ours very much. That being so in a straight fight, in my judgement, the issue is going to be very close and if any compromise be arrived at by which Sinn Féin could gather their northern forces to the constituencies, I would have extremely grave doubts as to the result.[11]

It was in this atmosphere of Home Ruler demoralisation and Sinn Féin resurgence that the Mansion House conclave commenced.

Dillon, who found the conference with McNeill a 'sickening experience' and a tiresome and disgusting business, got agreement from him that the seats be equally divided but could not agree on the allocation, rejecting McNeill's insistence on the 'cut and dried' proposals of the Dungannon convention. The negotiations dragged on through Monday and Tuesday, 2 and 3 December, with the deadline for nominations set for 2.00 pm on Wednesday. At twelve minutes to midnight, Tuesday, with negotiations effectively collapsed, Cardina Logue dispatched an anguished telegram to Archbishop Walsh in Dublin, the contents of which left no doubt as to the principal reason behind the hierarchical intervention:

Fear no agreement likely at Mansion House. Believe if Your Grace gave advice you could effect agreement, otherwise seats go, which would be a calamity already as educational scheme is being hatched at Belfast which would be ruinous to Catholic interests.[12]

When the IPP refused to accept the final Sinn Féin offer of East Down, South Fermanagh, South Armagh and East Donegal – an offer made after consultation with local Comhairlí Ceanntair – the matter was moved north to Armagh for arbitration. Whether or not Logue threatened to support Sinn Féin if the IPP refused to accept his offer of South Down, North East Tyrone, East Donegal and South Armagh, is unclear.[13] All that is certain is that the deal was made.

At first the Sinn Féin Executive repudiated the award and proceeded to nominate candidates in all areas. Later that day (Wednesday 4 December) the standing committee, at Michael Collins' instigation, accepted it with only the Limerickman Patrick O'Mara dissenting. But while the assent of the respective party leaderships was one thing, that of their rank and file was quite another.

Dillon, who admitted to Bishop O'Donnell on 9 December to having done and intending to do all in his power about the Ulster seats, reminded him that 'if you knew the intense bitterness amongst my friends in East Down, Derry City and South Fermanagh, you would more keenly sympathise'. Earlier Donnelly had told him that the feeling in his constituency was 'entirely for no compromise. Nationalists of South Armagh would never consent to a Sinn Féiner representative until they are beaten at the polls and not even then'.[14] In North East Tyrone, the outgoing Home Rule MP, Thomas Harbinson, expressed his confidence of defeating a Sinn Féiner and holding the seat in a three cornered contest.

Devlin had already told Dillon in his letter of 28 November of the split within the party ranks in East Down, voicing his concern that the seat would fall to the Tories if matters were not solved. Dillon had himself expressed similar worries. While Dillon's fears regarding Derry City were not to be realised, thanks largely to the binding influence of Dr McHugh, South Fermanagh came close to being a different matter. Crumley, the nationalist candidate, had announced on 7 December that he had no intention of withdrawing in accordance with the agreement. Four days later, on the urging of the Bishop of Clogher and after consulting Dillon, he announced his withdrawal. The *Fermanagh Times* of the following day, reported an AOH/UIL decision to vote unionist if the withdrawal went ahead. But discipline prevailed; when Crumley's name appeared on the ballot paper two days later (as did all those of all late withdrawals), he received only a derisory vote.[15] The split in the nationalists was not sufficient to give the seat to the unionist.

However, this was not to be the case in East Down. There appeals by Devlin[16] and the Bishop of Down and Connor, Joseph McRory, to the organisation to honour the Logue award, proved so unsuccessful that the original candidate's decision to withdraw was ignored by his organisation which then proceeded to fight in a triangular contest, securing the larger share of the nationalist vote but allowing the unionist to take the seat. In only one other constituency outside Belfast did the Home Rule vote exceed that of Sinn Féin; that constituency, South Derry, was not traditional nationalist territory and did not figure in the Logue divide. (It was in fact represented by the only Roman Catholic

Unionist MP in history. Sr Denis Henry.) Sinn Féin was on the offensive and knew it.

In those constituencies with substantial nationalist minorities, where the 'Carsonites' were sure of victory regardless of what agreement was concluded, a private initiative was taken by a section of the Antrim clergy. The *Irish News*, 10 December,[17] published a public appeal from Fr Nolan summoning priests from the affected constituencies to a conference in Toomebridge. This conference called on the 80,000 Catholics in the area, where no Home Ruler was running, to vote for Sinn Féin. But even amongst those summoned unanimity was not possible. One of them, Fr McCotter PP, wrote to the *Irish Independent*[18] disputing the paper's inclusion of his name in its report of Nolan's conference and rejecting the claim that Logue's letter, read in Armagh churches on Sunday 8th, contained advice to vote Sinn Féin. It had, he claimed, simply told the priests of the archdiocese they were 'free to support by their votes their honest convictions'. Likewise, he contended, the pro-Sinn Féin advice of McCotter's own bishop, McRory, at the St Vincent de Paul Society on Sunday 8 December, was applicable merely to the Belfast constituencies. Furthermore, McCotter claimed the conference represented a mere three parishes in County Antrim and was, therefore, totally unrepresentative of the areas involved. His own solution was that the nationalists in those constituencies should simply abstain.

But one constituency was to turn out the way both sides knew it would, the Falls constituency of West Belfast. De Valera had been invited to stand there on 19 September and had agreed to do so, against considerable advice. S. T. O'Kelly, had told the standing committee on 28 November, after attending a gathering in Belfast, that 'De Valera was going to get a good beating' in this Devlinite stronghold.[19] His decision to enter the lists, notwithstanding these caveats, may have been influenced by a party canvas of half of the total poll in the division which predicted a 55% majority for him.[20] A contributory factor may also have been the attitude of Bishop McRory, whom both Sinn Féin and the IPP saw as strongly republican in outlook. In any event, on 10 October de Valera's nomination was approved by Sinn Féin.

The Belfast contest pitted a Sinn Féin organisation which had undergone only modest growth in the city – eight Sinn Féin clubs was the total listed in December 1918,[21] the same as at the beginning of its new year recruiting drive – against a Home Rule machine which, in Falls at least, was fine-tuned by Devlin to a degree seldom seen outside the ward system of Tammany Hall, America.

On 11 December the *Irish News* carried the last 800 names and addresses of Devlin's 8,000 nominees. That his final election tally was to be 8,488 showed the personalised nature of his power in the city. His inaugural address on 7 December was pitched at workers, particularly women workers, stressing the themes of wage-slavery, unemployment and poor housing. Laced with statistics, it was an impressive indictment of the conditions he had spent his life opposing.

This and his solid support among the workers, particularly the mill girls, enabled him to thumb his nose at De Valera's view that the national question took priority, a view summarised by Devlin and the *Irish News*, in words that were to reverberate through Irish history as 'Labour can wait'. The cross-class nature of his appeal was shown by the presence among his nominees of vintners and clergy as well as by the staunch support of the *Irish News*.

The final total of 8,882 votes for Devlin to De Valera's 3,245 came as no surprise. While Devlin's organisation did not oppose Sinn Féin in any other Belfast constituency, the ability of the one unofficial Home Ruler who did run in an election in the city against them to secure a larger share of the vote, would seem to refute the suggestion that the rest of Belfast had followed the general pattern.

The IPP after the election
When the general election count took place later in the month, Sinn Féin emerged with ten members in Ulster to the IPP's five. Of these five successes, four were located within the soon to be sequestered six county area, to three victories therein for Sinn Féin. All of the twenty-three seats won by unionists in Ulster were concentrated within this region. Devlin later admitted to Dillon that only the Logue agreement enabled the Home Rulers to win any representation in the province outside of Belfast. The rest of Ireland presented Sinn Féin with a clean sweep, Waterford City electing the sole Home Ruler and three unionists returned, two of them on the university franchise. In total, 73 of

the 105 Irish seats went to the new party, leaving the pattern of Irish politics transformed. When viewed within this context, the Northern result may be read as a vindication of Devlin's strategy. He had indeed retained what he had aimed for, the 'nucleus of a small but effective party' to carry with him into the new dispensation.

The election had deepened the IPP's hostility to what it saw as a pro-Sinn Féin hierarchy. Though prudence dictated a diplomatic approach to the issue in public, there was no mistaking the injured tone in Home Rulers' private correspondence. As the South Armagh MP, Patrick Donnelly, remarked to Dillon on the bishops' pastoral of 1919, which extended its focus from the threats to Catholic education and Irish unity to the revived danger of 'secret societies':

> It is quite clear that while they do not care what slaughtering nationalists get in the south, they are very worried about Sir Edward Carson's new movement in the north. For the most part they have nurtured Sinn Féin and when they see one of the results, they are trying to get out of the hole.[22]

Ironically, both Dillon and a South Armagh IRA leader, John McCoy, were to see the Logue arbitration as branding their respective organisations as sectarian in the eyes of Protestants and increasing intercommunal hostility.[23]

Much as differences existed between the two parties, convergence increased between them on one issue at least, the peace conference. On 23 December an immense meeting of all shades of opinion, held in Armagh, invited President Wilson to 'visit Ireland and assure himself of its right to self determination'. Logue addressed a letter of support to the meeting.[24]

Dillon had earlier regretted allowing Sinn Féin to monopolise this issue. As his biographer remarked, his support for the Allied war effort left him better placed than Sinn Féin to present Ireland's case to a gathering of the victors.[26] Another point of convergence had become the issue of abstention. Once anathema to the IPP, the conscription crisis of 1918 had forced it upon them. In early 1919 Devlin told Bishop O'Donnell that attendance was undesirable for 'at least some time to come'. He cited as his reasons: the insignificance of the Irish section in parliament, seven out of 700; (the verteran Home Ruler T. P. O'Connor was re-elected for Liverpool); the likely hostility of an 'unthinking people inspired by passion and prejudice' to their parliamentary failure; and the perceived threat their presence might pose to Sinn Féin's bid for recognition at the peace conference. Their dilemma was acute; if they raised questions of policy in the House they were repudiated by Sinn Féin for their futility in doing so, and yet they had to defend fellow Irishmen, including Sinn Féiners, against violence done to them by the authorities.

Devlin's reservations were not shared by the other Ulster members when he met them at the request of E. J. Reilly, the East Donegal MP. They were elected, they stated, to attend and should act according to their mandate. Eventually they did, though in sporadic fashion and with varying degrees of enthusiasm. Later in the month, when Devlin thanked Bishop O'Donnell for correspondence on the party's educational proposals, he admitted it was the first communication he had received on the issue,[27] revealing just how much his party had been replaced in the consideration of the hierarchy by the Sinn Féiners. Devlin's fear for the 'Catholic interest' of Belfast, meant that the prospect of a body such as Belfast City Council having control over the primary education of children, would lead him 'without guidance, advice or mandate', to take the line he considered most effective. To make matters worse, an even bigger threat was looming on the horizon: a Home Rule Bill incorporating some form of partition at a time when nationalist Ireland had moved beyond Home Rule policy because of its supporters' seeming weakness on the partition issue. What was more, this was occurring in a parliament where the gap between conservatives and liberals had expanded from 20 to 230 in an uneasy coalition government, where the absence of the 73 Sinn Féin members left the 25 unionists as the predominant Irish voice. The events since 1916 had done much to erode sympathy in the House for nationalist Ireland – when coupled with the pivotal unionist position, this did not bode well for nationalist interests.

In July 1919 Churchill told Devlin that he intended to propose a settlement. By November, the latter, having sniffed the wind, could write that all talk was 'merely camouflage', and the result would be two parliaments, one for Ulster and the other for the rest of Ireland.[27]

On this issue of impending partition, two factions existed in the Commons' Irish standing committee established to draw up the Bill. One inclined toward the idea of a second parliament, the other towards county option. By the end of the year it was obvious this latter viewpoint would not prevail. When Dillon advised abstentions, Devlin who agreed in principal, expressed uneasiness lest his absence might cause trouble in Belfast where Bishop McRory was calling a meeting to condemn the Bill.

Dillon's advice by February was to allow Lloyd George to push through his scheme for two parliaments, 'hoping that the forces now at work will compel him to make the undivided province of Ulster the area of the northern parliament'. Conscious of his rejectionist mood towards any form of partition at home he added the rider, 'Being extremely careful neither in public nor in private to accept any responsibility for such a scheme'.

Devlin was to tell Bishop O'Donnell on 13 February that he was practically certain a six county parliament would be set up. This would mean 'the worst form of division', a permanent partition. 'Once they have their own parliament with all the machinery of government and administration, I am afraid anything like subsequent union will be rendered impossible.'[28] He proposed to attack the Bill from an Ulster point of view, giving reasons why the Catholics and nationalists could not, under any circumstances, consent to be placed under the domination of a parliament so 'skilfully established as to make it impossible for them to be ever other than a permanent minority with all the sufferings of the present day continued only in worse form'.[29]

Both Dillon's hopes and Devlin's fears were to be realised in the following ten days as the committee came down in favour of the nine county exclusion proposal, only to have the Cabinet reduce the area to six at the urging of the Ulster unionists. Nothing could have emphasised more dramatically the void left in the House of Commons by the policy of abstention.

As the Bill entered its committee stage, Devlin toyed with leaving the House, realising as he did the unlikelihood of a substantial alteration. He sought guidance from the Cardinal through Bishop O'Donnell, on whether to oppose the Bill or simply to leave it alone.[30] It was at this juncture that Devlin outlined to O'Donnell the government proposals, to which he had earlier agreed, to avoid the setting up of a separate northern party.[31] A parliament would be set up for the twenty-six counties while Ulster would remain under the direct rule of the imperial parliament, where 100 Irish members, 85 of whom would have been nationalists, would have the same power over government and administrative matters for the region as before. Devlin foresaw that the whole system would then have become 'unworkable' and the unionists 'would have been glad to come to the parliament of the twenty-six counties and to plead for union' Sir Edward Carson, he claimed, had stated repeatedly in the Smoking Room of the House of Commons that if these proposals were adopted, Ireland would by then be united.[32] Whatever the truth, it will remain one of the great imponderables of Irish history.

The Education Bill continued to cause problems. 'I will oppose it,' Devlin told O'Donnell, 'mainly on the ground you already understand, but chiefly I will oppose it on behalf of the hundred thousand Catholics in Belfast whom I represent and whose interests, more than the interests of any other class of people in Ireland, are involved under the new Bill'.[33] The previous year had seen little change in the hierarchy's attitude towards his efforts and he knew it. Enclosing a sample of threatening letters he had received practically every day, he commented, 'They rather amuse me but would it not be an irony of fate if I were assassinated for backing the bishops and priests of Ireland? I wonder would there be many of them who would regret the tragedy.'[34] How far the focus of power in Ireland had shifted was increasingly borne in on them. More and more the press was disregarding its once-favoured parliamentarians. The *Freeman's Journal,* Devlin complained, was trying to outdo the *Independent* in this respect under its new editor, Robert Donovan. Its conduct was 'contemptible', he claimed.

In the area to be affected by partition, the *Derry Journal* and the papers of the North West Publishing Company had long since gone over to Sinn Féin. While the *Irish News* remained loyal, even it was giving cause for concern to some of Devlin's followers. Devlin was having trouble with his own party as well. On the issue of abstention in the committee stages, Kelly of East Donegal and McVeagh of South Down, stood out in favour of attendance. On the day when Devlin conveyed this news to Dillon he had other news of a meeting in the lobby with Edward Shortt (McPherson's predecessor as Chief Secretary for Ireland) in which the latter confirmed that negotiations were taking place with Sinn Féin. 'The Sinn Féiners have beaten them and they recognise it,' Devlin commented.[35]

CHAPTER 2

The War of Independence

The focus of attention had long since shifted from Westminster to the guerrilla war being waged in Ireland. Beginning in early 1919, it had gathered increasing ferocity the following year, with the introduction of the quasi-military 'Black and Tans' to supplement the hard-pressed RIC, now concentrated in the larger towns. The pattern of IRA activity was uneven. In March 1921, a staff memo divided the country for operational purposes into the capital, Dublin; the 'war zone' counties of Kerry, Limerick, Cork and Tipperary; secondary country areas; and the six Ulster counties of 'Carsonia'. With Britain's military hold in Dublin successfully challenged for the first time since the reign of Edward Bruce, the military importance of Ulster had become the English lever for governing Ireland and it was necessary to attack it 'steadily and persistently' with all the 'focus that could be developed'.[1]

The five northern divisions of the IRA, established as part of the countryside re-organisation of the movement earlier that month, were exhorted against the enemy in a similarly magniloquent manner. Memos to three of the four divisions straddling the new established border envisaged the movement securing actual territorial control over large swathes of territory and seriously undermining the enemy economy. The 2nd Northern Division, encompassing all of County Tyrone and part of Derry, had been placed under the command of the Kerryman Charlie Daly, sent north by GHQ for the purpose.[2] According to GHQ a proper military grip of this area was essential for the breaking up of 'Carsonia' through the detaching of Derry, Newry and Enniskillen from Belfast. This was to be achieved by isolating districts through communication severance, followed by the establishment of a chain of IRA outposts. All of this would take place in tandem with a campaign of sabotage against the landed and business interests seen as the twin pillars of 'Orange ascendancy'.

The whole matter was, however, 'a particularly Ulster question and calls for a mature consideration by Divisional Staffs', the memo added. In the light of the actual performance on the ground in the area involved, this qualification must have saved many blushes at headquarters.[3]

While the Sinn Féin organisation in Tyrone had expanded from 36 clubs in February 1918 to 53 in September 1920, the Irish Volunteers had not grown at all, staying put at 15 branches. Actual membership had in fact increased by only 30.[4] The Sinn Féin victory in the June local elections, and the County Council's transfer of allegiance to Dáil Éireann, resulted in an upsurge of IRA activity. Poorly armed and badly trained, the highpoint of its offensive, the Cookstown Barracks attack of 18 June, resulted in the death of two volunteers. On paper, by the end of the year descriptions of the country in police reports had gone from 'satisfactory', 'fairly satisfactory' and 'generally peaceful' (descriptions which the other five counties continued to enjoy) to 'disturbed' and 'unsatisfactory'.

However, most of this activity was accounted for by smaller scale 'outrages', the sporadic digging up of roads, the cutting of telephone wires and occasional attacks upon vans of Belfast companies in connection with the Dáil Éireann boycott.[5] An exacerbating factor was the tendency of unionists to mobilise against Sinn Féin through the newly formed USC – raids, searches and arrests increased and reprisals also followed successful operations. The shooting of a constable in Dungannon in December resulted in the wrecking of houses in the town. 'Outrages' had leaped from 27 in July to 41 the following month. Pressure was being placed on the Volunteers from within the community, and in early September 1920 a 'peace meeting' was chaired by priests in Dungannon. While there were divisions between them on whether or not Sinn Féin was to blame, there was not doubt which way the wind was blowing.[6]

· The year's end saw the police report a decline in Sinn Féin activity in the county, and by the following March it was still described as 'fairly peaceful' despite an increase in IRA activity during the summer. This basically remained its condition until the Truce.[7] When Eoin O'Duffy took over the divisional command in March 1921, he found it necessary to scrap every company brigade and battalion in the area.[8] (He had little time for complaints of GHQ's failure to provide arms, having himself received only one rifle in his own Monaghan company and through raiding augmented the stock to 85.) The following March, when O'Duffy, in pursuit of his dream that the 2nd and 3rd Northern Divisions would become the two principal fighting areas, removed Daly from his command, the latter, who admitted having 'done but little', cited in mitigation not only the hostile loyalist community with which he had to contend, but also the 'apathy of our own civilian population'.[9]

In Derry the position was somewhat similar. By early 1918 there were eight Sinn Féin clubs with 425 members and four units of the Irish Volunteers with 198 members and 17 rifles. By August 1920, when the Sinn Féin organisation had expanded to 21 clubs and 1,455 members, the Volunteers had remained static. An increase of 50 members was counterbalanced by the loss of one rifle.[10] Only the outburst of serious sectarian violence in the city that summer served to provide them with a role. Lieutenant M. Sheerin of the Derry Brigade reported to Headquarters as follows:

> In the beginning of 1920 I had a company of about 50 men and was the only unit functioning in the city. 25% of these I held together by threats, the remainder were particularly unenthusiastic.[11]

About May 1920 the relationship between the Catholic and Orange element of the town became particularly bitter. It reached a climax in the beginning of June 1920 when, on a Saturday evening, four Catholic men were shot down in the main street. This appeared to be a signal for a general outburst and the Catholic quarter of the town was subjected to a fusillade for about two hours. Sheerin, in order to prevent his company getting involved, ordered a parade. Unfortunately, they discovered they could not get home without passing through the Orange quarter of the city and they were left with no choice but to defend themselves. The military men prepared to come to the defence of the Catholic population were not confined to republicans.[12] The following day, Sheerin reported, hundreds of 'British ex-soldiers' (i.e. Catholic ex-servicemen) were joining in as well.

> The RIC in our area surrendered through lack of supplies that is if it could be called a surrender. Though there was no one attacking them, they handed over their arms not to us but to ex-soldiers who by that stage had formed themselves into bands and were working independently. On the second

day of the trouble a prominent local member of Sinn Féin
who had been in jail was released. He was an elderly man
and had one time been an officer in the IRA. He was held in
high esteem by the clergy and through their influence all
Catholic units including Hibernians and Foresters, soldiers,
placed themselves under his orders. Dick McKee and Peadar
Clancy arrived in town about the same time as it was decided
the IRA would be placed under his orders and his experience
could prove useful.

Sheerin was appointed 2nd in command and took over St
Columb's College, holding his original company as a HQ garri-
son; the remainder, now swelled to several thousands, were dis-
persed in smaller groups to different sections. The sending to
the city of McKee and Clancy, both leading Dublin IRA figures,
and both of them close to Collins, was an indication of how seriously GHQ viewed the situation both as a crisis and an opportunity. Supplies of arms and ammunition were pouring in.[13]
Effectively, an ad hoc pan-Catholic militia, encompassing all
traditions, faced a similar grouping from the other side. Mobs
became active behind the lines, looting and burning, but 'police
pickets', formed from the various defence committees and frequently accompanied by Catholic clergy, meted out swift and
brutal corporal punishment. After about five days, the situation
was in hand and the Catholic defenders had control of 50% of
the city. 'Behind our defences,' Sheerin wrote, 'we could move
about freely. We had all preparations made for an attack which
would give us complete control of all the city on the west bank
when two additional British regiments arrive.' When the army
opened fire indiscriminately, the Catholic defenders, other than
the IRA, fled in terror. 'The discarding of rifles and ammunition
and the hasty disappearance of men, was not edifying.'[14]
Sheerin's men collected what arms and ammunition they could
and then went to ground. The IRA role as defenders availed
them little in the long run; the initiative passed to a conciliation
committee with heavy clerical and business representation.[15]

By October the city, still under curfew, was reported as 'fairly
satisfactory' despite the killing of a policeman in Bishop Street
on the 16th.[16] In April the Inspector General could conclude that:
'The nationalist politicians are doing everything possible to re-
strain the extremists and so far are very successful'.[17] The 'extremists' in fact were turning their attention westwards to

Inishowen with which it interchanged arms for an active service unit.[18] Friction between Frank Carney of Derry City and Peadar O'Donnell of East Donegal soon undermined co-operation and necessitated a GHQ inquiry on 21 May, but before the inquiry was complete, Carney and other leading IRA men were arrested by the British in Donegal.[19] By that stage discipline in the division had become so bad that Sweeney, the OC, was at HQ demanding authorisation to punish deserters.[20]

Back in Derry City, in the run up to the Truce, the IRA leaders were 'either interned or on the run'. The older people were reported as 'out of sympathy with them'. There was really 'no punch', and a lack of trust existed between the Volunteers and the ITGWU because of an attempt to woo members of the former into a citizen army. All in all it was a far cry from the grandiose plan for control in the north west by land and sea.[21]

Only in one divisional area did local reality come anywhere close to matching executive expectations, that was in the Armagh/South Down and North Louth region, comprising the 4th Northern Command of Frank Aiken.

The Sinn Féin growth in Armagh from the January 1918 by-election to the general election of the same year, had not been matched by a concomitant expansion of its military wing. In December 1918, when the country was 'very quiet', only one company of Volunteers was recorded. By August 1920, it had increased to three in a county 'far from satisfactory'.[22] From about May 1920 the South Armagh Volunteers had 'a fair amount of shotguns', obtained largely through raiding though this was counterbalanced by a scarcity of ammunition. In the Newry area, for instance, the stock of long-bore armaments which stood at a mere six rifles in the Newry area in 1919, had also been augmented by 'collecting all the 12 bore shotguns they could find'. South and north were later integrated with an Armagh brigade under Paddy Rankin as OC when Frank Aiken declined the post.[23] Often when discipline of the Brigade meant an unwillingness to act without GHQ direction, the initiative of local commanders forced the pace in its absence. Beginning with the unsuccessful attack on Newtownbutler barracks in December 1919, later followed up successfully in April, a series of operations continued through the year climaxing with the disastrous Egyptian-Arch ambush in December on the outskirts of Newry, which cost the lives of three IRA men, a loss overshadowing the simultaneous destruction of the Camlough RIC barracks. The period between this and the formation of the division in March witnessed a further degeneration, made worse by the deployment of the USC, a move resisted by the nationalists of both schools.[24] An example of this was provided in Armagh in November 1920 when the AOH County President and Secretary united with other Catholics on the Council to protest to the County Inspector of the RIC at the idea of 'political opponents and erstwhile rebels being established as guardians of the peace'. No necessity existed for them,' they stated, 'as most friendly relations exist between all shades of the population and with the RIC'.[25]

The GHQ memo to the newly formed 4th Northern on 25 April 1921 designated this area as 'the spearhead of the forthcoming attack on Carsonia', adding that: 'The general principle should be to consolidate our hold on the southern half of the divisional area as a base for incursions into the north.' While the broad strategic sweep of the memo, involving the destruction of the flax harvest, industries and communications, proved no more realisable there than elsewhere, on a tactical level they had somewhat more success. The Sliabh Gullion, Carlingford and Mourne areas became the base for training camps and flying columns, while at least one of the major sabotage operations desired by GHQ, an attack upon the country corps at Dundalk, was carried out with great élan at the Adavoyle embankment in June.

In the eyes of the GHQ the hostility of the northern territory had the 'comparative advantage of not having to worry about the inhabitants except to a very limited extent.' Furthermore, they insisted in bringing notice to them that 'aiding the enemy did not pay'. In practice, matters often worked out differently. The Kilkeel Battalion Commander had reported, in February, the termination of an ambush and the decision not to have any others in the district because of the number of unionists in the area. Furthermore, unionists were not the only hostile population with which militant republicans had to contend. Home Rule sentiment was far from being a spent force in a constituency where it had beaten Sinn Féin in a by-election three years previously. Even sections of the national movement, long since irredeemably Sinn Féin throughout Ireland, were more complex in character. As John McCoy reported, the GAA clubs in Armagh

were split evenly between Sinn Féin and the AOH.[27] IPP supporters, though believers in self-government for Ireland, were
not separatists. Strongly committed to membership of the
British Empire and what they regarded as its benefits, they were
rightly or wrongly viewed by the rebel movement as a fifth column and often treated accordingly. The two men shot as spies in
Armagh on 7 June were both prominent Hibernians.[28] A British
policy of reprisal culminated in the dispatch of the notorious
Igoe gang to the area in March.[29] Until the Truce in July, both
Armagh and Down continued to be described in the Inspector
General's reports as 'unsatisfactory', 'disturbed', and 'very disturbed'.[30]

The five battalions of County Fermanagh were divided be-
tween three divisional areas in March 1921.[31] The Fermanagh
Brigade, which included companies in Leitrim, Cavan and
Tyrone, was placed under the command of Sean McEoin, OC
Midland Division. It was mostly through the efforts of Sean
Carty, Secretary to the North Fermanagh Comhairle Ceantair of
Sinn Féin, that organisation was commenced in the county and
by December he had established 17 clubs in 'that half Orange
half Hibernian constituency'[32] and was, as a result, appointed
Sinn Féin organiser for the whole county. By August 1920 the
number of Sinn Féin clubs had increased to 30 with over 2,000
members. He was largely responsible for IRA organisation in
the county as Commandant of the Belleek company. But the
twin problems of sectarianism and lack of support from within
their own community were to bedevil the organisation, and
when Carty's men captured and burned Belleek Barracks in the
Autumn of 1920, local Catholic townspeople joined the police in
helping put out the fire.[33] The largest operation mounted in the
Fermanagh area consisted of the burning of 15 houses belonging
to B Specials and supporters in Roslea in February 1921. Carried
out with GHQ authorisation as a reprisal for the torching of the
Catholic portion of the town by the B Specials, it resulted in the
death of a constable, a sergeant of the USC, and the wounding of
seven others. Such activity could not continue without the risk
of civil war. Some weeks after the incidents, the Protestants of
the area approached the Catholic Church leaders for help, and a
meeting was convened of 'all classes and creeds from Roslea and
the surrounding parishes' with the Protestant Rector of Clones,
Canon Rudel, in the chair. It was a testament to its efficiency that

Fermanagh figured in police reports as 'fairly satisfactory' to 'quite satisfactory' until the Truce.[34] Cahir Healy later recalled arguing down a GHQ proposal for increased activity at a 1920 meeting of the IRA in Coa Hall. He opposed it on the basis that it led 'inevitably to sectarian warfare'.[35]

Along with the 2nd Northern, only one other divisional area lay entirely within the six county area, the 3rd Northern Division, comprising three brigades, the Belfast, Antrim and East Down brigades respectively. Throughout the War of Independence, in the words of the second in command, they were 'out of contact with Dublin for stuff and had to find their own war'. Despite these handicaps, the Belfast Brigade had roughly 1,000 men with 'fairly good supplies of arms' obtained before the war began from UVF and Redmondite stocks. A further supply of rifles was obtained from the National Volunteers in the summer of 1920, when a tornado of loyalist violence exploded on Catholic districts in reprisal for the killing in Cork of Banbridge-born Divisional Inspector Smyth.[36] This onslaught, which resulted in the expulsion of over 7,000 Catholics from shipyards and the death of 14 others, served to highlight the problem besetting militant republicans in the city.

Firstly, offensive operations against Crown forces on the pattern of the campaign in the south and west of Ireland were likely to provoke a backlash in which Catholics suffered most. Indeed, the triggers for the next two major outbreaks of anti-Catholic terror in August 1920 and July 1921 were operations carried out under the direction of GHQ. The first of these, the shooting of District Inspector Swanzy in Lisburn in reprisal for his role in the murder of the Lord Mayor of Cork, was carried out on Collins' direct instructions. The second followed the announcement of the Truce, five weeks into an escalated Northern Ireland offensive ordered GHQ. The increasing tempo of IRA activity in the city and its environs, from the spring onwards, had drawn forth the attentions of a death squad based at police stations in the city, most notably the Brown Street Barracks off the Shankill Road. In this situation the danger existed that a rival Catholic sectarianism involving purely anti-Protestant activity would be forced upon the IRA. In March 1921 GHQ reminded them that it alone could sanction offensive action and Seamus Woods, the future Divisional OC, complained in July that 'the Catholic mob' (was) 'almost beyond control'.[37]

Allied to this problem was the political character of the Catholic population in Belfast. As the election results had shown, they were still Devlinite in their affiliation. By September 1920, there were still only nine Sinn Féin clubs compared to 18 branches of the UIL and 25 of the AOH. That marked an increase since early 1918 of only one club. Republicans' sole area of growth was in the Volunteer strength which had grown from a company of 500 to a battalion of over 5,000.[38] Quantity was not quality, however, and a considerable gap existed in the movement between followers and leaders. As a veteran recalled, 'The officers in the Brigade, McKelvey, Woods and McCorley, came from families outside Belfast. The republican tradition went back generations in some cases (McCorley's grandfather, Roddy, was hanged in 1798 and is commemorated in a famous ballad). They played Gaelic football and many were language revivalists. Their followers were descendants of city bred men, they played soccer and were often little more than Hibernians with guns.'[39] Woods himself admitted to GHQ with characteristic honesty that:

Prior to the signing of the Truce in July 1921, the percentage of the Catholic population in the division that was in sympathy with the IRA was roughly 25%. Taking into consideration the proportion of the Catholic population to the whole our support in the division would have been something less than 10% of the entire civilian population.[40]

Added to this was the desperate financial position of the Belfast Brigade – 75% unemployed into the autumn of 1921 – and the IRA's lack of organisation in the No. 2 and 3 Brigade areas, Belfast, Antrim and Down hinterland. These factors may have been influential in GHQ's decision to send the one Belfast ASU which it did form, off to Cavan to fight. They may also have been behind Sean McEntee's fervent advocacy of the Dáil's Belfast Boycott, imposed on goods from the city in August 1920 in protest at the continuing expulsion of Catholics. McEntee was a 1916 veteran, at various times Vice Brigadier and Acting Brigadier of the Belfast Brigade, and held, according to a GHQ memo, 'pacifist views' which caused 'disquiet' in Volunteer circles in the north.[41] By enlisting the expelled workers' councillors in this project, he swung the considerable weight of Dáil Éireann behind their case and gave the Dáil a new legitimacy in previously Devlinite territory.

CHAPTER 3

The Elections of 1920 and 1921

Meanwhile on the political front, events were taking a shape of their own. With the Government of Ireland Act about to be introduced in February, the emphasis in the nationalist press was on unity against a common foe, as gains made in previous elections had to be maintained despite the divisions in nationalist ranks. The fact that the impending Municipal Elections in January were to be held under Proportional Representation made it possible for the non-unionist camp to display both the unity necessary and the diversity desired. In some areas such as the West Ward in Derry City, no contest took place as both sections of nationalism fought on a single ticket. Elsewhere the results displayed the degree to which the Home Rule party retained their original allegiance and how much the 1918 result had been obtained through an enlarged franchise incorporating those ineligible to vote in local elections. In Antrim the nationalists won 1,057 votes and ten seats, the Sinn Féin 266 votes and one seat. In Tyrone there were 12 Sinn Féiners to 19 nationalists; in Armagh 16 nationalists and 12 Sinn Féiners; in Belfast the nationalists won 12,261 votes to Sinn Féin's 5,640, whilst in the remainder of the province the figures were 9,9965 to 5,337. The transfer pattern revealed little in the way of joint allegiances. In Belfast, for instance, of the two nationalist candidates, Richard Byrne and Oswald Jamison's joint surplus of 314 only 11 votes went to Sinn Féin.[1]

The most unusual feature of the election was the emergence in strength of the Labour vote – its total of 27,504 votes in Ulster was second only to that of the unionists, and in Tyrone labourites held a balance of power, the nationalist strongholds in Omagh, Strabane and Cookstown returning two, three and four labour men respectively. The growing trade unionism of early 1918, pandered to by men such as the Independent Home Ruler Skeffington in the election of that year in South Tyrone, had shown itself again in the ongoing dispute with the Fultons in Caledon Mills. Now it was bearing electoral fruit. Labour failed to follow up the victory in the June rural and county council elections, calling instead for a republican vote. 'Down with the occupation, up with a free Ireland' its newspaper proclaimed on the eve of the elections. The elections, for such they were, comprising three contests, saw Sinn Féin and the nationalists again acting in unison if not in harmony. In Fermanagh six Sinn Féiners and five nationalists constituted a majority over the nine unionists. In Tyrone, Strabane, Cookstown, Dungannon and Omagh RDC fell to the anti-unionists giving them control of the councils. In the case of Omagh they swept the board but were outnumbered by the IPP in Cookstown, Dungannon and Strabane.

Sometimes the inter party co-operation gave rise to a feeling of oneness and a confidence of overcoming all obstacles. In South Derry, for instance, the degree of unity between Sinn Féin and the AOH produced joint celebrations for what was described as a 'Catholic victory' at the polls. They had 14 Catholics against 11 unionists on Magherafelt Council and eight Catholic representative on Derry County Council, Mr John Walsh told the meeting. The results had he claimed, 'silenced the croakers' who said 'Sinns' would not vote for 'Hibs' nor 'Hibs' for 'Sinns'. Father Rafferty was the 'Napoleon' who had led them to victory. They had the majority in south Derry and there would be no partition he concluded.[2]

Overall, however, what characterised the June 1920 elections, as the *Irish News* noted, was the apathy surrounding them. No doubt this stemmed from the fact that the 'Partition Bill' was then only at its committee stage and was being boycotted by nationalists. With the Bill passed into law and elections due in May, for the new parliament, a greater sense of urgency prevailed. Early in the New Year de Valera discussed the situation with Bishop McRory who suggested to him that Sinn Féin might be allowed a clear field. On 7 January Devlin wrote to Cardinal Logue telling him of a meeting in Dublin with De Valera at the latter's request at which they discussed the Ulster situation. Devlin, who claimed he had been unaware of the purpose of the meeting, placed before De Valera a series of proposals to secure 'joint and united action' in view of the 'grave peril' posed by the establishment of the Belfast parliament.[4] The four points which

De Valera agreed might be the basis for discussion and perhaps for adjustment were: firstly the impossibility of undermining the Ulster parliament by putting forward candidates to represent distinct interests; secondly, that as many as 15 or 20 seats could be secured by joint action; thirdly, that they come to an agreement on the division of seats 'leaving those opposed to abstention the right to determine whether to enter the parliament or not'; and finally each party was to be left free to pursue its own course. The first proposition De Valera would agree to but not the second and third, while the fourth Devlin felt would be a 'painful' policy if pursued 'in the face of a common enemy and a common danger'. A possible agreement between himself and De Valera would, he felt, be sanctioned by the 'general sense of community' and with the situation so grave and so many points of disagreement existing, 'all influences ought to be exercised in favour of bringing about a common and united policy'.[5]

Without bothering to inform De Valera, Devlin by his letter had placed the ball in the Cardinal's court, the church being the only institution capable of securing pan-nationalist unity. Apparently the strategy worked. When an agreement was finally reached, Dillon could write: 'No one likes this arrangement except the bishops and priests. All that can be said for it is that any alternative would be worse.' Both sides had already considered the alternatives.[6] On 13 January De Valera wrote to Collins suggesting the possibility of a boycott unless they were certain of at least one fifth (10 members) of the proposed parliament, otherwise 'the news would be boomed abroad' that these counties were a homogeneous unit.[7] If that condition were met, however, he felt the only possible merit in a boycott would be the fostering of sectional and class division within the unionist camp. Arthur Griffith, advised by the leading Tyrone Sinn Féiner, George Murnaghan, was in favour of this course. Collins could not make up his mind between the two alternatives and left it to the Cabinet to consider. They opted for participation but only on an abstentionist basis, after hearing analysis of the electoral outlook coupled with De Valera's instructions to 'Paudeen' O'Keefe, the Sinn Féin Secretary.[8]

It was an indication of how much they were reacting to events that they feared the prospect of independent nationalists taking a slice of the vote in the event of a boycott. Also the labour constituency was one on which it was felt a weather eye had to be kept. 'It will be our business,' De Valera wrote, 'to prevent the labour element from being confused by our entry into the election. We ought to be able to make them see that we are contesting these elections for principle and not for actual power in the northern parliament'.[9]

A conference took place in Belfast on the weekend of 18 February between Sinn Féin and UIL representatives. Agreement was reached on the issues of self-determination and opposition to partition but the tactic of 'abstention' remained a stumbling block. The UIL rejected it in principle and agreed to adopt it 'only until such time as an emergency would arise'. When this proved unacceptable to Sinn Féin, the UIL delegates, Jamison and O'Kane, proposed the twin alternatives of complete boycott or a scheme whereby the UIL would be allowed Belfast, Antrim and Down, while pledging abstentions elsewhere until all members of both parties agreed to attend. Though the standing committee of Sinn Féin rejected these proposals, as the Sinn Féin delegates predicted they would, compromise was inevitable. T. P. O'Connor told John Dillon on 12 March that if any deal at all was done by Sinn Féin, it would have to be on the terms of abstentionism as the alternative, that of entering an overwhelming unionist parliament 'with a ragged regiment of six or eight nationalists, confronted by the Orangemen on one side and with fire in the back from the Sinn Féiners on the other', was 'an impossible position'.[10] On St Patrick's Day 1921 an agreement was finally signed between the sides. Candidates would accept the principle of self-determination, pledge themselves to abstention, and to give second preferences to the other party on the 'anti-partition' ticket. There would be an equal number of candidates put forward by each side in each constituency. The agreement was kept from the press until details were ironed out, most notably the final item on selection quotas.

Finally, on Tuesday 29 March, beside an item announcing the deaths of 481 people in Ireland since the year began, the *Freeman's Journal* could proclaim that a united front existed in Ulster. All the northern bishops had expressed their approval to the newspaper's representative.[11] One modification of the 17 March proposal was the removal of the clause relating to candidate numbers and the insertion of one regarding the creation of parish committees to oversee electoral work. In the nature of things, these would have Roman Catholic clergy as their most influential members.

All but one of the candidates were either proposed and/or seconded by Catholic Church personnel, the Bishop of Dromore himself proposing De Valera in Down. That one exception, as it turned out, was Michael Collins. At the convention in Armagh strong opinions were expressed against him, principally by the local clergy. Some of them told the Sinn Féin secretary, Padraig O'Keefe, privately that the Cardinal might go so far as to 'write' against him.[12] Uniquely his proposers and seconders were both lay-men. One priest even suggested that the candidate selected at the last convention, i.e. De Valera, be chosen. Since he had already gone forward in Down another priest proposed the choice of Ernest Blythe. Collins was selected after a heated debate but only with the proviso that his selection be placed before HQ for ratification alongside the other options. It was a measure of how qualified was the hierarchy's conversion to Sinn Féin that militant republicanism's most celebrated practitioner should be treated in such a hostile fashion. Collins' running-mate, Frank Aiken, fearing that in the event of church opposition to 'the Big Fellow', he himself might secure the larger slice of the vote, appealed to HQ to be allowed to withdraw.[13] In the event both selections went ahead as planned, Collins topped the nationalist poll and the clerical backlash never materialised. Aiken, Collins' running-mate, lost his deposit.

The Home Rule party, Dillon had recognised, could not have put forward a candidate anywhere outside of Ulster. Reviewing their position there, Devlin considered it 'extremely difficult' to express any views as to the outcome.

> Everything is alright here in Belfast, I think we will win a seat in Antrim but I am not all sure as to Down (where disillusionment over the East Down debacle of 1918 still rankled) and whether we will win a seat in Derry, Tyrone and Fermanagh is equally uncertain, although local men tell me we will win seats in each of these constituencies'.[14]

In Tyrone only 40 out of 400 delegates turned up for the convention, most of them old men. The collection amounted to only £70, £50 of it coming from Harbinson, the Home Ruler and MP for the area.

In Armagh, the determination of the IPP's Patrick Donnelly to be the sole candidate meant that he would not accept the other name on the ticket. The names of John Nugent and Devlin himself were put forward by way of compromise. Devlin had to go to Dublin with the Belfast councillor Oswald Jamison to persuade Nugent, who was ill, to enter the contest. A list of problems beset the party – lack of funds, intimidation by USC, and the absence of any enthusiasm for party work.

Devlin felt, and all the activists from the constituencies agreed with him, that the agreement was not merely the best but the only course to have adopted, 'If we had stood on our own and fought the constituencies, I do not believe that outside Belfast we would have got a candidate,' he admitted bluntly.[15] On his estimation, he predicted five or six seats out of 15 or 16 was the maximum they could hope to obtain. In the event both they and Sinn Féin won six seats each, the largest nationalist vote in the six counties ever, though swamped by the more than doubling of the unionist representation since 1918, which produced 40 seats.

The number of Sinn Féin and IRA 'big names' in the line up – amongst those elected were De Valera, Collins, McNeill and Arthur Griffith – revealed the seriousness with which Dublin viewed the contest. The transfer agreement had proved a failure on both sides indicating the division not only between camps but between leaders and followers within them. Nonetheless, as the Home Rulers had promised in good faith to deliver on 2nd preferences, a corresponding arrangement by the Sinn Féin Standing Committee to hand the balance of the anti-conscription fund over to the IPP to compensate for the lack of finances, was honoured.

The UIL maintained its separate identity throughout, despite the similarity of the appeals in the common anti-partitionist cause. When Sinn Féin attempted to extract a pledge from candidates, one clause of which stressed 'the use of every effort to defeat the policy of partition in the Irish nation', Devlin insisted that the word 'constitutional' should be inserted before the word 'effort'. De Valera, as could be expected, did not agree.[16]

While Devlin's vote in the new West Belfast constituency exceeded the combined vote of Sinn Féin by more than 1,300 votes, it was a far cry from the margin of victory in 1918. The derisory vote for his running-mate, Richard Byrne, showed the personal nature of the appeal. Furthermore, Devlin's election in fourth place in Antrim was well beneath his expectation of being elected on the first count. Yet with only three-fifths of the Sinn Féin vote his party had secured an equal number of seats. There would be no doubting one thing; in a country where Sinn Féin had swept away all opposition for the second time in three years, his organisation had proven it was there to stay.

CHAPTER 4

Truce, Treaty and Aftermath

The truce of 1921 painted northern nationalists a deeper shade of green. Seamus Woods, then 2nd in command of the 3rd Northern Division of the IRA, could report that people were now flocking to them.[1] A representative from East Down could state that in this erstwhile Hibernian stronghold, the constitutional nationalists had transferred to Sinn Féin and handed over £1,000 collected from the Redmonite Volunteers.[2] But not all were prepared to worship the rising sun. A Fermanagh priest of Sinn Féin views complained to the party's standing committee of 'weak-kneed public representatives'.[3] That same month what he meant was made evident when the nationalist representatives on the County Council united with the unionists in an attempt to keep the Sinn Féiner, Thomas Corrigan, out of the secretaryship.[4]

The new post-Truce Sinn Féin was in a fighting mood. Most of those who spoke at the Standing Committee meeting ruled out passive resistance as the response to non-co-operative officials on nationalist-dominated local government boards. All had united in support of the Belfast Boycott. One delegate, whose zeal outran his grasp of international politics, suggested that America, Spain, France and Belgium be persuaded to boycott Belfast linen. The delegates were assured by Arthur Griffith that 'all Ireland would stand behind them in the fight'.[5] Behind this rhetoric was a considerably less impressive reality.

When Eoin McNeill, Chairman for the 'Committee for Information on the case of Ulster', the organisation formed by Dáil Éireann to work in tandem with the Treaty negotiations, went north to Enniskillen to a conference, he was disappointed to discover 'the whole local body without a clear policy or line of action'. He found a great deal of criticism of the envoys, particularly of Michael Collins. McNeill attributed this attitude to the remnants of the Irish Party spirit and the domination of the unionists.[6]

When he discussed the policy of non-recognition of the northern parliament with Archdeacon Tierney and Cahir Healy, he was told by them of the consequences such a policy would bring.[7] McNeill also brought up the question of non-recognition by Catholic schools of the Northern Education Authority and suggested that the schools which took the approach would have to be organised,[8] proposing the raising of the required £500,000 required from the rates of those who withheld payment due to Belfast. He was mindful, however, of the dangers of sectarianism developing from such an approach, a *caveat* invoked by De Valera to Dr Gillespie of Cookstown when the latter proposed a pan-nationalist organisation, including McRory and Devlin, to oppose the depredations of the northern government.[9]

Throughout the autumn, as negotiations continued in London, anxiety increased among nationalists in the six counties. In September, County Down nationalists of all shades met at Castlewellan to voice their opposition to partition.[10] The day before the Treaty was signed, Kevin O'Higgins wrote that the nationalists of Tyrone and Fermanagh 'complained that they were left without guidance or as it is pathetically put, "like sheep without a shepherd".' There was, he asserted, 'a complete absence of any settled policy', with nationalists looking to Dáil Éireann for a lead.[11] On 6 December the Articles of Agreement which became known as the Treaty were signed in London, conferring on Ireland Dominion status and providing for an Oath of Allegiance to the Crown. Under Article 12 a Boundary Commission was to be established to determine, in accordance with the wishes of the inhabitants so far as might be compatible with economic and geographical conditions, the boundary between the two states. A months period, 'The Ulster Month', was provided from the ratification of the Treaty by London in which the north could opt out.

On 7 December representatives of the six county nationalists met Eoin McNeill at Dublin's Mansion House. The Mayor of Derry gave vent to their disquiet at the thought that the London delegation had 'given away' what was 'fought for in the last 750 years'. 'We are no longer a united nation', he proclaimed. The Mid Derry MP and AOH member, George Leeke, voiced more specific grievances, in particular the Education Bill and the newly constituted USC. Fr McFeeley, predictably, also expressed worries over 'secularisation of schools'. McNeill was at pains to reassure them, telling them that 'non recognition' in a word was how the situation was to be faced and suggesting a 'practical programme of passive resistance'.[12] The next day an enlarged deputation was introduced by him to De Valera in the same building. De Valea began by assuring them that nothing 'irrevocable' had been done as the Treaty was not yet ratified, and ended by telling them he had 'no objection' if Derry recognised Dáil Éireann, thereby seceding de facto from the newly-formed northern state. He then listened to their concerns which resolved into the threats to both education and the franchise under a northern government.[13] One by one they voiced their views. The objection to a northern parliament depended solely on its power. They were quite prepared to recognise it for the 'Ulster month' and they saw as much hope for justice under an enlargement of the northern area as a diminution of it, provided it took place within an Irish state. This view was disputed by another delegate.[14] They wanted assurances that the policy of Councils pledging allegiance to Dáil Éireann could continue. As the Chairman of Armagh UDC commented plaintively, 'I only wish to do the right thing.'[15] The deputation got the assurances it required. The influence of these delegates meant that support for the Treaty radiated across the north. From 22 January Omagh Rural Council, Lisnaskea Board of Guardians and Tyrone County Council, all voted their support. The papers led the way. The North West Publishing Company chain, of which Alex Donnelly, one of the delegates at the meeting, was Chairman of the Board of Directors, swung behind it. On 10 December its *Frontier Sentinel*[16] proclaimed: 'Victory at last, Ireland enters on the path of freedom. The week of centuries mentioned by St Malachy has come to an end.' The Devlinite *Irish News* took a similar, if less ebullient tone. Its preference was after all for a solution preserving essential unity rather than for a Boundary Commission which would inevitably leave Belfast 'on the wrong side'. On 5 January it condemned as 'wreckage' Document No 2, the republican alternative to the Treaty which contained a different form of the Oath of Allegiance and lacked any alternative proposals on partition.[17]

Not all local authorities interpreted the non-recognition policy the same way as Tyrone County Council. On 7 December it recognised the Belfast parliament in expectation of a favourable Boundary Commission judgement. On 15 December Fermanagh refused recognition in accordance with its earlier pledge of allegiance to Dáil Éireann. Following on the terms of the Act introduced by the northern government earlier that month, the Council was dissolved on 21 December.

Sinn Féin and IRA – post-Treaty

The Treaty represented 'a new circumstance', Kevin O'Higgins told Cahir Healy in April, at the first meeting of the North East Ulster Advisory Committee, in reply to the latter's complaint that the Dáil's policy towards councils which cut their links with Belfast, was one of surrender'.[18] Cosgrave reconciled this position with the different approach of non-cooperation enjoined on northern nationalists the previous autumn, with a dazzling piece of casuistry, centred on southern self-interest. He told them that while the 'political situation' existing in Ireland during the lead up to the London negotiations 'required a little experiment as far as these councils were concerned' matters had been changed by the Treaty.[19]

That this was Dublin's view became alarmingly obvious to northern nationalists as far back as January, with the signing on the 23rd of that month of the first Craig/Collins Pact. This agreement, providing for the alteration of the Boundary Commission and the abandonment of the Belfast Boycott, was welcomed in the conservative and unionist press as a recognition of the new state. Nationalists were correspondingly outraged. Cahir Healy wrote on the 29th that Collins' proposal to scrap the Boundary Commission made some of them think he might be acting to their prejudice.[20] The nationalist Mayor of Derry, Hugh O'Doherty, had spoken of a possible 'grave situation' being created, while Bishop McRory conveyed to Dáil Éireann the disquiet of many Belfast Catholics at the lifting of the Belfast Boycott without any prior consultation with them.

A deputation of concerned nationalists from South Down, Armagh and Newry area, sought and received assurances of their future within an Irish State under the Treaty, whilst a similar assurance placated the six county Roman Catholic bishops, who sent a message to Griffith and Collins expressing 'satisfaction' that 'large areas of the six counties were to be transferred to the Free State'.

On the specific issue of the Belfast Boycott, a special missive from the committee overseeing it in that city, to the Dublin government earlier that month, had highlighted once again the unique vulnerability of the Catholics there, ' the Irish community in Belfast' as they were described.[21] Over 1,000 workers had been expelled, 300 traders burned out, a loss of earning power of £1,750.000 per year incurred, all with the objective by the perpetrators of 'driving from the city the most independent, most enterprising and nationalist members of our colony'. The use of the term 'colony' is indicative of how Belfast Catholics saw themselves as a marooned minority within a sea of loyalism.

Far from damaging the perpetrators, the Boycott 'unwittingly helped the pogrom' having forced the closure of premises on which republicans depended for work and the transfer of others to Dublin. While they did not wish to see the Boycott lifted or its efficiency as a punitive weapon blunted 'in the slightest degree,' they wished for a less self defeating policy. As a countermeasure they urged the granting of licences to certain firms. Such a condition would, they felt, 'Irishise Belfast' creating a 'compact force' in a city where 'foreign influence' was predominant.[22] The address which urged Dublin to show 'awareness from a national viewpoint' was signed by leading Belfast IRA members, Crummie and Smith.

The position of the IRA in the six counties had undergone an improvement since the Truce in terms of recruitment and morale. Woods could write of his Divisional area:

> With the signing of the Truce, the Catholic population believing for the moment they had been victorious and that the Specials and UVF had been beaten, all flocked to our standard with the exception of the aristocratic minority who prefer to live under with the British or northern government rather than an Irish one.[23]

The same attitude was reflected across the north in the growth of training camps in the other divisional areas. But difficulties continued to beset the movement. The OC of the 2nd Northern Division, Charles Daly, could write to GHQ on 24 August 1921 rejecting the claim that training had dropped in his command but admitting that there had 'never been much training done'. He went on to put the blame on the mentality of the nationalist population:[24]

> The cause which explains this is the same which explains the fact that there has been so few activities and so few of my orders carried out during hostilities. The slave mind and lack of enthusiasm and military spirit in the population in this part

of Ireland has a most paralysing effect. This has been my experience in Tyrone'.[25]

He complained of a lack of discipline among the young men in his command and welcomed the sending of instructors by GHQ but added the reminder in regard to the establishment of training camps in the division, that his orders 'as per usual had not been carried out everywhere'. A report from a Captain Andrews to the Director of Training in October, following a visit to the Breenagh Training Camp in Daly's Division, described the state of the Volunteers as 'very raw'. Of 29 men, with six exceptions, their 'mastery of soldierly duties' was 'nil', Andrews commented. The Tyrone experience was reflected in other parts of the nationalist north. A visitor to a camp in the 4th Northern Division area at Lurgan reported that it would be unable to continue much longer due to debt problems and organisational inefficiency. On a broader canvas the reports were favourable, reflecting as they did an improvement on the inertia of the 'Tan War'. The Belfast Brigade had established a foundry and was producing hundreds of grenades, working against time for the expected resumption of hostilities.

Like McKelvey, OC 3rd Northern,[26] who constantly used this phrase 'the resumption of hostilities' in his reports, Daly did not expect the Truce to last. Had he known it was likely to continue for as long as it did, he would, he later told GHQ 'have made more preparations and put the camps on a better footing'.

The signing of the Treaty ushered in a new phase for the northern IRA. Not only did it have confusing signals from Dublin to contend with, but the authorities, emboldened by a new sense of a legitimacy, became increasingly aggressive. Woods was later to characterise the period as one of demoralisation from which the Army felt it might never recover

General Cameron, the British Commander in the city, had informed Colonel Dalton of the Irish GHQ in Dublin that it was not his practice to communicate with 'a body not recognised by the established government'. Seamus Woods had noted this as 'a clear definition' of their status and expressed surprise that the Truce liaison office at St Mary's Hall had not been raided by them in view of the increasing harassment and provocation 'becoming daily more unbearable' at the hands of the 'old murder gang active during the war'. Particularly worrying to him was the ease with which officers' names could be obtained in the building. His fears were to be realised in March when a raid on the premises by military netted 'the names of practically every officer in the division'. As a result most of the Divisional officers and several Brigade officers demanded an inquiry, many of them calling for the resignation of the Commandment, Joe McKelvey. The enquiry, finally held on 30 March, was not attended by McKelvey who did not return from the IRA Army Convention in Dublin, summoned that month by opponents of the Treaty against the wishes of the Provisional Government's Minister of Defence, Richard Mulcahy. In McKelvey's absence Woods his deputy was elected the Commanding Officer of the 3rd Northern on 9 April. The pressure on the northern IRA was unrelenting.

The Convention resulted in an open breach within the army on the Treaty issue, following on the one in the Dáil in January. The newly established anti-Treaty IRA army executive repudiated the authority of GHQ and entrenched itself within fortified positions in Dublin city, with its headquarters in the Four Courts. By January 1922 there were four main groups of new political captives in the hands of the six county government: the 'Derry' prisoners under sentence of death after a botched escape attempt at Derry jail in which two warders were killed; the 'Dromore' prisoners captured after a raid by B Specials on a training camp in that area on 5 January; the 'Crannagh' group, captured after a gunbattle in December, and a small group taken into custody in Belfast in October. The sectarian savagery of the Ulster Special Constabulary had increased during the Truce in response to what was seen as the political success of the 'other side'. By 14 October the OC of the 2nd Northern Division could tell GHQ:

> Orange aggression and cowardly attacks on defenceless people in two of three areas of the division are becoming so serious that we must take active steps for their protection. The only solution is to provide arms in the Cookstown area. While the Volunteers are strong, without arms they are practically defenceless. The position of our people in the district was always bad but since the truce, it is becoming desperate.[27]

He went on to relate how on 15 September the Cookstown company was ambushed by a large group of armed Orangemen leaving one man seriously wounded and others badly beaten.

The attackers then shot up the area pouring 'volleys of rifle fire into the houses of Volunteers'. The result was that the Volunteers of the company were unable to stay in their own homes at night.

> They sleep together in a vacant house without even arms to protect themselves and in hourly expectation of being massacred. Raids on houses, indiscriminate shooting, holding up and ambushing helpless people at night, have become such common occurrences of late that they almost pass unnoticed except by the parties concerned.

In Dromore, scene of a particularly revolting triple murder by B Specials the previous April, the home of the IRA No 3 Brigade Quartermaster was flooded by over 100 men who ransacked the building and humiliated his sisters. One of the raiding party, a next door neighbour, had been tried and acquitted of the April murders. It was against this backdrop of one sided warfare, exacerbated by the handing over of 'Law and Order' services to the Belfast parliament in November, that an 'Ulster Council' of the northern IRA was formed, with Frank Aiken as Chairman, Sean McEoin, 1st Midland Divisional Commander as Deputy Director of Operations, and all the remaining Northern Divisional OCs on its executive.

Throughout January 1922 plans were laid for the arming of the IRA in the six counties, with pre-Treaty rifles exchanged for those handed over by the British to the Provisional Government. The kidnapping of prominent loyalists in response to the death sentences imposed on three of the Derry prisoners was also arranged. The first Craig/Collins Pact stalled both plans, the latter one being held over on Collins' instructions in anticipation of the Pact succeeding. When instead it foundered on two opposing sets of interpretations, the Ulster Council went into action, authorising abductions on 7 and 8 February of prominent unionists and B Specials from their homes and their removal to barracks in the south. Six days later a fatal altercation took place between the IRA and B Specials at Clones railway station.

On 17 and 18 March, Pomeroy and Maghera Barracks were attacked and captured by Volunteers of the 2nd Northern Division while a third attack in the same area was unsuccessful but resulted in the deaths of USC men.[28] Sean McEoin's 1st Midland Division attacked and captured Belcoo Barracks on 28th of the month. It is unclear whether or not the IRB trio of

Collins, Mulcahy and O'Duffy directing all of this were doing so with a view to keeping the northern IRA 'on side' in the event of the impending Treaty split. What is beyond dispute is that this was its major result. When the split came, only two Divisional heads, McKelvey of 3rd Northern and Charlie Daly of 2nd Northern, declared for the republican side. Daly had already been removed by O'Duffy and replaced by Thomas Morris, a local man[29] and ex-British army officer who had reorganised the IRA in South Derry during the War of Independence.

The 3rd Northern, as has been seen, did not follow McKelvey. Woods, who commented on the 'demoralisation' in the first three months of 1922, could later state that GHQ in that period 'did their best' to assist the six county IRA. Despite the lack of much in the way of practical support he recommended to the Division in March, that they back GHQ in the split in order to give 'the people who supported the Treaty a better chance of overcoming the position in the north'.[30] Yet a sufficient under-tow of disquiet existed to enable McCartan, himself a reluctant Treaty supporter, to write to a friend on the day after the signing of the second Craig/Collins Pact, with considerable exagger-ation: 'The IRA in the six counties all are anti-Treaty almost to a man. They, however, are out against partition rather than a Treaty. They feel they have been let down.'[31]

For the Provisional Government the most embarrassing re-minder of this undercurrent came in Tyrone when in January, 32 of 34 Sinn Féin clubs voted against the Treaty, ousting George Murnaghan in favour of an anti-Treatite. However strong the feeling may have been, it was not sufficient to shake their overall pattern of allegiance. Almost a month later, on 28 April, O'Duffy could account for the loyalty of all three brigades in the 3rd Northern Division and numbers one and two Brigades in the 2nd Northern, i.e. encompassing County Tyrone, which 'went with the Four Courts executive due to a misunderstanding' but were 'returning just as rapidly'. In the case of the remainder, one had repudiated its leader who plumped for the republic while the other was solidly behind GHQ.[32] The leaders of the 1st and 5th Northern Divisions Joe Sweeney and Dan Hogan, had come out in support of the Treaty with Aiken of the 4th Northern re-maining neutral. It was this last division which managed to give the best account of itself throughout the period, January to June 1922, when the north experienced what was in effect Orange-

Green civil war often equalling in savagery the one which began afterwards in the south. (By the time of the Four Courts attack on 28 June 16 IRA men had died in the north, more than in any of the previous years.) Aiken would later claim that 'at least 60 Specials' were killed in his division from Christmas to June. 'They never hit a nationalist but we hit back twice as hard. We had them cowed in our area.' Not all his retaliatory operations were against armed agents of the state. On 17 June 1922 at Altnaveigh, his men launched a gun and bomb attack on eight Protestant homes killing six, including a husband and wife. To this day the atrocity is recalled in northern loyalist circles.[33]

Nowhere was the position of minority now more desperate then in Belfast. January had been marked by gun and bomb attacks in the east and north of the city, resulting in the imposition of a curfew in the latter area. In February 44 people died in the city. In one incident six Catholic children were blown asunder when a loyalist bomb was hurled into their midst as they played in Weaver Street near York Road. On 22 February, as violence escalated, the Ulster Council authorised the formation of a Belfast City Guard of up to 72 men, partly to provide employment for otherwise destitute Volunteers. It was to be a flimsy shield against the hurricane of savagery unleashed on the Catholic population in the coming month, climaxing with the murder of Owen McMahon, his three sons and a servant on 24 March.[34] Writing in June to Churchill and the King, Lloyd George admitted that despite the presence of 9,000 troops and 48,000 Specials, 400 Catholics had been killed and 'another 1,200 wounded without a single person being brought to justice. Our Ulster case is not a good one,' he commented. Even though the Catholic population was not powerless when it came to retaliation – on Woods' calculations from 1 January to late May, 151 Catholics and 86 Protestants were killed, with 274 and 198 injured from the respective denominations – there was a grisliness about the McMahon atrocity which sent shock waves through the public sensibility.[35]

When Joe Devlin expressed his revulsion in the House of Commons, Churchill, while sympathising with him, coupled the condemnation of it with another atrocity, a politically motivated triple murder in a Galway city nursing home some days before. Churchill was throwing the ball back in the court of the Provisional Government and its inability to maintain control within its own jurisdiction.[36] With the situation in Belfast so obviously critical, a possibility existed for a trade-off on all sides. Under Churchill's auspices a conference was held in London on 29-30 March involving representatives of the three governments. Out of it grew the second Craig/Collins Pact, introduced with its theatrical fanfare of 'Peace is today declared'. Churchill was aware of Devlin's desire for an accommodation with the northern government. Devlin had made proposals in the House of Commons on 28 May suggesting the formation of a religiously mixed police force to replace the Specials. McRory had earlier called for an equally divided force and negotiations had been taking place between Craig and prominent Catholics of a unionist stamp. The Pact provided for the creation of an Advisory Committee to oversee the recruitment of Catholics into the Specials, for patrols and search parties of mixed religion, and for a conciliation committee representative of both traditions to oversee complaints and their handling. With the exception of the Secret Service, all police were to be in uniform and a record was to be kept of all arms issued.

Other clauses provided for the creation of a special court to try serious crimes, for the cessation of IRA activity and thereupon the organising of the special police outside Belfast on lines similar to those agreed for the city. Arrangements were to be made for the return of the expelled workers. £500,000 was to be allocated for relief projects, one-third of which would go to projects in Roman Catholic areas. Political prisoners whose offences were committed before 31 March were to be released.[37] The Pact in Clause 7 provided for a further meeting between the signatories 'during the month immediately following the passing into law of the Free State Constitution (when the northern government was due to exercise its opt-out concession under the Treaty). This meeting would consider whether means could be devised 'to secure the unity of Ireland' or, in the absence of such agreement, whether agreement could be arrived at on the boundary question' otherwise than by recourse to the Boundary Commission outlined in Article 12 of the Treaty.

The Pact was warmly welcomed by the national and international press as well as by the business community. Craig would enclose for Collins on 4 April a Resolution passed at a mass meeting of 'some 2,000 leading businessmen'[38] approving of the agreement and 'expressing hope' that the time would come when the revival of trade would 'permit the employment of all ex-service men and the return of those Roman Catholics of Belfast citizenship to those businesses where they were employed before the war.'

The Pact offered much to all groups who were party to it. To the British and unionists it held out the prospect of stability; to the Catholic minority an opportunity to have a say in the administration of the new state; to Collins a chance of superceding the Boundary Commission which he had never favoured. Its failure was seen as the failure of all the above to make these expectations converge. None of the participants was truly master of its own house. To begin with, the British government was an unstable mosaic that was to fall to Bonar Law's Conservatives later in the year. Within unionism, the right wing both inside and outside Cabinet, when not rejecting the Pact outright, was committed to the most niggardly interpretation of its clauses. The draconian Special Power Act, introduced as a sop to them the following month, was to have a disastrously polarising effect on inter community relations. Within the broad northern nationalist family not only did the obvious divisions between Home Rulers and Sinn Féiners still exist, there were the added tensions arising from the Treaty split which were fast pushing the south towards Civil War. All of this impacted on the republican movement north of the border.

The Sinn Féin organisation in the north was not identical with the IRA after the Truce any more than before it. Seán Milroy could report to Mulcahy in late September 1921 how the 'general attitude' of the Volunteers inhibited the organisation of the party. He had been told this by the Armagh organiser at a meeting in Belfast of representatives from that city, Down, Armagh and Tyrone.[39] It was not, Milroy hastened to add, based on any instances of specific hostility, but 'rather an atmosphere of aloofness on the part of the Volunteers and an implied attitude that the Sinn Féin clubs were not serving any useful purpose and that it was a waste of time and energy to trouble about them'. He advocated the issuing of a directive from headquarters urging the Volunteers to adopt a friendly and co-operative attitude towards the clubs.[40] A similar complaint was made by Vincent O'Sheil, the Dungannon solicitor and Secretary of Sinn Féin's Ulster Committee. The disquiet which arose after the passing of the initial post-Treaty euphoria added to the cleavage.

Immediately after the postponement of the Sinn Féin Ard
Fheis in February, a meeting was held in the Mansion House to
which only standing committee members and northern delegates to the Ard Fheis were admitted. The result was the creation
of a Sinn Féin Advisory Committee by the northern Sinn Féiners
under the direction of Eamon Donnelly. De Valera at this meeting 'denounced partition in every mood and tense'.[41] O'Shiel,
worried by the status of this committee, pushed through a resolution subordinating it to be the newly formed officer board of
Sinn Féin. He subsequently attended its first three meetings
where he defended Provisional Government policy against the
attempts of Archibald Savage, Eamon Donnelly and De Valera
to commit 'the whole six counties to a hopeless guerrilla war
with Craig's government'. Through stressing that Catholics, resident in the north (unlike the proposers), would be the sufferers
if such a policy were adapted, by May O'Shiel could happily report the committee had become a dead letter. In the meantime,
in Belfast where its influence was strongest due to the presence
of men such as Archibald Savage and Thomas Carolan, it continued to be a thorn in the side of those supporting the
Craig/Collins Pact.[42]

At the first and penultimate meeting of the Provisional
Government's North-East Ulster Advisory Committee, Belfast
delegates stressed the total separateness of the Sinn Féin and
IRA organisations in the city and how the former organisation,
since the Truce, had expanded to 12 clubs with over 1,000 members, many of them people 'not in the firing line' during the War
of Independence but now 'prepared to die in the last ditch'.[43]

The North East Ulster Advisory Committee had originated
in a suggestion of Aiken's who complained that the government's cause needed more effective contacts in the north than
Murnaghan and Milroy. Mulcahy conveyed the advice to
Collins who assembled its personnel by the simple expedient of
writing to those prominent Catholics in the north believed sympathetic to the Provisional Government. At its meeting on 11
April, less than a fortnight after the second Craig/Collins Pact,
where northern nationalism stood and where it was going, both
became considerably clearer. The conference highlighted the inefficiency of the Pact from the Catholics' point of view – no inquiry had been held onto the Brown Street murder gang, raiding
by the Specials had not stopped and release of prisoners had not

taken place. The responses to this varied from those – in the minority – willing to break the Pact outright, and those, such as Dr McRory, prepared to push the demand for an inquiry 'to breaking point' but worried of the consequences for Belfast Catholics if they were seen to break it. In the attitudes expressed, both to this question and the related one of Catholic recruitment to the Specials, it revealed the east-west of the Bann divide which was to become of greater importance in the years that followed. As one delegate commented, 'The Pact is all about Belfast'. While delegates from there saw no difficulty in getting their followers to join the constabulary if certain conditions were met, Gillespie from Cookstown and Healy from Fermanagh were adamant that only the Hibernians in their area would accept such an offer.[44]

An exchange involving a Derry delegate, the prominent Sinn Féiner Patrick Hegarty, encapsulated the difference:

'The IRA split last week,' he said, 'and there was dread the pogrom would start once more, but inside one hour the IRA and the Hibernians and the people of Derry that are deadly opposed to each other united again. At the last pogrom in Derry half a dozen houses was all that was burned of Protestant property and that was one of the principal reasons why the city remained quiet. The Freemason Gang has more to lose.'

It was quickly pointed out by Bishop McRory and a Belfast priest that the analogy was invalid. Derry enjoyed easy access to the Free State and had a Catholic majority. 'One might as well be talking about London,' McRory commented. The question was raised of how the Roman Catholic population would approach the issues of 'education' and 'local government' within the new constraints imposed by the Treaty. McRory had been worried about the position of St Mary's Training College. It had been largely on his urging that the boycott affecting up to one-third of Catholic secondary schools had been introduced in February. His message now was simple. 'If there is any disposition not to recognise the Belfast government in this matter or in any other matter, I am quite prepared to stand out and let our people suffer on. For I understand,' he added ominously, 'there is every likelihood of their being recognised in other matters.' Events behind the scenes proved him right. Lord Londonderry had already approached the Provisional Government for an accommodation on the education question. In the light of such developments Archdeacon Tierney of Enniskillen told the delegates he 'would close with the northern authorities at once' if schools under the Catholic managers got the right to adopt the programme and timetables of southern Ireland.[45]

Further confirmation of McRory's point was provided at the meeting itself in the rejectionist remarks and cold shouldering attitude of the southern ministers. For instance, on the issue of local government there was, it was stated, a limit to the extent to which Dublin would subsidise the dissident northern Councils. Despite the encouragement given to public bodies in the north to declare allegiance to Dáil Éireann, no 'regular policy' had been inaugurated to deal with 'local government up there', as Cosgrave admitted. Neither 'the purse of Dáil Éireann' nor that of the Provisional Government was 'a bottomless one' in the changed situation, he told them.[46] Healy voiced his feeling of grievance at this situation. 'They were put out of existence for recognising An Dáil and today we hear that the Dáil recommends a policy of surrender. It may be a good policy but it is not a palatable policy,' he said. It was in this context that O'Higgins made the comment on the 'new circumstances' created by the Treaty and accused Healy of not stating the position fairly. There were in any event differences among northern nationalists on these issues. Cosgrave told the meeting that only one Council, Newry, had 'stood out and fought a good fight' – all the others recognised the English government or the British Local Government Board 'at a time when there was a life and death struggle in the south'. The Hibernians' presence on Fermanagh Council made it doubtful that abstentionists had a majority there,' he claimed, adding that those Councils which cut their links with Belfast had done so since the Treaty when 'a different situation had arisen'. In this altered context the action of Fermanagh County Council was to Griffith 'merely a moral gesture' to which he was 'utterly opposed. It didn't help us' and 'it gave away all that had been fought for', he claimed.[47] By way of explanation, Alderman Hegarty from Derry recalled that the Home Rule Mayor of the City had prevented the Sinn Féin members from carrying a resolution of allegiance to Dáil Éireann. As a result only one of non-recognition of the northern parliament was able to get through.

The southerners were not slow to exploit this theme of northern nationalist disunity. 'The class of people that we have got down here from the north to discuss local government,' said Cosgrave, 'always send down a peace man and a war man and they put up to us what we are to do. There is always a negative and a positive policy.' 'You remember,' he remarked in reference to the December Mansion House meeting, 'where the Mayor of Derry was contradicted by another man from the city and they both said they represented that particular area.'[48] It was a typical exercise in 'buck passing' by a leader of mainstream Irish nationalism. Northern Catholics had been entangled in an enterprise in which their position made them more vulnerable than any other section of the nation. They were then blamed for the contradictions resulting from that vulnerability which the pursuit of that project inevitably exposed and exacerbated.

Despite all its reservations and objections, Dublin typically baulked at the idea of recommending that the dissolved councils be reinstated. That trenched upon the 'policy of abject surrender' deprecated by Cosgrave. Instead it was to be 'left to the chairman of each body' to decide. If they had a nationalist majority they would get back under the terms of the pact, O'Higgins assured them, otherwise the strategy of the Boundary Commission would be better served by leaving the Commissioner appointed by Belfast in place.[49]

The IPP since the Truce

Since the Truce the Home Rule movement in the north had receded into the background as the republican/unionist conflict took centre stage. In September they had watched with bemused contempt as the English born-Milroy collected information in the north for Dáil Éireann while studiously avoiding them.[50] On the Treaty Dillon reported in late January that the nationalists in Belfast and the six counties felt 'let down badly', confessing himself 'anxious … none of the old party should make themselves responsible for it'. But new realities of power within Ireland could not be ignored, and in February Devlin who had been 'bitterly attacked' by some of his followers for his meeting with Collins at the Shelbourne Hotel in Dublin, took Dillon's advice not to go to the House of Commons for the time being.[51] When he returned to Westminster and it was to voice the grievances of his constituents at the horrific violence of that the following month. Dillon had no doubt in his mind who bore the ultimate responsibility for the carnage, telling T. P. O'Connor that:

> The Sinn Féin activity is a deliberate policy ... to goad the Orangemen to fury. In private they do acknowledge their policy and are quite proud of the results. When anxiety is expressed as to the fate of the Catholics of Belfast and the six counties, the reply is that of course in great revolutionary moments there must be bloodshed and suffering.[52]

Devlin lent his support to the second Craig/Collins Pact but feared being displaced by Sinn Féin as the representative voice of Belfast Catholics. This anxiety underlay his comment to Dillon that an agreement was 'no good in Belfast without guidance and organisation by somebody who knew how to do these things.'[53] It was a worry reciprocated by republicans, unsure of how to deal with such a resilient opponent.

The North East Ulster Advisory Committee had discussed the idea of Devlinites joining the Catholic Special Police Force due to be established. Some feared their presence, others such as Archdeacon Tierney of Fermanagh welcomed the idea.[54] They, along with the De Valeraites, were seen as the pact's chief opponents in the Catholic community. A suggestion that their councillors, Oswald Jamison and William Hazlett, be appointed to the Relief Committee produced the unusually bluntly expressed Sinn Féin accusation that 'they had more in common with Protestants' and would be 'Protestant for Corporation work'.[55] That denominational terminology, so at odds with the party's expressed inclusiveness, could be used at all said something about the depth of such ideas within sections of the movement. That it should be used ascriptively to reject rivals within the nationalist community showed that such exclusiveness did not stop at the religious divide.

It did not come easily to Devlin to sit on the sideline and watch as Sinn Féin made the running. By April, in Dillon's eyes, he was 'evidently anxious' to go into the 'Ulster parliament'. O'Connor approved his instinct but felt the time was 'not ripe'.[56] They may have noticed the drift of Sinn Féin supporters back to the IPP throughout the spring, a police report stating that the republicans were 'daily losing ground' to them.[57] Bishop McRory's discomfiture as the new order bid fair to threaten church interests gave the IPP a certain 'schadenfreude', Dillon gloating that he had messed things badly and was reaping the result in great unpopularity.[58] In fact, unknown to the Home Rulers, the pace of events had forced the bishop to adopt a more inclusive approach. While they felt McRory shared the reluctance of Griffith and Collins to do business with Devlin – a suggestion made to him by Churchill – on 7 May the bishop, after approaches from prominent Catholics, was writing to Collins asking him 'not to refuse' to meet him. In this respect McRory was ahead of opinion within official circles in the emergent southern state.[59]

As far on as June the Provisional Government were still refusing to have dealings with Devlin, describing him to T. P. O'Connor as 'an extinct volcano'.[60] A confidential government memorandum could state in early 1923:

> Since partition and the triumph of Sinn Féin the AOH and UIL have been particularly destroyed in Ulster. Save for the city of Belfast, the UIL has completely disappeared.
>
> The AOH by reason of its official status as a Friendly Society has been able to hold together the badly shattered framework of its system. It is and has always been robust in Belfast which is natural, seeing that it is the city of its birth. After Belfast it is strongest in East Down, South and Mid-Antrim, County Derry and County Armagh. In Tyrone it is practically a dead letter save for certain outlying portions of the east and south, with a spot or two in the mid Division. Fermanagh might still contain about nine or ten lodges which keep up the paraphernalia and formalities of a country board.[61]

That Devlin would use that power base, however constricted, to threaten its position, remained an abiding worry for Dublin.

CHAPTER 5

The Collapse of the Northern IRA

Six weeks after the signing of the pact and a fortnight after the introduction of the Special Powers Act how matters stood for the northern Catholics become clear from the meeting of the Free State's Ulster sub-Committee held on 15 May in the Grand Metropole Hotel, Belfast. The Pact, the chairman admitted, was 'still in existence' but had not been honoured by their side 'since 2 May'. Their opponents had not, they felt, 'honoured it since they signed it'. The strategy to be adopted was one of brinkmanship, placing the onus for breaking the Pact on Craigavon's government for whom the 'most unpleasant thing was not the breaking of it but the pretence on our part of keeping it on'. The 'pretending game' would be played in the hope of securing concessions on the issue of prisoners and increased representation on the labour committees, issues to which the northern Catholics and the southern government accorded different priorities.[1]

In all of this they were conscious of division within their own ranks. Under the terms of the Pact, Relief Committees were to be set up for the disbursement of aid. With Collins holding out for full representation of the minority by the White Cross organisation, while Andrews, the Minister for Labour, wanted a Home Ruler Councillor and an expelled worker included, Fr Laverty had 'gone behind their backs' and arranged a deal with Andrews for lower representation on the committee than had been envisaged. The Bishop of Down and Connor, suspected of being behind the compromise, was 'one of the biggest sinners of the lot', one delegate remarked. Not that Laverty's action was their biggest problem.[2] The De Valeraites and Devlinites comprised between them 'the majority of the Belfast Catholics', the Chairman, General Seamus Woods, acknowledged. The former section provoked Protestant retaliation, then united with the Devlinites in a joint criticism of the Provisional Government for failing to protect them. 'They want to let us down,' he concluded. Added to this was the continuing rural/urban divide within northern nationalism, reflected in the creation of two information offices, Clones, Co Monaghan and Belfast. 'The north western position,' as Dr Russell McNabb, a leading Belfast Sinn Féiner, reminded them 'was not the same as the north eastern'. Over-riding everything was the fear expressed by O'Shiel of Craig breaking the Pact 'with tremendous explosion' forcing 'all the Catholics' to 'put their hands up and submit to the northern government'.

To counteract this situation and make the government impossible, they proposed to the Provisional Government, 'a campaign of destruction inside the six counties, coupled with the creation of a committee to bring into focus' once more the Boundary Commission, 'the one thing' according to Healy which 'ruffled' the unionists and which 'for some reason of his own, Mr Collins practically scrapped'.

Bound up with any consideration of the position of Catholics in Belfast was the position of the IRA there. At the meeting of the Ulster Advisory Committee in Dublin in April 1922, Woods had described the Pact as agreeable to the majority of the Catholic population. Whereas during three years of war the IRA had 'put up little fight as the civil population backed the enemy' the situation had changed since the Truce. As Dr Russell McNabb told it they now had the 'support of the whole people … of every Catholic in Belfast and were getting along famously when the Pact came'. Commenting on the incendiary campaign against unionists' property he rhapsodised about beautiful fires in Belfast each night, asserting that the burning campaign, if coupled with some arms, would bring unionists to heel. 'If they thought we were going to resume it again would be a deterrent to them' he concluded. Replying to this Collins acknowledged that Dublin had 'for many good months' done as much as possible to get property destroyed, adding that 'unionists thought a great deal more of property than of human life'. But more sober counsels prevailed. Mulcahy, the Minister of Defence, gave his opinion that the cost of paying for such destruction would eventually fall on an Irish government rather than a British one. Other voices, principally that of Bishop McRory, also deprecated the idea. He outlined the starkness of the situation as he saw it: his flock was more dispirited, discouraged and cowed than ever before, the whole Stanhope Street district was deserted, 'our poor people are huddled in the Falls area and sleep on the floor'. Large parts of Belfast, he told them, could not be entered by the IRA for the purpose of incendiary attacks. And even that policy where possible would be counterproductive. 'I can assure you that if you burn houses you will intensify the slaughter and the men who do the burning will have to run away and hide,' he told them, warning that it was impossible to do anything, even incendiarism, 'which will not bring down on you a terrible punishment.' Woods' testimony reinforced this. The Falls, he stated, was the only area in which a fight was possible, everywhere else in the city the nationalist people were 'striving for existence'. Volunteers faced the prospect of 'dying for nothing' or getting up to 15 years imprisonment with little prospect of release. 'Sooner or later,' he predicted, 'we will have to clear out of Belfast.'[3]

The next month was to be crucial for the movement. As the 'law and order' section of the northern Cabinet got its way and pursued a policy of repression, climaxing with the introduction of the draconian Special Powers Act at the end of April, the Pact while never formally abandoned by either side, receded into the background.[4]

From mid-April onwards abduction of loyalists by the IRA, particularly its 4th Northern Division, took place as a surety for the release of prisoners (those kidnapped earlier in the year had been released in exchange for Hogan's freedom and the reprieve of the Derry prisoners). The infliction of flogging under the Special Powers Act provision, on those found with arms, increased the sense of terror in nationalist Belfast. An Ulster offensive had been under contemplation by the Northern Council since before the Pact. At a meeting of the council held in Clones on 21 April, each commandant supplied a note of the required war material for forwarding to GHQ.[5] A date was fixed for the operations inside the north and a fortnight allowed for the 'transport of stuff'. The following day, 22 April, Woods held a Divisional Council meeting at which all agreed the whole six county IRA should strike at once. Almost from the start things went wrong. While No 1 Brigade (Antrim) and No 2 (Belfast) were ready for action, the position was different in No 3 (West and East Down).[6] There the commandant, Patrick Fox, declared for the anti-Treatyite executive, having previously supported

GHQ. Even though most of his officers failed to follow him, sufficient members of those recruited since the Truce left the movement, necessitating the scrapping of two battalions. Arms were coming to Belfast through the 4th Northern Division. 300 rifles and 1,000 revolvers were given to Aiken by O'Duffy that May and June. The 4th Northern itself got about 400 rifles and 500 hand guns plus some Thompson sub-machine guns.[7] The secret arming of the northern IRA involving collusion with antitreatyite factions, continued up to the eve of the Four Courts attack which initiated the southern Civil War. On 25 June, just two days before it, Aiken was told by O'Duffy that the 500 extra rifles promised to him would have to wait. All this notwithstanding, the northern IRA was by this stage undoubtedly well armed. In late April O'Duffy could state, probably with some hyperbole, that 75 per cent of pre-Truce guns were in their hands. The 800 men of Belfast No 1 Brigade by the summer had 181 rifles with 11,000 rounds of ammunition, 308 service revolvers with 7,400 rounds and 5 Thompson guns with 1,220 rounds. Unfortunately for the planned offensive, much of the 'stuff' failed to reach the area in time. When the oil-tanker en route to the Antrim Brigade broke down in Carrickfergus, Woods had to request a postponement of three days from the Chief of Staff.[8]

The offensive when it finally came was a fiasco. The attack on Musgrave Street RUC Station on 17 May was not followed up in the other Brigade area for two days. The delay in the case of the No 3 Brigade in Down meant this area was soon flooded with Special Constabulary from Newry. As Newry lay within the 4th Northern Divisional area, Woods sent his second in command to see the Chief of Staff, Frank Aiken, who promised to commence operations.[9] As McCorley later recalled, the 4th Northern failed to go off while the 2nd Northern, comprising the Mid-Ulster area, went off too soon. Woods kept the men in Antrim and Down 'under arms' in the hope of reinforcements. When these failed to materialise he gave the order to disband.[10] With the introduction of the most sweeping provision of the Special Powers Act on 20 May, internment, and over 400 IRA suspects lifted, the movement was firmly on the defensive. After that it was downhill all the way for his Division, the 3rd Northern. Brigades Nos 2 and 3 were virtually destroyed within five weeks by demoralisation. No 1, Belfast itself, remained active through May and

June, the campaign of incendiarism discussed by the Ulster Advisory Committee and by the cabinet continuing until the government called it off in July. In June alone 85 burnings were carried out.[11] But defeat was on the way for the IRA in the city. Having braved the ferocity of the northern State, the attitude of its own people was to be the rock on which it finally perished. As Seamus Woods acknowledged, they had 'backed the enemy' during the war. Dr Russell McNabb had been equally frank to the Northern Advisory Committee: 'It is our people who are going to beat us and they are not united.' Their support had come only belatedly through the IRA's role of defenders, not through any adherence to national ideals. Now the tide began to ebb again. Woods wrote in June:

> There is a feeling among the civilian population we are not recognised by GHQ and that our orders come from the executive. Most of the priests are under the impression also and some of them in fact have said from the pulpit they will not give absolution to anyone who is a member of the secret military organisation. They have refused to hear Fianna Boys' confessions. The people who supported us feel they have been abandoned by Dáil Éireann, that the fight was no longer a national one in common with all Ireland. They feel all the suffering is in vain and they cannot see any hope for the future. The people who did not support us are only too glad of the opportunity of assisting the enemy and practically all over the Division police barracks are stormed with letters giving all available information against the IRA and their supporters. We have captured such letters and in most cases suggestions have been made to the police as to how best they could cope with the situation. In some cases, they regret they did not give this information years ago.[12]

In one memorandum after another the same point was rammed home:

> The latter (ie the Catholics of Belfast) constitutes the most difficult part of our problem and anything that has been said about them is in no way exaggerated ... we are coaxing the population to a great extent and are daily losing ground. The tactics the enemy are adopting are having the desired effect. If they succeed everywhere as they are succeeding in Belfast, it will not be long until the northern government have complete recognition from the population of the six counties.[13]

That was written on 14 July. Seven weeks previously he had told
GHQ:

> If operations were started on a general scale in the six coun-
> ties and a policy of war decided on, I am afraid I would be
> completely compelled to mete out capital punishment
> among the Catholic population.[14]

By this time the nationalist districts of Belfast were ringed with
military blockhouses, the Specials patrolled in armour plated
cage cars invulnerable to IRA rifle fire, surveillance was so intense that one Ulster Advisory Committee delegate from the city
was stopped at seven checkpoints on his way to the railway station.[15] All the while murderous assaults with official collusion
continued against the population. 46 Catholics died violently in
May, and 1,000 fled the city for Glasgow in June. In a population
where republicanism never secured electoral superiority, a vel-
vet glove policy of 'fraternisation' by the police provided the
final straw. Woods, commenting on Catholic morale, could
state:

> The northern government, having commandeered buildings
> on the Falls Road, have issued instructions to their troops to
> avoid aggressive action as much as possible in this area, to
> fraternise with the people and to try and restore a spirit of
> confidence in them. These instructions are being carried out.
> The Specials, whenever they come into contact with our peo-
> ple, have declared that they are not here to interfere with
> anybody provided they are not interfered with. The civilian
> population, war weary, tired of the long drawn out struggle
> and with never a strong national outlook at best, are only too
> anxious to acquiesce and I'm very much afraid are at present
> giving information.[16]

From the home side of the fence Dillon could assure T. P.
O'Connor that the B Specials were 'most civil and obliging and
were rapidly establishing friendly relations with the Catholic
people.'[17]

The split within the Belfast IRA also played its part in the debacle. The anti-Treatyites, though never numerically significant,
mounted operations which had undermined the attempts of the
mainstream movement to establish itself. On 31 May, for instance, the shooting of Specials by the Executive forces resulted
in reprisals by the USC on Catholic districts and the near capture

of IRA officers. The Executive forces also carried on an arson campaign of their own which helped to alienate Catholic opinion. The torching of 'McLaverty Brothers', which employed large numbers of Catholics, and the burning alive of 13 horses in the 'Noble and Carrier Stables' in Seaforde Street, were two widely condemned actions, but the shooting dead in a hold up of a Catholic, Mr Devine, Manager of Hughes Bakery, brought matters to a head between the two IRAs. Arrests by the GHQ faction of the alleged culprits produced counter arrests by the Executive troops. A stand-off situation lasting several hours followed before cooler counsels prevailed and all men were released. In the view of GHQ supporters, the Executive members were 'desperadoes' some of whose leaders – in Ballymacarret and the Markets – had been cashiered from the movement before the split.

As the summer progressed, matters became worse. The long days, Woods pointed out, were a 'serious drawback' and it was 'impossible to travel under cover of darkness' due to the heavy military presence. This, combined with the fact that they saw 'no sign of receiving support from any of the other Northern Divisions to relieve the pressure on them, was further undermining morale. The Brigade with a 75 per cent unemployment rate before the Truce, was near starvation.[18] Many left for jobs in Dublin, despite appeals by Woods to the government not to accept them and an IRA edict demanding that they first seek permission. The other divisions were in fact in no position to help Belfast. Communication from the 2nd Northern Division for the month of June reported 'no action from the IRA or executive troops but almost daily activity from the enemy'.[19] Another report on Catholic morale in 'the greater part of County Tyrone and in the overwhelmingly Protestant part of County Derry', describing it with some under-statement as 'not good', went on: 'Since the burnings and murders became general several families have been living in fear. Many go to bed at night fearing they might be burned out under the cover of the curfew.' Protestant morale was not much better. In the Maghera district the custom of joint turfing on Glenshane Mountain had ceased.[20] Across the divisional areas raids, arrests, arson, intimidation and curfews were everyday occurrences. Even in the 4th Northern, which Aiken had committed to the republican cause in the south's Civil War when his 'neutrality' was not respected, there was disquiet reported amongst the northern Catholic population, particularly in Newry, at the IRA's recent offensive.[21]

In the south throughout early June, northern policy was reverting back to the 'Treaty Position'. Beginning with a cabinet meeting on the 3 June, which decided on a policy of 'peaceful obstructions', this approach continued through the month. The policy of the second week in June was to involve concentration on Belfast and an 'avoidance of the border question'. The Minister of Defence reported that the Dáil's control of the policy in the city did not extend beyond keeping 'small bands of men employed in incendiarism'. Notwithstanding the Cabinet's belief in the salutary effect of 'reprisals', there was a realisation that the policy of hostage taking could not be resumed and an awareness of the sectarian effect reprisals could have in Belfast. In this context the shooting of William Twaddell MP in Garfield Street in May was agreed to have been 'bad policy'. The southern election could be read as an endorsement of the Treaty. Collins, who had already broken his pre-election pact with the anti-Treatyites, certainly viewed it as such.[22]

The Four Courts Executive, despite its continuation of its own Belfast Boycott, had ceased to be a rival for the loyalties of northern Catholics, and British pressure was increasing culminating in an ultimatum following the shooting dead of Sir Henry Wilson on 22 June outside his London home. This action, carried out with Collins' apparent collusion, was probably the last in this secret war against the northern State. The death of Sir Henry Wilson, Military Advisor to Craig's government and the scion of an Anglo-Irish family, was blamed on the anti-Treatyites, and resulted in the British demand for the removal of their Dublin garrisons. A series of incidents, beginning with the arrest of the Director of the Belfast Boycott – still acting on what he believed to be a joint operation with GHQ – ended with the attack by Provisional Government troops on the Four Courts with British artillery in the early hours of 28 June, plunging the south into Civil War.

As the conflict spread the northern IRA continued its appeals to Dublin. On the approach to be adopted, O'Duffy received a query from the 2nd Northern on the subject of giving evidence when charged in the northern courts. On 24 July Woods told Collins that the majority of the people favoured the 'peace policy' and the recognition of the northern government, most of his officers feeling that no other option was open to them. Mulcahy communicated reports which he had received to Collins who, on the 24th of the month, told him he would ask the government for 'an indication of the lines of future policy' towards the north. Conferences had been held on the subject during the month.[23]

The 2nd Northern Division had effectively collapsed by the end of June. Most had fled across the border into Donegal and were accommodated in barracks at Moville, Lifford and Letterkenny. Only a Flying Column of never more than seven men remained, constantly moving to avoid capture. The Divisional OC, General Thomas Morris, was already *hors de combat* after being wounded. The Provisional Government had accelerated this disintegration by refusing monetary assistance. In Fermanagh the dislodging of the IRA from the Belleek/Pettigo Triangle by the British army in a contretemps which almost broke the Treaty, had shaken the 1st Northern Division. West Fermanagh, still led by Sean Carty, found itself isolated and under pressure from the Sligo republican Seamus Devins to join the anti-Treaty side. Reports exist of a conference decision as early as 22 July to conclude the fight in the north east as the position had become hopeless. The remaining volunteers were to be brought to the Curragh for training. Even before that, men had been arriving there from the 3rd Northern area. From April 1 1922 to December 31 a total of 1,685 men left Belfast to join what was soon to be called 'the Free State army', many of them wanted under warrant by the northern government. Only 246 had returned by February 1923. In January of the new year a further 1,150 left.[25] The final decision was taken at a conference of northern IRA leaders at Portabello on 2 August, presided over by Collins himself. The fight in the north would be called off, the men would come to barracks in the south, be trained under their own officers, would not be required to join operations outside the six county area and would resume the fight in the north under a six county command. 524 later came to the Curragh under this arrangement. Collins reverted to his old fighting self at the meeting, promising he would tell Lloyd George 'what he could do with his Treaty' when the Civil War was finished.[26] This rhetoric concealed the fact that he was already over one week into the pursuit of a different policy, one involving the consideration of and conciliation of those whose views he had previously opposed – the unionists and the Home Rulers.

None of this was really too surprising when one examines his record in its totality. He had been an opponent of the Belfast Boycott. He had met Joe Devlin after his first pact with Craig and was chided by Mulcahy who advocated the isolation of the northern Home Rulers. The IRB, to which he belonged, took a moderate line on resistance in the north in its magazine *The Separatist*. In one issue P. S. O'Hegarty had compared the IRA position there *vis à vis* the unionists to that of the Black and Tans in southern Ireland. A few hours after receiving Woods' dispatch of 24 July he called in the man who was to be the instrument of his new policy, a Protestant British army war veteran with northern connections, then resident in Sutton, Captain Edmund Loftus McNaghten.[27]

PART TWO

1922-1935
'They would find a hundred reasons for leaving us to paddle our own canoe.'

'Out of power, they (the southern political parties) would use us. In power, they would find a hundred reasons for leaving us to paddle our own canoe.'

Cahir Healy
Ulster Herald, 20 October 1926

CHAPTER 6

Collins' Northern Initiative

After a verbal briefing later in the evening of 24 July in Collins' office, McNaghten was forwarded a memorandum by him on the 27th putting 'in more definite shape' the plans Collins had in mind for him. He was authorised to make a general inquiry among political personages and businessmen regarding the position in the north of Ireland, particularly in regard to its relationship with the rest of Ireland. Collins wrote:

> You will understand from my conversation, what our feeling in the matter is – that we wish very heartily for a united Ireland – that there is a general desire among thinking people to deal in fair terms with our north-eastern fellow countrymen. You will recollect what I said in relation to the question of getting the maximum value from the anti-partition feeling which undoubtedly exists among certain elements in the north east which are, for the moment, not in agreement with us politically. The real need is to do something to consolidate this feeling, to bring into closer association the parties who have a common disinclination towards division of the country so as to avoid what will be to them and to us a real catastrophe.[1]

All those visited by McNaghten, on foot of these instructions, were from groupings previously tabooed by the southern leadership: Unionists and Devlinite Home Rulers. His contact-men with both groups were the 'Catholic Craigites', Raymond Burke and Hugh Dougal. Burke, a shipbroker and Consul for six nations in the city, and Dougal, proprietor of a carrier firm, had acted as link-men between the Dublin and Belfast governments in the negotiations of the spring. Burke, in helping to secure the release of kidnapped loyalists, had expressed the hope that the northern government would speed the day when northern Catholics recognised it by dealing with Devlin rather than with Collins. His help for the latter on this occasion was undoubtedly prompted by the belief that he was helping achieve this aim by a different route. The northern cabinet were thinking along similar lines when they discussed the visit at their meeting on 4 August.

After lunch in Belfast, McNaghten met with the 'Ulster Defence Association' a group of Protestant businessmen concerned with the effects of the Belfast Boycott, still maintained by the Four Courts executive against the north east. He told them that the unofficial boycott would be maintained by the Republicans for as long as Roman Catholics were maltreated by the Belfast government. The 'remedy was in their hands' he reminded them, a point which they acknowledged.[2]

He then discussed the situation with fifteen prominent Home Rule Catholics including Martin Hopkins JP, the McCanns, fishmongers, and JPs William Hughes, Managing Director of Keegan and Company, mineral water manufacturers, James Kennedy, a leading member of the Ancient Order of Hibernians, Councillor Oswald Jamison, and Councillor T. P. McCarthy, editor of the *Irish News*. During the remainder of his visit he was driven by Burke and Dougal to meet with leading lights of the Unionist commercial and political establishment, including Colonel Spender, Cabinet Secretary, James Craig's secretary, Mr Blackman, the Ministers for Labour and Home Affairs, Andrews and Dawson Bates, and the directors of the city's largest industries including the Gallagher brothers, grain importers, and J. H. Stirling of the world's largest flax spinning companies at York Street. He also interviewed Bishop McRory and Fr Laverty, interviews which may have been arranged for him by Frank McArdle, probably the only Sinn Féiner in the city involved with his visit. The upshot of his report was firstly that a 'practically unanimous detestation of partition' existed among the prominent businessmen of both sides. Little by little this discontent among the Protestant section could be utilised by the Dublin government. *Festina Lente* ('hasten slowly') was the recommended motto.[3] Secondly, a unanimous desire for peace existed as well as a genuine willingness to recognise the ongoing injustices endured by the minority. As examples of these, he cited the one-sided use of internment – 259 Catholics and only one Protestant on the prison ship *Argenta* – and the re-employment in a loyalist district of Catholic men put out of work at the Falls Baths when it was commandeered by the B Specials. Thirdly, there was an 'earnest desire' that Catholics should take their seats in the northern parliament where they would be guaranteed a warm welcome. Among the Catholic business and professional class the support for attendance was 'almost universal'. The only condition which they attached was the support of the government for the redress of their grievances.[4]

Attendance, they felt, would mitigate much of the savagery displayed by the government in recent months. The flogging sentences imposed under the Special Powers 'would never have been given and miscarriages of justice avoided'. 'It is fact,' McNaghten stated, 'that large numbers of Catholics in Belfast, both Nationalists and Free Staters, are recognising the northern government and have exercised the franchise. They pay rates and taxes, they take their full share in the life and the community, some of them are magistrates and they are perfectly prepared, on certain terms being granted them – which terms Colonel Spender assured me would create no difficulty – to support the entry of Catholics into the northern parliament'. They 'strongly urged' on McNaghten that the southern government should recognise 'temporary partition' and that Catholics in Belfast 'should be given instructions' to recognise the new parliament.

All of this was seen as a first step on the long-term goal of a united Ireland. The only dissenter from this view whom McNaghten met was Bishop McRory. He held that recognition of the northern parliament was conditional on its acceptance of Dublin jurisdiction and 'though this must mean many years of unrest and suffering and even bloodshed, his Lordship (was) prepared to face it'.[5]

Fourthly, it was represented to Collins' emissary both by Catholics and Protestants that 'in order to pave the way for a United Ireland' a small representative conference of Craig, Devlin, Collins and 'one or two others interested' should meet and formulate an agreement on common matters to be approved by both parliaments. After a time the mutual association would lead to greater confidence, they felt.

Before leaving Belfast, McNaghten met Craig who had just returned from overseas. Craig expressed the view that the Catholics of Tyrone and Fermanagh would vote against union with Dublin but could not cite evidence to support this view. 'None of us,' he assured Craig, 'will talk about unity until the Free State government is master of its own house.' McNaghten left believing that the nucleus of a provincial parliament 'existed in the growing pride felt in the Belfast legislature and the nucleus of an all-Ireland one in the Council of Ireland'. His final recommendation called on the southern government to utilise the feeling among political and business figures of the unionist community which tended towards Irish unity. In the case of the latter group he relied on 'stern but simple facts of economics to push them in the required direction'.[6]

'A third string to our bow,' he claimed, was 'our own people domiciled within the jurisdiction of the Belfast government – theirs will be an insistent voice crying in the wilderness ... when the Boundary Commission had concluded its deliberations'. He went on, 'There may be a reconstruction of the policy of Catholic abstention from the Belfast parliament ... with the House of Commons as a pulpit they could preach the gospel of unity and preach it more powerfully and insistently than from any other forum ... Huckleberry Finn ... asserts that 'some fleas is good for dogs'; some form of opposition even if it occasionally causes irritation will be good for the Belfast parliament and logically such opposition should come from the Catholics and Nationalists.'[7] With this current of protest augmenting the other two, it would, he concluded, 'become a raging torrent which no government will be able to withstand'.

McNaghten's report was dated 7 August; on 1 August, a cabinet sub-committee had been set up to reconsider northern policy; on 11 August Ernest Blythe, a member of it, reported to the government and recommended an abandonment of the military campaign in the future in the north, acknowledging it could never achieve the measure of support which attended operations in the twenty-six counties. A continuation of it would only mean the total extermination of the Catholic population; 'the events of the past few months made that evident'. The boycott policy was likewise ineffective ... 'many governments controlled less territory than the northern one ... even the pettiest and most poverty stricken government clings to life', the document stated, and it continued 'the prospect of unification if the north goes out next January will depend upon our showing a friendly and pacific disposition towards the northern government while letting them come up against the full logic of partition.' To that end Catholics were to disarm and 'outrage propaganda' to cease.[8]

The question of the northern teachers, which the Dublin government had been attempting to dispose of since the Craig/Collins Pact, was to be dealt with in consultation with the northern government. As the cabinet decision of 19 August had been seen as an abandonment, even a betrayal, of an earlier policy adhered to by Collins, a *Dolchstosselegende* had arisen of the honest soldier destined not to reach his thirty second birthday, outmanoeuvred by cynical civilian politicians.[9] In point of fact, it was nothing of the sort. Even though Collins' support for the IRA in the north and his co-operation with the republicans was unknown to most of his cabinet colleagues, the incendiary campaign in Belfast that summer was discussed at a closed session of the entire cabinet.[10] The meeting of the North East Ulster Advisory Committee had pre-figured the changed attitude on the schools and local government issues. Most significantly, McNaghten's report, undertaken on Collins' initiative, prevailed over Blythe's recommendations. Northern Catholics were not encouraged to enter the northern parliament and were specifically discouraged from offering bail when interned by the northern government.

Naturally, those nationalists unaware of the role accorded to them by Dublin in this wider game plan, were to experience a bitter sense of betrayal. Seamus Woods often quoted remarks made in late September after a visit to Belfast, that 'the attitude of the present government towards its followers in the six counties' was 'not that of the late General Collins' was understandable, coming from a man unaware of how complex that policy was.[11] Cahir Healy's letter, written from the *Argenta* prison ship the following day, struck a familiar note.[12] In the light of a statement made in the Dáil by Cosgrave, he wanted clarification on the issues of recognition as the oath of allegiance was being taken by public boards in the north without Dublin's disapproval, the question of the teachers and above all else the issue of 'going bail'. As for his own plight and that of his fellow internees, he could reach only one conclusion: 'We have been in custody since May last … so far we have been abandoned to Craig's mercy … we must look after ourselves, I think.'

CHAPTER 7

In the Shadow of the Boundary Commission

It was McNaghten's advice which prompted O'Shiel to pressure nationalists to contest the seats of Tyrone and Fermanagh in the Westminster elections. The presence of the Home Ruler Harbinson as running mate of Healy reflected not only the common bond of anti-partition but also the degree to which Sinn Féin then set the agenda. Dillon wrote to T. P. O'Connor in September that a 'poisonous little faction, especially in Tyrone, hate Devlin ... a large number of priests are of course more bitter than ever and look on Joe Devlin as the enemy ... Harbinson is an utterly worthless selfish person completely in the hands of the Murnaghan gang.'[1]

Harbinson's role in opposing partition at the 'Black Friday' meeting in June 1916 won him Sinn Féin respect. Both seats were held for the anti-partitionists. An attempt was made by the Dublin government to win another seat in Derry, sending McNaghten there as a candidate – as a Protestant Home Ruler he had relatives in the Derry Protestant community. The attempt backfired when the nationalists and Sinn Féiners in the city, resenting the imposition of a candidate, called for a boycott. The seat was won by the Unionist – McNaghten's cousin.

It was indicative of the lack of unity between even pro-Treatyite northerners that Murnaghan in Omagh was the conduit for Dublin's finances to McNaghten's campaign.[2] On 11 October a deputation including Harbison, Donnelly, Lynch and Collins and two northern priests, were introduced by Murnaghan to the President and O'Higgins. The meeting, as representative as the one with De Valera the previous December, produced the same set of grievances. This time, as in the case of the abolition of PR, matters had a new sense of urgency, as one delegate remarked 'the Boundary Commission is our only hope'.[3]

The conference of northern nationalist representatives

promised by O'Shiel since the previous February, met on 22 and 23 November in the Mansion House, under the chairmanship of Sean Milroy.[4] They appointed a committee to oversee the collection of evidence for the Boundary Commission. Home Rulers and Sinn Féiners were united in this exercise. J. H. Collins, the Newry Sinn Féiner, had advised the Dublin government to raise no objection to the presence of former opponents on deputations.[5] The republican tide was ebbing in the north as a secret report in late September, sent to O'Shiel by an ex-organiser in the north, made clear:

> It is quite probable that the Hibernians will once again gain ground in the north east. You had the spirit alive in every chapel area ... we no longer hold a grip on the people. They see the futility of our actions in so far as they are concerned ... besides a considerable proportion of them were always luke-warm Sinn Féiners.[6]

O'Higgins himself acknowledged, at the 11 October meeting, that many who called themselves Sinn Féiners felt that they had been abandoned by Dublin. Despite this the newspapers of northern nationalism west of the Bann – *Derry Journal*, *Tyrone Democrat* and the North West Publishing chain – continued to support the government. Only the *Irish News* gave them difficulties. Devlin, notwithstanding the antipathy in his area to Dublin's behaviour and the desire of many of his supporters, particularly the Vintners Association, to enter the northern parliament, made no move in this direction. A factor in this may have been the Catholic bishops who Dillon reported[7] were 'blocking' such attempts. Pressure continued on the Dublin government to nominate its commissioner. Cosgrave, in exasperation, proposed deciding on a course of action and 'carrying it out regardless of what anyone thinks'. 'Devlin himself publicly contradicted the editorial writer in the *Irish News* who said a Boundary Commission would not be set up.[8] By July, when the Free State had appointed as its Commissioner Eoin Mac Neill, O'Sheil could write that while relations had previously been 'rather strained' between UIL and Sinn Féin electorates 'that phase has now happily passed and these people can be relied upon to stand by us for the Treaty.'[9] But within the hostility of Michael Lynch's North West Publishing Company group to the *Irish News* it was not difficult to discern the old animosity. In June, the flagship of the fleet, the Omagh based *Ulster Herald*, supporting the NEBB denial that the *Irish News* was the voice of northern nationalists, stated:

> The forces which are calling for a speeding up of things are the same forces that bitterly opposed Arthur Griffith and the Sinn Féin leaders for many years. It would be nothing short of criminal, however, for the nationalists of the minority areas to drag along with them into the Belfast parliament mirage the nationalists of Tyrone and Fermanagh, parts of Derry South and East Down and South Armagh, when a clear majority are in favour of incorporation.[10]

Throughout the year discontent bubbled beneath the surface in the nationalist north, with the east/west divide demarcating those sceptical of Dublin's assurances from those willing to take them at face value. The creation by the Free State of a customs border on 1 April drew a stinging editorial in the new issue of the *Irish News*[11] stating that the border had now been 'stereotyped by deliberate action of the Free State government'. The 'starting point' for all reasoning people, it asserted, was that the nationalists of the six counties must travel alone on the road marked out for them. By contrast, the *Dungannon Democrat* allowed its columns to be used by the Dublin government's North East Boundary Bureau to tell readers that 'real or simulated alarms occasioned in some quarters' over the erection of tariff barriers had 'given way to a clearer appreciation of reality'.[12] In May Kevin O'Higgins, whose government had recently emerged victorious in the south's civil war, said he was at one with Devlin in the latter's view expressed at Magherafelt that the Boundary Commission should have been set up at the time of the Treaty.[13] That same month O'Shiel attacked the *Irish News* for allegedly urging a policy of submission by northern Catholics, and the *Fermanagh Herald* took issue with its suggestion that the commission be dropped.[14]

An added source of anxiety was the education question. The Lynn Commission, which had caused such concern to nationalists, had become the basis for Lord Londonderry's Bill, introduced in March 1923, and passed into law that October. From March onwards a series of protest meetings were held across the north. In May a conference of clergy had taken place following the statement against the 'treatment of Catholics' issued by the six northern bishops in October, which laid heavy emphasis on the Catholic schools 'forced under control animated by hostility towards Catholicism'.[15] The increased involvement of clergy in the organisation of these gatherings was noted by police. Arrangements were made secretly and were announced only at Mass on Sunday. RUC Inspector Gilfallan wrote of the 11 November Cookstown meeting attended by 100 people. The topics discussed at that meeting were representative of those discussed at the others: Clause 12 of the Treaty and the Boundary Commission; the taking of the oath by public bodies and individuals; the injustices of gerrymandering; USC behaviour; the abolition of PR; and, of course, education.[16] A feature common to all of these gatherings was their discreet nature; mostly, as at the Derry meeting chaired by the ex-Mayor O'Doherty, attendance was by special invitation, and 'proceedings lacked enthusiasm of any kind and were in every sense tame'.[17]

Public representation and attendance continued to be an issue. The Catholic hierarchy had unsuccessfully pressured Devlin to enter the northern parliament in October[18] but, still loyal to Dublin's strategy, he had refused. At local level the nationalist representatives of several bodies had taken the oath 'under protest' and sometimes despite threatening letters from the remnants of the IRA.[19] A circular from John D. Nugent of the AOH to the Omagh meeting in November called for a decision on attendance 'to end the ridiculous situation existing of some priests taking the oath and others refusing to'.[20] Cahir Healy, as has been pointed out, complained in September 1922 of Dublin's failure to give a lead in this matter.

A more serious situation had arisen on the *Argenta* prison ship itself. In June 1922, 340 men had been interned there and another 110 languished in nearby Larne workhouse. With the movement collapsing in the north and civil war raging in the south, the feeling was of 'having struck a reef in a nationalist storm', Healy recalled.[21] The prisoners, most of whom were Free State in sympathy, maintained a common unity in the face of their jailers. Their 'long faces,' he wrote, 'were not caused by the wretched conditions on the ship' but by 'those political storm waves that day by day broke in upon us from Dublin and the press.'[22] By January 1923 the situation had become tense as the men saw no prospect of being released. Against a background of continuing unrest south of the border, 'a state of despondency' developed.[23] The announcement by the government in Dublin that northern Catholic teachers were to take the oath – as 95% of them subsequently did – was particularly upsetting to the internees as they had been told to refuse release. As the internees as a body had refused to recognise the Release Committee, a 'little rift in the lute' followed when the nine teachers on board were ordered to go before it.[24] Yet the attitude towards the Dublin government's delay remained one of understanding. In late February Healy could write that 'even with Catholics clamouring to be taken from under the heavy hand of Craig with his gerrymandering, legal commissioners and his over-zealous Specials', the Free State could not 'easily risk' a Boundary Commission 'beset as they were by active Republicans'.[25]

As spring gave way to summer he described, amidst his thoughts of the 'winds blowing regally on Island Magee', how letters to the men revealed a lack of appreciation by the wider community for their non-recognition policy. One priest in Clogher, County Tyrone, had written to some South Tyrone men ordering them to appear before the committee, having been assured by Colonel Topping of the Home Office that they would be 'probably discharged in a week'. Healy doubted this, remembering the case of the men in Larne workhouse who had been given these assurances and were still not at liberty nine months later. In regard to his fellow internees, no such moves were possible until the situation became 'more defined'.[26] One cannot fail to be impressed at the continuing loyalty of the internees to the Free State government, whose major concern seemed to be that they would be released as part of a Devlin/Craig package deal concluded behind Dublin's back and involving Catholic recognition of the state. As late as May 1923 information supplied to Sean McKeown in Dublin by an ex-internee named Sheehan, showed 50% absolutely loyal to GHQ, 5% neutral and only 25% with 'irregular sympathies'. That was a drop from 80% estimated as loyal in late October 1922 but it was still significant. By 26 August, some two months before the outbreak of the hunger strike, the Army Command[27] in the ship could calculate that 184 out of 390 internees were 'loyal to GHQ'.

On the subject of the conference to be held between the governments, Healy warned Dublin that it would be valuable 'only if through it we could secure a national unity', for no arrangement could be considered as satisfactory which would exclude permanently any part of Ireland from a national assembly.[28]

The hunger strike, which collapsed after three weeks and three days, was very much a republican affair. Led by Mick McCartan, a cousin of Dr Patrick McCartan, it never included, on Healy's estimate, more than 20 Free State supporters. Stressing this fact, Healy suggested to O'Shiel that the time was ripe for a government initiative to have the internees released on the same terms as those in the south. O'Shiel, who regarded Healy as 'one of the sanest and most far-seeing leaders of what may be described as the Free State section of nationalism in the six counties', took up the issue with his government and the British. But in Dublin Civil Service circles the initiative was spiked. McDunphy was advised to tell him it was 'too late to move as to A ... no outgoing government would risk the criticism which might follow an attempt to force Craig's hand.' Besides, they did not know what the election outcome would be.[29]

The advice given in McNaghten's reports continued to inform Dublin's policy on the boundary question, O'Shiel even citing the Latin tag from one of them, *Festina Lente*, (Hasten slowly) as a suitable motto in a memorandum the following April.[30] In this respect, the south's policy represented a logical continuation of that finally adopted by Collins in the summer of 1922. O'Shiel recognised as much in May 1923 when he wrote that:

'The late General had never made any secret of his dislike of the Boundary Commission as a settlement *per se* ... feeling that though the territory of the Saorstat might be broadened, the gulf between the Saorstat and the population would also be broadened ... the ultimate object was not the securing of more territory but the securing of national union ... hence the Boundary Commission was a weapon in the diplomatic war for national union and our aim should be to extract from it and its by-products every ounce of value'.[31]

The possibility of using Clause 7 of the Craig/Collins Pact as the basis for a settlement as the last resort was still spoken of by O'Shiel in May 1923. This aspect of government policy explains its tardiness both in the appointment of a commissioner of its own and in pressing for the establishment of the Commission once he was appointed. The man chosen by the Executive Council, Eoin Mac Neill, was picked supposedly because he was 'a minister, a northerner and a Catholic'.[32] A related factor behind the delay was the fluidity of the electoral position in

Britain. The election of 1922 resulted in a Conservative victory and the devastation of their coalition partners, the Liberals, now divided into Lloyd Georgeites and Asquithians. The beneficiaries were the rising Labour Party which more than doubled its representations, taking almost one third of the total poll. The election of November 1923 produced an even more intriguing situation. The Conservatives dropped from 346 seats to 259. Labour rose to 191 while the Liberals at 111 recovered sufficiently to emerge with 159 seats. Liberal support for a motion of censure in January 1924 resulted in the first Labour government in British history taking office, under the leadership of Ramsey MacDonald.

In July 1923 O'Shiel could state, after interviewing the leading British establishment figures, Devonshire, Cope, Jones and Mosley, 'seldom if ever has the stock of our nation and our race stood higher in the estimate of the English than at present. They have a respect for us they never had before'.[33] The reason for this lay in the Free State's recent victory over the republican forces, and this in maintenance of the treaty. In order to keep its side of the bargain, it had not hesitated to sacrifice some of its best citizens and saddled itself with a debt of twenty-five million pounds. By Christmas 1923 the Free State government had still not pressed for the establishment of the Boundary Commission and was weighing the pros and cons of doing so. The delay in setting it up had been all in their favour so far, O'Shiel felt:

> Peace has been established, a loan floated, the hunger strikes broken, a civil police force established, while the last election had altered the composition of the British House of Commons in our favour and left the Conservatives too weak to give much support to the Belfast government.[34]

And he expressed once again the reservations about the idea of a Commmission:

> The Boundary Commission is not an ideal solution because it does not necessarily lead to national union and might easily lead in an opposite direction. It would be no solution at all if it was not carried out in the spirit in which we believe it ought to be carried out, and it is extremely doubtful if a Conservative government would ever carry it out in that way.[35]

A conference prior to it would, in his view, enable the Dublin government to ascertain the aim of the other parties. With the Irish government indecisive on the question of a Commission, the British government worried by the shakiness of the position, the Conservative opposition menaced by their own pro-loyalist die-hards under Salisbury, and the northern Governor refusing to appoint a Commissioner, the issue was shunted into a conference in London in early 1924. O'Shiel had staked out the Free State's opening position in late 1923. 'We must allow ourselves any amount of scope to retreat back to an unshaken Article 12 position.'[36]

North of the border it evoked widespread nationalist cynicism. The *Irish News* editorial repeatedly condemned it while the *Fermanagh Herald* and the *Derry Journal* expressed their strong reservations, the latter publication on 11 February going so far as to predict its breakdown as inevitable.[37] Cosgrave proposed as a basis of agreement a local Ulster parliament with the 'withdrawal of all penal acts against the minority'. Cahir Healy, one of the two northern anti-partitionist MPs, writing in *The People*, foretold civil war if the Commission was not set up.[38] The attitude of northern Catholics towards the six county state had changed considerably since 1921. Sinn Féin supporters, as well as Home Rulers, were prepared to accept its workings on a day-to-day basis as a tactical necessity if nothing more. In Fermanagh, one of the areas most likely to benefit from the Commission, a representative for the area encountered this change in attitude when he returned after almost two years incarceration in February 1924. Cahir Healy MP, twice elected for the Fermanagh and Tyrone constituency while interned on the *Agenta*, was released in 1924 and was subjected to an order by the Home Affairs Minister, Dawson Bates, under the Special Powers Act, excluding him from returning to his home area. Upon his arrival in Fermanagh he duly announced his intention of defying the order. He recalled the response: one woman, whose brother was interned, told him he was acting 'very foolishly. The people don't care,' she reminded him, 'They have left the dependants to shift for themselves. You have been away for two years, enjoy your freedom'.[39] Healy, having failed to take her advice, was re-arrested. While in the dayroom at Enniskillen barracks awaiting removal to Derry jail, he witnessed 'a regular stream' of people arriving to seek permits for a charity dance organised by the Catholic ladies of the town. The 'new freedom of the north', he later remarked, 'was hard to comprehend. The people have to make the best of things and one cannot blame them if they seem a trifle more complacent than one would expect'. When mainstream Sinn Féiners, with the power and promise of the Treaty behind them, found themselves marginalised by their own supporters, this situation pressed *a fortiori* on that minority of northern republicans who opposed the Treaty and emerged the losers in the south's civil war. Early in January 1924 a Free State Intelligence Officer could report from a conversation with a prominent County Down 'Irregular' that great disillusionment existed at headquarters. Their failure to organise Ulster counties, lack of co-operation and apathy was complained of from the 'few existing remnants' and no headway was being made in any direction. The County of Armagh was described as 'hopeless' and 'with the exception of small groups in Newry and in Tyrone and Fermanagh, which were deemed too insignificant for any purpose, the outlook reported was by no stretch of the imagination favourable.'[40] Reports from all six counties stressed the normality prevailing. Attempts at reorganisation were still going on, with released internees appointed on a county basis for the purpose. For most internees, however, of whatever persuasion, held by either government, release meant simply an attempt to rebuild their lives. Seamus Mallon, formerly of the 2nd Northern Division, had returned from service on the pro-Treaty side in the south to head an organisation of unemployed northern nationalists which he hoped to extend to Derry. Whilst on a visit there he claimed that 'little interest' was being taken in the Boundary Commission by the 'average nationalist' who felt 'let down'. This feeling that the Commission was ineffectual he attributed to the prevalence of 'irregular progaganda' in the area.[41] Even though republicans were largely southern in composition and had little to differentiate them from the Free State on the Ulster question – De Valera Document No 2 accepted the Boundary proposals of the treaty – they hoped to harness the disillusionment of the nationalists. In the expectation of achieving this, they decided to enter the Westminster General Election precipitated by the fall of the Labour government in the 'Zinoviev letter' election of 1924. On Saturday 11 October De Valera announced Sinn Féin's intention to contest all seats.

Both nationalists and pro-treaty Sinn Féiners had planned to hold their own separate contests in the normal way to decide a policy, until the clergy intervened. On Sunday 12 October[42] it was announced at Masses throughout Tyrone that a conference was to be held in Omagh the following Thursday. Dean Quinn of Dungannon said it did not matter whether they were Hibernians or Sinn Féiners, 'the issue was purely a Catholic one'. It decided in favour of abstention.[43] Similarly, in Fermanagh on 14 October Archdeacon Tierney urged Catholics to 'have nothing to do with the election', commenting that after the elections of 1922 and '23 everyone knew where they stood.[44] The republicans found themselves handicapped on all sides: lack of both workers and speakers for their campaign, the forces of the northern State ranged against them, harassment of supporters in the south and finally a boycott imposed on their activities within the Catholic community. On 20 October[45] Cahir Healy described the northern minority as 'sick to death of Dublin intermeddlers, none of whom cared a straw what happened to the six county nationalists. They simply play them off as a pawn in the southern game.' And it became clear from his remarks that he was not referring merely to the anti-Treatyites but to the republican struggle in the War of Independence as well. 'I am glad to think that I was one of those responsible for turning down (at Coa Hall) their proposals of blood and fire five years ago.' He wanted, he concluded, a sane policy north and south. It was a reminder once again of how qualified the support for militant republicanism had been in the north east, even among those whose Sinn Féin credentials were flawless.

The election results were a disaster for the republicans. Only in one constituency, Armagh, did more than 10,000 Catholics support them. There Dr J. T. McKee secured 11,756 votes and over 28% of the poll. North Belfast recorded the worst result with 1,192 and 3.4% for Hugh Corvin. The two candidates in Fermanagh and Tyrone, one of them a local man, County Council Secretary, Thomas Corrigan, received less than 7,000 votes each. In 1923 over 90,000 votes had been cast in the constituency for Healy and Harbinson. In West Belfast, almost won by Harry Midgley in 1923 with Catholic votes, after Devlin's decision not to run in the new constituency, the republicans secured only 2,688 preferences. An IRA veteran of the period recalled the atmosphere in the Grosvenor Road/Divis Street area off the Falls Road:

> Feeling was so bad against us that known IRA men or repub-
> licans weren't safe in travelling through the 'Loney', as the
> Cullingtree was called, but there were sound republicans liv-
> ing in that area though they had a hard time sometimes.[46]

This rejection of republicans did not imply any surge of enthusiasm for the soon to be established Boundary Commission. From
December 1924 until the summer of the following year, Stephens
and McCartan, the leading figures of the North East Boundary
Bureau, toured the areas on the Commissioner's itinerary, meeting the agents, discussing the presentation of the case and
sounding out opinion in the locality. Beginning with County
Armagh in December the reports sent back painted a depressing
picture of a disillusioned people. 'My impression both in
Armagh and Newry,' McCartan wrote, 'was that very considerable apathy prevailed and that great scepticism existed about
the Boundary Commission being effective.'[47] In Armagh the
idea of any boundary aroused 'nervousness' while in Newry a
republican leaflet, 'The Betrayal of Ulster', based on an article by
Fr Isidore Mooney in the anti-Treatyite *Éire* newspaper, was
being circulated to damaging effect.[48] Other counties had a similar story. In Limavady there was a 'great deal of apathy', in
Magherafelt the sceptism of the local parish priest, an IPP supporter, infected his parishioners.[49] The Aughnacloy and
Dungannon areas of County Tyrone were 'quite apathetic',
many in the county interpreting the co-operation with Devlin as
an indication that 'no good result' could be expected from the
Commission and believing that Dublin was attempting to force
them into a Belfast parliament under Devlin's leadership,[50]
while in Fermanagh 'people were very sceptical about receiving
fair treatment' and feared a policy of 'rectification which would
dismember the country'.[51]

Throughout the spring and into the summer of 1925 the
Boundary Commission heard evidence from the areas under
consideration. Even though Craig had pledged non-co-operation,
several unionist dominated councils (nationalists had boycotted
the 1924 local elections in protest at the removal of PR and the alteration of boundaries), including Fermanagh County Council
under Basil Brooke, agreed to give evidence. The hearing of the
case breathed new hope into the nationalists of the north.
Stephens, leaving Derry City after the hearing in May, reported
that 'the depression which was noticeable for the past few

days,[52] has entirely disappeared in the general satisfaction with the presentation of the case among those responsible for it.'[53] Tyrone left him feeling that the case had been well presented in the western half of the county where there had been 'apathy and scepticism' before the Boundary Commission visited. An opportunity existed, he felt, for organising nationalists' opinion in the north.[54] In the eastern half of that county, where ties with Belfast and distance from the border had made the 'apathy more marked', the impression he formed left him with the feeling the Boundary Commission was consolidating nationalist opinion.[55]

Throughout the summer and autumn of 1924 matters continued along familiar lines. In June a motion by Milroy on the subject was defeated in the Dáil. In July Justice Feetham began his tour of the border. Among the northern nationalists the sense of muted dissatisfaction laced with hope continued to prevail. On the same day, 16 August, that Devlin in a speech at Dundalk called for a quick resolution of the matter, an *Irish News* correspondent pointed out that any solution would leave not less than 70% of northern nationalists inside the northern State. In September Kevin O'Higgins, in response to a meeting on the subject in Derry by nationalists of both schools, pledged as 'our trust' to ensure that 'just as force is not being used to keep within our State areas whose inhabitants dislike its jurisdiction, so areas whose inhabitants desire it and passionately resent their present plight, shall not be forcibly kept out'.[56] Behind the scenes neither the British nor the Irish governments had their hearts set on the Boundary Commission. The refusal that month of Belfast to appoint its Commissioner and the dark reminders from prominent English politicians that large scale transfers of territory were not contemplated,[57] were all ominous signposts to the futility of that course. In October, when the Boundary Bill was introduced at Westminster, MacDonald, the Prime Minister, expressed hopes that the Bill need not be brought into operation at all.[58] Earlier, on 25 and 29 September, O'Higgins had circulated the Executive Council with a memorandum of a possible offer to be made to the northern government before the Bill became law.[59]

It reiterated that the Boundary Commission had 'never been regarded' by Dublin 'as the most satisfactory' solution, a fact which could be seen from the 'alternative put before Northern Ireland in Articles 14 and 15 of the Treaty, the Craig/Collins

Pact' and the 'Appeal to Northern Ireland of Cosgrave on the eve of their voting out'. It acknowledged that any new Boundary would leave untouched such important questions as the 'alienation of the condition of those of our supporters, probably the majority, who would still be left in Northern Ireland or the larger questions of the future relations between north and south'. It admitted to approaching the Boundary Commission 'with a feeling of uncertainty' and proposed in its stead a package deal whereby an all-Ireland authority was established, with the powers enjoyed by Westminster under the 1920 Act transferred to it. Under its auspices common matters such as customs, excise, fisheries, etc, affecting north and south would be dealt with and tariff barriers between the two States would end. As concessions to the Catholics in the north, PR would be restored, gerrymandering abolished and the B Specials disbanded. The northern minority, it stated, would enter the northern parliament. Only 'minor alterations' would be made 'by consent' to the border.[60] With no positive reply to these proposals, the Boundary Commission began operations on 8 November.

From the start it was to prove a flawed instrument. The confidentiality of its proceeding was not respected by Fisher, the representative appointed for Northern Ireland, who enjoyed an unhealthy relationship with Craig's government. Wishful thinking by O'Shiel, based on decisions by similar post-war international tribunals, missed an essential point. Only in one case, that of Schleswig-Holstein, involving a defeated Germany in dispute with Denmark, were the wishes of the inhabitants given priority as the basis for partition. In the other cases a different yardstick was used. The wishes of the majority in the Aaland Islands in favour of secession from Finland was overruled in favour of a form of regional autonomy, whilst in Silesia the settlement recognised the takeover in the area by Poland. The hearing of the Free State case in counsel had given indications that in Feetham's view the second clause of Article 12 restricted the first.[61] In a discussion of the issue of the Belfast Waterworks, located in the nationalist Mourne area, but supplying the city, he insisted that:

> The very manner in which the words 'In accordance with the wishes of the inhabitants' are used, shows that it is intended to be a qualification upon the wishes of the inhabitants. The word 'inhabitants' implies area. Suppose it is suggested that

Belfast was at the present time the seat of the parliament and government of the area and then any dimution of the area of the parliament and government would prejudicially affect Belfast. Is that a circumstance to be taken into consideration in determining whether or not you are to give effect to the wishes of the inhabitants of say South Down or South Armagh?[62]

In the area where the Boundary Commission could have no effect, matters were proceeding along a different track. Devlin was under considerable pressure from several quarters to enter the Belfast parliament. The pressure reportedly was strongest from the Vintners Association but was 'scarcely less strong from the AOH and the nationalist working class elements'.[63] It was claimed that the Anti-Prohibition Society had agreed to support financially those who entered the parliament. Among these nationalists most strongly in favour of attendance were Vincent Devoto, owner of the *Irish News,* and Richard Byrne, Alderman for Falls. At a conference Devlin argued for a middle course; his people who, he stated with justification, had suffered more than any others in Ireland had no prospect of representation in a Dublin parliament and could not forego representation in a northern one indefinitely.[64] He did not, however, wish to fragment nationalist unity by entering the Belfast parliament before the Commission had given its decision. Those most opposed to even temporary postponement included T. S. McAllister from Antrim and John Hanna, former secretary to Redmond.[65] A more immediate reason for the emphasis on unity was the Stormont general election called by Craig for 3 April. Coming in tandem with a border tour and mobilisation of the B Specials, it served as a show of unionist strength in the middle of the Commission's work. Nationalists were able to join forces in 1921 after half a decade of divisiveness. Now after three years of co-operation, unity between pro-Treaty Sinn Féiners and Home Rulers was a much simpler prospect. The idea of a conference had originated in the Sinn Féin ranks and met with Dublin's approval. Cosgrave had earlier sent Eamon Duggan north to meet the Cardinal who apprised him of the poor state of nationalist organisation and finances.[66]

Early in 1924 when Healy, on being released, had gone south to meet Cosgrave and O'Higgins,[67] they told him, on a drive through the Wicklow mountains, that they would not attempt to give guidance to northern nationalists on electoral strategy. The 'proactive' stance adopted by them over a year later may have been due to a fear that the vacuum in nationalist politics would be filled by either republicans or Labour, or as O'Shiel feared in the south, by an alliance of both.[68] Alternatively it might have simply reflected a determination to beat Craig at his own game. In any event, the expenses of the candidates were paid by Dublin.[69] Devlin was shown the list of delegates invited to the conference and was invited to make additions. He was also asked to be its Joint-Chairman with Alex Donnelly but declined in favour of Harbinson. The 'greatest good humour',[70] it is recorded, prevailed at the conference which resulted in a joint pro-Treaty Home Rule panel of twelve candidates, six from each side. Only eleven were eventually nominated, eight of them being proposed by Roman Catholic clergy. According to reports, Devlin was 'particularly pleased' by the unity in the ranks of nationalists. It was at the conference he first met with Cahir Healy in what was to be the beginning of a lifelong mutual respect. However, some echoes of the old divisions between Sinn Féiners and Home Rulers persisted between the pact candidates. Devlin claimed that in Armagh Nugent's candidature was being opposed, a claim denied by Lavery, the Sinn Féiner, but supported by Fr McKenna and also by the AOH of the country.[71] Nugent's views of the Boundary Commission may well have jarred on pro-Treaty susceptibilities. After all, even his fellow Home Rulers were given cause for concern. T. P. O'Connor, writing to Dillon the previous August, confessed himself 'startled' at Nugent's view that a reduction in the six counties would be 'prejudicial not beneficial' to northern Catholics who could otherwise conclude a deal with Craig on gerrymandering and PR in return for leaving the area untouched.[72] It may have been this fact which explains the drop in his vote to 4,991 from his 1921 total of 6,857. He finished as a runner-up to J. H. Collins, the pro-Treatite, and lost his seat.

The anti-treaty Sinn Féin also approached the election with interest. On 12 March their Advisory Committee had met to decide matters, with all areas except Tyrone represented. The delegates were strongly in favour of contesting the election, if organisation and funds permitted, but in the light of their weakness in both areas they opted for an offer of agreement with the nationalists as an alternative. The depths of animosity towards former colleagues was clear in the proposal of the Fermanagh delegates, that Sinn Féin contest all seats 'in case Cahir Healy or any other nationalist should enter the field'. At the Standing Committee meeting Art O'Connor's proposal of a boycott failed to receive a seconder. That of Mrs Sheehy Skeffington and O'Donnchadha, to contest regardless of the outcome seemed likely to succeed. A compromise proposal by Sean Lemass and Gerry Boland was then put, advocating a pact with Devlin in default of which the seats would be contested. By nine votes to seven it was passed.[73] The request to Devlin, which involved a reference to the 'farce of the Boundary Commission', met with 'a polite and reasoned refusal'.

In all but one of the six constituencies which they contested the Sinn Féin performance was disastrous. The exceptions were South Down, where De Valera was elected without a contest in his last outing as President of the party, and Armagh where Eamon Donnelly pushed J. H. Collins into fourth place and won from J. D. Nugent, despite a smear campaign in the *Frontier Sentinal*, alleging Sinn Féin support for the B Specials, an equation the North West Publishing Company newspapers seemed to make with opposition to the Free State. In Fermanagh and Tyrone, where no Sinn Féiners were elected, co-operation between pro-Treatyite and Home Rulers reached its apogee with the transfer to Harbinson of all but 242 of Donnelly's 2,905 vote surplus, electing him on the second count.

The nationalists had reason to be pleased with the overall result. 10 of their 11 candidates were elected, Devlin himself securing a record vote. Three Labour Party members were also elected – Jack Beattie, Sam Kyle and William McMullen, in East, North and West Belfast respectively, the latter on Devlin's surplus.

On the 27th, just over a month after the election, Devlin and McAllister entered the northern parliament. The decisive factor in bringing about the step may well have been pressure from the Roman Catholic hierarchy on the educational question. The bulk of nationalist Ireland expected and understood the decision because by that stage the pre-1922 hostility towards Devlin had largely vanished from Free State government circles. Dillon, writing to T. P. O'Connor from strikebound Ballaghaderreen in May 1925, could relate how Cosgrave was 'extremely anxious to cultivate family relations with Joe and the northern nationalists'.[74] When Devlin, at a banquet in Dublin on 1 May, expressed the predominant Belfast nationalist view that the Commission would not solve the northern problem, his view was echoed one week later by O'Higgins. Speaking in Howth he asserted:

> The Boundary Commission will not solve the political problems that exist in the north east. It will only, one hopes, gradually and fairly delimit the problem. Perhaps only time can solve it.[75]

In July the commissioners concluded their hearings and left for London. The next three months were to be a time of constant newspaper speculations as to the nature of the award. Most of the forecasts envisaged a two way transfer, with the entire Inishowen Peninsula going to Northern Ireland in some predictions, eliciting protests from Derry nationalists and Donegal Hibernians. The *Independent* of 27 October concluded from the manner in which evidence had been heard:

> The Commissioners appear to have been interpreting Article 12 in a manner that suggests that whatever adjustments take place they will be compatible with economic conditions rather than with the wishes of the inhabitants.[76]

On 10 October the Free State Governor General, Tim Healy, wrote that while he felt the fears about Inishowen were groundless 'yet it is possible that Feetham might join with Fisher to affect such an amputation'.[77] Within a month they were both proven correct when the Tory newspaper *The Morning Post*'s revelations of 7 November confirmed their worst fears. In exchange for strips of the northern territory, portions of the south including a large fertile slice of East Donegal were to be transferred to the north. The *Belfast Newsletter* published a similar forecast the same day. The *Irish News* at first pooh-poohed the *Morning Post*'s prediction as just another one of many. Soon it was to become obvious that this was not the case. Even before the journalistic bombshell, disquiet west of the Bann was discernible in a correspondence from Healy to O'Higgins:

> With reference to your letter when you requested me to write to you, I would be obliged if you could get a decision of the Executive Council on the following:
>
> Will the Saorstat representatives submit Boundary line for consideration?
>
> Will Executive Council approve of any boundary that does not involve substantial areas?

Will representatives of the area to be partitioned be consulted on these matters?[78]

Ominously, beside questions one and three the word 'No' had been written in blue ink.

As the validity of the *Morning Post* revelations came to be accepted, anxiety had mounted in the nationalist north. On 17 November the *Derry Journal* called on the Free State government to take action to prevent the transfer of East Donegal. A deputation of Strabane nationalists went south to meet the government on the 17th.

By 21 November McNeill had resigned from the Commission and two days later the remaining Commissioners issued a statement pointing out that he had agreed with the position as far back as 17 October. Amidst mounting clamour from the Labour Party and individual border TDs, McNeill relinquished his position on the Executive Council and his resignation speech of 24 November described how Feetham had held the view that the Government of Ireland Act of 1920 created a *status quo* which could be departed from only 'when every element and every faction compelled them to do so'. The Commissioners, empowered by law to carry on in McNeill's absence, announced their intention of doing so and when Thomas Johnston of the Labour Party asked for a statement of policy, Cosgrave and O'Higgins requested time to consider the situation. The following day Cosgrave went to London for the first of a series of conferences with the British and with Craig, culminating in the agreement of 5 December. During the negotiations the Free State side came face to face with its own self-deception as much as with British duplicity. They had believed, largely on the strength of ambiguous utterances by the treaty signatories Lloyd George and Birkenhead, that the Commission would 'delimit more fairly than the 1920 Act' the northern boundary. Birkenhead's more recent pronouncement on the subject, in which he predicted the opposite, should have given them pause. Now as Feetham was to remind them at the meeting with the Commissioners secured by O'Higgins through the British Prime Minister Baldwin's agency, 'the instrument in which the Free State trusted had broken in their hands'.[79]

It was to be the supreme irony that Cosgrave should recall the breakdown of the pre-war Buckingham Palace Conference on the issue of six counties or four, only reluctantly to agree with

Chamberlain who reminded him that the Commissioners' function was not the transfer of the two majority nationalist counties. For the successor to the Sinn Féin party, which had outflanked the IPP on the partition issue, more had come to mean less. Worse still, they faced a fate similar to the IPP if they returned empty-handed. No member of the Executive Council believed they could face the Dáil and keep a majority even in their own party, O'Higgins himself acknowledged. The government, he told the British, would be certain to fall. This was despite the absence from the 139 member Dáil of the 48 republican deputies.

On 1 December O'Higgins claimed that the controversy could only be kept off the 'physical plane of direct action' if the Executive Council were able to supply the people with 'some safety valve'. The concessions he had earlier suggested by way of a 'safety valve' related to the treatment of northern nationalists and involved the restoration of PR, the abolition of the gerrymandering of constituencies, and the demobilisation of the USC. This latter force, overwhelmingly Protestant in composition, was now swollen to 45,000 members. In the twenty-six counties, two and half years after the conclusion of a civil war, the security forces consisted of 6,000 Civic Guards and 15,000 soldiers.[80]

If an alleviation of the plight of nationalists was impossible, O'Higgins enquired as to the likelihood of concessions in some other form. Such concessions would, he claimed, 'deaden the outcry of the Catholics in the north east' and 'prevent that outcry finding an echo in every one of the twenty-six counties in the Free State ... The position would no doubt be invidious but the Roman Catholics in the north would, it seemed, be let down in any case'. Cosgrave (who at one stage broke down in tears) had suggested that a compromise might be made on the economic front. He had earlier spoken of the south's adverse balance of payments, with one-third of its farmers living on uneconomic holdings of less than £10 valuations. An article in the *Irish Times* that November had suggested a trade off between Article 5 of the Treaty, committing the Free State to a share of Britain's public debt, and Article 12.[81] In the event this was what happened.

On 3 December in the Colonial Office the Boundary Commission Report was suppressed; 'burned and buried' in Cosgrave's words, with the agreement of the Commissioners themselves and Craig's collusion. In return the existing frontier was recognised, Free State liability under Article 5 was cancelled, compensation was to be paid by the Free State for 'Malicious damage done since the 21st January 1919' (i.e. Ireland's 'War of Independence'). The 'Council of Ireland' provisions were done away with and all remaining prisoners released. An 'Ultimate Financial Settlement' was to be reached the following March. Cosgrave later used the phrase 'damn good bargain' to characterise the deal concluded.[82] Northern nationalists who had been led to believe in the Boundary Commission recoiled in horror. The *Derry Journal* of 4 December strongly condemned it and that[83] same day T. P. McCarthy, the *Irish News* editor, took a more sophisticated line of disapproval reflecting the uniqueness of the Belfast Catholic position. In an editorial entitled, 'The Financial Factor' he wrote:

> The Council of Ireland never materialised, the southern parliament never came about, but a council could have been set up and was not. Article 15 had gone by the boards like Article 5 and Article 12, and the nationalist and Catholic people are left altogether and absolutely to their own devices … they must begin the task of organising themselves in self-defence for the preservation of their few rights that remain to them and the recovery of those rights they chose to sacrifice when they depended upon the specious assurances of gentlemen … of the NEB and refused to organise and act together before they had been gerrymandered out of the public boards, disenfranchised by the thousands and relegated to a position of almost helpless and hopeless inferiority in the country of their birth … they consoled themselves with the 9th Beatitude 'Blessed are they that expect nothing for they shall never be disappointed.'
>
> The Free State government will find no difficulty in justifying their action to the people of the twenty-six counties. The nationalists of the six counties must look ahead, examine their political resources, resolve and utilise them … avoid the tendency to indulge in recriminations which is inherent in the Irish nation.[84]

West of the Bann the tendency to 'indulge in recriminations' was more pronounced. The *Irish Independent*, strongly pro-agreement, could not find a single nationalist in Strabane who approved it.[85] The North West Publishing Company chain of papers was particularly scathing: 'The nationalists of the border have been callously betrayed,' thundered the *Frontier Sentinel*, 'Nationalists never clamoured for good government from Belfast but struggled instead for the unity of Ireland; they have been so unblushingly betrayed by the latest bargain.'[86]

Editorials in this and their sister papers continued this theme into 1926. Yet even from the depths of their chagrin, the nationalists of rural Ulster were beginning to reassess that tradition. Healy, on a deputation to Dublin with fellow MPs O'Neill and Harbinson, commented:

It is a betrayal of the Free State in its alleged support of our case since 1921. Time will decide if the betrayal will not bring its own retribution. John Redmond was driven out of public life for even suggesting partition for a period of five years. The new leaders agreed to partition for ever.[87]

Eight years later, while electioneering in Derry, McCarroll, proprietor of the *Derry Journal* and a former Sinn Féiner, expressed similar sentiment, revealing not only resentment at betrayal but also at wasted opportunities. Attacking southern republicans coming north to oppose his election, he recalled:

The shameful pact of 1925 which handed over nationalists to their political foes bound hand and foot … at that point (1922) northern nationalists might have struck a bargain for themselves. If they dared to, they could have secured the continuance of Proportional Representation and control of several public bodies in the north now gerrymandered away from them. But they trusted in the people across the border to get the last ounce out of the Treaty and they left them a free hand.[88]

One group stood to benefit by the situation, the republicans. Despite their lack of a clearly defined northern policy, they were at least untainted by association with the agreement and had of course opposed in arms the Treaty from which it was a development. The possibility existed that northern nationalists might warm to them. Even before the agreement on 30 November, the *Irish News* had written:

If Mr De Valera shows the same determination to help in securing the position under the treaty in the same spirit in which he discussed the boundary, no one will seriously bother himself about his academic views or abstract beliefs concerning the republic.[89]

Whilst in Dublin on the deputation after the agreement, Harbinson and others had attended an indignant meeting in the Shelbourne Hotel at which republicans spoke. Three months later, writing of the split in Sinn Féin which resulted in De Valera's formation of Fianna Fáil, the *Frontier Sentinel* of 13 March stated:

> The republicans have come badly out of all crises and the one which promised to be most useful to them – the betrayal of the six counties for a pecuniary advantage – left them weaker than before. To lash themselves into fury over the most abstract things and ignore the living present is nothing short of childish speculation. Their concern over the abolition of the oath test is ridiculous enough to provide material for a new version of pigs might fly.

It followed that when these people adopted a less doctrinaire approach in matters which scarcely impinged on northern nationalist consciousness, while addressing themselves to those matters which did, those selfsame northern nationalists might look with different eyes upon them.

CHAPTER 8

Nationalists after the Agreement

The Free State government had promised the British it would use its influence to bring the remaining northern nationalists into parliament. Cosgrave's intermediary in this attempt was, strangely enough, the representative of the *Morning Post* newspaper in Ireland, Mr Bradsheet. Devlin simply told him that the question of participation was a matter for the representatives themselves.[1] Pressure from quarters other than the discredited southern government was to be decisive in forcing the nationalists to enter the parliament. Most significant was that coming from the Catholic hierarchy, concerned about the inferior position of their 'voluntary' schools.

In March 1926, Leeke, McGuckin and O'Neill were mandated to go in. The representatives of the western constituencies continued to abstain – a reflection of the lingering Sinn Féin influence. Collins, Donnelly and Healy all came from that tradition, while Harbinson and McHugh, the other absentors, had long been under the influence of Sinn Féin. Those who had taken the plunge continued with their efforts to entice the remainder into following their example, emphasising the benefits of a united effort. Devlin complained to Healy in November 1926 that without 'assistance, advise and help our work in parliament will be of an almost futile nature'. At the Ladies' Day parade of 1927, H. K. McAleer, President of Tyrone AOH, reiterated his St Patrick's Day view that abstention was 'a fruitless and unsuccessful policy'.[2] The *Irish News* editorial of 18 August 1927 seized on the example of De Valera's entry into Dáil Éireann and commented that the precedent set by men 'who walked into the Dublin Assembly' could be followed as 'logically by the Lagan as by the Liffey'.[3]

On 22 August, McHugh wrote to Healy asking his advice on the matter. In reply to his query as to whether all argument against it 'had vanished into thin air', Healy told him that

Harbinson was going to attend the following October 'to oppose the new gerrymandering scheme'. While he was 'desirous' to wait for a decision of the people, Harbinson feared that if they did so they would 'have lost any little political and social rights they possessed'. Healy felt, however, that the agreement of three years before not to enter without a conference meant that one ought to be called.[4]

In August McHugh told him that a decision taken then would lead people to say they were 'stampeded by Fianna Fáil' and suggested that Healy 'sound opinion' on the subject. Healy followed his advice. Alex Donnelly told him that he felt it was unlikely that the Fianna Fáil party would 'hold their ground' at the next southern election. Lynch, the councillor and *Ulster Herald* proprietor, was non-commital. Though, like Donnelly, he himself did not favour attendance at the Belfast parliament, he hoped for 'united action'. Harbinson, however, continued to put them 'in an awkward position' having 'made up his mind' to attend. For years his IPP allegiance had been subsumed into the dominant Sinn Féinism of his constituency. Now it had reasserted itself.[5]

Healy admitted in October that Harbinson had 'stolen a little march' on them by his decision to take his seat. The day before he wrote, a conference called by the clergy of Tyrone and Fermanagh had met and authorised attendance.[6] Northern nationalists were united at last but no organisation existed to underpin the new approach.

Throughout that autumn discussions continued between them on the formation of a party with a common policy. The prime movers behind it were Healy and Devlin. The latter's influence was reflected in the emphasis on pensions, tenant purchase agreements and unemployment benefit, inserted within the programme. With remarkable prescience Healy suggested to Fr Coyle that 'Fianna Fáil ought to aim at gradually improving the social services of the Saorstat as this might constitute a barrier to national unity'. De Valera's party was the one to which they now looked as their source of support south of the border. Healy wrote:

> Northern nationalists can expect nothing from the party which betrayed them … they (Cumann na nGael) can never retrace new steps upon the slippery slope they took when they signed the agreement of 1925. Therefore, it seems to be

that we can do much by creating a good understanding between northern nationalists and Fianna Fáil and adopting on
both sides a policy which will be mutually acceptable, thus
setting a stepping stone across the river that divides the
people of this country ... If Fianna Fáil can use such political
machine as northern nationalists possesses for the furtherance of its national ideals, it would be a big stroke as well as a
great step for the whole country.

The proposals were considered by the Ard Comhairle of Fianna
Fáil on 19 January 1928. Feeling it 'in no way' contradictory to
the policy of Fianna Fáil, they sent Lemass and Sean T. O'Kelly
to meet with Healy and Devlin in Belfast with a view to a merger
of the organisations.[7]

Characteristically, the northern nationalist MPs consulted
their respective bishops on the process. Donnelly met McKenna
on 7 February. O'Neill and Collins had met the Bishop of
Dromore earlier. Healy told Devlin, who was ill (he entered a
nursing home later that month), that 'everywhere' the reception
was 'splendid and cordial. I honestly think that we have caught
the tide at the flood'. On 13 February the proposals were placed
before the bishops.[8]

Problems remained, however. Harbinson told Healy on 20
February that the bishops 'did not wish openly to identify themselves' though he continued to hope 'for their silent support'.[9]At
the 200 strong conference called by the nationalist MPs at St
Mary's Hall on 28 May, the new mood among northern nationalists at last assumed an organisational form with the creation of
The National League of the North. In its title it evoked memories
of Parnell, a figure whose memory would be respected by all
factions. Its clericalist character was emphasised by the presence
of five priests on the executive council and the Fermanagh clergy-
man, Archdeacon Tierney, as one of its joint secretaries. Devlin
said they had 'no means other than the northern parliament for
making their voices heard'. Before setting out they had 'consulted
the northern bishops and secured their approval'.[10] The increased emphasis in the League's programme on social amelior-
ation reflected the Devlinite populism of West Belfast and the
fear of being outflanked by Labour on these issues.

At one organisation meeting after another the grievances
aired were the specific ones of their communities: treatment
under the Craigavon regime; gerrymandering; inequalities in

public employment; the USC; sometimes the issue of unbought tenants and almost always the threat to Catholic education. Anti-partitionism *per se* was conspicuously absent from the message. Above all the emphasis was on unity between brother nationalists. 'The nationalists of the six counties,' wrote Healy, 'form about one third of the population. It is well known that in the recent past they walked under different banners. We do not live in the past. The best use of history is as a guide pointing towards the future. So we made up our minds that whether we called ourselves Hibernians, Sinn Féiners, or nationalists, we were going to face the new day with a new message and a new outlook.'[11]

Yet old divisions were not so easily laid to rest. Healy was told by McAllister, the Antrim MP, that at their first meeting held for the Ballymena/Toome district, John Clarke of Glencar had 'denounced in very unmeasured terms the late John Redmond'. Canon O'Donnell, the convenor of the meeting, had protested. McAllister pointed out to Clarke that if their party had pursued that course in discussing the immediate past 'there would have been no League and much chaos'.[12] Among the staunchest defenders of the policy against the criticism which inevitably followed it were nationalists of the Sinn Féin tradition. The most promising of them, Cahir Healy, writing in the *Irish News,* 15 September, replied to these critics:

> We have been charged with (1) subordinating the national demand to a purely political end, (2) drawing a sectarian herring along the national path. Both charges happen to be untrue.
>
> In the very forefront of the National League of the North we put the national unity of Ireland. How this is to be achieved is something we must be allowed to work out in our own way. Living in the north and experiencing all the inconveniences that an active profession of nationality there means, we surely ought to be the best judges of our own position.
>
> If at times we talk of over-taxation, inefficiency, emigration and the hundred and one ills of which our people suffer, that is not evidence of our being content with a truncated nation. It merely means while we are working for the major we must content ourselves with the minor things as well ... we do not consider overmuch the quality of stepping stones that bring us across a swollen river.[13]

He also rejected the sectarian charge by reiterating the League's objective aimed at fostering 'a spirit of conciliation and co-operation among all creeds and classes'.

A similar approach was taken by his one-time Sinn Féin colleague Joe Connellan MP. In his capacity as editor of the *Frontier Senitel* newspaper he roundly condemned those who opposed ameliorative efforts by nationalists on public boards, stating that it was the duty of Catholics to see that the 'government-made inferiority' was ended. The removal of these disabilities would be far from satisfying the demands of the National League which aimed also 'for the social uplifting of all the people and the promotion of a united Ireland cherishing its distinctive tradition, 'but at all events it would be a beginning'. Until then the emphasis was to be on the restoration of lost rights, he concluded.[14]

The League which faced into the 1929 Northern Ireland and Westminster elections retained this approach. According to its manifesto, this was its first opportunity to 'assert its claim to the full and unconditional rights of citizenship'. Since the foundation of the state every 'effort made by the minority' to 'take its part' in the 'common task' of developing 'industrial and commercial prosperity' had 'been turned down'.

The Belfast government had 'a doleful litany of missed and misused opportunities' of 'broken pledges, disappointed hopes and unfulfilled expectations' ending with the abolition of PR. 'The nationalist aims in regard of the sundered portion of Ireland have been malignantly represented' the manifesto asserted. 'No party or no section of a party in Ireland has declared or indicated their intention to force Northern Ireland into any system of government without its willing consent.' As 'positive achievements' of the National League it listed improvements in social welfare benefits and pledged as its 'future policy' to make further advances along those lines.[15]

This common denominator of welfarism illustrates how strong the Devlinite influence within the movement actually was. Some weeks previously the *Irish News*, organ of Devlinism, had seen fit to rebuke the Hibernians for 'an excess of zeal' within the organisation, reminding them that they were 'but an arm of nationalism though a strong one'. The National League had, it stated, 'bound together all classes of nationalist thought' uniting the northern nationalists 'in a brotherhood of right'. A look at the line up for the May election demonstrated this fusion of the factions. Of the eleven nationalist candidates, six came from the IPP tradition and five from that of Sinn Féin, though one of the latter, Alexander Donnelly, was a former Home Ruler. Through the presence of candidates such as Donnelly, himself the Managing Director of the North West Publishing Company, and Joseph Connellan, *Frontier Sentinel* Editor, the major west of the Bann newspaper chain was linked with the *Irish News* in a common cause. McCarroll, the Derry MP, was of course also editor of the *Derry Journal*. Of the National League candidates he was also, at forty years of age, the youngest. In occupational terms, five were wealthy businessmen, two were solicitors and two others were newspaper editors.

A feature of all those from the IPP tradition was membership of the AOH. Only one of them, Hubert McAleer, in Mid-Tyrone, stressed his GAA connection on his election profile, something common to most Sinn Féiners. A retired national school teacher turned auctioneer and merchant, he alone of the IPP component had received a third level qualification. Of the five candidates from the Sinn Féin stable, only the two newspaper editors, McCarroll and Connellan, had not obtained similar educational distinctions. The occupational differentiations between the former IPP, five of whose six candidates were engaged in commercial employment, and the former Sinn Féin, all of whose men were engaged in intellectual work, was once again emphasised. There were no manual workers from either camp in the race.[16]

The nationalist press, in particular the *Irish News*, showcased the election, offering money prizes for the most accurate forecast. In the event, the nationalists did well – with a total of eleven, all their candidates were elected. Six of their successes were unopposed. In the new parliament they were joined by 34 unionists, one Labour man and two independent unionists. The nationalists elected to the Belfast parliament could do little but make speeches in support of Catholic interests and representations on behalf of their constituents.

Within the lifetime of the parliament they had withdrawn in exasperation at the indifference of the unionists to their grievances. Devlin's heart was never in the role of representative in Belfast, his Westminster seat having vanished in the 1922 carve-up and he had never re-contested the new West Belfast seat with its small unionist majority. In 1924 he had been assured that he would be welcome to contest the Westminster seat of

Fermanagh Tyrone as Harbinson's running mate.[17] Despite the latter's willingness to allow him he refrained from accepting the role until 1929 because perhaps of the hostility towards him by Harbinson's string-pullers – Murnaghan and his associates. However with the attenuation of inter-nationalist hostility in the post-1925 atmosphere, matters had begun to mellow so that following Harbinson's death in 1930 Healy contested as Devlin's running mate in the 1931 Westminster election and won the seat. In the aftermath of his withdrawal from the Belfast parliament, he and Healy approached De Valera and Sean T. O'Kelly with a revival of the 1928 proposals for a merger with Fianna Fáil. De Valera turned him down and refused to offer guidance to them on whether or not they should return to Stormont.[18] According to reports, Devlin made overtures also to republicans on the issue of a possible union of forces. No record exists of any result from this alleged meeting.[19] After a few more weeks in the political wilderness he was called to a meeting of the northern Catholic hierarchy in May 1933 who prevailed upon him to return to parliament at the October sitting. But, as Healy recalled, it was to be a qualified attendance only. They would 'neither become an official opposition' nor 'tender a day by day attendance, agreeing to attend only on occasions when they had something special to talk about or some statement to make'.[20]

When the *Irish News* at the end of 1930 looked back on the year just gone,[21] it designated the controversy over the Education Bill introduced in April its 'most outstanding event'. The Roman Catholic approach had up till then been, if anything, more accommodating than the Protestant one, which after all had held out strongly for Bible education in the schools. In the 1926/27 academic year, the primary schools of the Christian Brothers, the last remnants of the southern-instigated schools boycott, accepted the jurisdiction of the northern Ministry of Education.[22]

Even after the publication of the controversial proposals, Mageean, the recently installed Bishop of Down and Connor, held out the prospect of his church's acceptance of the 'four and two' system. At the INTO conference that month, he told delegates that it could be considered if its factions could be 'limited to the purely secular side of education'.[23] A few weeks later, priests of the Down and Connor diocese presented proposals which included modifications to the Bill 'so as to secure' that 'all matters including selection of teachers' should be 'subject to those who represent church interests'. The visit by a group of twenty prominent Catholics led by the Bishop of Derry to demand, it would appear, government finance for the voluntary schools – as the concessions on Bible instruction had effectively turned the state schools into Protestant ones – proved unproductive.[24]

It was to be the signal for a co-ordinated campaign of protest by northern Catholics, utilising all channels, which culminated in the May 1930 concession by Craigavon of a 50% grant for the building and enlargement of elementary schools in the voluntary sector. Even though Cardinal McRory described the situation as 'disappointing' and harked back to the pre-1923 position, it was to serve as a framework within which his church could strengthen its role in its community over the next forty years.

In tandem with this struggle for Roman Catholic Church control in education, went a fight on the political front against what was seen as the alien force of socialism within the Catholic community. The bitterness was on public view in the 1929 contest for the Falls seat between Richard Byrne and William McMullen. But it was played out most sharply in the contests for local government seats in Belfast Corporation. The nationalist approach to their Labour opponents was a mixture of the well worn 'Red Scare' argument, a welfarish programme which they portrayed as being in advance of the Labour one, and a resentful view that Labour were stealing 'their'seats.

During the corporation elections of 1930 an article in the *Irish News* of 10 January[25] entitled 'Catholicity and Labour – How interests conflict', related how the Poor Law Guardian member, James Collins, speaking in the Dock election campaign, accused Labour of opposing them in their upholding of Catholic education. 'Their aim' was 'to drive religious teaching from the schools,' he said, before going on to allege that Labour used their representatives in Dock Ward to prevent Catholics from getting employment. The example of Russia was invoked as evidence of how dangerous it was not to have Catholic representatives on public boards. The nationalist policy, Collins said, 'did not follow but led Labour'. He referred to the improvements in accommodation and rent reductions they had obtained and praised the work of Catholic welfare organisations.

On the day of the election the *Irish News*,[26] in an editorial entitled 'A Socialist Mystery', accused Labour of having 'split the progressive vote in three wards while in a dozen others the reactionary one goes unchallenged'. The defeat of Sam Kyle in Dock, Murtagh Morgan in 'Smithfield' and J. T. Keenan in 'Falls' was hailed by the *Irish News* as a 'rout' of socialism, though in all cases, except Smithfield, the candidates lost by less than 400 votes. A similar approach was adopted in the Westminster general election of 1931, when Campbell contested West Belfast and Devlin joined Healy in Tyrone and Fermanagh. All were at pains to emphasise their populist credentials. Devlin and Healy were 'fighting for farmers and agricultural labourers'. Campbell was waging the 'same fight for the working class'. Devlin recalled the 'headline' they 'set to the world in the provision of cottages for agricultural labourers' in the days of the Irish Parliamentary Party, while stressing that both he and his running mate were 'friends of the farmers'. He was neither a 'socialist nor a reactionary', he assured the electorate. 'I worked with the socialists when they sought for the betterment of the people, and voted against them and helped to defeat them when they refused to do justice to the Catholic schools in England'. The equation of Catholicism with Irish nationalism was made the most of by the *Irish News*. In an editorial entitled 'The Menace to Catholic Ireland', they advised northern Catholics against believing that the bishops' Pastoral Letter referred only to the Free State. Lest anyone forget the message of the Pastoral Letter they reprinted it with its sulphurous strictures against communism – 'a blasphemous denial of God', 'materialistic' and 'aimed at the overthrow of Christian civilisation' – going on to tell readers that 'it also meant class warfare, abolition of private property and the overthrow of family life'. Referring to Spain, a country which would loom much larger in their consciousness before the decade had passed, it bemoaned that 'great Catholic nations have fallen. A monarch who once bore the title of His Most Catholic Majesty, has become almost a forgotten exile.' (In April 1931 King Alfonso XIII abdicated, ushering in the second republic.) In case anyone still failed to link all this up with the nationalist campaign, their election address was printed in the opposite corner of the same page.[27]

The victory of De Valera in the southern general election in March 1932 was warmly welcomed throughout the border counties. The day after the new Dáil met (19 March) the *Frontier*

Sentinel reprinted from its issue of 12 December 1925, 'Border Nationalists Deserted' and recalled the Omagh meeting of that December which denied the authority of the Dublin government to do what it had done. Now with the De Valera victory the settlement imposed upon them was, it seemed, in the first stages of being dismantled.[28] Consequently, when De Valera called a further general election in January 1933 to establish a clear majority for his party in the Dáil, and rid himself of his dependence on the Labour Party, the border nationalists flew to his defence. Healy, Collins and Connellan crossed the border to participate in the Fianna Fáil election campaign, Healy in Donegal and Cavan, Collins in Louth and Meath, and Connellan in Cavan and Louth. An election fund started for Fianna Fáil in Down raised £100.

Connellan, in the *Irish Press* of 15 January, condemned Cosgrave and 'his friends in Freemason and Tory camps' and hailed De Valera for his 'ten months of wise and patriotic government' … legislating for 'the poor and down-trodden in keeping with Papal Encyclicals'. He appealed to all nationalists in the border counties to support Fianna Fáil, his headline of 28 January in his *Frontier Sentinel* newspaper proclaiming that 'Nationalists have been too long abandoned.'[29]

At the celebration in Newry after De Valera's victory, Connellan told the crowd it was 'nobody's business' whether one was 'a Hibernian or a republican of long standing' nor where anyone was in 1921 or 1922 or even last year. What mattered, he contended, was 'where they stood today'. Not only 'old republicans' but AOH supporters and long time opponents of De Valera 'supported him on this occasion', he stated.[30]

The mainstream republican movement had disapproved of the National League. IRA Chief of Staff, Maurice Twomey, in a letter to McGarrity in 1931 described it as 'sectarian'.[31] Instead he pinned his hopes on a coming together of Catholics and Protestants under the impact of worsening economic conditions. An opportunity came for them to test their strength in the election called by the northern government at the end of 1933. Candidates were nominated in Foyle, Belfast Central, South Armagh and South Down. While none of the republicans were nominated by clergy, all the nationalist candidates in Tyrone, Fermanagh and Derry were. In the latter constituency, the IRA candidate, Sean McCool, faced McCarroll, editor of the *Derry*

Journal, whose proposer was the local bishop. The *Journal* in repeated editorials lambasted the IRA as 'vote splitters' and communists, a theme taken up by Cahir Healy when he spoke in the constituency and recalled with horror how the bishops' Pastoral of 1931 had been described as 'infamous' in *An Phoblacht.* McCarroll was, he asserted, the 'champion of national and Catholic interests'. McCool by contrast was backed by 'the people who came out to defend Gralton' (a left-winger deported from Ireland by De Valera). The elision of past differences was evident in his claims that nationalists of 'old and new schools' supported McCarroll. The latter, despite his victory, later confessed himself 'disquieted' by the 3,000 votes received by his opponent.[32]

The Belfast contest produced the usual alliance of the Catholic Church and the *Irish News* in support of Devlin, who only reluctantly agreed to stand when approached in London by a deputation led by Joseph Campbell. In what was to be the last election of his life, his margin of victory dwindled to 2,700 votes. The nationalist vote in South Armagh split between Patrick O'Neill, the official National League candidate and prominent Hibernian, James G. Lennon, enabling the republicans' Paddy McLogan from County Laois, to take the seat in what was to be their sole victory of the campaign. In South Down the nationalist convention at Castlewellan had split between two candidates. A compromise proposal was put forward that De Valera, who had held the seat in 1921 and 1925 but withdrawn from the contest in 1929, be selected. Initially he had refused, citing his 1929 view that nationalists should first resolve on a united policy, but later at the Fianna Fáil Ard Fheis he relented and allowed his name to go forward as a candidate for the constituency from which he was barred by law. His about-face outraged the republicans who had already nominated their own man in opposition to the National League. Though relations with De Valera were becoming frayed since his election, they still remained his allies. Now for the first time a clear breach emerged. *An Phoblacht* of 2 December condemned his entry as a 'factionalist', one made at the invitation of the 'Hibernian machine' which it recalled had attacked republicans, including De Valera himself, 'when he came as a candidate to the north in 1918, 1921 and 1924. 'His stand in this contest,' the writer asserted, 'will be represented as being the same as in the previous elections and by those who were his bitterest opponents then.' The IRA Army Council, in a supplied statement, had placed the onus for splitting the vote on De Valera, remarking that his denial of political treatment to republican prisoners in the south hardly left him in a position to object 'to the same methods being used by the Craigavon government'.[33] On 9 December this issue of the prisoners was again raised in a hard-hitting editorial entitled 'Fianna Fáil becoming Anti-Republican'. While the De Valera intervention can be seen as the supreme example of how much the divide of Sinn Féin/Hibernian, and indeed pro- and anti-treaty, had vanished among northern nationalists, it also served to emphasise the widening gulf between his organisation and the IRA. Early in the New Year he told Joe McGarrity, 'If this country is not to be a Mexico or Cuba, a basis must be found or else the party that has got the majority here will have to secure order by force'.[34] The stage was being set for a confrontation with his old comrades. Though the republicans trumpeted McLogan's victory, they remained conscious of their lack of roots within the nationalist north. Most of their candidates, McLogan included, had come from over the border as had the majority of their speakers. An article in *An Phoblacht* in October 1934 serves to emphasise this divide, a gulf which was to remain for the next thirty-five years until the civil rights movement unleashed forces which were to give republicanism, for the first time in history, a substantial indigenously northern base of support. Under the headline 'who let the north down?' the anonymous writer answered his own question bluntly: 'The north let itself down', before going on to berate the northern Catholics for their sense of grievance and their historical refusal to embrace the separatist tradition. 'Self pity they say is the prelude to senility. If that be so the nationalist people of the north are well advanced in their dotage', he jeered, recalling the solidity of their opposition to Parnell, the Devlinite decision of 1916, and the continuing strength of the Home Rule organisation among them in 1918. He continued in a similar vein:

> Up to the early part of 1920 the number of active volunteers there was infinitesimal. It was only the sectarian riots in Belfast and Derry which drove large numbers into the ranks of the republican army. It was a gesture of self-defence and nothing more ... when the treaty came, nowhere was it supported more scurrilously and venomously than in the six

counties. The numbers who joined the Free State Army from the north east was far in excess in proportion to the relative geographical dimension of those who joined in the rest of Ireland.[35]

'Again,' the writer asked, 'who let the north down?' He then went on to remember the Boundary Commission and the nationalist support for it, remarking that the 'same slavish dependence' was once again manifesting itself in the attachment to the Free State, and to De Valera. All these condemnations were qualified by reference to the small minority of 'active conscientious re-publicans' who were present in the north since 1798.

On 18 January 1934 the ailing Joe Devlin died, his passing mourned across the political divide. A convinced Home Ruler he had met the Sinn Féin challenge and emerged through the dark passage of the early 1920s to become a figure commanding the support of most Belfast Catholics and courted by the Dublin government. In his life he had straddled many divides, that be-tween clericalism and a reformist workerism in Belfast, between AOH and ex-Sinn Féin in the enforced unity brought about by the collapse of the Boundary Commission, between east and west Ulster in his acceptance of a parliamentary seat for the Fermanagh-Tyrone constituency. Towards the end of his life he had been moving towards an accommodation with republicans. With his passing no successor could be found with a similar talent.

Devlin's death was a blow to all northern nationalists but particularly to those in Belfast. In April a representative confer-ence was held in St Mary's Hall, presided over by Senator T. J. Campbell, for the purpose of consolidating the nationalist forces. Campbell stressed their common bond of anti-partitionism, and their 'earnest wishes' for the welfare of their fellow countrymen beyond the border from whom they had 'never been separated in spirit'. James McSparran, one of the organisers, told the con-ference there was 'no reason' why the northern minority should be 'tied to any policy or any party in the Free State'. Comment-ing that it was 'pitiable' to see so many northern nationalists 'like a herd of sheep without leadership, ideas or any present policy', he went on to describe as 'incomprehensible' that the mentality of the minority had descended to such a plane that they were prepared to drift leaderless and rudderless at the mercy of their political opponents. Referring to the south he recalled how

'Leaders of both parties had declared that the position in the six counties would remain as at present for an indefinite period, therefore, the nationalists of the area must rely upon themselves.' The 'vast number' of 'evils' which they endured 'could only be remedied by the organisation' he stated in conclusion. Alderman Byrne claimed that when united they were 'a powerful force ... for the cause of Catholicity', while William Fulton claimed that the Hibernian organisation had decided that 'a basis for unity must be formed'. James Collins, one of the few non-AOH members present, asserted that every attempt had been made to hold a representative conference.[36]

The Belfast nature of the gathering was shown by the fact that only one of the speakers, John D. Nugent, the AOH General Secretary, came from outside the city. The first challenge they faced was the retention of Devlin's own seat in Central. No by-election writ had been moved by May, partly because of their disorganisation but also because, as the Labour party was not slow to point out, a June date would coincide with the holding of the Catholic Truth Society Conference in the city and facilitate the playing of the religious card. Any interference with the seat from outside the nationalist nexus was regarded by them as a form of *lese-majeste*. When Beattie and Midgley raised the issue of the writ in early May, the *Irish News* described their threatened action as 'ungrateful if not an impertinence'.[37] The nationalists blocked the attempt and the by-election was not held until June as Labour had predicted. The nationalists selected Campbell as their candidate and commenced a vicious sectarian campaign in what the *Irish News* described as 'Catholicism's hard battle'. Campbell was careful to pitch his campaign between the socialism of McMullan, his main opponent, and the Labourism of the constituency, a middle course well trodden by Devlin before him. While expressing his concern at the 'trend of Labour towards revolutionary socialism' and promising not to 'travel that road', he assured his listeners they would 'go as far for the just rights of workers as any party and further'. In the view of the Falls MP, Richard Byrne, even the party itself had acknowledged the entitlement of Catholics to the seat.

McCarroll, in from Derry to support Campbell, also made an issue of McMullan's religion. 'Was it not an insult to Catholic workers,' he asked 'that they must look for leadership to non-Catholics who subscribed to principles which no Catholic could countenance?'[38] Leeke, the Mid Derry MP, likewise hailed

Campbell as a 'champion of Catholic rights' and asked if McMullan favoured grants for Catholic education. A prosperous hotelier, he also played the workerist card, telling his listeners that before the British Labour Party came into being, the nationalists at Westminster had defended their rights.[39] The third candidate in the constituency was Harry Diamond, head of the newly formed Anti-Partition League, which aimed to undertake a policy of abstention from Stormont, the co-ordination of all anti-partitionist forces, in tandem with the setting up of a publicity branch which would galvanise overseas opinion on the issue of the border. Campbell dismissed the abstentionist tactic as a failure and made fun of the idea of arousing world opinion. 'Czechs, Slovaks, Yugoslavs and Germans will be listening with bated breath at the wireless and the border will fall soon after the activity gets underway.'[40] He attacked the APL for calling him sectarian, asking if support for Catholic schools and condemnation of anti-Catholic boycotts made him so, and pooh-poohed their republican credentials by producing a copy of *An Phoblacht* in which most of its founders were accused of failing to support 'a real abstentionist' in the November 1933 election. Campbell emerged a clear winner with the APL a derisory third.

Within the IRA the objective of linking national and social liberation revived in the early 1930s under the impact of the campaign against land annuities, the Outdoor Relief struggle of 1932 in Belfast, and the upsurge of working class militancy.

After the failure of an earlier organisation, Saor Éire, in 1931, largely due to opposition from right-wingers in the IRA leadership, a similar move was made in 1934. When the traditionalists, Sean McBride and Maurice Twomey swung the Executive and Army Council against it, its proponents resigned from the movement. From their decision eventually grew the Republican Congress of IRA leftists and nationally-minded trade unionists which met in Rathmines under the chairmanship of William McMullen on 29th and 30th September 1934. Almost from the start the Congress was a failure with a split developing between the IRA/Communist party faction and the Citizen Army Republican Labourites on the issue of 'Republic' versus 'Workers' Republic'. Nonetheless the months between the Athlone manifesto issued by the IRA defectors in April (calling for the establishment of a Congress) and the September meeting were anxious ones for the mainstream movement which sought to prevent further defections. This was as true in Northern Ireland as elsewhere, though its appeal varied on a rural-urban basis. In Belfast, roughly fifty volunteers, about a quarter of the active strength in the city, were inclined towards the new departure. In Derry not more than five or six; in the whole of Tyrone, ten would have been the maximum. Shortly after the Athlone manifesto, in an attempt to enforce unity, Maurice Twomey called an Extraordinary Meeting of the movement at the Donegal Street ITGWU Hall in Belfast. At the meeting, attended by 'about 200 volunteers', all present were called upon to 're-attest'. Those who refused were requested to leave. About twenty, including Jack Mulvenna and Jim Straney (who was to die on the republican side in Spain) left the hall.[41]

Relations with the official movement in the city were strained but not severed. Though the Dublin based *Republican Congress* newspaper recorded a 'tying to the railings' of a volunteer who joined and an attempted kidnapping of another. Mulvenna discounts the first claim and remembers the second simply as an attempt by IRA volunteers to seize a gun from Paddy Largey, the OC of the Markets McCracken Company, who had failed to 're-attest' and was required to return his weapon. The attempted seizure, which occurred as Largey walked with Mulvenna and another volunteer down Donegal Street, was beaten off.[42] Largey had presided with Gene Thornbury at the joint organising committee of Congress in the city in June and had been instrumental in the formation of Connolly clubs in Rosemary Street, The Markets and Ballymacarrett, helping to bring speakers, including Gilmore and O'Donnell, to the city.

The July 1936 revolt of the Spanish Generals against the democratically elected Popular Front Government of the country, sent the Irish Catholic Church into a frenzied identification with the Falangist forces. Long before the Vatican had issued its official endorsement of the Franco forces, McRory was assuring worshippers at the shrine of Blessed Oliver Plunkett in Drogheda, 'that there was no reason any longer for doubt as to the issues at stake in Spain'. His sermon also included an attack upon the Republican Congress, 'a very serious development ... one for the state to take note of'.[43] That section of the left which did not tack to this prevailing view endorsed by all nationalist newspapers in the north was to be the chief loser most specifically in the stormy election of 1938. In Dock, Harry Midgley, whose support for the Spanish Republic had included a debate with a Roman Catholic priest, Fr Sexton, in late 1936, the publication of a pamphlet rebutting Catholic Church attacks on the Popular Front, and the offer of hospitality to Spanish sailors at his home in Belfast, was pushed into third place by a clericalist indepen-dent, James Collins (later to join the Labour party) and defeated. Despite the allegation of certain historians that Midgley's failure to remain in Belfast during the 1935 riots was the key factor ac-counting for his defeat, he had been re-elected in 1936 to his cor-poration seat a few weeks before the outbreak of the civil war. It was a glorious opportunity for the nationalists who had sup-ported Collins to make good the threat enunciated by McSparran, after their victory in Central in 1934, that having dri-ven Labour out of Central they 'would drive them out of Dock also'.[44] In Derry the Labour Party, smeared with the same red brush by their opponents, did not fare any better, coming bot-tom of the poll in the municipal elections of May 1938.

By that stage clerical nationalism, now fortified by the Vatican endorsement of the Franco cause, had ratcheted its pro-paganda to an even higher pitch. McRory could state in January 'that if ever there was a war for God and Christian civilisation' it was the 'war waged by General Franco and the youth of Spain'.[45] Those Labourites who took this line, as did the Newry-Armagh branch, proposers of a pro-Franco motion, portrayed their action as a defence of workers' rights, and became the unexpected beneficiaries of clerical support or at least lack of opposition. When Senator McLaughlin of Armagh, prominent clericalist businessman and AOH member, fell foul of those clergy in the south of the county by opposing their policy of abstention-ism in the February 1938 Stormont election, he found he could no longer rely on their support. After his surprise defeat by Labour in the May 1939 council election he wrote to Healy of the 'combination we never knew existed' which defeated him. 'Catholic workers, unemployed B Specials and Orangemen'.[46]

For the republican tradition, the Spanish conflict drew away its most progressive elements, some of whom had already affili-ated to the Congress. Many were among the 170 volunteers who left to fight for the Spanish Republic, under the leadership of for-mer IRA leader and signatory of the Athlone manifesto, Frank Ryan. Of the 19 volunteers from Northern Ireland, mostly from

Belfast, only seven returned. With the radicalism in the IRA marginalised, its right wing moved in. As one veteran of the period told the writer, 'a lot of queer people came into the movement'.[149] Activists like the Fusco brothers, second generation Italians and admirers of Mussolini, infected the organisation with their thinking. The way was paved for the appearance on the scene of the 'belt and boot' brigade which enforced discipline along the lines of the European fascists. Some volunteers, encountering this disturbing phenomenon on their release from prison, left the movement as a result.[48] It was no accident that when O'Duffy recruited his detachment for the Francoist cause, Belfast was the only place where members of the IRA were prepared to join.[49]

PART THREE

1935-1945

'The completely wrong attitude from a national viewpoint.'

'As usual, northern Catholics are left to their own resources, so any movement by nationalists in the north is bound to be driven underground and will possibly and very probably lead to a pro-German feeling here in the event of an Allied invasion. This would be the completely wrong attitude from a national viewpoint.'
Patrick Maxwell MP to Cahir Healy MP, 5 June 1940

CHAPTER 9

The 1935 Westminster Election and after

The death of Joe Devlin and the rising strength of republicanism set the seal on the fortunes of the moribund National League, already falling apart under the weight of its own regional factionalism and its manifest failure to achieve its purpose in the face of unionist intransigence. Amongst its rural members abstention from Stormont was setting in gradually. The West Tyrone MP, Alexander (A. E.) Donnelly, had left the Belfast parliament in April 1934. McCarroll admitted to Healy in November of that year to having 'no desire to open my mouth there' except as a means of raising the grievances of constituents. The mid-Tyrone NW-Tyrone MP, Hubert McAleer, held on until October 1935, a reflection of his Devlinite outlook, his departure on the eve of the republican challenge in the Westminster election indicative of the degree to which even the moderate nationalist tradition had been pulled along by events. With his fellow Hibernian, Joe Stewart, in East Tyrone already gone, only the two Belfast MPs, T. J. Campbell and Richard Byrne, were eventually left in attendance.

By 1935 the gap between the northern communities was wider than at any time since the early twenties, as the frustration of nationalists, their growing attachment to Fianna Fáil and the increasingly vicious sectarian utterances of Stormont ministers pandering to the bigotry of Orange Lodges, all interacted to produce a polarisation which did not begin to decrease until the late 1950s. With the July riots in Belfast leaving over 2,200 Catholics homeless, and burying the working class cross-community alliances of the 1932 Outdoor Relief strike, the republican electoral intervention that October formalised the new mood. To the IRA and its supporters, the smell of victory in their nostrils since the Stormont election of 1933, the announcement of the Westminster poll for 14 November was too good an opportunity to miss. By 28 October six republicans had been entered for the contest, one each for Derry, Down and Armagh and two for the joint constituency of Tyrone and Fermanagh. West Belfast and Antrim had followed suit by 1 November. The mainstream nationalists were not slow in reacting to the republican presence. On 29 October the *Irish News* editorial (written by Belfast Central MP, T. J. Campbell who had succeeded Kirkwood in the chair) predicted that the 'unfortunate intervention' would render the efforts of the nationalists 'worthless' and, recalling the setback of 1924 when Sinn Féin had last contested a Westminster election, asked if they wanted a repetition.[1]

Wearing his other hat as a parliamentary representative, Campbell chaired a nationalist meeting for West Belfast a few days later which decided not to put forward a candidate. In a lengthy statement afterwards they voiced the hopelessness of Belfast Catholics in the prevailing climate, commenting that nationalists realised they were 'engaged in a fight for existence', that every census since 1861 had shown a declining Catholic population (reduced from 33 to 23 per cent) who, with most private and almost all public employment closed to them, were not prepared to 'dissipate their energies in a hopeless fight on a register with a unionist majority of 15,000'.[2]

Both the *Irish News* leader and this statement made specific reference to the one area where the minority population returned representatives to London which they were likely to lose in the event of a split vote, the sprawling two-seat western constituency of Fermanagh and Tyrone. For it was there that the biggest drama of the entire election was being enacted. When the republican announced their candidates, Martin Gallagher, 1920-22 Brigade commandment for the 2nd Northern Division, and Thomas Daly, a brother of Charlie Daly OC of that same division executed by the Free State government in 1923, it caused consternation among the outgoing MPs, Cahir Healy and Joe Stewart. On 23 October they contacted De Valera assuring him that most nationalists in the area were Fianna Fáil supporters and requesting a meeting to discuss a situation which would, they felt, lead to unionists gaining and retaining the seats. De Valera told them he was unwilling to intervene in disputes between northern nationalists, an answer in keeping with his non-committal response to Healy's overtures to him following the July riots. When Archdeacon Tierney of Enniskillen, hearing of the deputation's failure, hurried to Dublin some days later to meet the Taoiseach he received a similar rebuff.[3]

The nationalist committee which had mandated Healy to contact De Valera met on 31 October at Ballinadden, Fivemiletown, to appoint delegates to the convention called for Omagh on 1 November, pledging to oppose outside groups who might put forward candidates. That convention, presided over by Archdeacon Tierney, lasted five hours, and resulted in a vote of 128 to 27 in favour of abstentionism with both Healy and Stewart re-nominated. The reality of the republican presence could not have been lost on the delegates meeting in St Patrick's Hall. Throughout the deliberations IRA chief of staff, Maurice (Moss) Twomey, harangued a crowd less than a hundred yards away.[4]

With neither of the two nominees acceptable to republicans, and a 'strong body' in favour of co-operation, attempts to secure a compromise continued over the weekend of 2 and 3 November. An eight-man plenary committee put forward a number of proposals including a third name on the ticket, joint representation by republicans and nationalists, and a possible later review of the abstentionism decision. All of these suggestions and others, including one of a joint appeal to De Valera, were turned down by the republicans. Shortly before the close of nominations a compromise was agreed between the committee and Donnelly, the republican director of elections, whereby two local nationalists, Patrick Cunningham and Anthony Mulvey, would be invited to go forward.[5] Cunningham, a large farmer and one of the few Sinn Féiners to oppose the treaty in the area, first heard his name had been proposed when a deputation aroused him from his sleep on the morning of 4 November.[6] He accepted for the sake of unity. Mulvey, editor of the *Ulster Herald*, had been sympathetic to republicanism since his days as a journalist in his native Leitrim.

At a meeting held in Enniskillen later that day, Twomey hailed the decision as a reflection of the spirit of the 1918 election. Amongst the Belfast executive of the moribund National League of the North, the decision aroused a 'feeling of disgust'. Parliamentary representation was, they stated, one of the League's principles, adding that the 'present situation' would not have arisen had the decentralisation of the organisation not been persisted in' by Cahir Healy.[7] The *Irish News* however swallowed its reservation, rejoicing on 11 November in 'priests and people co-operating to secure victory at the polls'.

Interestingly Twomey's opponents from the Republican Congress split of the previous year also gave the campaign wholehearted support, though its leader George Gilmore had written to Healy, when the issue of seats hung in the balance, asking him to convene a conference in Dungannon of nationalists and trade union representatives, as the nucleus of an all-Ireland assembly, to forestall a descent into the 'old Sinn Féin wilderness' of negative abstentionism. The initiative proved abortive when Healy told Gilmore he had no authority to call such a gathering.[8]

The message of republicans on the hustings was the traditional one of communal unity, leavened with social conscience in deference to the mood of the times. Twomey denied that a difference existed between a nationalist and a republican, saying simply that the only true example of one was the other. Their manifesto linked the social with the national, stressing that only the 'mass of the people' united in a free nation could end an unjust order which was 'impoverishing and degrading a large section, depriving them of their dignity as human beings'.[9]

In this frame of mind, Protestants were repeatedly exhorted from platforms to return to their true 1798 allegiance, the July riots in Belfast depicted as an example of the 'lengths which England would go to foster hatred', and the outgoing MPs, Healy and Stewart, castigated as the spokesmen for 'a Catholic party'. It was an approach irksome to a section of Belfast Catholic opinion. One such person, writing in the *Irish News* of 9 November, declared:

> The republicans tell us there is no sectarian issue but almost every Catholic realises that the major issue is a sectarian one. Territorially Catholics have lost and are losing ground. In 1920 there were two Catholic streets off York Road, Weaver St and Stone St; today there is not a single Catholic left on this side of Millfield and Brown Square.

The correspondent condemned the introduction of 'extraneous issues such as imperialism' stating that it would not be the soldiers of the republic who would be in the frontline but 'the girls and women in the mills and factories who stood their ground last July.[10]

A feature of the republican campaign was the preponderance of people from the twenty-six counties on its election platforms, a point later used against them by nationalist spokesmen. At the opening meeting of the campaign in Armagh, three of the five speakers were from Dublin, in Derry two of the four were from south of the border, in Down southerners made up eleven of the sixteen people addressing the crowd. Without the help of local nationalist networks it is difficult to see how the vote would have been mobilised. The leading Fermanagh republican, Sean Nethercott, later admitted that he had only five men enrolled in that county to control a total of eighty-five booths, though 'matters were more satisfactory in Tyrone'.

In the recriminations following the result, this was to be a major bone of contention with nationalist representatives and supporters. Healy, criticising the 16,284 votes obtained by Charlie McGleenan in Armagh, alleged that the polling stations were so inefficiently manned the result there was less than half of what candidates from the minority had obtained in the past. At the Fianna Fáil Ard Fheis in December, the Devenish curate, Fr Coyle, made a particular issue of the southern origins of republican personnel. This elicited a reply from the abstentionist Stormont MP, Paddy McLogan, reminding Fianna Fáil that no such objections were raised by the party during De Valera's cross-border electoral foray of 1933.[12] Later in the spring of 1936 *An Phoblacht* was attacking 'so-called nationalists who questioned the right of republicans to enter the campaign' but whose special resentment 'is reserved for those outside the six counties'.[13] Criticisms notwithstanding, the final election tally could be read as a vindication of the republican strategy. The vote in Armagh and Down, where no nationalist had stood for Westminster since the State was formed, marked an improvement on Sinn Féin's 1924 performance, most markedly so in Down where the vote leapt from 8,911 to a solid 20,330. The decline from the almost 41,000 strong opposition Liberal vote in the constituency in 1929 was accounted for by a corresponding increase in the unionist total. Only in Belfast was a decline in the anti-partitionist vote registered – Charles Leddy's 20,013 to Campbell's 1931 vote of 23,006. The two compromise candidates, Mulvey and Cunningham, were of course returned for Fermanagh and Tyrone with a slightly larger vote than that obtained by Healy and Joe Devlin in the previous election. The unionist vote underwent an increase of several thousand in all the contested constituencies, spurred into action by the nature of the new opposition.

Sectarian politics was to bedevil those on the other side who tried to make a cross-community appeal. James Blackiston Houston, one of the two unionist candidates in Fermanagh Tyrone, wrote to Brookeborough complaining that the poll had been on a strictly religious basis with no attempt made to enlist the support of Roman Catholics. When during the campaign he had suggested a visit to the Roman Catholic Bishop of Clogher, nobody was prepared to accompany him. He was advised to keep the visit a secret and told it would lose him the funds of the unionist association. Though, as he assured Brookeborough, he was not naïve enough to believe it would have won a single Catholic vote, it was still important that the 'bogey of religious division' would be 'driven into the open'. Disputing that Catholics were automatically disloyal, he recalled their record of imperial service and reminded Brookeborough that the Stormont parliament depended on the goodwill of the entire electorate. The policy of individuals at local authorities had been to drive the minority community into the opposition camp. 'No Catholic can join the B specials,' he told Brooke, concluding prophetically that unionists would one day have to give an account of their stewardship and 'must be prepared to answer the question "have you been tolerant to the Roman Catholics?"' Coming after two years of the most public anti-Catholic utterances by unionist leaders, this appeal fell on stony ground. Brooke, author of the most egregious of their remarks at the previous year's 12 July gathering at Newtonbutler, writing later to the Prime Minister, Lord Craigavon, commented that 'Jim Houston made me hot under the collar once or twice. I put it to him bluntly he had a "sit on the fence" outlook.'[14]

The approach of people like Brookeborough prevailed over that of those like Blackiston Houston. J. M. Andrews, the Minister for Labour who was to succeed Craigavon as Prime Minister in 1940, until Brooke's 20 year reign began three years later, and who had himself boasted earlier of the absence of Catholics employed at Stormont, felt the 'only relief' in the election result was its disclosure of the 'number of downright disloyalists' in the contested areas.[15] At a time when the northern minority population still had a foothold in the administration of the state – 17% of the RUC was Catholic in 1935, the percentage within the ranks ranging from over one third of its head constables and county inspectors to one seventh of its constables – this mood in the unionist hierarchy was ominous. That year saw the resumption of the electoral manipulation begun in the 1920s, climaxing with the Derry gerrymander of 1936 which gave the unionist minority in the city a clear majority of seats on the corporation. A similar transformation was achieved that year with the nationalist controlled Omagh Urban Council. The Armagh Board of Guardians had already been disbanded two years previously to be reconstructed with a unionist majority in 1946.[16] Northern Ireland, in its policies of employment, housing and policing, was consolidating into the pattern of sectarian rule that would not shatter for another three decades. In the face of this onslaught, the need for nationalist unity had seldom been so paramount, yet never had it been so lacking. The Westminster election had illustrated once again the traditional east/west divide, republicanism's lack of an indigenous northern base, and as demonstrated by the Catholic rate of abstentionism, its inability to win over more moderate elements. Throughout 1936 northern nationalism could be seen in its component parts as each strove for a way out of the political morass.

That April, in a lengthy feature article,[17] a special correspondent of the *Irish News* captured the confused and often contradictory nature of northern nationalism. After a tour from Belfast to Derry via Newry, Enniskillen and Omagh there were, he concluded, almost as many brands of nationalism in the six counties as there were nationalists. For convenience he divided them into 'the peace with Stormont' group and 'the no truck with Stormont' group, this latter faction 'quite significant' in South Armagh, South Fermanagh and South Tyrone.

A conversation he had with an old native Fermanagh leader 'conveyed the clearest impression of the anti-Stormont group. "300 years ago there was not a blade of grass in the country that was not owned by a Catholic Celt." Today,' the old man finished with a gesture which swept in imagination over such objects as the statue of the British General Cole which dominates Enniskillen, 'the shops in towns and villages have signboards sporting the planter origin of their owners and the country mansions of the Brookes and Archdales.' When he said '300 years ago' there was, the correspondent felt, a note of injury in his voice as if it only happened yesterday. It was impossible to conceive of a Belfast or Antrim nationalist similarly 'plantation-conscious' – for them the events of the seventeenth century had become merely an 'historical fact, sufficiently remote for its consequences to be accepted philosophically'.

On the issue of partition, the writer noted a clear difference from those in the border counties:

> The wound is just as raw as on the morning of the Anglo-Irish Treaty which cast six Ulster counties out of the Irish nation, as raw as on the morning of the Boundary Commission which set its seal on the casting out.

To this mindset the abolition of PR, the gerrymandering away of nationalist electoral control in Fermanagh and Tyrone, was a 'salt-rubbing process, a re-enactment of the Penal Laws with Lord Craigavon the Simon Lagree of the Ulster plantation'. By contrast 'in and around Belfast' partition had also become a historical fact with:

> Nothing like the same amount of gerrymandering is taking place. Some of those who have been forced to have dealings with Stormont have been impressed by the courtesy and kindness of Stormont officials. One public representative, who had 'run many errands to the leaders of the six county government' told the reporter, 'I have never been refused anything I asked for.'[19]

The view of several members of this group the *Irish News* synthesised as follows:

> Stormont is here to stay in our generation. We must recognise it for the sake of our schools and for the social services. Why should we not recognise it fully and become the official opposition in the six county parliament, attending for all the social legislation, showing by our criticisms of it that we have men amongst us just as anxious for the welfare of the six counties as any unionist leader and just as able to provide that welfare?

At present, an unidentified representative told the correspondent, only three were attending parliament with any regularity as a party ('if this could be said to be a party').

He contrasted this with the time when the Irish Parliamentary Party addressed the 'great social and economic issues', regretting that those matters were now the province of socialists and independents. To border nationalists, the paper noted, an attitude such as this was heresy, a deviation from the obligatory obsession with partition.[20]

Nationalists after the election

No strand of minority political opinion was more troubled by the situation than Hibernianism. With the republican challenge looming in October, the AOH leader, John D. Nugent, had toughened his anti-partitionist language to the point when it was cited in private correspondence by the Minister for Labour, J. M. Andrews, as the type of rhetoric which antagonised unionists.[21] Early in the year Nugent set out his plans for an organisation to 'unite all sections' of the Catholic community, his first requirement for membership excluding those groups 'under the ban of the church or any body associated with communism'. (A list of these, culled from James J. Hogan's booklet *Could Ireland Become Communist?* (Dublin 1935) was provided and included the IRA.) The second condition rejected as unsuitable the suggestion that Fianna Fáil should organise north of the border. This would, Nugent maintained, lead to party competition. Likewise it was proposed that northern nationalists abandon all involvement in southern electoral politics. The final clause reaffirmed the rejection of anyone who refused to accept the legitimacy of the twenty-six county State. All conditions reflected the fears and hopes of an organisation strongly pro Fine Gael in character – fears of a socially egalitarian republicanism and of a Fianna Fáil resurgence among northern Catholics, hopes of an inter-nationalist unity based on a common conservatism and acceptance of the southern State.[22] But with northern nationalist opinion turning increasingly in the direction of Fianna Fáil, such an initiative was doomed from the start to have nothing more than a sectional appeal.

The republicans too sought a united front but on terms different from those of the Hibernians. Early in June they announced that proceedings to form a new nationalist organisation were under way, a series of meetings having already been held towards this objective involving various shades of abstentionist opinion ranging from the IRA to the Donnelly wing of Fianna Fáil. That the issues uniting them were less important than those which divided them became obvious when the conference finally took place on 15 June in St Mary's Hall, Belfast. No representatives of the National League or Labour organisations were invited and those of Cumann na mBan and outdoor relief who turned up were refused admission. As well as being abstentionist, the parameters of the hypothetical organisation were implicitly being set as socially conservative and male. But even this was not enough. When the conference got underway, presided over by Hugh Corvin, an Andersonstown accountant, and including such luminaries as the abstentionist Westminster MPs Mulvey and Cunningham, the absentee South Armagh member for Stormont, Paddy McLogan, and the former Nationalist Poor Law Guardian member for Falls, Harry Diamond, differences developed immediately over attitudes to the southern State. A draft constitution submitted by Diamond's Anti-Partition League became the subject of a republican amendment repudiating the authority of both parliaments. After a heated debate lasting five hours, thirty delegates including Corvin and Mulvey walked out. In a clear indication of their pro Fianna Fáil orientation, both of them joined with Cahir Healy two days later as a deputation to De Valera to discuss the minority's grievances.[23]

Whether encouraged by De Valera in the matter or not, the mainstream nationalists, no doubt sensing their growing irrelevance, were making moves to regain the initiative. A little over a week after the St Mary's Hall meeting they opened a new office in Castle St, Belfast. Throughout July nationalists in Derry, Armagh, Fermanagh and Tyrone worked behind the scenes to produce a new organisation,[24] culminating in a convention at Omagh on 26 July with powers to draft a constitution and with an emergency executive, including Cahir Healy and the AOH member for Mid Derry, George Leeke. But it was one thing to unite nationalists of the Hibernian and non-Hibernian stamp west of the Bann; to do so in Belfast was quite a different matter. A lengthy conference held in the city on 19 August with T. J. Campbell among the nationalist MPs present, was only partly successful in this regard. When the new organisation finally saw the light of day in September as the Irish Union Association, both he and the other Belfast nationalist MP, Richard Byrne, were noticeably absent.

The inaugural meeting (attended by 100 delegates, including 20 priests) pledged: to strive for the 'national unity and independence of Ireland; to seek the co-operation of all Irishmen in that objective; to promote a national outlook; to secure social services for all citizens, and to attend to registration.' Significantly there was no discussion of abstentionism, the focus being fixed firmly on the attainment of the widest unity possible. The organisation committee appeal in late October stressed its freedom from sectional conflict, pointing out that in previous incarnations of the northern national movement the 'principle of democratic control was regarded as limited'. It also acknowledged as 'painfully evident the apathy and disunion among nationally-minded people'.[25]

At the formation of branches in Omagh and Cookstown that month, R. H. O'Connor described it as a 'democratic organisation open to all'. A. E. Donnelly told his listeners it was 'primarily an organisation formed to enlighten public opinion and to compel definite action to be taken in relation to partition'.[26] Its clericalist character was obvious from the start. Its constitution, which was submitted to Cardinal McRory for approval, specified in Article 7 that included in each 'Coisde Condae' (i.e. County Committee) would be all the clergy of the area. McShane, the parish priest of Omagh, shared the joint secretaryship with Nugent, and the organisation of branches in Fermanagh was specifically delayed by Healy until Archdeacon Tierney of Enniskillen returned from holiday in Portugal.

With the formation of the IUA minority politics could at least be said to have a centre to counterpoint its extremes of Stormont attendance, militant republicanism and Labourism. Both these latter two traditions were to be increasingly incorporated into the clericalist conservative consensus, their radicalism washed away in the tidal wave of 1930s reaction, heightened by the responses to the Spanish Civil War that summer (see pp 117-118).

But this centre was to be an unstable one. The orientation of the new movement towards Fianna Fáil not only ran the risk of alienating its Hibernian members, it also faced the greater hazard of finding its house built on sand if De Valera's party failed to match the expectations reposed in it. But for the moment all of this was obscured, with only the old east/west division within nationalist politics seeming to exist. In this spirit George Leeke joined with Healy and Mulvey in April 1937 to lambast the predominantly Catholic Ballycastle council for its 'slavish attitude' in sending a congratulatory telegram to the new monarch, George VI.[27] Leeke's fellow Hibernians, the Belfast MPs Byrne and Campbell, had also sent greetings.

Nationalists and De Valera's Constitution
That December, when the IUA's joint secretary Reverend McShane condemned a certain mentality prepared to acquiesce

in the status-quo, he referred to a 'ray of hope' which the year had brought.[28] That 'ray of hope' was the May 1937 Constitution of Eamon De Valera with its apparent claims in Articles two and three striking a responsive chord among nationalists, particularly those of the western and border varieties. Cahir Healy had told the *Irish News* that nationalists were on the whole in favour of it. Even if it offered them 'no prospect of immediate release' it was, he said, 'at least comforting' to them 'to know they were not forgotten'. The Omagh based North West Publishing Company chain of newspapers went further, hailing it as 'righting the wrong wreaked by the Act of 1920' and recalled in vivid detail Cosgrave's role in the 1925 agreement which it was felt had now been superseded.[29] Support also came from Bishop Mageean of Down and Conor.

But the greatest effect was to be on the minds of those like Eamonn Donnelly who saw in the constitution the basis for a new nationalist organisation committed to abstentionism which would seek admission to Dáil Éireann. Having clashed with Healy on the issue of moving the IUA in this direction (Healy had told him that abstentionism as defined by Arthur Griffith was merely a tactic not a principle intended only for a definite period and a definite situation),[30] Donnelly branched out on his own, forming in late 1937 'The Northern Council for Unity'. Traditional republicans like Peadar Murney of Newry and the poet Alice Mulligan rubbed shoulders with Fianna Fáil supporters Mulvey and Corvin on its executive. The many priests present at its formation included the IUA joint secretary Reverend McShane.

By this time the IUA was already beginning to disintegrate. When such differences could exist between two native born northern nationalists like Healy and Donnelly, both formed in the pre-civil war Sinn Féin tradition, it did not augur well for united action with those of a different stamp. Because limits there certainly were to the penetrative power of De Valera's constitution within the nationalist north, no areas being more resistant than the heartland of Hibernianism from Belfast to the Sperrin mountains. East Tyrone MP and AOH leading light, Joe Stewart, wrote to Healy telling him 'little or no interest' was taken by the priests of the area in the document and the expansion of the IUA suffered as a result.[31] Though Stewart had promised in October 'to start branches soon', he admitted that many of his constituents 'distrusted' the organisation.[32] For this reason the nationalist press had held aloof from the IUA fearing that to give it full support would alienate its Hibernian readers. Mulvey, in his capacity as editor of the *Ulster Herald*, admitted as much, confessing himself 'afraid' that such support might spark fears of an abstentionist move.[33]

However, as Healy privately acknowledged, it was not opposition but 'apathy' which was to prove its real undoing. On 13 October when they held a meeting in Newry which advocated a total boycott of Stormont institutions, no elected representative was present. A delegation was chosen afterwards to meet De Valera. Healy, fearing the worst, rejected a call by Foyle MP Patrick Maxwell to summon an Ard Fheis in November which would, he felt, only produce worse dissent. As he had privately admitted to Maxwell, only a few districts outside Fermanagh had ever established branches, and three quarters of Tyrone remained unorganised, with the remainder of the county not in a position to send delegates.[34] F. J. Nugent, the Omagh registration agent, had earlier told Healy that the organisation was 'generally regarded' as having ceased to exist.

In this situation voices were raised which had hitherto remained silent, voices hostile both to the policies of abstentionism and of dependence on De Valera. The Belleek hotelier and Hibernian, Senator John McHugh, claimed De Valera lacked any 'real plan' for the abolition of partition, calling on him to demonstrate otherwise. He condemned as an illusion the reliance on the Free State, remarking that his frequent visits there convinced him its inhabitants were not prepared to make sacrifices in the cause of unity. His suggestion was for a conference of nationalist businessmen 'who have made themselves leaders of their community', from which politicians would be excluded.[35] Despite the hostility shown to him by the *Derry Journal*, support for his outburst came from his fellow AOH parliamentarians, the MPs Byrne and Stewart, as well as the former *Irish News* editor, J. P. Kirkpartick.[36] It was a sign that the Hibernian tradition was becoming more assertive, pulling strongly against the current of abstentionism.

At a meeting in the Avenue Bar in Belfast on 9 December, eight of the nine nationalist MPs pledged themselves against the practice, promising non-co-operation with other parties and rejecting the idea of becoming the official opposition. And they took a side swipe at Mulvey's support for De Valera, pointing out that in strict logic his and Cunningham's 1935 election pledges bound them not to recognise the Dáil as well as the northern parliament.[37] The sole absentee from the meeting, Patrick O'Neill MP for Mourne, (unavailable due to illness, he died shortly afterwards) would have agreed. Three days earlier he had informed Healy that he was never in favour of abstentionism, acknowledging the death of the IUA 'if indeed it every had a life' and lamenting that northern nationalists had been without a leader since Devlin's death, expressed his doubts that matters would improve even if they were to get one.[38]

The abstentionist idea was far from dead, however, and was about to receive its most powerful boost in years. With the clerical administration of Newry and Armagh on the side of the Northern Council, it was soon to find fertile ground in the Armagh and Down areas where both McLogan and De Valera himself had been elected on abstentionist tickets. They got their opportunity when Craigavon, worried both by the south's constitution and a possible deal on partition under the Anglo-Irish talks drawing to a conclusion in London, called an election for February.

In South Armagh, where legislation requiring an oath debarred McLogan from standing, the pro-boycott groups carried the day at the convention in Camlough. In Mourne, despite reported divisions among the clergy (it was after all O Neill's seat and he was no abstentionist) the candidate, Joseph Smyth of Saul, announced his withdrawal to the praise of the *Frontier Sentinel* newspaper. That seat was also left vacant. In South Down the convention invited De Valera to stand once more. In his reply declining the offer, he expressed regret that a common policy among northern nationalists had not proved possible and denied that the election would be a true index of anti-partition feeling. The convention then fell back on the boycott tactic, handing another seat by default to the unionists. South Armagh City seemed set to go the same way but for the emergence of the veteran Armagh city Labour councillor, Patrick Agnew, whose action in filling the vacated seat earned him the reprobation and undying enmity of the Catholic establishment.[39]

The boycott tactic presented the mainstream nationalists with a problem. Healy and Maxwell argued for a compromise situation involving token attendance before withdrawing en masse, an idea which won considerable press and political support in the nationalist community but failed to win the support of republicans in Belfast and Fermanagh, who rejected it out of hand. Healy had contacted De Valera but received no reply. Senator McLaughlin, prominent Hibernian and Knight of Columbanus, who confessed he had a 'great deal of trouble' getting Smyth to stand in Mourne, reported a similar lack of response from Dublin.[40] Interestingly, Mulvey's son told a Belfast historian in 1978 that the boycott tactic was De Valera's idea, and certainly the pro-Fianna Fáil *Irish Press* had openly advocated such a course, to Healy's great displeasure.[41]

Whether or not the strategy was adopted at ground level depended, as with so much else in northern nationalist political life, on the attitude of the local clergy. In West Tyrone it had been a close run affair, with the Omagh convention at one stage seeming to swing in favour of it. The Reverend McShane had commented on the number of priests defecting to the idea. Even though the threat failed to materialise, that area remained potential territory for the abstentionists, with Stewart telling Healy that its MP, A. E. Donnelly, was 'the weakest link' nationalists had got.[42] In Stewart's own territory of East Tyrone things were very different, as he acknowledged, largely because the clergy there, as in the south of the county, regarded the policy as 'out of the question'.

Overall the election results showed the number of nationalist seats down by three, two in unopposed returns, a total of 16,167 votes or 4.9%. It was the lowest nationalist vote ever recorded in the Roman Catholic community. It was an unimpressive tally, particularly galling to those outside the spell cast by Fianna Fáil. One such person, Louis J. Walsh, the former Antrim Sinn Féiner and internee, by then a Cumann na nGaedhal appointed District Justice in Donegal, wrote to Healy in late February bemoaning the loss of seats, the Omagh group's reliance on Fianna Fáil advice, and the failure as he saw it of abstentionism. Expressing himself 'glad to hear' of a 'reaction against this policy', he advised Healy to start a new nationalist organisation if the London talks between Chamberlain and De Valera failed to produce an outcome.[43]

The London talks had not been a major theme in northern nationalist political discourse until the calling of the election. From then on, the fears of Lord Craigavon became reflected as their aspirations. 'The reaction of northern nationalists is one of hope that the convention in Downing Street will lead to the unity of the country,' the *Irish News* proclaimed. A year earlier, in an editorial entitled 'Northern Catholics and the London talks', it had acknowledged that the 'Government of Ireland Act cannot easily be repealed', but neither was it intended to be used as it is now being used 'to penalise the majority'. It had then listed the grievances, the remedying of which was a condition of an amicable settlement.[45] This change in tone in the traditionally less border-obsessed Belfast press testified to the hopes raised by the new constitution. And the Catholic Church weighed in, with McRory in his New Year's address condemning the 'outrageous bigotry of the ascendancy clique', expressing surprise that Britain had not taken steps to prevent it, and pointing to Tyrone where a majority was not only separated from those on the other side but 'still have to feel that in the enforced separation they have no hope of even-handed justice'.[46] It was a carefully worded statement which avoided aligning the church with any strand of northern nationalism while voicing the resentment common to all. Earlier he had spoken of the possibility of anti-partition unity with a national figure agreed upon for president – a call welcomed by the Northern Council for Unity as an endorsement of its ideas.[47]

The nationalist representatives, meeting in the Avenue Bar in Belfast to discuss the situation, welcomed De Valera's placing of partition on the London Agenda and approved McRory's suggestions. All were agreed that partition was the paramount issue, with everything else as Patrick Maxwell asserted 'of secondary importance'. The Mid Tyrone MP, H. K. McAleer, expressed the hope that the Irish delegation would not fail to deliver on the issue while Stewart stated that any settlement made with the south which did not provide for the abolition of partition would be unwelcome to northern nationalists. On the question of abstention he remarked privately in a revealing aside, 'Fathers Magann and Coyle should be interviewed before any move was made on the issue' and that nationalists 'should be slow to take any definite steps' without first being aware of De Valera's attitude to the progress of the negotiations'. 'I do not believe in throwing out the dirty water until we get in clean water,' he concluded.[48]

On 11 March a united convention of nationalists of South

Down, South Armagh and Mourne took place pledging support for De Valera following an earlier decision to begin the establishment of branches in Down and Armagh. On St Patrick's Day McRory referred to the 'sacred places' cut off from their people, while the Northern Council of Unity reiterated that any scheme which left partition intact would be merely a partial solution. On 21 March the newly elected nationalist MPs agreed to stay away from Stormont until the London Talks had concluded. No definite decision was arrived at on abstention. When a majority failed to turn up at the meeting called for 4 April to consider the issue, the Belfast MPs Byrne and Campbell, together with their fellow Hibernian Senator McLaughlin, of Armagh, went ahead and returned to Stormont. The *Derry Journal* rounded on them 'to make it more disgusting it comes at a time when unionist parliamentarians are complaining that the absence of a party at Stormont is reducing the proceedings to a lifeless farce'.[49] Campbell and Byrne were to feel a sense of justification when the London talks finally concluded. 'We would regard it as a betrayal of our interest if he ignored the problem of partition by getting trade and defence agreements only,' Cahir Healy had said in February after a meeting of nationalists with De Valera and McEntee in London. The final outcome in April ended the 'Economic War', as had been expected, in return for a total payment of 10 million (the value of the annuities) and the opening of the Irish and British markets to each other. Most significantly from the Irish point of view, it involved the return of the ports still occupied by Britain under the terms of the treaty. There was no concession on the partition issue though De Valera had drawn from Chamberlain the admission that it was an anachronism.

The *Derry Journal*, which had in March assured its readers that De Valera would never 'barter the national claim for any material advantage', confessed itself 'disappointed' but took heart from De Valera's reassurances in the Dáil. The eight anti-partitionist MPs placed on record their profound disappointment that partition was not included, but congratulated De Valera on 'the completion of another step in the reunification of the country'.[50] Long-term critics of De Valera's strategy, like Senator McHugh of Pettigo, felt fully vindicated. Recalling how he had described De Valera's Ard Fheis statement, 'The time is now ripe for a National movement' as 'vague and unsatisfactory', he confidently proclaimed that the London settlement proved him right and that he was more satisfied now than ever that 'De Valera had no real policy' regarding the north and was merely using the northern minority for his own purposes.[51] The Northern Council of Unity, as a supplement to their congratulations of De Valera for the agreement, proposed that the 'Government of Ireland' should consider the safeguarding of 'old established industries now in jeopardy in the six counties' by allowing them duty free access to the Irish markets. It was an oblique acknowledgement of how the 'economic war' had widened the gulf with the north to the detriment of the border regions.

Throughout the following months the Northern Council for Unity continued its organisational drive through Down and Armagh, helped considerably by the Roman Catholic clergy of the area. Seven priests in all were on the platform at the creation of a branch at Mullaghbawn, County Armagh, including McShane from Omagh, McGettigan from Derry and the Vicar General of St Malachy's in Belfast.[52] Early in April a delegation from the Council, including Fathers McComiskey, McCorry and McShane, were introduced to De Valera by Aodh De Blacam. They proposed that a six county president be appointed; that the Éire government provide them with funds and organisational help; that a permanent liaison office between north and south be established; that the abolition of the oath in Belfast parliament be made a priority in the negotiations; and asked for government help in broadcasting their case. De Blacam, recalling the 1,000 copies of 'Facts and Figures of the Belfast Program' printed under the auspices of Desmond Fitzgerald's department in 1924 which the then government decided not to publish, proposed a book publication on similar lines. To the first suggestion De Valera claimed 'nothing useful could be done' as 'no one group' could decide who was to be president. The question of organisation was, he told them, a matter for themselves. On the abolition of the oath, he ruled out any exclusion of Northern Ireland from benefits of any trade agreement reached and denied that he would make such matters and concessions on PR and fair treatment under Stormont 'part of any agreement with the British'. He expressed the hope that the abolition of the oath would only come with the end of partition. The question of funds was 'primarily one for the organisation to deal with by private subscription'. As for broadcasts they would, he stated, 'have to be carefully balanced and any propagandist tendency would have to be avoided'.[53]

Peadar Murney, the leading organiser, attributed much of the progress in Armagh to Fr Corry, the parish priest of the area.[54] Elsewhere the appeal of the organisation was more limited, though Antrim was described in May as having held 'a few conventions', the Reverend Hughes PP being the directing influence. The deputation to De Valera claimed with considerable hyperbole to represent 'two thirds of nationalists in the six counties outside Belfast'. The council received a bad blow later that year in August when the aging Donnelly, despite the publicity of having been arrested by the RUC at Newry and fined for defying the 13-year-old exclusion order on him, failed to gain election to the southern senate. The magnitude of his failure was startling – he received only one vote. Coming on top of the London agreement it was a reminder of how different priorities were on the other side of the border. Clearly the nationalist movement was not getting its message across. Furthermore, they were hard-put to agree among themselves. The 'working arrangement' envisaged by Fr Maguire of Newtownbutler for the general election and essayed by Healy, had, as we have seen, fallen through. Even though Northern Council members were careful to avoid impugning the other anti-partitionists, it seems likely that their intransigence was blocking united action.

As late as September 1938, Healy could write to Murney asking that their disagreement on attendance should not outweigh their common anti-partitionism. Derry, Fermanagh, Tyrone and Belfast had agreed upon attendance. 'That the people of South Armagh and South Down hold a different view, however, should not prevent our co-operation with them upon a vital principle. (We) would welcome a United Front. It is as if a house was on fire and we would have to ascertain the views of members of the Fire Brigade before asking them to put it out.'[55]

A conference in Dungannon on 11 October between the Council for Unity and nationalist MPs produced an agreement. Less than three weeks later, the Northern Council for Unity held the first meeting in the new campaign to right 'the most cruel wrong since the Treaty of Limerick'. Calls were made on the government in Dublin to take action and analogies were drawn with continental minority problems – the resolution of the

Sudetenland question at Munich had earlier been raised on Unity Council platforms. Mulvey, speaking at this meeting, denied that northern nationalists were 'not unanimous'.

A deputation later went to Dublin to meet De Valera to discuss partition. That same week De Valera sent a message of support to a meeting in Derry. All Nationalist organisations – Northern Council of Unity, IUA, National Association of Old IRA and AOH – were included in the goodwill note which promised support in the drive to end partition. Cahir Healy on the platform contrasted the situation of the Catholic minority in the north with that of the Germans in Czecho-Slovakia. The 'Zero Hour had arrived,' he said, 'for the removal of the unnatural border.' Reverend Peadar McConmy, a curate from the mainly Protestant Waterside, Derry City, recalled the Roman Catholic teaching in the constitution. 'Ireland,' he stated, 'is a distinct and ancient nation.'[56] He appealed to two classes of people to study the document: the republicans and 'the main body of the six county Protestants'. Of the latter he asserted, 'there was a small minority claiming to be simply British garrisons holding that part of Ireland for Great Britain.' 'They had,' he maintained, 'no right in Ireland.' The main body of Protestants were 'not in that category', he conceded, they 'were Irishmen' whose hearts were in the land in which they lived. They were estranged from us by one cause, he concluded, a 'religious bigotry created and kept here for political purposes'.

This attitude towards northern Protestants, conditional in its acceptance of them and self delusive as to their beliefs, was repeated later that month in an *Irish News* editorial entitled, 'The Present State of Ulster'. It dealt with a report of how Hugh O'Neill, the former speaker of the Northern Commons, had said regarding the Munich Pact 'that if it was right for Germans, Poles and Hungarians to leave Czecho-Slovakia and go with their own country, then it was equally right for the Protestant minority in Ireland to be governed by the government it desired'.[57] Sir Hugh should have said 'that it was equally right for those people who refuse to belong to the historic Irish nation to betake themselves to the land of their hearts desire', the *Irish News* editorial maintained. Significantly neither unionists nor nationalists saw fit to view matters from the standpoint of the Czechs nor to see the Munich Agreement as a violation of their country's integrity.

Shortly after the nationalists' visit to Dublin, De Valera gave further encouragement to the campaign. Maxwell, asked to comment on the meeting, said that matters were developing quickly and 'would develop even quicker over the coming winter'.[58] Cahir Healy could write that De Valera desired a series of meetings 'across the north', whilst Canon Maguire of Newtownbutler could promise Healy 'a big contingent from the other side of the border' at the next meeting in that village. The Fianna Fáil general secretary, Erskine Childers, was detained and later released after attending this meeting in the village, which took place despite a government proscription. The ban which 'turned the town into an armed camp' in the view of the *Irish News* was raised at Stormont by Campbell and Byrne and defended by the authorities on the pretext that the gathering was 'provocative'. Maxwell, who still kept alive the semblance of the Irish Union Association in Derry with its room in Butcher Street, had the idea of placing 10,000 adhesive labels with a 'partition must go' motto on envelopes to America. This plan was, he told reporters, approved by De Valera. He (Maxwell) expressed the hope that the series of meetings in the coming twelve months would create a situation 'where a long pull and a strong pull' would end partition. Throughout the following year, anti-partition meetings were held in both the north and Britain at which calls for the removal of Catholic grievances on gerrymandering, discrimination, education and the Special Powers Act were mingled with the line of the Northern Council of Unity, that 'No mere concessions were required but the freedom of Ireland from Rathlin to Berehaven'.

South Armagh became the focus of a special anti-partition drive with the formation of anti-partition clubs in a succession of villages in February. The enthusiasm, however, concealed an underlying despair. In April a meeting of all strands of northern nationalism expressed its 'deep concern' at the apathy and indifference in the twenty-six counties on the vital question of partition and requested the government to set up 'without delay' a radio service on the subject.[59] By May 1939 the campaign had clearly run out of steam.

Privately, in a lengthy statement, nationalist deputies made known their despondency to De Valera.[60] It began by assuring him of their intention to avoid any 'reference that might be construed as offensive' and reaffirmed their admiration for his 'integrity', going on to describe as 'nothing short of a miracle' the ability of the northern minority to retain 'any semblance of national feeling' after seventeen years of government from Stormont and London. It characterised them as 'the loyal minority to whose lot has fallen the duty of holding for the nation that part of its territory that has been most menaced by a powerful nation with the assistance of a local sectarian group'. Many of them had, it stated, 'already sought safety in silence and had been advised by some influential people among them to turn their backs on the rest of Ireland which they declared had betrayed them in pursuit of its own selfish ends or used them simply for party political catch cries'. Another threat to the national spirit, in their view, was 'The English dole system and other social services' which they admitted were 'on a greater scale' than elsewhere in Ireland. These they said had been repeatedly used by unionists and numerous 'bread and butterites calling themselves Labour men' to deflect people from Irish nationalism.[61] The document continued in this despairing tone:

> Undermined and assaulted time and again, the spirit of the people has often flagged and they almost ceased to regard themselves as belonging to Ireland. Patriotic bodies like the Gaelic League have heroically strived to preserve some vestige of Irish tradition but they have often been as voices crying in the wilderness and, even when they have made progress in some small way, it is to be feared that the prospect of qualifying for jobs in the twenty-six counties has been more an incentive among the youth coming under their influence than the hope of serving the cause of Irish nationalism where it most needs to be served.[62]

A further danger cited by the deputies was the 'great number of families, especially in urban areas, connected – some of them for generations – with the British armed forces'.[63] Even though these people were 'not invariably hostile' most of them regarded England 'in anything but an unfriendly light'. 'Notwithstanding all this the minority have been inspired from time to time to great heights of enthusiasm. They felt that they saw in the early victories of Fianna Fáil and in the conclusion of the Economic War more than a gleam of hope for the early abolition of partition. They followed with deeper interest than admiration, the sensational doings of Hitler and Mussolini on the continent, believing that with the Treaty of Versailles in the melting pot, 'Ireland would come fully into her own and that, before the present stage, partition would be a thing of the past'. The deputies felt it was a considerable achievement to have kept the 'National Spirit' alive as long as they did and rejected the criticism often made in the south of Ireland, that they should have united 'in a great anti-partition campaign that would electrify all the rest of Ireland and the Irish throughout the world'. They doubted that any other people 'so absolutely abandoned to their slender resources' would have succeeded so well.[64]

With the end of the Economic War and into 1939, the hopes of the nationalists were high, they said, but 'now day by day there is a steady decline and a reversion to the despondency that prevailed from the days of the bogus boundary commission till 1932.' The increased activity of both the army and the B Specials was adding to the demoralisation. The actions of the IRA against this backdrop of despondency and seeming abandonment sent a 'momentary thrill of joy' through the minority who 'raised them to the level of the Fenian patriots' and sought 'parallels for their intrepidity and outspokenness ... in Sullivan's Speeches from the Dock. 'It is a momentary thrill,' the document went on, 'but it gets us nowhere'.[65]

They, therefore proposed that the Irish government take the initiative in broadcasting Ireland's case to the world, pointing out that promises had been made 'probably in perfectly good faith' which were not kept, either through inability or inactivity. It was felt that offers made to northern unionists only consolidated their intransigence and, therefore, the London government should be the target of any such campaign. A Board of Propaganda should be set up to spread the message worldwide. An indication of the imminent danger to the minority was the decline of their numbers in Tyrone and Fermanagh. At the 21 October meeting with him they had cited the drop as 2,269 in Fermanagh and 3,183 in Tyrone. Furthermore, as a counterweight both to the increasing threat of conscription in the war which now seemed inevitable and to the IRA campaign then gathering momentum, they proposed that the southern government assert its legitimacy by opening the ranks of the army to northern Catholic volunteers. Finally, they urged De Valera to make a statement on partition in response to an agreed statement of their own submitted in advance, 'such a reply we respectfully suggest in view of the great depression that has set in, should be completely emphatic and spectacular', the document concluded.

CHAPTER 10

The Second World War

While De Valera did protest successfully on the conscription issue the following May, as we shall see shortly, nonetheless, by late November, over two months into the Second World War, the balance sheet of nationalist expectations looked decidedly unpromising. Murney proposed to Joe Connolly that a 'representative delegation' go to Dublin 'to clarify matters'. Among the headings which he wished to discuss were the failure to make a statement on whether the government adoption of neutrality was recognised by the belligerents as one which embraced all of Ireland, the 'political silence' since the war began 'which had deprived' the nationalists 'of all direction', and the refusals to open the ranks of the Irish army to northern Catholics, 'a denial of their Irish citizenship which caused pain and offence', Murney stated, contrasting it with the open door policy of the British Army towards Irishmen. Finally, there had been a complete failure by the south to give preference to six-county products, more than two years after nationalists had issued a call on the matter.[1]

But it was the exclusion from the Irish army which cut deepest, emphasising as it did the reality behind the rhetoric of the 1937 constitution. Whatever Fianna Fáil politicians might assert from platforms, whatever hope six county Catholics might have placed in it, still on the rebound from betrayal by the opposing group of southern politicians in 1925, here at last was the moment of epiphany. The northern nationalists were nobody's children. De Valera had already told a deputation of theirs in April that the retention of the twenty-six counties was too valuable to be risked in any attempt of reunification.[2] But his efforts on the conscription issue the following month went some way towards compensating for it. Now, for a second time since its foundation, the southern state had entangled northern nationalists in an anti-partitionist venture which it could not bring to fulfilment.

There was only one direction in which some were likely to turn and De Valera, recognising this, had warned against it at the April meeting.

Patrick Maxwell, the MP for Foyle, wrote to Cahir Healy early in June 1940 giving voice to this deep sense of abandonment which the closure of the army in the wartime emergency had engendered, commenting that northern Catholics were 'as usual left to their own resources'. 'In such a situation of course any movement by the nationalists here is bound to be driven underground and will possibly and very probably lead to a pro-German feeling here in the event of an allied invasion.' 'This,' he was careful to qualify, 'would be the completely wrong attitude from a national point of view.' In his estimation everything boiled down to whether the Dublin government had a twenty-six or thirty-two county viewpoint.[3] Later in the month he returned to the theme, telling Healy 'it was now more obvious than ever' that Northern Catholics were 'left to their own devices'. And as it was time 'something was done by ourselves', he would be glad to know what decision the conference arrived at.

The conference in question was the latest in a series held in Armagh city under Cardinal McRory's auspices with a view to achieving inter-nationalist unity, previous attempts having foundered on such issues as the meeting's representiveness and Dublin's fear of IRA infiltration. This latest gathering had been held in secret but early in June *Irish News* journalists 'got wind of it', Senator McLaughlin told Healy. Peter Murney, for reasons McLaughlin did not understand, had some opposition to a 'suggested meeting'.[4] Both the 'future action' of which Maxwell wrote and the suggested meeting referred to by McLaughlin meet with no elucidation in a review of the national press of the period. But a confidential Garda correspondence helps fill in the blanks on what exactly was happening behind the scenes in that fateful summer of 1940 which saw the Nazi war machine triumphant over France and poised to invade Britain.

The report marked 'Top secret' and dated August 1940, describes how a meeting of the Northern Council was held that month in Dublin to which representative of the Axis countries were invited. All except the German minister wrote expressing inability to attend. The German minister, Edouard Hempel, told Peadar Murney at the meeting that the Third Reich had lost confidence in the IRA. 'It was decided,' the account went on, 'to place the Catholic minority in the north under the protection of the Axis powers.' Two further meetings of the body were held in Dundalk later that month. Among those northerners in attendance were John Southwell from Newry, John Joe Murray of Lurgan and Banbridge based Padraig McGillis. Significantly all meetings were chaired by Senator Thomas McLaughlin of Armagh City.[5]

As McLaughlin, a prominent Armagh businessman, AOH member, Knight of Columbanus and probably the nationalist closest to McRory, was not previously a member of the Northern Council of Unity, having always stood apart from them politically, his presence as chairman poses a question (so far unanswered) as to the Cardinal's own involvement. However, in the light of what we now know subsequently transpired, a letter written on 19 June (with German troops in Paris and France only days from capitulation) takes on a deeper and more sinister complexion. From McLaughlin's fellow AOH member, the East Tyrone MP, Joe Stewart, to Cahir Healy, it refers to a meeting of the hierarchy the following week, stating that, 'his Eminence should know the contents of the document' and that McLaughlin 'could do the needful'.[6]

In November, when Donnelly set about forming a new organisation 'more vital than the Council', John Joe Murray approached both the German and the Italian legations and was promised support in the form of anti-partitionist propaganda on Axis-controlled radio stations. Karl Petersen of the German Embassy attended the meeting. When these happenings[7] are taken into consideration, it becomes easier to understand the evidence from Hempel's diary of references to 'growing sympathy for Germans among the Irish clergy in the Autumn of 1940 and of McRory's susceptibility in June of a possible German action for the return of Northern Ireland'.[8]

McRory continued to be a thorn in the side of the Allies, complaining in September 1942, to David Gray's chagrin, 'of British and US troops overrunning the country against the will of the Irish nation. In February 1944, when he stated that Éire treated Great Britain well by not having joined the Axis forces, 'bearing in mind how Ireland had been treated in the past', Spender wrote in his diary that reconciliation between Catholics and Protestants in Northern Ireland was impossible 'whilst the leading men of the former expresses views of this character'.[9]

The 1940 departure in northern nationalist politics had a

sequel in July of the following year with the arrest of Cahir Healy MP and his internment as a 'security risk' in Brixton Prison. When Senator McLaughlin approached the Department of External Affairs in Dublin in August, he was told that Dulanty had 'in a personal and unofficial way' spoken to the Home Secretary, Herbert Morrison, and Sir Alexander Maxwell, permanent Head of the Home Office. 'Release,' they were told, 'was somewhat remote in view of the extreme imprudence of Healy's letter to Father Maguire of Newtownbutler.' When McLaughlin then suggested going to see Churchill, the Department advised against it on the grounds that the British might leak the contents of the offending letter with 'very serious consequences for the other nationalist MPs in the six county area'.[10] Furthermore, 'liberally-minded Englishmen' who sympathised with his plight would be alienated. A secret memorandum confirmed the contents of Healy's letter, intercepted in the mail by the wartime censor: 'In the event of a negotiated peace the Germans should be left in no doubt as to the wishes of himself and his politician friends as to the help they could give to Germany,' it stated. Brookesborough's claim in Stormont that Healy had written to the German minister in Dublin is at least plausible in the light of this evidence.[11]

As earlier reports from Dulanty, immediately after Healy's arrest, confirmed, the British government was unaware of the 'repercussions in the form of public protest, indignation meetings and so on' which it had given rise to among northern nationalists, and were 'not disposed to help the person any longer than what they regard as the security interest demands'. While this behaviour by northern nationalists was obviously in large measure an expression of the timeworn motto of Irish nationalism – 'England's difficulty, Ireland's opportunity' – it must also be seen in the context of the admiration displayed towards Fascist ideas in Catholic Ireland at that time. Even Hitler's Germany – the dictatorship least favoured in the Irish papers, on account of its later difficulties with the Roman Catholic Church – was described as follows in an *Irish News* editorial of 16 January 1939, entitled 'Nazis Anniversary'. It assessed their six years in power: 'No matter what one may fault about the Nazis ... their crowded hour of glorious life has been packed with thrills for Europe ... they have been denounced as gangsters, yet they have succeeded in restoring Germany's absolute sovereignty.

Their determination to persecute religion cannot be justified, yet they remain the greatest political bulwark against communism.'[12]

The Catholic Social Conference the previous November in St Mary's Hall had been told, in a lecture 'Swastika versus Cross' by Reverend Dr Ryan, that 'while there might be some point in the Nazi reaction against the abstraction of Liberalism which overlooked as it did the definite natural tendencies arising out of soil, tradition and loyalty to one's own people, they went too far in 'erecting these things into something to be worshipped'.[13] As a critique of Nazism it hardly placed him in the same category as those of his martyred brothers in Christ who died in German concentration camps.

The republican movement made a dramatic re-emergence in January 1939 with a series of mysterious explosions in England, one of which killed a porter in Manchester. It was the beginning of the S Plan, master-minded by Sean Russell, with a view to forcing the issue of British withdrawal. A separate bombing offensive had developed in the north from 1937 onwards, beginning with the 'hardy annuals', as the Veteran Republican Joe Cahill recalls, of the customs posts, the Armistice Day celebrations and the marching season. In July it widened to include commercial premises and power installations. From the wrecking of the Donegal Street office on Armistice Day 1937, to the following year, a total of 13 bombings and two accidental explosions had taken place.

As a campaign it lacked a coherent strategy. 'No great purpose was put into organising it,' Cahill recalls. It was simply a case of 'where you can strike, strike, when you can hit, hit'.[14] In late November a premature explosion at Castlefin, Co Tyrone, killed two IRA men and seriously wounded a third. Opposition was not slow in coming from the predictable quarters. The Ulster Protestant League (formed in 1931 ostensibly for the protection of Protestant employment during the recession), already reconstituted under the leadership of men like former B-Special Alexander Robinson, 'The Buck Alex', in the Docks area, began a sporadic arson and bombing against Catholic churches and AOH halls.[15] State repression also increased. Throughout 1938 extensive police raids took place on Catholic areas across the north, Northern Council of Unity members being among those visited.

Peadar Murney's house near Newry was raided after the Castlefin explosion. Finally, at the outbreak of the Second World War, the northern government introduced internment. In a movement in which the Falls Company, its area of greatest strength, had one rifle for every twelve men and one small arm for every six, this might have proved fatal. But an unexpected lifeline had been thrown by the British government itself – conscription.

Even before the outbreak of war, the northern Cabinet had discussed its introduction and proposals for its extension in the event of an all-out conflict. In May 1939, when its introduction was first mooted, an explosion of outrage took place among northern nationalists. Cardinal McRory proclaimed a 'moral right to resistance', a view endorsed in a statement issued by the five northern bishops. De Valera, under pressure from northern nationalist representatives adamant that Catholics would never agree to serve in the northern forces, sent J. W. Dulanty, his representative, to London to meet Chamberlain. The meeting was productive and Chamberlain assured him it would not be introduced but, to avoid the impression of having yielded to De Valera, delayed the announcement until after the Cabinet meeting. Chamberlain, Dulanty recorded, was 'relieved not to seem happy at the decision'.[16]

When the blow fell again almost two years later to the day, the reaction evoked a certain sense of deja-vu, but once more the vehemence of nationalist opposition was unmistakable. The bishops reiterated strongly their 1939 view and in McRory's words, the proposal amounted to 'a people already subjected to the gravest imposition in being cut off from one of the oldest nations in Europe, now being deprived of the fundamental rights as citizens in their own land'. He warned of 'disastrous' consequences if the decision was implemented; it would, he said, be likely to 'arouse them to indignation and resistance'.

Across the north protest meetings were held, uniting all sections of nationalist opinion from Labour traditions to the republican one. Jack Beattie recalled the Home Rule crisis of 1912 when, as a 'minder' for the visiting Winston Churchill (then a supporter of Irish self-government) 'he and others' had to save him from loyalist attack. Alex Donnelly reminded his constituents that it was only twenty years since the Black and Tans operated in Ireland. Mulvey stated bluntly, 'we will not have it' and, recalling the 1939 resolution of Ulster nationalists, called for an all-Ireland movement to defeat the proposal.[17]

Throughout the week at mass rallies in Belfast, Armagh, Newry, Omagh, Dungannon and Enniskillen, the 1918 pledge was revitalised. In a dramatic show of opposition, all parishes in the north were to be encouraged to sign, and behind the scenes the Dublin government was making its views known to Whitehall. Matters had changed since the appeasement approach of Chamberlain. Churchill, Dulanty reported, 'went off at the deep end' at the 22 May meeting, accusing the Irish of having thrown away an historic opportunity for reunification. He was prepared, he told the Irish High Commission, to face whatever problems might arise in a conflict when 'Britain was fighting for her life'. Though he admitted to having had sympathy for Ireland when he signed the treaty, this, however, changed when De Valera repudiated the agreement and 'made scrap iron of it'.[18] On the 26th, when Dulanty met him again, Churchill subjected him to a 'terrifying harangue'. Walking around the room he recalled the First World War sacrifice of Redmond and Kettle and told Dulanty, who accused him of treating the north 'as if it were Yorkshire', that the Ulster people 'are a valiant people'. To Dulanty he sounded 'like the old Tory voice of forty years ago'. On a visit to Bevan the following day, Dulanty was given a cool reception and left feeling they 'were by no means out of the woods'.[19]

Within hours, however, as pressure on Britain to moderate its decision, notably from the United States and Canada, increased, the Cabinet relented. Churchill, in his statement to the House of Commons, admitted that the imposition of conscription would be 'more bother than it was worth'. The reaction of northern nationalists was one of jubilation. A very satisfactory result, said A. E. Donnelly. T. J. Campbell was more verbose:

'Conscription has been stalled by the rock of a determined pledge which bound people to resist it at all costs. Gratitude is due to the Cardinal Primate and hierarchy for their weighty warnings and to our countrymen in Éire for their act of goodwill.'[20]

One group who claimed the withdrawal of conscription as its achievement was the IRA. Despite the attrition of internment – 320 men locked away by December 1942, most of them in an overcrowded prison hulk, the *Al Riydah* moored in Strangford

Lough – the fear of conscription kept the movement, if not vibrant, then at least numerically strong. When GHQ sent a representative north in late 1941 to explain the demoralising Stephen Hayes affair, there were over 1,000 Volunteers in the Belfast Rotunda Hall to hear him speak. (Hayes, the IRA's Chief of Staff, had taken refuge in a garda station after being held by the organisation as a suspected informer.) The Hayes affair resulted in a northern take-over of the movement, such as remained of it in the south under the weight of De Valera's repression.[21]

In the north, with the release of Hugh McAteer in November 1941, the army embarked upon a more vigorous course. Previously activity had been confined to sporadic sniping at police patrols, frustration of the blackout in Catholic areas and isolated incendiarism. The anti-British, but less than pro-German, feeling had resulted in information on Belfast defences being supplied to the German spy Herman Goertz[22] which may have been used by the Luftwaffe to pin-point targets in the April 1941 raids on the city.

As was often the case with IRA activity, it was to be the operation which went wrong that provided the movement with its greatest uplift. Such a situation presented itself in April 1942, with the death of a Roman Catholic RUC man, Constable Murphy, in a shoot-out following an abortive ambush designed to divert police attention from the Easter commemoration. The six men arrested after the shoot-out were tried for capital murder and on 30 July sentenced to death at Belfast Crown Court. Nationalist opinion was once again electrified at the thought of the largest mass execution at Britain's hands since the 'Black and Tan War'. The hanging, scheduled for 18 August, was postponed because of the men's appeal but with its failure on 22 August all efforts in nationalist Ireland were directed towards saving the mens' lives. Petitions for reprieve were organised in all church areas, with Eamon Donnelly in overall charge of the operation. On the ground, the clergy arranged the collection of signatures. In Armagh the Administrator, Dr Quinn, organised house to house signing; in Newry, the Reverend McComisky collected 8,000 signatures; in Omagh, where Reverend McShane presided, 3,000 signatures were obtained. As was the case with the conscription crisis, representations were being made behind the scenes by Dublin. Realising the effect of American pressure in 1941, De Valera's first approach was made through David

Gray, the American Ambassador, in a meeting arranged for 19 August by Joe Walsh of the Department of External Affairs. De Valera stressed that the 'men did not conspire to murder' and rejected Gray's contention that 'analogous circumstances' existed in the south where the Dublin government had, since the outbreak of war, allowed two men to die on hunger strike, executed four and shot dead another in military custody. De Valera claimed that these executions took place 'with great reluctance' and only 'after superhuman patience' had been shown. He had, he claimed, the 'almost unanimous support of public opinion. He also denied that the Irish government was unfriendly towards the US, claiming that its neutrality was benevolent towards America.[23]

By 28 August, with the executions scheduled for 2 September, J. W. Dulanty was in London patiently explaining the Dublin government case to Herbert Morrison, the Home Secretary, in a meeting arranged by a high level member of the British Cabinet, sympathetic to Ireland. Dulanty again denied any similarity with the draconian policy of the southern State, which was to claim another execution victim before the year was out. He got Morrison to acknowledge that he, too, was 'as extremist as the next fellow' in his 19s and 20s, and when he riposted that he 'did not go around shooting people' told him that 'Battersea was not Belfast', a point which Morrison accepted.[24]

As the fatal shots were fired by two people, Morrison felt it would be 'dreadful' to hang somebody else besides Williams merely on suspicion. Dulanty replied that 'it would be worse to hang all six'. The meeting concluded with Morrison promising nothing beyond that he would 'see what he could do'. By 1 September all but Williams were reprieved. When Dulanty met the Labour leader and Deputy Prime Minister Clement Attlee on that date to secure a reprieve for Williams, Attlee expressed annoyance at what he saw as the Irish government moving its ground. It had, he felt, originally taken the line that 'six to one would be an outrage and told him with some asperity that they were not going to re-try the case'. 'What about the poor policemen so cruelly shot?' he asked Dulanty.[25]

Questioned by Dulanty as to what government would 'prohibit meetings, send armed police into the homes of respectable citizens, damage their furniture and insult their nationality', Attlee replied that there were 'two sides to the question'.[26]

Despite hopes held out by Maffey, the British High Commissioner, of a last minute reprieve, Williams went to the gallows on 2 September, the only republican ever executed by the northern State.

In the emotive impact of the execution a by-election was called for the Falls Constituency, following the death of the sitting MP, Richard Byrne. His parliamentary colleague, T. J. Campbell, miscalculated badly by announcing that the seat would be contested in the nationalist interest against the Northern Council for Unity whose candidate, Eamonn Donnelly, was, of course, pledged to abstention. The divide between the Council and most of mainstream nationalism had become blurred during the war and became even more so in the new mood of the Williams affair. Senator Thomas McLaughlin of Armagh, Donnelly's erstwhile opponent, served as secretary of the reprieve committee. Likewise it was to be another AOH representative, Joe Stewart, who moved the writ for the by-election. He also backed Donnelly. With Donnelly's role as head of the Green Cross Organisation, the votes of prisoners' and internees' families were his for the taking notwithstanding the opposition of republican purists. Campbell's candidate, McGouran, finished a poor second. The still worse performance of the Labour candidate was deceptive.

The following February another by-election occurred, this time for the West Belfast seat at Westminster held by the unionists since 1922. The nearest they came to losing it was in October 1923 when Harry Midgley, a Protestant trade unionist and member of the Belfast Labour party, came within 2,050 votes of the sitting MP. The possibility existed that a candidate of left-wing views, with cross community support, might take the seat. Such a candidate emerged in the form of Jack Beattie, Stormont MP for Pottinger, who went forward for the Labour ticket. Beattie did not fit easily into any northern Irish stereotype. He served in the British army during the Boer War, rising from a boy batman to an officership in the Hussars. He had worked as a blacksmith and later married the daughter of a wealthy builder. A Protestant in religion, he championed the cause of Catholic voluntary schools and went with the flow of pro-Franco feeling in the Catholic ghettos,[27] thereby avoiding the fate of Harry Midgley. Anti-partitionist in politics, he sought placement for his sons in the RUC. His activity in support of the Outdoor Relief Strikers was still remembered with gratitude on the

Shankill. Faced with such a figure and with an independent unionist in the lists to complicate matters, the mainstream party knew it would have a fight on its hands. Its only hope of victory lay in a split opposition vote. A meeting of the Donnelly group had already been held in St Mary's Hall, with a view to contesting the seat.

Emotion had subsided since November and funds were scarce when Ted Lynch, a nationalist senator, and owner of the Monico Bar, emerged with sufficient money for a campaign. The Andersonstown accountant Hugh Corvin, of the Northern Council, was nominated to contest the seat. But the support of Lynch, an anti-abstentionist, seemed incongruous to at least one person on the platform, Sean McKeown. After making discreet enquiries he discovered that Lord Glentoran's agent, Billy Douglas, the Unionist Party Secretary, had approached a Glengormley republican, Pat Bradley, in an attempt to force a contest. McKeown shortly afterwards in the Monico Bar overheard a call from Douglas to Lynch. Suspecting collusion he withdrew from Corvin's campaign.[28] Beattie was supported by former nationalists Councillor Frank Hanna and James Collins who stressed the compatibility of his ideas with Papal Enclyclicals. Great emphasis was laid on the social benefits that would accrue from a pro-Beattie vote particularly in the light of the Beveridge Report (named after the economist who had chaired an inter-departmental House of Commons committee in 1941/42 which proposed a community scheme of social insurance without income limit). The continuity of such benefits with Joe Devlin's achievements was also stressed. From the Corvin camp, Donnelly spoke of a 'thirty two county parliament being set up after the next general election' in accordance with the Atlantic Charter. On the issue of social services he did not want to see the Beveridge Plan applied to Ireland – as an article in the *Irish Weekly* had showed it would allow 'a married man to live with a lady who was not his wife'.[29] The republicans decisively rejected any dealing with Corvin, Hugh McAteer in a statement describing him as a 'self-styled republican' who would never receive any support from them'.[30] Lacking the backing of this crucial subculture, and with nothing but abstentionism to distinguish his appeal from that of the moribund nationalist organisation in the city his chances of success were slim. When the votes were counted he lost his deposit with a lowly 1,250 votes to 7,551 for the Independent Unionist and 14,426 for Cunningham, the unionist party candidate. Beattie with 19,936 emerged victorious.

The Williams case had given a temporary lease of life to republican militancy in the north. Material was brought in from the south for a retaliatory offensive as the outcome of his appeal became clear. Despite the finding by police of a large arms dump stockpiled at Hannahstown and the shooting dead of a Volunteer guarding it in late August, the offensive went ahead maintaining its intensity throughout September and October, then gradually petering out towards the close of the year. It was perhaps indicative both of the inflamed situation after the execution and of the role taken in that situation by the Catholic Church, that both Cardinal McRory and the Bishop of Down and Conor, Dr Mageean, refused to comment on the double murder of an RUC man and a B Special at Clady later that same week.[31] But neither this splurge of activity, the dramatic prison escapes from Crumlin Road and Derry jails following on it, nor the hierarchical ambivalence towards it could conceal the downward trajectory of the organisation. Even when the conscription threat had kept the numbers high there had been problems. One Falls Road volunteer recalled the efficiency of police Intelligence on the movement. 'All information they got, came from the Catholic population,'[32] he told the author. In an attempt to stem this flow several executions were carried out. It was the difficulty which had confronted Seamus Woods as IRA OC for that divisional area in 1922 (see pp 65-67) – a nationalist population prepared to support republicans only on its own terms and liable to revert to a different mode of behaviour if circumstances changed.

Despite the sense of oneness engendered by such events as the conscription crisis, unity of northern nationalists remained elusive. In July 1941 a Dublin newspaper could characterise them as 'tied to a policy drift', four of the six MPs abstaining from Stormont, all four senators attending, and factionalism so pronounced that no agreement could not be reached on the holding of a convention following the death of the mid Tyrone MP Hugh McAleer.[33]

Increasingly the various strands of mainstream nationalism looked towards the changing configuration of world politics as a way of resolving their situation. Though Corvin in the Falls by election had dismissed the Atlantic character as 'merely a restatement of what President Wilson had said in 1918', others saw it differently.

In November 1944, shortly before his death, Donnelly told Healy of 'contacts which should be revived abroad' making particular reference to the Soviet Union as a likely 'big influence in the readjustment of the new world'.[34] Only in the self referential moral universe of northern minority politics could someone as relatively progressive as Donnelly (he was the Fianna Fáil TD least sympathetic to Franco and his Irish supporters) entertain the notion that a country which lost 26 million lives defeating Nazism would look favourably on overtures from a people whose representatives had attempted collaboration with it. In a similar vein of unreality the *Irish News* enthused that the 'tens of thousands who volunteered should in the eyes of the prejudiced constitute a positive contribution'.[35] Healy alone seemed to grasp the hard facts of Weltpolitik. 'The attitude of neutrality,' he stated in March 1944, which 'the people rightly insist on maintaining', had hurt Churchill and his followers. Therefore if the proposed conference came about 'they would do their worst and their best to exclude Ireland on the grounds that it did not help the allies'.[36]

Notwithstanding his rhetoric of a 'nation ready to march' when the war ended, Healy also warned against the foolishness of forgetting that affairs were not 'helpful' either north or south of the border and they would not be any nearer the goal of a united Ireland.[37] A *contretemps* earlier in the year involving Sean McEntee had highlighted the difficulties they faced with the South. McEntee, commenting on a paper delivered by Sean Ruane of Coras na Poblachta in the Mansion House, opposed the Donnelly idea of giving seats in Dáil Éireann to northern anti-partitionists, stating that he knew of 'no plan' that 'would of certainty end partition'. Healy, in the pro Fianna Fáil *Irish Press* a week later, recalled 1925 when 'the first party washed its hands' of northern nationalists and suggested 'the other party' was now doing the same, repudiating as a 'red herring' the suggestion that division between northern nationalists were to blame.[38]

The Belfast-born Catholic McEntee had presented problems for his fellow northerners before. De Valera was seen in a vastly different light. The evil memories of 1939 and 'betrayal' had been replaced by better ones of solidarity with the minority during the conscription crisis and other events. Above all his neutrality policy, culminating triumphantly with his famous reply to Churchill, placed him head and shoulders above all other southern politicians in the eyes of many northern Catholics, including those of the Hibernian tradition. The response of one such person, T. J. Campbell MP for Belfast Central (who attended throughout the war and was soon to accept a northern judgeship), said it all: 'Mr De Valera had given Churchill his tit for tat, the Englishman had met his match.'[39]

It was clear therefore that when the anti-partition drive resumed in the post-war world it would be characterised as it was in the 30s by dependence on De Valera and illusions about the helpfulness of foreign governments. Its failure then previsioned the debacle which was to overtake it in the 1950s. There had been a disastrous inability to get its message across in Britain, an inability of northerners and southerners to formulate a common approach, and there had been fissiparous tendencies within northern nationalism, used by Dublin as in the 20s to excuse its own inaction, but in themselves largely a result of that same failure to act. Most ominously there was a massive grassroots apathy, strong enough to kill an organisation like the IUA, and a growing contentment with the British Welfare State tending to undermine opposition to the union, as northern nationalist MPs had privately admitted in 1939. However in the new world ushered in by the Allied victory, nobody, least of all northern Catholics, expected the past to repeat itself.

PART 4

1945-1956

'You people in the twenty-six counties were more interested in the price of beef and eggs.'

'Whilst we lost Irishmen have been kicked around the streets of Belfast and Derry and burned from our homes, you people in the twenty-six counties were more interested in the price of beef and eggs.'
Eddie McAteer, Galway, June 1948

CHAPTER 11

The Foundation of the Anti-Partition League

In the summer following the defeat of Germany, when elections to both the Stormont and Westminster parliaments took place across the six counties, nationalists faced into each of them in a buoyant mood. Not only did they draw comfort from the San Francisco conference and the outline UN charter which followed, with its emphasis on national and individual rights, but developments nearer home also seemed to hold promise.[1] Within the British Labour Party, which was swept into office under Clement Attlee that July, the existence of a coterie of MPs deemed sympathetic to the minority's position, which was later to coalesce as the Friends of Ireland group,[2] led many to the conclusion expressed by a prominent nationalist that a British government more favourable to Ireland had not existed within living memory.[3] From the other side of the border high ranking people had hinted at a new initiative. Opening the campaign at Rosemount for his Foyle seat at Stormont, Patrick Maxwell MP spoke of 'the anti-partition council' to be established after the election in co-operation with fellow nationalists from the south.[4] In a similar vein, while electioneering for a fellow nationalist in Falls, the mid Derry contender Eddie McAteer spoke of the necessity of having representation on this proposed all-Ireland body.

The idea of an all-Ireland Anti-Partition Council may have had its origin in the Donnelly wing of Fianna Fáil. Certainly nothing said by the spokesman of that or any other southern party between the elections and the foundation of the League in November tended to depreciate the idea. Michael Donnelan of the Farmers' party had suggested in the Dáil a movement of north and south to abolish the border, failing which an appeal to the World Peace Conference should be adopted.[5] At the Fianna Fáil Ard Fheis a week before the inaugural meeting of the League, a motion to a similar effect was passed.[6] The nationalists therefore, saw their organisation as the willing tool of a wider strategy to be left to De Valera's discretion. The remark made by Malachy Conlon, newly elected MP for South Armagh, to the *Irish News* after his election encapsulated the feeling. 'Not for over twenty years had there been such unanimity among nationalists in the six counties'. He felt confident 'it would strengthen the hand of Mr De Valera in whatever action the national leader would deem advisable'.[7]

This mindset may go some way towards explaining their contrasting attitudes towards internees and political prisoners in the two jurisdictions. While they campaigned vigorously on their behalf in the north, meeting Warnock on a deputation before the election, sitting on the Green Cross Committee and championing them from the hustings in Belfast and elsewhere, they indignantly rejected any attempt by unionist spokesman to equate the behaviour of the two states despite De Valera's extension of internment at a time when the northern government was phasing it out. Only in May 1946 in the face of revelations of atrocious prison conditions endured by republicans under De Valera's rule, dramatised most graphically by the death that month of IRA Chief Sean McCaughey on hunger and thirst strike, did northern Catholic politicians feel the need to go with the flow of public outrage. Some including Healy (who privately supported De Valera's policy on the matter) and McAteer (who did not) attended an indignation meeting at Hamill Street, Belfast at which the southern government was denounced. Harry Diamond, the newly elected Republican Labour MP for Falls, later laid a wreath on McCaughey's grave. When feeling subsided on the issue, however, even those nationalists sympathetic to the republican position hedged their bets. When the IRA man Harry White was sentenced to death by a military tribunal in Dublin later that year, Eddie McAteer who supported White's case refused to allow discussion of the issue at the Derry branch of the organisation.[8]

Of the six outgoing nationalist MPs all but one were returned unopposed – the aforementioned Maxwell who saw off an unofficial Labour challenger. Three newcomers, James McSparran, Mourne, Peter Murney, South Down, and Malachy Conlon, South Armagh, made up the complement of ten combined with the anti-partitionist left wing seats of Harry Diamond in Falls and Jack Beattie in Pottinger. It constituted the largest anti-partition block ever elected to the Belfast parliament. The claim by Malachy Conlon after his election that such unity had not existed among the nationalist people for over twenty years seemed at first glance incontrovertible, yet a closer look revealed a more complicated picture, one where the labour and conservative nationalist traditions sat in uneasy alliance. The only nationalist loss was in Falls where labourite Harry Diamond saw off an attempt by their candidate, McGlade, to retain the seat won by the late Eamon Donnelly. In what was to be the beginning of the end for nationalist representation in the city. Conlon's own constituency of South Armagh provided an even better illustration of the conflict between the traditions. Paddy Agnew, the outgoing Labour MP, had taken the seat unopposed in 1938 by ignoring the nationalist boycott. In the June 1945 election he found himself the butt of what a contemporary described as 'one of the most unscrupulous campaigns known to Irish political historians' in which the devoutly Roman Catholic Agnew was vilified as a 'communistic atheistic Jew' and, despite being the father of seven children and adopting two others, was accused of being a proponent of birth control.[9]

The decision to end abstention – a decision enthusiastically supported even by those close to the republican tradition like Diamond and McAteer (though opposed somewhat paradoxically by the Hibernian Joe Stewart) cannot be seen in isolation from the perceived threat to Catholic education. Episcopal pastorals the previous February had issued dire warnings on this score and the defence of the 'pearl of great price', as T. J. Campbell MP termed it, figured prominently in the election manifestos of nationalist candidates.

The invitation to 'all nationally minded groups and representatives' to meet in St Patrick's Hall, Dungannon, issued by McAteer and Conlon, followed naturally in this climate. The meeting on Sunday 14 November 1945 was attended by 480 delegates including all nationalist representatives and several priests. The Bishops of Derry and Dromore sent messages of support. In the statement of aims, published both before and after the meeting, the contours of anti-partitionist policy – and its attendant deficiencies – could be clearly seen.[10] (The absence of Diamond – who originated the Anti-Partition League title – from the meeting did not reflect any snub by the League. He later spoke from their platforms.) Aside from the usual objectives it stressed, 'equal rights to all people in the matter of education and the promotion of a spirit of co-operation among all creeds and classes'. Decoded, this meant support for Roman Catholic segregated education and a concept of the State and of class derived from papal encyclicals.

The report of the APL's formation also referred to the 're-unification of our country in accordance with the principle of determination as encouraged by leaders of the UN and the re-establishment of friendly relations between this country and Great Britain in order that the Irish nation may play its rightful part in the creation of world peace ...' As an *Irish News* editorial of 5 August 1946 remarked, 'We have settled all trouble with the English except partition and when that trouble is settled I think no doubt there will be nobody more friendly with Great Britain than this country.'[11]

De Valera's attitude to the League may be taken as one of welcome. On 12 December he stated that the time was 'overdue' for a 'big drive to end partition'. At the inaugural meeting of the League of Fermanagh, at which Healy launched his pamphlet *The Mutilation of a Nation,* Healy stated, 'De Valera had promised us help and had received the news about the founding of the Anti-Partition League as one of the best things he had ever heard.'[12] But in accordance with the belief as to where the ultimate responsibility for partition lay, and their new found faith in the British Labour party, it was to England that focus shifted in June 1946 after six months of organisation in the north. Within a year the euphoria had turned sour, and by March 1947 the Fianna Fáil General Secretary Tommy Mullins was sounding a warning that Labour was trying the patience of the Irish people.[13] By October Lennon, at rallies in Glasgow and Merseyside, was recalling the refusal of Ede, the Home Secretary, to meet them in Belfast the previous month, while McAteer was referring to a small body in the Labour government stultifying our efforts. McSparran in the spring of 1947 went further describing Labour policy as 'Ultra-Tory'.[14] Speaking at a meeting in Belfast in December over two years after the League's foundation, and eighteen months after entry into England, he could only offer by way of achievement an assertion that but for their efforts the unionist government would have been worse![15]

Clearly a change of strategy was called for, but there was a problem. The Irish in Britain might be, in Malachy Conlon's words, 'the army that we in the north of Ireland need', yet, as Senator Lennon put it, whatever 'government rules in England will always remain Imperial'. McSparran, referring to the Labour government, would not say its supporters were against them but 'the leaders or a majority of the leaders were'. Faced with such impotence they turned to the only agency powerful enough to press their case – the Dublin government. At the opening of a branch at St Malachy's in Belfast, McSparran heralded the change, remarking that 'they could not see why the issue was not made a national one by whatever government was in power in Éire'. Conlon picked up on this theme that the League was going to go south. Political developments across the border beckoned. A new party formed in June 1946, Clann na Poblachta, had gone from strength to strength pooling a number of currents of dissatisfaction, including teachers' grievances, and the republican prisoners issue. Its leader was a former IRA Chief of Staff, Sean McBride, the son of an executed 1916 leader. Significantly for the APL, McBride's northern policy, proposed the opening of the Oireachtas to northern representatives. Writing to Cahir Healy on 13 January 1948, weeks before the south's general election McBride described the proposal as the most constructive ever put forward, claimed it as a possible basis for anti-partitionist unanimity, and inquired as to the attitude of the APL. In conclusion he told Healy that 'tremendous progress' was being made and he wished to see the League taking 'a more definite stance on the matter'. Healy in reply reminded him that the late Eamon Donnelly had promoted the idea without success for years within Fianna Fáil. Significantly he also pointed out to McBride that the APL appeal for funds, addressed to all out-going Dáil deputies, had elicited only three replies.[16] Healy accompanied Lennon, McAteer and McGurk to Dublin in the last week of the campaign, addressing a rally of several thousands in the city centre in an attempt to make partition an issue.

The new inter-party government which replaced Fianna Fáil after sixteen years of unbroken dominance, was a mosaic of many traditions, with a tacit compact to play down the border issue for the sake of unity. This fact was reflected both in its composition – the vocal anti-partitionist Con Lehane was not included – and in the low key approach adopted on the issue throughout 1948.[17]

The APL did its best to change this with a speaking campaign in the south which proved markedly unsuccessful. Launching the campaign in the west, McSparran urged his audience to give the lie to the writer Sean O'Faolain who had claimed that support for the APL did not exist in the twenty-six counties. By the summer, an anguished Eddie McAteer was making a confession of failure to a gathering in Galway, accusing southerners of being 'more interested in the price of beef and eggs' while northern Catholics were being driven from their homes.[18]

All of this was to change before the end of the year, not from any newfound southern altruism concerning the northern minority but through the wounded pride and inter-factional rivalry of southern politicians. In the spring after the formation of the new cabinet, De Valera, eager to outbid McBride's republicanism, embarked on an anti-partitionist world tour. That autumn the inter-party government announced in Canada, following a snub at an official banquet, the decision to repeal the External Relations Act and leave the British Commonwealth, proclaiming Ireland a Republic.[19] Spurred into action by the changed political climate, Brookeborough, the northern Prime Minister called a Stormont general election for 10 February. Without consulting the APL, the Taoiseach, John A. Costello, convened a conference of the south's political parties at the Mansion House which floated a fund to aid anti-partition candidates in the northern election. The demand made by this all-party anti-partition Mansion House Committee for a British withdrawal from Ireland was, as one of its present day admirers points out, more extreme in its wording than that of the Provisional IRA.[20] It also undertook a number of publications including the books *Finances of Partition* by Ó Nualláin, *The Indivisible Island* by Frank Gallagher and a trilogy of pamphlets on discrimination, gerrymandering and the border.

The declaration issued in May 1949 in response to the Ireland Act came as the culmination of six month's activity. Those months saw the peak of southern intervention in northern affairs between 1925 and 1985 with a consequent solidification of the unionist camp. They saw southern Ireland spend more than was necessary of money gathered at 'chapel gate collections' – a setting which to Protestants seemed sectarian – to contest northern seats which could not be won. They saw the Republic proclaimed to mixed feelings among northern Catholics, ranging from those, probably a majority, such as Healy, who saw it as a symbol of hope, to those like McSparran who welcomed it publicly but slated it behind closed doors, to others like Mulvey who condemned outright the raising of hopes without consultation or the likelihood of fulfilment.[21]

Those years also saw the Northern Ireland Labour Party finally split along the fracture line of partition which had been threatening to open for so long. One result of the February election was the decision by McAteer, mandated by a meeting, to seek admission to the Dáil. On 5 March he sent a carefully considered letter to the Minister for External Affairs, McBride, pointing out that he recognised the practical difficulties as well as the desirability of keeping clear of any controversial 'domestic issue' on the other side of the border, but requesting a 'token attendance', being concerned merely with the symbolism of the thing. He had discussed the matter with the MPs including Frank Hanna and all were in agreement with the news. Con Lehane raised the issue in the Dáil. The Attorney General, Cecil Lavery, was asked by the government to prepare a memorandum on the subject. After much postponement of its consideration, the idea was ruled out by Costello in reply to a question of Lehane on 5 July 1949. He cited 'legal and other difficulties' but left open the question of giving them a right of audience in the Seanad.[22]

On 10 January 1950 when Attlee announced a general election for 23 February, McBride expressed the hope that the two Westminster MPs of Tyrone and Fermanagh would make a start by taking their seats in one or other House of the Oireachtas.[23] That election reflected once again the accessibility of the militant republican tradition to the Clann na Poblachta party. Former IRA Chief of Staff, Hugh McAteer, and Crumlin Road prisoner, the Belfast OC Jimmy Steele, were both candidates on a United panel. Government speakers, including McBride and Browne, addressed meetings in Tyrone and Fermanagh thundering out the anti-partitionist message. This stance of the Clann na Poblachta government conferred a sense of legitimacy on the IRA while drawing republicans into an increasing identification with the southern State. Brian O'Higgins, speaking at the re-burial of one of the victims of De Valera's draconian policies, Paddy McGrath, an event attended by Dr Noel Browne and other government ministers, remarked, 'the men were put to death as criminals, outlaws, enemies, of Ireland. Today that judgement is reversed even by those who were and are their opponents and they have been acknowledged to be what we have always claimed them to have been – true comrades of Tone and Emmet.'[24] Increasingly, at republican commemorations the emphasis was on avoiding confrontation with 'fellow Irishmen'. Hugh McAteer, who had left the movement but still retained his links with them, told the Dublin government that a possibility existed of the IRA accepting the authority of the southern State.[25] It was in this context that Standing Order No. 8 barring operations against southern forces was introduced in 1954.

It was indicative of the mood of disillusionment with the British Labour party that conventions held before the election had bound both Mulvey and Healy to non-attendance of Westminster, a decision both resented. Cunningham had announced his decision not to go forward again. In all it was a far cry from the euphoria of 1945 when both he and Mulvey cited the new administration as their reason for ending ten years of abstentionism. So irritated was Mulvey by the decision that he sought and obtained a reversal of it at a new convention at Omagh. Defending his action to the *Irish News,* he waxed lyrical on the benefits to be gained for his constituents, claiming that only some elements from East Tyrone and South Derry had favoured abstentionism as a matter of principle. Both his election and his remarks testified not only to the localised nature of republicanism in the constituency but also to the wide gap between appearance and reality in his own seemingly 'republican' victory fifteen years earlier.

The South Armagh by-election and the issue of Dáil seats
Another effect of the February election campaign was to redirect the APL's attention southwards, the southern intervention having reawakened hopes in an organisation increasingly becalmed in the political doldrums. It was 'unanimously agreed' by the League to submit another request to the southern government for the admission of its representatives to both houses of the Dublin parliament. Clann na Poblachta policy continued to offer encouragement and, in late January, Con Lehane had tabled a Dáil motion requesting that legislation be introduced for this purpose. On 17 February Sean McBride expressed the hope that Healy and Mulvey when elected would 'make a beginning by taking their seats in one or other of the Houses of Parliament of

the Republic.[26] On 16 May Sean McNally, the League's Honorary Secretary, wrote to the Taoiseach requesting a meeting between a deputation of theirs and 'leaders of the Dáil and Seanad'. Costello brought their letter before the Committee of the Mansion House All-Party Anti-Partition Conference who told him that 'no purpose' would be served by it as the opinions of at least some of the political parties on this subject were well known. He conveyed this decision to the APL in July, but told them that a meeting of the deputation with the government would be possible. Before this he had turned down a memorandum by McBride on the subject of granting a 'right of audience'.[27] McBride had argued it would be 'the logical first step' in converting 'the southern parliament into an all-Ireland one' as well as publicising the issue abroad and increasing co-operation with the northern MPs. Costello met with the deputation of six nationalist MPs, two Senators, three APL members and four members of the Dublin based Anti-Partition Association including its Chairman, Councillor T. P. O'Reilly. On the deputation also was Charlie McGleenan, the League's candidate for the South Armagh vacancy, caused by the death of Malachy Conlon. McSparran, the leader of the deputation, said their main purpose was to secure a decision on their proposal for admission. Costello referred once again to the decision of the Mansion House All-Party Committee and expressed himself satisfied that general Dáil agreement on the issue would 'not be possible'. McSparran claimed that the Mansion House Committee was concerned only with the administration of funds and that the Dáil was the proper agency for its consideration. If the government made it a 'matter of policy' the Dáil would accept it, he contended.

The Taoiseach, however, regarded 'substantial general agreement' as a precondition for putting the proposal in the first instance. McAteer viewed this as placing the proposal in a different category from other proposals brought before the House and asked whether it implied that some of the political parties 'supporting the government were against the proposals'. Costello then told the deputation he was prepared to offer an alternative which might make for closer contact between the government and northern anti-partitionists. However, as the deputation stated their intention of making known to the press the result of the meeting, this new proposal would have to be treated in confidence.[28] When Cahir Healy requested that they first be told what the proposal was, Costello refused to let them know. With the deputation unable to agree on the selection of a smaller group from their number to discuss the proposal, as Lennon had suggested, they decided to withdraw. When the results of the meeting were disclosed to the press, Healy at Derrygonnelly the following week said they had not been informed who the dissenters in the Dáil were. He pointed out that both McBride and Browne were 'in town' but had not attended. Referring to the 'delight of the Tory press', he asserted that northern nationalists could ease their position considerably if they were prepared 'to allow the National hare to sit (ie. soft-pedal or abandon anti-partitionism) during their lifetime.' He was sure they could secure 'some public positions here and there', and a due proportion of the RUC and the Civil Service'. They were not, however, thinking primarily of their own convenience or gain. They wanted first and last the unity of their country and they would not exchange that demand for anything else. Stating that 'Koreans, Indians or Pakistanis would not accept partition' he claimed that the northern nationalists if they did so, 'would be repudiated by future generations'.[29]

With the by-election in Armagh looming, discussions between Labour and nationalists took place as part of Dublin's desire for unity. On 6 June, the day after the monthly meeting of the APL executive, McSparran, McAteer and McNally met the Labourites Harry Diamond, Jack Macgougan and Sean McKearney. It foundered when Diamond's proposal of a 'liaison committee' to make binding decisions on both parties proved unacceptable to McSparran. Though the writ had not at that stage been moved for the by-election, McGleenan was generally perceived as the candidate to be and had announced he would seek a mandate from the voters to take his seat in the Dáil. When the by-election took place in December, McKearney opposed McGleenan in the Labour interest, Agnew having withdrawn for health reasons. The contest highlighted not only the divisions between the two groupings who continued to co-operate under the direction of Dublin in the organisation of unity meetings, but also the growing APL estrangement from the government of the Republic. McGleenan's victory of 5,581 votes to McKearney's 3,026 was hailed by McSparran as a 'clear indication of the disgust and resentment which the electors feel at the efforts of the Irish Labour Party to wreck the only movement which has made any progress towards consolidating the drive for Irish unity'. 'It was,' he said, 'a warning to Irish Labour to mind its own business.' They, as the APL, had 'endeavoured' to 'keep out' of 'Free State politics' but might have to 'reconsider the wisdom of that policy'. Senator Lennon asserted that the intention of the APL in selecting McGleenan was to get the concurrence of the electors on admission to the Oireachtas. The presence of the Labour leader William Norton on the government side when the deputation had gone to Dublin was recalled by McGleenan. The Labour party, he stated, had 'thrown a block in the drive for unity'. Before long antipathy towards Labour in APL ranks reached such a point that the second 'unity' meeting had to be postponed. Fianna Fáil, with an eye to the main chance, had helped in stirring the pot with an endorsement of McGleenan's candidacy by Frank Aiken, De Valera's henchman.

Almost simultaneously with the South Armagh election result the focus shifted to Belfast. The nationalist organisation in that city had been in retreat since the war years, its last parliamentary seat vanishing in 1946 when T. J. Campbell resigned to accept a judgeship. The subsequent by-election was won by Frank Hanna, then of the NILP, in a purely inter-Labour contest. Attempts to regain their influence on the corporation under the banner of the 'Inter Party Group' ended in failure at the elections in May of that year. By the 1950s they had been reduced to a role on the sidelines watching the infighting for winnable seats between the multiplying Labourite factions and backing the most conservative. In November a by-election occurred for the Westminster constituency of West Belfast owing to the disqualification of the incumbent, the Reverend Godfrey McManaway (also a Stormont MP for Derry City), who had taken the seat from the Irish Labour MP Jack Beattie the previous February by a margin of more than two and a half thousand. On this occasion Beattie lost to McManaway's successor, Thomas Teevan, by a mere 913 votes.

Even thought the abstentionism among the 1,500 odd republican voters who supported Steele on the previous occasion, was almost certainly the cause, nationalists saw it as another victory. The man organising the unity meetings on Dublin's behalf and maintaining a watching brief in its interests, was an ex-British Army officer of literary tastes, Captain Seamus McCall. Casting a cold eye on the APL's triumphalism, he reported on 26 November that in the event of likely Labour losses in both seats the League would 'get a new lease of life and be more puffed up in their own estimation' becoming 'more intractable than ever'.[30] By 10 December he considered this assessment 'an understatement'. 'They are just at present impossible,' he told the Department of External Affairs in Dublin. 'They take the view that they have defeated not only Irish Labour but also the Irish government and the All-Party Committee. For they pretend to believe that both the latter were behind the challenge to their power in South Armagh' and 'openly assert' that the contest was 'engineered' by 'the people in Dublin' in the hope of being 'saved the embarrassment' of having McGleenan claim his seat in the Dáil. Some of the League members boasted that the Labour party 'was now a dead letter in six counties' politics' and claimed the abstentionism in West Belfast resulted from 'annoyance' at Labour's attempt to 'steal the League's seat in South Armagh'. McCall offered a withering assessment of both the League in South Armagh and the area it represented. It was, he claimed, 'too much under the influence of men to whom removing the border is simply a euphemism for the transfer of ownership of the fleshpots of place and patronage'.[31] The result of all this was 'political stagnation' as far as the 'lower strata' were concerned.

Of McGleenan's constituency he had this to say:
Touring around such areas as South Armagh is rather like going back a whole generation in Irish history. The gombeenmen still operate there the old style. 'Grinders of the faces of the poor' still flourish and there are a variety of small time racketeers as well. The one important change is that they now have, as probably the biggest of all, the smuggling racket. And unfortunately putting down all the people who are doing well out of these rackets – including the smugglers who would be put out of business if the border were removed – find their best 'protection in the League and share with the League a lively hatred of anyone who tries to muscle in on their territory.[32]

Of both campaigns McCall could record that Labour were caught unprepared by the West Belfast election and were 'seriously hampered' in South Armagh by the absence of press support as well as being victims of whisper campaigns about 'communism', coupled with sentimental appeals for loyalty to the memory of the late Malachy Conlon. The League speakers also associated them with British Labour, the Ireland Act and the 'socialisation of education' he wrote.

McCall deprecated any panic by Dublin over the League's success. The 'Nationally minded people are on the whole behind the anti-partition movement but they are not behind the Anti-Partition League' he claimed, noting that McSparran eschewed the later term during the campaign as a means of establishing himself as the overall anti-partition spokesman and placing the 'partitionist' tag on the Labour party. McCall noted also that, in spite of the APL's 'easy victory', their vote was 'only a third' of their 'total register strength' and 'only a half' of that received by the non-abstentionist APL candidate the previous February. That being the case, it could not then be construed as representing the 'clear decision' in favour of Oireachtas representation claimed by a League spokesman. It was pointed out also that McSparran and every other APL MP and Senator except McNally (the League Secretary) and Lennon and Connellan (who 'live practically in the constituency') carefully refrained from publicly associating themselves with McGleenan and took no part whatsoever in the election until the result was known. Furthermore, McGleenan, as a native of the constituency, had a distinct advantage.

On 9 February Deputy Con Lehane submitted a motion calling for the granting of a 'right of audience … in as much as the citizens of South Armagh have recently elected Charles McGleenan for the express purpose of representing them in Dáil Éireann'. McNally, the APL Secretary, wrote to Costello on the 26th to say he had been informed McGleenan would call to Leinster House on 1 March and seek admission.[33] On 1 March, as McGleenan listened in the public gallery, Costello told the Dáil that the motions on this subject should be 'discussed in a calm atmosphere free from any heat' and their 'subject matter approached solely with a view to determining whether or not the matters mentioned in these motions do or do not assist an early solution of the problems of partition'. He promised a debate on the subject after Easter and a free vote on the subject. But the sequence of events which became known as the Mother and Child controversy supervened to sweep his government from office in April of that year.

When a deputation met the new Taoiseach, Éamon De Valera, on 3 August, it was obvious how large an educative role the events of the previous year had played among northern nationalists. The deputation, consisting of MPs McSparran, McGleenan and Senators Lennon and McNally, raised as its primary concern, the formation of the Unity Council and their wish that it should represent all the anti-partitionist MPs and Senators. They claimed that they were the voice of 90% of northern nationalists and should, therefore, be the Council's principal component with the possible addition of Diamond, Hanna and the QUB Independent Dr Eileen Hickey, who were not members of the APL. A five person committee could then be chosen with these three accounting for one member.[34] They rejected the view that the committee should liaise with all political parties and expressed preference for direct negotiations with the government. Only as their fifth point did they raise the question of representation in the south and then only of 'one or two representatives' nominated to the Senate. De Valera explained at length the difficulties involved in this proposal similar to those in cases of Dáil representation. He promised, however, to consider the request.[35]

On the problem of partition the general policy of the APL was, they said, to attend the Stormont parliament. The case of McGleenan was, they acknowledged, 'exceptional'. They warned the six counties against moving in the direction of the British Welfare State. 'Majority opinion' in the six counties, one member said, 'tended to be conservative politically and was likely to remain so' with 'little likelihood' of 'labour interests gaining a majority'. The deputation then went on to state that 'apart from gerrymandering and certain other matters, some of the grievances of the nationalists in the six counties were not perhaps so great as it would sometimes appear. Conciliatory methods would probably secure the best results. As a means of ending partition, sabre-rattling speeches were unlikely to achieve much and abuse achieved nothing,' they told De Valera. 'The six counties government was facing many difficulties and advantage should be taken of this,' was their final word on this issue. On the question of whether 'from the viewpoint of ending partition' Dominion Status for the north was preferable to continued UK membership, they felt Dominion Status more likely to perpetuate partition.[36] References to a 'federal solution' were, they felt, open to misunderstanding with its implication of 'two co-equal parliaments in Ireland'. On the Ó Nualláin study, *Finances of Partition*, then in preparation, they qualified the view that the northern government was subsidised by Britain with the reminder 'that the six county area was a valuable asset to Britain, particularly as a dollar earner'. They proposed instead a study on the subject entitled *What Partition costs the Six Counties.*

North and south, funds were proving a problem. In the Republic, De Valera stated, the Mansion House Fund was not 'hypothecated' and he would consider proposing a Dáil vote of monies for publicity purposes. Up north the APL funds were at a low ebb, a deputation told him. It was 'almost impossible' to raise the £1,000 a year expenses of the League as 'there were too many collections already'.[37]

In the meantime the matter of the Unity Council continued to exercise minds. The idea of the council may be said to have had its origins with the Mansion House Committee's Conference of 16 April 1949, which urged the improvement of APL organisation in the six counties. Jack Macgougan, the Irish Labour Party Secretary in the North, had written to the Committee in December 1949 stating the view of his party's Northern Council that a 'Central Co-ordinating Authority' of overall national opinion be created.[38] The clearest formulation of the idea came on 25 May of that year in a report from McCall to the Mansion House Committee. Under the heading 'Northern Advisory Council', he suggested as an alternative to seats in the Dáil the setting up of a Council of Ireland somewhat on the lines once envisaged by the British but with the northern representation drawn from the anti-partitionist MPs. Such a council might then be able to give the 'much needed must be obeyed' direction to anti-partitionist activities in the north'. As a 'simpler compromise' he proposed a 'Northern Advisory Council' consisting 'mainly but not exclusively of nationalist MPs and Senators, APL and Irish Labour'. This he felt would provide them with the same sense of influence as would seats in the Dáil by enabling them to act in an advisory capacity to the Irish government.[39]

The inclusive result of the 'Unity' meeting in June 1950 has already been noted. The effort of the following month made 'only slight progress'. Though all national organisations were invited, none except Sinn Féin formally replied. The proposal which Costello hoped to disclose in secret to the July deputation, he outlined in a letter that September to the APL. It proposed a 'small committee representative of six county anti-partition groups which would maintain liaison and close contact with a small group of members of the government'.[40]

Negotiations continued over the summer and autumn. Finally in November McCall could report a breakthrough. On the fifth of that month at a meeting in Belfast, the second such 'convention' to be held on the subject, a decision was taken to set up a Unity Council. On closer examination the result was not the milestone it appeared to be. Only eighteen people attended the meeting comprising eight organisations, some of them decidedly unrepresentative of northern nationalist opinion (the Ulster Union Club and Clann na Poblachta) and others (the old IRA, the Tyrone Republican and South Derry Organisations respectively) without a clear profile. But the APL was there as was the Irish Labour Party (though both Jack Macgougan and Victor Halley were unavoidably absent), and Joseph Connellan of the Irish Citizens' Association. It was impossible not to notice the flaws in the structure, however. The meeting was acrimonious, most opposition coming from the APL which expected the lion's share of representation and the decision to appoint a council of one delegate from each of the eight organisations was not endorsed by them. In the event only three organisations – Irish Labour, Clann na Poblachta and Ulster Union Club – supplied names. McCall, to 'clinch the business', announced the establishment of the Council, leaving 'metaphorical blank spaces to be filled in'. He was to discover over the coming years just how difficult a task this would prove to be.

As has been described, the South Armagh by-election forced a postponement. Despite the hostility expressed during the campaign to the All-Party Committee, McCall did not believe they had lost interest in the Council. Senator Lennon had expressed himself in favour of it and the APL Secretary McNally gave 'the impression' of 'rather looking forward to the next meeting as an opportunity of rubbing in their victory over Irish Labour'. The first meeting in early January was a failure due to the 'flu epidemic. The second, on 21 January, was more significant. Even though McCall admitted to 'difficult patches' during its four and a half hour duration, in which it proved 'impossible to keep the south Armagh election out of the discussion' – one motion from the Tyrone Republican Association proposed the exclusion of Labour on the grounds that it took its orders from Dublin, and

the Newry based Irish Citizens' Association refused to attend
because of the by-election affair – the meeting was on the whole
satisfactory.[41] Despite the opposition of the League executive to
the equal representation of Labour, and their demand for a
council of 'all the elected MP's and Senators', tentative agreement was secured for a council where three seats went to the
League, two to Labour and one each to the other affiliated organisations. Approval was also gained for a proposal making all
elected public representatives (who were members of one or another of the affiliated organisation) members of the representatives' council. This, McCall felt, would prevent the 'county
members from swamping proceedings'. With the unsuccessful
visit to the Dáil in March of McGleenan and six other APL members, where they heard Costello's statement from the visitors
gallery, the League executive hardened its approach. Throughout
April McCall complained of 'continued' stalling and obstruction
by the APL delegates 'making the whole thing look like the conference of the foreign ministers deputies in Paris'.[42] A meeting
on 6 April saw a row-back to the original demands on the composition of the Council. A further irritant to McCall was their
view of themselves as the leaders of the APA in the south, the
League for an Undivided Ireland in the US, and the anti-partitionists in Britain. 'The element of truth in this is very slight,' he
remarked, recalling how during the 'Journalists invasion' of
Belfast in 1949 not a single one of their number had to his knowl-
edge sought an interview with any member of the League'. And
that was how it had remained. So clueless was the APL in dealing with the foreign media that when, in 1950, a Canadian journalist sought a meeting with McSparran the latter had to telephone McCall beforehand requesting his help.

A meeting of the League executive was called for 16 April
after Labour objected to what they saw as 'packing of the jury'
by the League. As McSparran, the Chairman, Healy and the
other key members were not present, an extraordinary meeting
was held on 26 of that month. The day before, Connellan, Healy
and McNally assured McCall that his proposals would be carried. 'But,' McCall ruefully recalled, 'they reckoned without
McSparran.' Under his Chairmanship a vote on the subject was
disallowed and McCall, who was excluded from the meeting,
was handed a typed note informing him that the meeting resolved 'that any decision with regard to the proposed Unity

Council should be deferred until such time as a decision is arrived at in the Dáil on the question of admitting thereto six county representatives'.[43] The non-League delegates toyed with the idea of setting up a council in their absence or accepting McCall's suggestion (put forward he admitted 'only as a threat') of Dublin 'selecting' an advisory committee. In the event neither idea was followed through.[44]

McSparran had originally been an opponent of the Dáil seats idea, his new-found hard line stemming from his fear of what might lie ahead. He told the APL conference, on 28 March in Belfast, that the only alternatives to the 1945 foundation of the APL was to allow the 'idea of Irish Unity' to 'perish' or have it 'dealt with as in 1916'.[45] There were flood tides and ebb tides 'in the struggle', he said, accusing Dublin of having 'betrayed the people of six of the best counties Ireland had'. On 4 April McSparran had clashed with the *Irish Press* newspaper in Dublin over its editorial treatment of a speech of his. 'You now adopt the anti-partition movement as one sponsored by your party, possibly even by your journal,' he wrote. He gave credit to De Valera, and the Fianna Fáil secretaries Mullins and Little 'for services rendered', but 'would be pleased', he felt, 'to have enlightenment on the services rendered by other prominent leaders of the party' recalling the 'repeated appeals' for coverage made unsuccessfully by northern nationalists.[46]

The APL and Labour

The APL had begun its existence in a state of illusion about both the helpfulness of the Dublin and London governments. The years that followed had been one of hard realities, frustrated ideals and wasted effort. Now as the fallout continued from the Ireland Act and relations with Dublin were put once again somewhat shakily back on track, those with British Labour had been shattered beyond repair. At last they were dealing with 'known' enemies rather than alleged friends,[47] McSparran stated as he supported Anti-Partition League candidates against that party in the 1950 Westminster election, all of whom received only a derisory vote.

But it would be a mistake to see this hostility as something deriving either suddenly or gradually from differences of grand policy on the national question alone. A wide gulf existed between the philosophy and worldview of a clericalist, rural, middle class, ageing organisation and that of secular urbanised social democrats determined to make good the wartime dream of a more egalitarian Britain.

The extension of the Welfare State system to Northern Ireland provoked, in Patrick McGill's words in the Senate many years later, 'taxes on an industrial scale upon an essentially pastoral community'.[48] The only difference between the Tories whom he detested, McSparran said in January 1950, and Labour whom he also detested, was that there might be enough money in the kitty to pay for the social services if the Tories got in.[49] To northern nationalist politicians, who had seen nothing wrong with European clerico-fascist regimes and who championed Catholic control in education and the social services, the secularising drive of the Attlee government touched a raw nerve. Later that month McSparran, speaking of the Labour government's attitude, said, 'those who wished to feel secure in whatever privileges they had in regard to the faith had only to see the contempt with which Labour received the proposals of the British bishops on education, their attitude to Franco's Spain, their hostility to the collaborationist King of the Belgians and their haste in recognising communist China'.[50] There was also, *sotto voce*, the fear that the welfare state would corrode the 'national feeling' on which they battened – the very morning of the Browne resignation an *Irish News* cartoon by 'Sciandor'showed L.E. Éire anchored to independence while HMS Britain towed away the north through waves marked 'taxation'.[51]

The right-wing hostility displayed by McSparran did not stop at the political platforms. He was instrumental in blocking an attempt at introducing rent controls on northern landlords [52] and, McCall told Dublin, swung the northern Bar against a scheme to introduce free legal aid.[53] Even where co-operation continued with the Friends of Ireland, a noticeable difference in emphasis existed also between the two groups towards the disabilities suffered by the northern minority. To the 'Friends' these injustices constituted the problem, to the APL they were merely aspects of it. When the *Irish News* in May 1950 posed a series of questions to Brooke, then departing for a tour of America, only one was on 'gerrymandering', one was on 'the flag', nine were on 'partition'.[54] Joe Stewart reconciled this position with the more pragmatic one which many of his audience remembered from the Joe Devlin era by assuring them that there would be 'no end to discrimination while partition lasts'.

Bing's pamphlet, *John Bull's Other Island*, published at the height of the feud with Irish Labour in South Armagh, was coldly received by the APL, one of whom dismissed it as a 'Transport House Manoeuvre'.[55] And they differed also on ultimate objectives. In October 1951 the Irish Ambassador in London told the Secretary of the Department of External Affairs that Bing had described Dominion Status for the north as the 'goal the APL should seek'. Failing that, they should strike for total integration with Britain.[56]

The distance between the APL and the Friends of Ireland was highlighted by others besides Bing. The 'eagerly awaited' debate in the House of Commons in May was, the Ambassador admitted, 'a failure'. Only Michael Foot 'came near to attacking partition', all other speakers 'directed their shafts not at partition but at six county Toryism,' he complained. 'The damaging implication' was that 'if ... a better government' existed at Stormont 'everything would be rosy in the garden'. Neither was the case made against the government on the grounds of religious discrimination 'wholly convincing', he complained. It was negatived by the claim that Catholic local authorities discriminated against Protestants, that the low percentage of Catholics in the RUC resulted from their attitude to the force, and that Catholic voluntary schools in the north were more favourably treated than those in England. Above all else, the publication by Dr Noel Browne of his correspondence on the Mother and Child Scheme 'hit them a grievous blow, particularly among the left wing of the party'. Sam Silkin, in conversation with the Irish Labour Party Leader William Norton, described the Browne affair as a 'cold douche for Labour supporters'.[58]

The early co-operation between the APL and labour did not survive the South Armagh by-election. Indeed the willingness of the League to withdraw from South Down in the general election earlier that year and give Jack Macgougan a clear field against the unionist was unmatched by a readiness to encourage support for him. Only the intervention of McCall at the APL meeting prevented the publication of a statement in the press condemning Macgougan as an intruder. Even so, an election edition of Connellan's *Frontier Sentinel* had urged in a large banner headline 'South Down MP (i.e. Connellan himelf) says spoil your vote'. Ostensibly advice for the electorate in Britain, who were not within the newspaper's readership, there was no mistaking the real target of the demand. Other manifestations of

what McCall termed the 'imbecile jealousy' towards Macgougan
in the constituency included the 'red scare', the forced withdrawal of personation agents and, when much of the electorate
turned out under pressure from the clergy (whom McCall had
approached), the casting by some of pro-unionist ballots. The
view of Labour as a 'troublesome lot ... always anti-Irish' and 'a
pro-partition group ... only a burden'[59] are typical of the senti-
ments expressed in private APL correspondence.

Within Labour itself, troubles arose particularly in Belfast.
The West Belfast branch, which always maintained its distinc-
tiveness within the Irish Labour party, soon found itself at odds
with its own sitting MP, Jack Beattie, the February 1950 election
highlighting differences within the party when on a dispute
over finances in the midst of the campaign the Regional Council
decided to suspend canvassing. Beattie lost the seat and subsequently failed to regain it in the November by-election. His
moment of triumph had to wait until the Westminster election
of the following year when he recaptured it by 25 votes after a
lengthy recount. Much of this resentment, particularly between
Beattie and Diamond, who had called the meeting of the
Regional Council in February, was of a personal nature. Beattie
was, as his close associate James Kelly told this writer, 'very
much a one-man band'.[60] The dispute flared up at the
Administrative Council meeting in December with a resolution
passed on the 13th to establish a committee to investigate the situation. Halley, Diamond and McGeever prevented a quorum
for its next meeting on the 30th by leaving the room. Matters
resurfaced again in March 1951, with a decision taken to dissolve the Regional Council.[61]

Diamond continued to pursue his own initiative. Early in
July he fought Beattie for the Aldermanship of Smithfield, having resigned his seat in Falls to do so. He was heavily defeated,
with only 312 votes to Beattie's 1,402, whether despite or because of his use of the sectarian issue against Beattie is unclear.
His action rebounded on him still further in November when his
candidate, McGovern, was defeated for Diamond's own seat in
Falls by an even larger margin. Diamond himself declined to
run, allegedly for health reasons. In September eight members
including Diamond, Halley and McGovern were expelled.
Three of them were councillors. In retaliation they issued a manifesto condemning the Belfast General Branch as 'crypto communist'.

The attitude of the APL to all of this was shown in the endorsement by Healy, McSparran and Lennon of McGovern in the November by-election. The League's earlier attempt to turn this infighting to its own advantage ended in electoral disaster when its candidate, a local freak-show owner, came last in the July contest despite an intensive registration and reorganisation drive.

When one casts a closer eye over the events of those months, many of the contradictions within Labourite politics in Catholic Belfast spring to light. Diamond shamelessly played the religious card against Beattie ('Freeman or Freemason?' his posters proclaimed) and the anti-communist one against Jack Macgougan, Beattie's election agent, yet Diamond's own chief lieutenant Victor Halley was (like Macgougan) a Presbyterian, as were others who had entered Irish Labour politics from Diamond's socialist republican party route. As far as opposition to communism was concerned, when the vacancy first occurred Diamond unsuccessfully attempted to persuade a veteran of the 15th International Brigade to go forward against Beattie. Halley himself had served on several committees in support of the Spanish Republic in Belfast during that conflict. Diamond, who had once described the APL as a sectarian manoeuvre and who had lost votes to them in July, found himself a semi-detached ally of theirs in the battle to regain his own vacated seat. Though Diamond after his expulsion excoriated the Irish Labour Party, his group after disaffiliating had petitioned William Norton for permission to register as a separate branch. Even the circumstances of the original vacancy were suspicious. The retiring councillor Vincent Kelly, a member of Diamond's group, may have been pressurised into taking the action he took 'for personal reasons'. Clearly parochial power politics rather than any deep seated ideological clash underpinned the division. Yet a polarisation was nonetheless developing between a seemingly sectarian version of Labourism and an apparently more pluralist and secular one. For the moment, to its credit, the Catholic population seemed to prefer the latter returning the Protestant Jack Beattie, a man whose commitment to anti-partitionism was equalled by his attachment to the benefits of a continued link with the British Labour movement. And this was happening at a time when Ireland was increasingly marching to a different drum.[62]

The collapse of the first Coalition government over the Mother and Child scheme had dramatised more clearly than any other single event the clericalist character of the Southern State. Though many critics have since lambasted Dr Browne for his alleged political immaturity in failing to separate the IMA objectors from the Bill's hierarchical opponents, the fact remains that the solution his Fianna Fáil successors reached was made possible only by the insertion of a means test and was first submitted to the Cardinal for his approval.

The reaction in the north to the events, which became a major weapon in unionist propaganda, was on the nationalist side quote low key. The *Irish News*, while approving of the bishops' action, did so in the context of an editorial condemning the welfare state – the subject of regular condemnation in its columns and bishops' pastorals. McSparran at Stormont defended the right of bishops to advise members of the southern legislature but only when unionist MPs raised the issue.[63] Later in the year Independent Nationalist MP for Queen's University, Dr Eileen Hickey, debated with Dr Browne at the university, the motion that 'the welfare state is an indispensable component of a modern society'.[64] McCall, moving through nationalist circles at the time, took particular note of this absence of response among APL members. Only one of them, Senator McNally, mentioned the affair to him at all and he seemed curious to know if Dr Browne was a Protestant.[65] Behind the scenes, however, some expressed their disgust.

Cahir Healy, also a leading member of the County Fermanagh Knights of Columbanus, in reply to a series of proposals made by Canon Maguire of Newtownbutler, wrote when he came to the heading entitled 'social justice':

> The Bishops made no representation in regard to northern Catholics. They in fact never mentioned us. Are we neither of the nation or the church? Dr McQuaid had never once said that he is opposed to partition. The bishops should have made their representation openly and not secretly. The Constitution offers all people equality of treatment. Would Protestant doctors and nurses be accepted in any 'Mother and Child' scheme acceptable to the Bishops?[66]

The following months would be crucial, he told Maguire, concluding with the tart reminder that he was 'wary' of 'dragging our Lord Bishops into things ... after Dublin'. Such a comment, coming from the quarter it did, spoke volumes both on how badly the Roman Catholic hierarchy had overreached itself and on how partitionist its mentality was.

CHAPTER 12

The APL Adrift

In July the new administration dealt with the question of northern seats. De Valera told Dr Noel Browne in the Dáil on 5 July that the admission of the northerners would be 'a futile gesture … open to serious objections' involving 'power without responsibility'. A similar rebuff had been received by McGleenan in May.[1]

Finally, on 19 July, a motion by McBride and John Tully on the subject (by the remnants of Clan na Poblachta) was put to a vote of the Dáil and defeated by 82 votes to 42. Of the Fine Gael deputies, 19 supported McBride's motion while 11 opposed it. All the Labour party and Clann na Talmhan members supported it as did nine of the 12 Independents. The entire Fianna Fáil party voted against it.

McCall had already advised the government on the impracticability of the idea, quoting from McAteer's letter of 5 March 1949 to the then Minister for External Affairs.[2] At that time the Attorney General, Cecil Lavery, advised the government that constitutional changes would be required in order to facilitate such a move. His opinion on the subject to the government on 12 March 1949 had, however, suggested 'right of audience in either House accorded possibly under rules of procedure and certainly by legislation'. This memorandum had however been withdrawn by the government later in the year. McCall's report read by the Taoiseach in May 1951 stated that members of the Anti-Partitionist League had made it clear to him that a 'right of audience' would be exploited mainly for publicity purposes, 'for proclaiming over and over again that the credit for everything which has been done towards ending partition has been done by them and that the government has done nothing'. Referring to McSparran, he warned that 'those who at one time described the 'seats in the Dáil' proposal as 'foolish stunting' now wished to press it forward for the purpose of embarrassing the government and in the hope of taking to themselves the power to make and unmake governments in the Republic'.[3] He then went on to restate what he had earlier told Dublin about McGleenan's election. It was being used as a stalking horse for the selfish agendas of Leaguers who did not share McGleenan's principles. Mc Gleenan, whom he described as 'honest and sincere but far from bright and seldom consistent', represented a League which had opposed abstention and was supported by prominent anti-abstentionists motivated by fear of a minor seccession and a consequent reduction in their dwindling numerical strength.[4]

Whereas in Sinn Féin days, 'abstention, which McGleenan sincerely believed in, was an assertive and dignified, even dangerous policy' in 1951 it was merely an 'aspect of the political inertia' which was 'the despair of all those who are the real victims' of the six county regime.[5] Together with 'semi-abstention' and half-hearted attendance' it 'disenfranchised nationalists' and, whatever its motivation, was a 'policy of futility. He blamed a number of those clamouring for admission to the Dáil for having made 'many of our former friends in the north abandon the struggle as hopeless', describing 'absentee MPs' as being 'as useful in the Ireland of today as absentee landlords were in the Ireland of yesterday'.[6] Were these people to be admitted to the Dáil, it would increase the belief in physical force as the only means of redress.[7] The Stormont parliament, though not offering 'the Irish minority' any hope of changing the system, at least enabled them to mitigate its severities and curb its excesses. What was 'needed' among nationalist public representatives, therefore, was a 'policy of political and economic alertness and a willingness to carry the fight into the enemy camp'. Instead they had indulged in 'preaching to the converted, the soliciting of funds, and the making of promises, without evolving anything approaching a polity or achieving anything approaching agreement on methods', McCall claimed. As a result, he contended, the 'political following' of the League did not permit them to 'return' a single member for Belfast or even to secure representation on the City Corporation.[8]

A survey of the APL's heartlands painted a similar picture of demoralisation and lack of public support. In Derry, the leaders of the League 'were able to mobilise only a dozen followers to begin their St Patrick's Day procession'. In the rural areas the APL's political inertia had 'lost them the active support of the

younger generation' and, though there were 'virile national elements' who sought 'guidance and practical leadership', few of
them were active between elections with the League. Indeed,
some were quite ill disposed to it and the 'latent strength' of the
movement 'would remain that way so long as the League leaders refuse to face reality'.[9] Healy himself had acknowledged in
May that of the 21 clubs in existence in Fermanagh only 13 had
even bothered to affiliate.[10]

The real attitude of mainstream nationalist politicians to Dáil
representation was echoed by Healy in a letter to Fr Maguire of
Newtownbutler the previous November:

> We were asked to go to Dáil Éireann at the last convention;
> that is why we went. I never had any hope of sitting there.
> We have no work to do in the Dáil and we are needed outside
> badly, yet a large section of our people think something won-
> derful would develop if we went there'.

The question of an anti-partitionist umbrella organisation con-
tinued under the new government. Whilst in opposition De
Valera had met with Harry Diamond, Frank Hanna and Dr
Eileen Hickey, members for Falls, Central and Queens
University respectively, and on 2 February he told the APL
Secretary that agreement existed on the creation of an Advisory
Council consisting only of parliamentary anti-partition repres-
entatives, the three aforementioned MPs wanting senators ex-
cluded.[11]

The League for its part seemed determined to sabotage the
idea in any form. On 14 March when Eddie McAteer MP and
Senators P. J. O'Hare and Sean McNally met De Valera and his
deputy, Frank Aiken, they told him to withdraw an earlier proposal for a sub-committee of the Council offered to them by
Costello as a consolation prize following the rejection of their request for Oireachtas representation. They also presented Dublin
with a formidable wish list, stressing amongst other things the
desirability of having cattle from the twenty-six counties exported
directly to Britain rather than passed through Enniskillen, calling for the inclusion of the six counties in Radio Éireann's coverage, asking for a legal adviser to deal with discrimination cases,
and requesting a six county representative on delegations to the
Council of Europe. In addition, they expressed their hopes for
action on the question of the oath and for money from the Anti-
Partition Fund.

The attempts at forming such a council sputtered on in-
effectually as the years went by.[12] When the issue of Dáil
representation surfaced again in November 1954, the Taoiseach,
John A. Costello, confessed himself in a letter to the League
Secretary Patrick McGill, unaware 'whether or not it is still in existence'. In tandem with all of this the Republic's anti-partition
drive had begun to run out of steam. The Minutes of the
Mansion House Committee for 26 June 1951, record not only a
refusal of Senator McNally's request for the holding of an Irish
Race Convention, but also a decision not to make a contribution
to the Armagh branch for the Belfast High Court action which
they successfully took on the tricolour ban, nor to support financially the nationalists charged in connection with the incident.
Financial assistance was also turned down for the Derry Branch,
whose candidate, Frank McCarroll, had contested the
'McManaway by-election' in 1951. Furthermore, the mobilisation of 'the far flung Irish race' on which the All-Party
Committee had placed such store had proven itself a failure.
After a promising introduction to the US Congress in July 1950,
John Fogarty's resolution in support of an All Ireland plebiscite
was defeated by 266 votes to 130 in September 1951.[13]

Writing in November 1953 to Brian Durnan in the
Department of External Affairs, Conor Cruise O'Brien, the third
secretary, noted that 'our campaign against partition which has
as its main constituent the effort to draw an American support
… will get precisely nowhere when it comes up as it must
against the rock of religious prejudice'.[14] The only way to operate in a situation where the Irish demand was portrayed as the
'handing over of a Protestant population to a Catholic power'
was 'to win over the Protestants of the north'. As a first step he
proposed the removal of Roman Catholic symbolism from the
southern state. His list of 'offensive symbolisms' which included
the broadcast of the Angelus on Radio Éireann was rejected by
Monsignor Kinnane of Maynooth and was heard of no more.[15]

A report to the Mansion House Committee on the 130
branches of the Ireland League in Britain stated, in reference to
the movement's failure in the US, that it was 'doubly difficult' to
succeed in Britain, as unlike the United States 'where anti-
Britishness could be flaunted with impunity' and occasionally
with advantage, 'anything suggestive of it in Britain had for obvious reasons a poor market'. 'Doctors, businessmen, writers,
actors, BBC employees and other Irish people of professional

and educational attainment were likely to give the APL a wide berth for that reason. And yet, they concluded, 'that section was important to enlist if they were ever to create a climate of sympathy and understanding towards Ireland'.[16]

In Northern Ireland the APL was having its own difficulties not least being the ameliorative impact of the British Welfare State about which they had complained so loudly in August. 'Political ineptitude among the local nationalist leaders in the six counties,' McCall reported in March 1951, ' is having a bad effect on our people generally. I was disheartened to find in the smaller towns in the six counties, considerable complacency, a tendency to fall victims to unionist propaganda, a belief that – with munificent Social Welfare benefits – they were better off as they were, and a definite trend towards accepting the present state of affairs as 'not too bad'. He complained of the petty prejudices and party feeling blinding nationalist newspapers and preventing united action.[17]

The failure of the Mansion House Committee to support McCarroll in the Derry by-election, coupled with a refusal to assist Congressman Fogarty in coming from America to lead the St Patrick's Day procession in Derry, left Eddie McAteer further disillusioned. He was proposing to play a 'lone hand' and, harking back to the ideas of his 1945 pamphlet, was considering the organisation of a civil disobedience campaign which he felt the Mansion House committee 'ought to finance'. He had lost faith in the APL which was, as McCall reported, 'in general disfavour in Derry' at least when measured by participation levels. O'Neill, the Westminster MP for Mid Ulster, noted McAteer's estrangement, complaining in March 1953 that he was 'interested only in Derry and did not believe in the League', an opinion of him endorsed by Conor Cruise O'Brien. It was reported from that city that nationalists there felt the situation was 'explosive', the Welfare State benefits not having had the anticipated demoralising effect on their majority 'which consisted mostly of the poorer people'. Derry nationalists were sceptical of Dublin's proposals to distribute pamphlets as a means of penetrating unionist opinion – they had seen the few Protestant nationalists in the city boycotted by their co-religionists and criticised what they saw as the 'fraternisation policy' of the Irish government. This policy of cross-border co-operation on such common matters as transport and electricity had led Terence O'Neill, unionist

MP for Bannside and later Home Affairs Minister, to praise the Fianna Fáil government as the most realistic Dublin administration to date. Especially irksome to the Derry nationalists was the attendance of an ESB representative from the Republic at a luncheon in the city connected with the Erne scheme. To them it seemed a betrayal of the boycott which they had organised of the gathering.[18]

The continued influence of the Catholic Church on politics in the city was illustrated by the decision to cancel the banned 1953 St Patrick's Day demonstration there on the insistence of Dr Niall Farren, the local bishop, who 'disapproved' of 'anti-partition stunts' and, being more 'interested in the economic advancement of the Catholic community than in any political concern', had 'kept a tight rein' on the strongly anti-partitionist clergy.

The Derry experience was not exceptional, with the League increasingly fragmenting on regional lines. The most significant of the factions, the 'Omagh Group', centred around those MPs and Senators with interests or involvement in the North West Publishing Company group of newspapers with its headquarters at the *Ulster Herald* office in Omagh. These included West Tyrone MP, Roderick O'Connor, the Managing Director of the *Ulster Herald*, Senator Lynch of the Lynch family of Omagh, proprietors of the newspaper chain, the *Ulster Herald* editor Senator Patrick McGill, the *Fermanagh Herald* editor, Senator P. J. O'Hare, and the editor of the Newry based *Frontier Sentinel*, Joe Connellan MP. The two MPs at Westminster, O'Neill and Healy, were both associated with the group, Healy holding a directorship of the *Fermanagh Herald*.

Interfactional resentments and rivalries characterised the relations between these nationalist fiefdoms. The Derry group, for instance, was highly critical of the Westminster performance of the aforementioned MPs, considering it 'too respectable'. Westminster, McAteer felt, was useful only for the staging of 'stunts'. Though in O'Neill's view abstentionism from Stormont was no 'longer a live factor', it was still being advocated for the Westminster parliament. It was widely maintained in the constituency, he acknowledged, that both himself and Healy were 'doing no good'. In what was probably a reflection of the Omagh Group's greater influence, the Department of External Affairs' film on housing discrimination was made on Fintona – an obscure town in the gerrymandered Omagh RDC, suggested to

Conor Cruise O'Brien by O'Neill – rather than the more obvious and blatant example of Derry which McAteer would obviously have preferred.[19]

Within the League there was a widespread hostility towards what was described as McSparran's 'absentee leadership'. McSparran, it was felt, would relinquish his chairmanship if anyone could be found to replace him. It was typical of the fragmentation and demoralisation that no contenders were in line for the job. The APL was falling apart, as the Irish Union Association and others had before it. Even though in theory Antrim was the only area unorganised outside Belfast, in reality, as McGill admitted to Healy in February 1953, many of their branches existed 'only on paper' and no lifeline was coming from the Dublin government to rescue them from extinction.[20]

Later in February McBride told Healy that 'partition' in the Republic was 'in the doldrums' and that De Valera was proposing to wind up the Mansion House Committee.[21] From the nationalist point of view this was regrettable. Southern assistance was once again required when the abstention issue bounced back on the agenda in the Stormont general election of October 1953. The victory of the republican militant, Liam Kelly, in Mid Tyrone and the impressive performance of Kevin Agnew in Mid Derry, highlighted the growing abstentionist feeling. Agnew was supported on his platform by Clann na Poblachta members McBride and Tully. Kelly, a co-op manager, founder of the Saor Uladh organisation after his expulsion from the IRA, pitched his appeal to the McBride nexus, accepting as legitimate the 1937 Irish Constitution. On the ground a significant section of the clergy had defected both to abstentionism and to his camp. Two of his chief advisers were priests.

A sidebar result of the 1953 election was the quiet departure from the scene of all but two of the AOH representatives in parliament, Joe Stewart, MP for East Tyrone, and McSparran in Mourne. Mid Derry had never been regained by them after Leeke's death, Mourne passed out of their hands after McSparran's retirement in 1958 and the defeat by Kelly of Edward Vincent McCullagh, who had regained the Mid Tyrone seat for them on McGurk's death in 1948, ended Hibernian representation there for all times. The process of co-operation, ongoing since the 1920s, had rendered this particular form of inter-nationalist animosity, a thing of the past. When Canon

Tom Maguire of Newtownbutler wrote to Healy in March complaining of the latter's attendance of an AOH organised Easter
March, Healy expressed himself 'hurt by the allegation that he
had sold out to the AOH' adding that:

> I was just as much opposed to them as you could be: I was
> never in their ranks. It is over 40 years since the incident of
> the Belfast convention (i.e. the acceptance by Home Rulers in
> 1916 of contemporary exclusion). All of the persons who fig-
> ured in it have long since been gathered to their fathers. Most
> of their descendants would be found on the side of Fianna
> Fáil today. I don't think you should punish children for the
> sins of their fathers.

Earlier Healy had told him, 'We cannot go back to 1918 …
whenever we need the Hibernians for nationalist or parochial
purposes they are available; they are all Irishmen'.[22]

Even before the election, however, the alarm bells were ringing within mainstream nationalism and all efforts were being
directed towards the one source which they felt could save
them, the Irish government. After its impact had sunk in, the
question of entry to the Dáil was once more top of the agenda. In
April 1954 McSparran, at a large Easter Commemoration in
Dublin organised by the Anti-Partition Association, called for a
'right of audience' in the Dáil. On 17 July, a deputation of APL
MPs attended the general council of County Councils in the
Republic to seek their support for admission to the Oireachtas.
In May, Stewart and a Dungannon priest met Costello with the
same request. In August O'Neill reported to Healy that 'opposition leaders' had been approached on the subject 'as had De
Valera on behalf of Fianna Fáil'. Notwithstanding their past
record, O'Neill continued to believe that Fianna Fáil would be
'more sympathetic'. A favourable response would, he maintained, 'resolve a difficult problem here by cutting the ground
from under the abstentionists feet'. Anticipating a republican
challenge at the next Westminster election, he cited as the main
object the preservation of the Fermanagh and Tyrone seats 'at all
costs', warning that they were 'in present circumstances' a bit
apprehensive and expressing doubts that they could command
'sufficient united effort in the future'.[23]

In late October the APL adopted a resolution calling for
nationalist admission. On 5 November Healy, Stewart, McGleenan
and Gormley had a discussion with De Valera on the subject in

his room at Leinster House. Of those four, only McGleenan had ever viewed the issue as a matter of principle. Indeed Gormley had argued against that very proposal in the manifesto of Agnew, his Mid Derry opponent. De Valera, as in the past, turned them down. The refusal, the APL leadership said, was heard 'with a sense of shame'.

The gap with Labourite Belfast was once again emphasised when Diamond wrote welcoming the decision. As an alternative to the 'impracticality' of Dáil seats, he proposed an eight point programme of action including defence of voluntary schools, ending of discrimination, unequal local government franchise, extra legal powers, a campaign for full democratic rights and maximum north-south co-operation. Keeping up the pressure on Dublin, Canon Maguire wrote to De Valera on 30 November conveying the sense of desperation: 'Our people are leaderless – have no policy – do not attend Stormont four out of nine – they fight nothing as a body. They are hopeless and we are helpless and though Kelly's declaration at the election has stirred the spirit and may do good, it might,' he cautioned, 'lead to an outbreak and do harm.'

Healy had admitted to the Canon their difficulty in keeping their 'lads at Stormont'.[24] Whether attacked from one side by abstentionists or from the other by such as Ernest Blythe, who suggested a policy of nationalist dissolution within the north as a prelude to community agreement, the nationalists continued to look to Dublin for succour. In a debate with Blythe – whom the APL denounced as 'one of the guilty men of partition, now blaming the victims for the effects of his own betrayal' – Lennon their representative proposed that Dublin should assist Catholic education, establish industries along the border, provide finance for more clerical houses, extend the Arts Council to the north, set up a government ministry for reunification and finance all from the public purse.[25] Nothing on these lines was of course forthcoming. In April the impotence of the League was emphasised when during Sir Anthony Eden's visit to Belfast they requested a meeting with him. Not only did he not reply, he reaffirmed his support for partition and the Belfast parliament.

McAteer on 30 March confirmed a 'falling off in formal organisation' but denied there was any 'falling off in the determination of the people'.[26] It was whistling past the graveyard. Throughout 1954 the attentions of these same people were increasingly being directed to events outside parliament. Liam Kelly, jailed for six months for making a seditious speech at his victory celebration, was, in July, nominated by the Taoiseach John A. Costello to the Southern Senate on the urging of Sean McBride, whose party held the balance of power since the May 1954 elections. Both the occasion of his nomination and of his release were marked by huge demonstrations in Pomeroy. On the latter occasion 10,000 people filled the tiny village to hear speakers including Sean McBride. When the RUC attempted to seize the tricolour, a serious street battle ensued which wrecked the village and left scores injured. This incident resulted from the new legislation on the flying of the tricolour, the 'Flags and Emblems' Act, pushed through Stormont by the unionist government after its High Court defeat on this issue in the Armagh case. As the legislation went through parliament nationalist opposition was sporadic and ineffectual. Only five of their number turned up in February during the committee stage. 'Fortunately for us,' Healy recalled, 'it had to be postponed'. They had not turned abstentionist but 'believed only in a theoretical attendance'. Abstentionism, in his view, had been tried for ten years and proved futile. Were a convention to be summoned it could only end in 'some groups walking out and showing our disunity upon the very issue that does not matter'. Healy and Gormley had earlier waved a tricolour in the house at Canon Maguire's suggestion. Gormley was suspended for the incident.[27]

A further problem facing the Nationalist representatives was that a majority of the APL executive comprised non-parliamentary members, leaving it open to manipulation by unelected pro-abstentionists. With the republican threat growing, Maguire told Healy in April that they were 'creeping back to 1916'.[28] At a commemoration of the rising at Knocknafallon, Healy had commented scathingly on the Easter Rising as a 'Dead Sea Apple' for people north and south – reminding his audience of Pearse's acceptance of the 1911 Councils Bill which both the Irish Party and the hierarchy rejected. It was a theme to which Healy would return.

In July 1954 when Conor Cruise O'Brien brought the English Jesuit and Oxford Lecturer, Fr Wingfield-Digby, to the north for the purpose of 'indoctrinating' him on the state of affairs there, and met the usual nationalist informants – McAteer, the Omagh Group, and Senator Lennon as well as figures in Belfast such as the Irish Labour Party Councillor Mary O'Malley – a picture presented itself of a society in a state of flux.

Since the Gough barracks arms raid in July, IRA training and recruitment had increased particularly in County Tyrone. There was 'universal approbation, even glee' amongst nationalists at the arms raid, all were agreed. McAteer spoke of 'very general satisfaction' that 'the Dublin government had not condemned the raiders'. In his view, it raised the morale of a population which had 'been rather cowed and defeatist'. All were agreed that this approval was given 'in more or less sporting spirit' without reflecting on the 'consequences or logical conclusion' of the policy which the raids represented.[29] The IRA was not yet a political force and Kelly's movement had 'little or no influence' outside his own immediate Mid Tyrone area. Abstentionism was, however, gaining ground especially in Tyrone and Fermanagh, with a bid likely to be made for the Westminster seats at the next British general election.[30] The abstentionists were divisible into those who treated the policy 'as an end in itself' and those who regarded it as a preparation for the use of force. O'Brien's informants could speak with authority on these points. Some had IRA contacts while Lennon was related by marriage to Liam Kelly.[31] On the consequences of a renewed IRA campaign there was divided opinion that bloodshed would alienate the Catholic population and provoke reprisals.[32] The APL itself was drifting. McAteer repeatedly emphasised that they were 'not committed to anyone of action' and would support 'anything that seems to promise even partial results'.[33]

On 28 October a Dáil motion by Jack McQuillan calling for a 'right of audience' was defeated even more conclusively than in 1951 with all of Fine Gael uniting with Fianna Fáil to oppose it. Costello proposed the reconstitution of the Unity Council which had not met since 1952: 'Let me say it is a poor thing but mine own. I started it … it made some progress but never reached fruition' he told the Dáil.[34] As part of its case against Dáil representation the government quoted comments on the subject by the nationalist members, most notable the rejection of the idea by Healy and Traynor at the Fermanagh national Convention, on the grounds that it would force the APL into 'taking sides' in southern politics, something they had not done since the 1930s. Furthermore, Costello told the Dáil, he had not received correspondence from any northern representative in support of the idea.[35] This was not altogether true as Healy had written to Costello enclosing a ten-point memorandum on the subject, the thrust of which was that the Republic of Ireland Act would be given substance by permitting right of audience to the Westminster MPs.[36] The Stormont seats were, he acknowledged, a different matter. This change of front was caused not only by the vote for Dáil admission at the Omagh convention and the feeling of 'almost all of our people' that there should be closer relations with the Republic. There was also the looming threat of the extra parliamentarians. As he reminded Costello, 'the position has changed somewhat of late since the elected representatives of unoccupied Ireland have elected to the Senate one who has not been following a constitutional course hitherto. If the Dáil takes no further steps it will be assumed that the physical force policy is the only one which meets with approval down here.'

Following the defeat of McQuillan's motion, McAteer wrote to Costello asking that the northern representative be accorded simply 'a courtesy audience'.[37] On the refusal of the request he commented that 'the two main parties … are determined that no reproachful voice from the north will disturb their Kathleen Mavourneen policy on partition'.[38] A request from the APL Secretary, Senator McGill, for clarification of government policy brought a promise from Costello to 'facilitate an Advisory Council if it still existed'.[39]

Under the impact of the growing militancy in the north, a gulf was opening also between the APL and its southern supporters, the Anti-Partition Association, long known for its hard-line stance. The APA, at its November 1953 Ard Fheis, passed a resolution favouring abstentionism in the north until Kelly was released unconditionally. It was in fact a compromise motion devised by the Chairman, Eoin (The Pope) O'Mahony, to avoid a more extreme suggestion that abstention be adopted without time limit.[40] But despite their explanations to the League and their protestations of non-partisanship the damage was done. The following March, Healy told O'Mahony who had asked for his help in the forthcoming Easter Celebrations, 'It will be difficult to work up any enthusiasm for your day this year after the resolution … which meant a repudiation of the northern MPs, especially those from the two counties of Fermanagh and Tyrone'.[41] When Patrick O'Reilly, the APA President, wrote a week later to Healy attempting to distance the Association from those who 'let loose ... steam' at conventions, Healy told him that his letter did not clear him 'of wanting' to 'dissociate' himself from the APL: 'clearly you think another more in line with your policy here than we are. You adopted their ideas and rejected ours.' For a considerable time he had witnessed a drift into extremism by the Association and a consequent 'turning away of the public from your Association'.[42] Their 'stupid resolution,' he told him, had 'shattered' the determination of the northern branches who were willing to spend up to £500 a year on bringing bands from Northern Ireland to Dublin for the parade. 'Do you think we enjoy being spat upon?' Healy asked.[43] And this was the representative view in the League. As Healy could tell O'Reilly, he had for long been a defender of theirs when others 'thought they saw the direction' in which the APA was 'drifting'.[44] The APA continued its efforts to 'keep going without loss of friendship,' as Maire Comerford put it, in the situation created by the entry of republicans. Healy considered her request an 'extraordinary document', accused her of regarding the League 'on the same level as Sinn Féin and Clann Uladh' and told her openly to go to Sinn Féin and 'your new found allies' for support in organising parades. 'Do you think we have lost all self-respect?' he concluded by asking.[45]

Throughout early 1955 northern nationalists continued their discussions with the Taoiseach, John A Costello, on the securing of greater north-south co-operation. After a meeting on 17 January with Eddie McAteer, Michael O'Neill, Joe Stewart, Patrick McGill and Cahir Healy, agreement was reached for the holding of regular consultations.[46] With Sinn Féin committed to contesting the forthcoming Westminster election Conor Cruise O'Brien was sent north in February to prepare a report for the government. The picture he painted was one of widespread nationalist demoralisation. Healy in his role as Westminster MP was 'widely regarded as written off' in the constituency and had announced he would not be going forward. O'Neill, the Mid Ulster MP was, in McAteer's view, 'overawed by Westminster'. McGill regarded him and the rest of the Omagh Group, himself included, as 'out of touch with the younger generation of active nationalists'.[47] O'Brien concluded that, 'with the exception of McAteer who was exceptionally energetic and sanguine and one or two others who were simply cynical', the APL executive including Healy and O'Neill were 'tired and bewildered' by the seeming impossibility of ending partition.[48] McAteer realised that the clergy would endeavour to prevent a three-cornered contest and, with its unrivalled contacts in the IRA and Fianna Uladh, was attempting to work out a deal with Sinn Féin. O'Brien hoped for the success of this strategy as such a deal would, he felt, reduce the Sinn Féin momentum.[49] He had earlier proposed the inclusion of Fianna Uladh on the Advisory Council as a means of dividing the republican forces and slowing 'the drift towards violence'.[50] McGill, in a reflection of the confusion gripping the APL, had enquired of the government as to whether or not there should be co-operation with Sinn Féin and Kelly's organisation.[51]

The republicans for their part were in no mood for co-operation with anybody, buoyed up by the rising tide of militancy following the Armagh and Omagh raids. 'We had the bit between our teeth. After the Easter Commemoration, it was a straight gallop to the Westminster elections in May,' IRA Army Council member Ruairí Ó Brádaigh recalls.[52] A series of shootings by the B Specials, one of them fatal, ratcheted up the tension.

In this fast changing climate the APL was still hoping for a lifeline from the south.[53] On 22nd April Costello reported to the Cabinet a discussion which he and the Minister for External Affairs, Liam Cosgrave, had with a group of nationalist representatives in regard to arrangements for contesting of the seats on 26 May. Following consideration of the Taoiseach's report, the Cabinet appointed a Ministerial Committee to keep 'the situation under review' and take any action thought 'necessary and desirable'.[54] The following day Healy, O'Neill, Stewart and McGill met officials in the Department of External Affairs. They complained of the way in which anti-partition activity in Britain and elsewhere had tended to 'bog down' and reiterated their request for a separate Departmental Publicity Bureau. On that same theme, they expressed concern at the performance of the Irish News Agency[55] and the publication arm of the Mansion House Committee, whose proposed handbook on partition had not yet appeared. They were pessimistic about their chances in the Westminster election but felt that Sinn Féin's lack of personation agents, and the abstention of moderate nationalists, would lead to the unionists taking the seats. They confessed to divided counsels on the question of whether or not to put forward a can-

didate. Despite the influence of the church on nationalist politics, which all acknowledged, there was little chance of the
Cardinal using his influence against the physical force candidate.[56] A major interest of the clergy was to 'prevent deep splits
among their flocks'. As such advice would have the effect of
'splitting, even destroying, many social, charitable, sporting and
other organisations under church patronage' the 'clerical influence', while not pro-Sinn Féin, 'would be in the direction of
avoiding conflict'.[57] A crucial factor in determining many voters
would be the attitude of Dáil Éireann. If both the Taoiseach and
Eamon De Valera were to endorse jointly the official League
candidate that would be decisive for a great many people, they
claimed. O'Neill attributed much of Liam Kelly's support in Mid
Tyrone to the publicity he received on Radio Éireann, which
gave the impression to voters that the Dublin government was
backing him against the APL candidate. Were the long promised
Unity Council to come into being and endorse candidates, the
backing of the Taoiseach and De Valera 'might be possible', he
hoped. The view in the ministry was that this suggestion was a
'ticklish matter' and could only be 'passed on' to the government.[58] Strangely enough the week before, when Costello met a
deputation from South Armagh including McGleenan, he told
them that the decision on admission to the Dáil was 'for the
moment' and 'not necessarily final'. He was, however uncon-
vinced as to the merits of admission he said.[59] It was indicative
of how Dublin was prepared to play politics with the situation.
Costello was leaving the door ajar for the most hardline elements, a sop no doubt to McBride who was backing his minority
government. Yet like De Valera, whose deputy Frank Aiken
had, it will be recalled, endorsed McGleenan in the crucial 1950
by-election, he had no qualms about slamming that door firmly
shut when they or any of their more moderate colleagues attempted to cross the threshold.

Sinn Féin emerges
Originally Sinn Féin had intended to run prominent republicans
for the winnable Westminster seats of Mid Ulster and
Fermanagh and South Tyrone, but because of the emotional pull
of the Armagh and Omagh raids, prisoners made up the majority
of the nominees.[60] The nationalist convention at Omagh, confronted with the determination of Sinn Fein to go forward,

decided not to field a candidate. E. V. McCullagh advocated this course in order not to reveal the divisions present at the convention which he felt was by a majority opposed to the candidate Tom Mitchell. Mitchel went forward proposed, by Fr McIntyre of Strabane, the seconder of Michael O'Neill at the previous convention in 1951. At the Fermanagh South Tyrone convention in Enniskillen, Philip Clarke was nominated by Canon Maguire of Newtownbutler. The Canon himself had attempted to secure a council seat earlier in the month and ended up losing it to the unionists. He later complained that the people had preferred to vote for Tories than for him.[61] Cahir Healy, in an impassioned speech, opposed the candidate on the grounds that the Sinn Féiners were southern interlopers and were gearing up for a physical force policy. In remarks which were later to be misconstrued by unionists as support for violence, he stated that he was 'not opposed to physical force' but 'the time selected should offer some chance of success'. He argued against abstentionism as having been tried for ten years since 1935 and then abandoned. On the question of registration, on which the nationalists had spent 'thousands of pounds keeping up the register', he predicted that the Sinn Féiners' lack of a northern organisation would allow the register to fall into decline and lead to unionist control. The nationalists would be 'nobody's children', he predicted. After three hours of debate, the convention, by a majority of 114 voters to 71, chose Clarke over Healy's nominee, Frank Traynor of Ederny.[62]

In occupational terms the Sinn Féin candidates were predominately manual working class and white collar employees. Mitchell was a Dublin Corporation labourer, Clarke a Civil Servant and other candidates included labourers, a bus conductor, a baker, a brick layer and a sheet metal worker. In a replay of 1935 most of those speaking on their platforms came from the south, many of the same people covering several constituencies. One IRA Army Council member regards this fact as deceptive. There were, he asserted, many northern republicans working 'on the ground', their lack of visibility a result of their vulnerability to RUC harassment. On his calculation 40-50% of those involved in the campaign were six county republicans, the remainder made up of regular nationalist workers determined to hold the seat.[63] Sinn Féin in its election manifesto stressed that the 'winning of seats' was not regarded by them as an 'end in

itself', the results would not 'affect' the 'determination of republicans to forge ahead towards their objective'. Neither, they
asserted, would the number of votes cast be looked upon as
'something in the nature of a plebiscite affecting in any way
Ireland's right to unity'. That 'right' was, they claimed, 'inalien-
able and non-judiciable and must never be put in issue through
a referendum of a section of population nor of the people of the
county at large'. The election was simply 'an opportunity for
people to renew their allegiance to Ireland and to demonstrate
to England and the world' their view on the question of the
union with Britain. There was no question of their speaker seeking an endorsement for a campaign of physical force. Michael
Traynor, the Sinn Féin secretary and himself a candidate in
South Antrim, stated in Fermanagh that 'they were a constitutional movement advocating only constitutional means. 'We are
not,' he told his listeners, 'asking Irishmen and women to go out
bearing arms for freedom; we are only asking every man to do
his duty to his neighbour, the Christian duty of seeing that they
are well clothed and well housed.'[64] As befitting an organisation
which had sent the copy of its inaugural constitution to sympathetic clergy for vetting, he was at pains to deny any 'smear' that
they were a communist organisation.[65] The APL had admitted
privately to Dublin's representative that this allegation which
they themselves rejected entirely, was believed by members of
the Roman Catholic Hierarchy.[66] Only Seamus Sorahan broke
ranks on issue of violence with an intemperate speech in High
Street, Belfast, disapproved of in Army Council circles, and even
he had stated on Clarkes's platform in Enniskillen that they
were 'not there to preach the doctrine of physical force'.

One activist, who would later distinguish himself as a left-
wing opponent of militant republicanism, welded together the
national and social questions and had Traynor claiming that as
'realists' they knew 'only a united Ireland could solve the problems of unemployment and emigration'.[67] He also gave expression to the double-think at the heart of the nationalist and republican view of Protestant unionists. At the June victory parade in
Dungannon, he defined the enemy as 'the British forces' telling
northern Protestants who 'wished to fight alongside them' that
they were 'Quislings who forfeited the rights of Irishmen'.[68]

Only in Belfast did Sinn Féin face a serious non-unionist opponent. There Jack Beattie fought desperately to retain the seat

regained by such a slim margin in 1951. He stressed that he was a representative of Irish Labour, the party in power in the Dublin government and told his electors he was 'at all costs prepared to resist physical force', that he 'believed in the democracy he lived under' and that Sinn Féin's policies would lead to a revival of the troubles of the 1920s.[69]

The final Sinn Féin performance across the north, 152,310 ballots to a unionist total of 442,647, looked impressive on paper. But it had been boosted by the contesting of seats in areas untouched by nationalists and unwinnable, making it the largest non-unionist vote until then in the history of the north. On close examination, the returns in the winnable constituencies of Fermanagh South Tyrone and Mid Ulster, reflected not vigour but decline. Mitchell's poll was more than 4,000 below that obtained by Michael O'Neill in 1951 while the 1951 result in Fermanagh South Tyrone which helped win that constituency, an entry still unmatched in the *Guinness Book of Records,* had fallen by 2,288. Relative to the 1950 performance the republican vote revealed a drop of over 2,000 on Hugh McAteer's showing in Derry but an increase of over 7,000 on Jimmy Steele's vote in West Belfast, an achievement which, taken with the slump in Beattie's to 16,050, exposed the cumulative effect of the dissent faced by the latter within his party over the years. Not in a single constituency did Sinn Féin's tally exceed that obtained by Labour in 1950 and only in one did it come anywhere near it (within 2,000 votes in South Down). In all the Belfast constituencies Labour beat Sinn Féin into third place.

In Fermanagh South Tyrone, Clarke was disqualified by court order and the seat given to the unionist. The Mid Ulster election was referred to the House of Commons which ordered a second contest. On 11 August Sinn Féin put forward Mitchell again. The *Dungannon Observer* of 23 July noted, 'Once more it will be a straight fight between the unionists and Sinn Féin. There will be one important difference however. On this occasion the Sinn Féin candidate will have the active and whole hearted support of nearly every anti-partitionist in the country.' The results went some way towards proving it right. Mitchell increased his mandate to 30,392 – a climb of over 600. The unionist vote rose by a little over 100 to 29,586. For the second time in three months the Dublin labourer, serving ten years as guest of Her Majesty, was returned as the Honourable Member for the Mid Ulster Constituency.

On this occasion the authorities did what they had already done in the case of the Fermanagh South Tyrone result; the unionist runner-up Charles Beattie was awarded Mitchell's seat by court order. Thus it appeared the matter had finally been laid to rest.

At the end of July, with the by-election campaign still ongoing, the Department of External Affairs in Dublin sent Conor Cruise O'Brien, Eoin McWhite and John Belton to visit 'anti-partition centres' in the north and ascertain the lie of the land. Outside members of the Omagh Group there was unanimity that Sinn Féin would win the Mid Ulster by-election, a view also endorsed by Senator McGill, regarded by them as the 'shrewdest member of the group'. On their assessment of Sinn Féin's strength one councillor, O'Doherty in Derry, put the figure for 'real Sinn Féin supporters' as low as 3%. An 'important qualification' was added, 'it is only too clear that support for a policy of fighting partition by any and all means – including terrorism where this can be effectively used – is very much more widespread than support for the present Sinn Féin organisation'. McAteer and O'Doherty put the figure for 'any and all means' as high as 70% and stressed that it included 'Derry and Ulster nationalists generally'. 'How much of this is genuine and how much merely theoretical – representing a determination not to be outdone by Sinn Féin – is difficult to estimate', the report commented.[70] The general opinion was that Fianna Uladh would 'fizzle out' as it had 'no real political policy' and that the Stormont seats were safe from Sinn Féin partly because that organisation – unlike Kelly and McGleenan – felt itself debarred by the oath from standing. In addition, nationalists remained confident that the large majorities by which they held their Stormont seats made them immune to any Sinn Féin challenge. Regarding the possibility of a government crackdown on the IRA in the south, it was believed that the Omagh group and McSparran favoured 'locking up the people who were doing the recruiting for IRA', something which Monsignor Arthur Ryan of Queen's University felt would be the most useful means of promoting better north-south relations. McAteer was opposed to 'any such idea' as long as 'that movement confined itself to non-military activities in the twenty-six counties'. He despised the Omagh Group for having opened the door to Sinn Féin through their 'lethargy and inactivity' and regarded many of their remarks as a case of 'sour grapes'.[71]

On the issue of north-south co-operation, Belfast nationalists – it was reported – were 'inclined to favour such a policy'. Diamond and his friends who tended to 'flirt with the IRA' were 'not very important exceptions' to this trend. The Omagh Group who had declined in prestige had not any strong opinions on the subject, though Michael O'Neill supported it and hoped for its extension. McAteer, who retained his power in Derry undamaged by the electoral intervention, represented the 'most extreme section of official nationalism'. He was 'unenthusiastic' about it but, it was emphasised, 'did not oppose it as a line to be taken by the government in Dublin'. Like most nationalists outside Belfast, this was different from their co-operation with Stormont which after the World War Two analogy of McAteer's pamphlet, *Irish Action*, they dubbed 'collaboration'.[72] No objections were likely to be raised to Dublin's continuing policy, the deputations reported, provided cognisance was taken by the government of the discrimination suffered by northern nationalists. The exposure of issues such as the Mater Hospital would continue to retain nationalist confidence in Dublin, it was felt.

On the question of where the APL was going, the Omagh Group wished to transform it into a formal party organisation. As things stood, there had been little change since the state was formed.[73] In Westminster constituencies conventions were chosen on a basis of two from each parish, at after-Mass meetings. In the case of Stormont the pattern varied; in East Tyrone the AOH provided all the machinery and nominated the candidate, in another, each parish priest nominated two delegates whilst in a third the nominees of all Catholic organisations, including the St Vincent de Paul and the AOH, went forward. The Omagh Group proposed to put forward their ideas at the League executive meeting. Eddie McAteer rejected the Omagh idea and claimed that the nationalist organisation, 'odd as it looked to outside observers', answered local needs 'quite well'. With his opposition the Omagh proposals would be unlikely to succeed, it was reported.[74] Since the Omagh Group intended to seek a Dublin subvention for the work, McWhite, Belton and O'Brien advised against such a course in the absence of unanimity on the issue. The League was first to be required to show 'some signs of attempting to put itself on its own feet'. The southern government pledged to continue its links with the 'Irish Association' whose 150 'hand-picked members' commanded weight in business and upper middle class circles in Belfast. It was already, they had been told, 'having a distinct effect on the tone in relation to 'the south' among the 'upper social layers' in Belfast.[75]

The *Observer* chain of newspapers, run by the Mallon family of Dungannon, had developed into an important ally of republicans and a counterweight to the North West Publishing Company's influence. The Irish Embassy in Washington reported in February 1954 that Oliver Mallon and his brother Austin, editors and publishers of the *Observer* newspaper in Dungannon, had championed Liam Kelly's cause among the Irish Americans. At the Hotel Commodore in New York, Oliver Mallon spoke of Liam Kelly as symbolising the spirit of the men of the north and told the *Irish Echo* newspaper that he 'advocated the adoption of a more vigourous policy'. 'It would appear,' wrote Joe Horan to his Departmental colleague Conor Cruise O'Brien, 'that Messrs Mallon and Co are the representatives of the Liam Kelly organisation recently started in the six counties'. A former IRA Army Council member recalled to this author the greater 'objectivity' of the *Observer* group in its coverage of the IRA campaign.[76]

The Dublin government continued to maintain a watching brief. When Belton and McWhite went north again in September to assess the situation, little had changed since their July report. Any analysis of Sinn Féin, they concluded, was rendered more difficult by their ability to attract the 'voting support of a large body' of nationalists ordinarily opposed to them. This ability, they felt, derived from the fact that voting Sinn Féin was the only way of expressing opposition to unionism. They did not feel that the movement had the 'wholehearted support' of either believers in physical force, e.g. Hugh McAteer, nor of the 'abstentionist' group, though many in both camps would tend to choose Sinn Féin preference to the APL.[77] The report went on:

> Estimates of the effective strength of Sinn Féin in northern nationalists prepared to give support either by 'active service' or sheltering men on the run etc., range around the 5% mark. The personnel concerned here are mainly concentrated in rural areas consisting largely of the farm labouring type and the sons of small farmers who have no family or other responsibilities. Their educational level is low. On the whole their sincerity is not doubted. The character and integrity of the men now under prison sentences here has, we are informed, even won the respect of many unionists.

Though it concluded that Sinn Fein's voting strength averaged 23-35% of the nationalist electorate, both McAteer and Professor McCauley in Derry were chary of accepting the figure. The ability of the IRA to pull off a successful coup a few days before an election would, according to them, 'have an electrifying effect on the voters'. Contrariwise, with public memory so forgetful, it would take only a 'few failures' to make Sinn Féin disappear.[78]

The Iveagh House analysis discounted the possibility that the largely symbolic Westminster election victories could be translated onto the plane of everyday policies:

> While there are differences of opinion as to the value of attendance at Westminster, all shades of nationalist opinion are agreed that representation at Stormont is the only protection the minority have against the more vicious forms of discrimination and exploitation. Ecclesiastical properties (e.g. the Mater Hospital, Belfast) and education matters give the church a vested interest in Stormont and the majority of nationalists will never oppose the wishes of the church. If Sinn Féin were to be so rash as to try to enter the Stormont elections on some sort of abstentionist basis, they would alienate most of their support and solidify their opponents in the nationalist camp.[79]

On attitudes within the Roman Catholic Church, the Omagh Group confirmed for the deputation what the elections had made obvious – that 'a few priests' had 'certain Sinn Féin sympathies' thought it was not clear whether or not this simply reflected 'abstentionist' feeling on their part. Senator Lennon, who was on 'close friendly terms with Cardinal D'Alton', did not expect him to go beyond his remarks of the previous December when he warned the clergy in his diocese against encouraging support for Sinn Féin. The capacity of the issue to divide parishioners would, Lennon felt, make priests on the ground 'reluctant to take a stand'. The complexity of the hierarchial attitude was summed up by Monsignor Arthur Ryan when the deputation made contact with him the previous July. Asked if the hierarchy were 'anxious, willing, able or prepared to come out openly against Sinn Féin', his reply was 'anxious, yes; willing, no; able, yes; prepared, no'.[80]

Virtually all those Belton and McWhite met confirmed that the 'nationalists were suffering under an acute sense of frustration' and that Sinn Féin's success reflected this. More disturbingly from their point of view, the movement had 'not been successful in attracting young men. It generally recognised' they commented, 'that there is no early prospect of ending partition and the importance of ensuring that the nationalist movement continues on after the present leaders, who are in their middle forties and upwards, pass away is considerable'.

Even though the department officials remained sceptical about the Omagh Group's idea of a 'Nationalist and Anti-Partition Party' knowing that 'such would not be welcomed by all shades of opinion', they stressed the importance of 'strengthening the League as the most immediate step'. When the League members' criticism of 'lack of leadership' from Dublin was met with queries as to what Dublin 'could do to help them', they listed their wants, the most important of which was the making of a public declaration on behalf of the Dublin government expressing its 'whole-hearted support for them'. Such an official statement would, they all agreed, be 'the most effective single weapon against Sinn Féin that the League could have and use'.[81] Other requests made by the League had in the past foundered on objections from Dublin. Air time on Radio Éireann had, for instance, been turned down lest it provoke 'retaliation from the BBC'. Belton and McWhite felt, however, that a formula could be devised to satisfy this request without producing such a response. Such a scheme might, in their view, influence the 'floating vote, generally in this context the poorly informed rural people'. Likewise the demand for government support could be met by a public declaration. They warned Dublin that 'ill advised if honest statements' … that no solution to partition existed should be 'dropped or at least not given publicity since they were having 'a most depressing effect on northern nationalists', and they noted in conclusion the complaints from McSparran and others that the appointment of Liam Kelly to the Seanad – a house to which the APL members had not been admitted – was an 'official blessing on Fianna Uladh' and implied a reflection on the League.[82] On the issue of registration and financial assistance, Dublin had already turned down the League's request for a paid registration agent in the north, an idea which Healy in any event did not approve. Nevertheless, 'universal agreement' existed that nationalist registration in the north 'was in a bad way and that a definite danger was present of losing the existing majorities'. Apart from Derry, generally regarded as the most efficient body in the six counties, the position elsewhere was mixed. Fermanagh was 'fairly good' but had 'room for improvement' as many had dropped from the register. Armagh had 'fallen to pieces' since the League was set up and was in the process of being reorganised. Mid Ulster had 'broken down'. O'Neill estimated, a loss of 1,000 voters per year.[83] Only in Newry, where a citizens protection organisation was set up by Joe Connellan, who still remained on the League executive, had 'anything positive been done'. Worst of all, of course, were those areas where nationalists' chances of winning were non-existent. Although no seats would be gained there, it was 'felt desirable' that the 'leakage be stopped' as these areas contributed to the total APL vote and a decline accordingly strengthened the case for partition.

On the co-operation policy, a fine line had to be walked where condemnations of Sinn Féin by northern nationalists were concerned. The APL view, despite its hostility to this organisation, was that such language merely encouraged the unionists. Across the spectrum APL representatives united on this from the McAteer group in Derry, who felt that to condemn Sinn Féin was 'to do Stormont's dirty work for them', to McSparran who confessed himself 'fed up', a term he used repeatedly, with comments which would, he felt, simply result in unionists increasing their demands.[84] The crucial fact in the making of such condemnations was the context in which they were expressed. 'They stated quite bluntly that ... a good opportunity had been lost to throw the blame for the rise onto the physical force element into Stormont' and they 'would have welcomed' the 6 September condemnation of the republican movement by a Dublin minister had 'this point been made that Sinn Féin and IRA activities were only the result of Stormont's intransigence' and disregard of the minority's constitutional rights.[85] Such a statement would, they felt, have the added advantage of embarrassing Stormont in its dealings with Britain. McAteer stated that he himself would make a speech on these lines when Brookeborough next called for extradition but would prefer if a Dublin minister spoke instead.

The reaction of northern nationalists to the Irish Association ranged from a 'certain amount of goodwill' in Belfast, where 'old Queen's University men' like McSparran regarded it in much the same innocuous light as a university debating society, to the 'rather cynical attitude' in Derry which viewed it as a

'coffee cup coterie'. 'It's not a bad thing' they added, by way of
qualification. Senator Lennon doubted its effectiveness but was
prepared to join if it 'would do any good', a course advised
against by McWhite who felt his position in the APL would suffer as a result.

McWhite's conclusion on the nationalist attitude to the
north-south co-operation policy was that while 'various elements of the nationalist press, such as the *Derry Journal*, could
never publicly welcome it for fear of being accused of collabora-
tionism, the policy was generally favourably received in nationalist quarters'.[86] Lennon considered it an 'excellent proposal'
and a useful means to 'knock down barriers in employment'. If
an anti-discrimination clause was made a condition for receipt
of funds he felt it would be 'generally welcomed' by nationalists.
Similarly McAteer considered 'an orangeman as good as anyone
else' when the question arose of filling jobs in the south where
trained personnel were in short supply.[87]

This point also tied in with the attempt to revive the APL.
There was general agreement that prominence in nationalist
politics was a bar to advancement in the northern professions.
The requirement on the use of Irish excluded them from many
positions south of the border, McWhite stated, laying emphasis
on the 'problem of attracting young men into the nationalist
movement' – a serious problem which 'will soon have to receive
serious attention'.

The Omagh Group, looking to the future, said they were
'prepared to fight all comers in any forthcoming election'. This
'general stiffening of the APL against Sinn Féin' was welcomed
by McWhite as a 'definite improvement'.[88]

Sooner than anyone expected, the opportunity came to put
all of this to the test when at the end of the year the House of
Commons disqualified Charles Beattie from his Mid Ulster seat,
as the holder of offices of profit under the Crown, and forced a
third election in the constituency.

The 1956 Mid Ulster by-election
When on 14 January the APL announced they would oppose
Mitchell, it looked at first as if a straight fight would take place
between two schools of nationalism for the seat. With this in
mind, the *Belfast Telegraph* on the 16th advised unionists to take
the 'long term' rather than the 'short term' view, reminding its

readers that 'if Sinn Féin was the common enemy as we believe it is when the long term view should prevail'.

The point was well taken. A unionist convention presided over by the Duke of Abercorn decided by a large majority not to enter the lists. As expected, the Sinn Féin convention on the 21st selected Mitchell again and the nationalists, meeting shortly afterwards, chose Michael O'Neill, the former Westminster MP. Despite the entry of a Dungannon shopkeeper, McQuaid, running as a 'business candidate', it still looked effectively like a two-horse race. Then ten minutes before the close of nomination an auctioneer and livestock salesman, George Forrest from Dungannon, emerged to fight in the unionist interest. Disclaiming any hostility to the OUP, he said simply that loyalists should have the choice of a Protestant candidate. As no less a person than the British Prime Minister, Sir Anthony Eden, had been rebuffed by Brookeborough when he wrote protesting at the idea of a contest 'between one Sinn Féin faction and another, letting the violent and non-violent Sinn Féins fight it out'[89] and as the Unionist Association in Mid-Ulster had endorsed the idea of non-participation, the emergence of Forrest 'like a hedgehog in spring', in Cahir Healy's words, seems almost inexplicable. It became clear the following June when the newly elected Forrest sought admission to the ranks of Official Unionism. Abercorn admitted to Terence O'Neill, whose support he sought for Forrest's admission, that a backbench revolt, largely centred on the B Specials in the constituency, had occurred. As a result both he and Dame Dehra Parker, who had pioneered the original abstentionist decision, found themselves 'on a sticky wicket'. She in particular had 'incurred a great deal of unpopularity'.[90]

In his election address Michael O'Neill stressed what he saw as the 'misrepresentation' of the Mid Ulster nationalist electorate 'twice within the last twelve months for a policy of unlawful physical force'. Particular stress was laid on the word 'unlawful'. The nationalist stand was taken clearly on the presumed right of the Dublin government to be the only body entitled to achieve Irish unity by violent means. P. J. Gormley, as one of the few Nationalist MPs to support O'Neill openly, stated at an eve of poll rally in Magherafelt, where the Sinn Féiners followed the Nationalist on the platform:

> This is not an election for a seat at Westminster; it would probably go to Forrest. This is really a referendum of nation-

alist opinion on whether they held that the proper authority to use force in the six counties against the British is the Irish government. Many of us would prefer a policy of force by the government in Dublin but the authority rests solely with them and not with individual well-wishers.[91]

Sinn Féin, in its election manifesto, invoked the 1918 election. It claimed:

The electorate will be able to demonstrate to the world the right of an ancient and historic nation to its complete and absolute freedom and independence. The policy which Sinn Féin is pursuing in relation to what is termed the Irish government is clearly defined in its National Union and Independent programme ... the main concern is to get the British forces out of Ireland and the use of physical force in the twenty-six counties is not contemplated.

Members of the republican movement, it averred, did not seek 'civil war with fellow Irishmen or sectarian strife', the threat of physical violence deriving from the 'presence of foreign soldiers on Irish soil and not from the activities of Irish men who bear arms in support of British aggression'.[92] O'Neill's manifesto emphasised Sinn Féin's character as a southern party which had, it claimed, simply obtained nationalist votes in 'the face of a common enemy'. He invoked the warning issued by the Roman Catholic hierarchy in January, read at all Masses, proclaiming to their flocks that 'sacred scripture gave the right to bear the sword and to use it against evil doers to the supreme authority and to it alone'. It had followed on an earlier condemnation made by the Cardinal of communism which, he claimed, was 'quick to utilise national grievance such as the enforced and unnatural partition of our country and trade on the revered name of history for its purposes'.[93] O'Neill's use of these statements and of others issued by the Dublin government[94] failed to save him from disaster. When the votes were counted he had lost his deposit with 6,421 votes; Mitchell retained 24,124. On a reduced unionist vote, Forrest took the seat. The *Derry Journal* on 11 May commented:

The result of the Mid-Ulster by-election is one that the Irish government cannot afford to ignore. Twenty four thousand nationalists voted against a candidate who rightly, in our opinion, held that the solution of partition was the responsibility of the government and Dáil. This was not a vote in favour of physical force, it was a clear indication of dissatisfaction with the national leadership or the lack of it ... the Dáil – government and opposition – was on trial and found wanting.[95]

Ten days after his defeat, O'Neill called to the Department of External Affairs with his tale of unreciprocated loyalty. He had 'little specific to say', McWhite commented, 'and seemed to be searching more for our reaction than anything else.' O'Neill complained that the lack of speakers was 'absolutely fatal ... they were going for election on the basis of the policy of the Irish government and from the viewpoint of their constituents the lack of speakers, radio support, or some official endorsement made liars out of them'. When 'asked for evidence of this support' O'Neill said they had nothing and were therefore 'accused of trying to use the pronouncements of the bishops and the Taoiseach for their own ends'. This made them feel 'particularly bitter' as 'they were not regarded as liars, false patriots and bad Catholics'. Despite the strictures of the bishops, the clergy of the constituency had failed to fall into line. O'Neill complained 'that some openly supported Sinn Féin, others by their actions, e.g. advising local convents not to vote and denying the use of the church halls to the APL, put them on a par with the episcopally condemned republicans. As the clergy more than any other group were the beneficiaries of the APL's presence at Stormont, he felt it would be 'their own fault' if Sinn Féin abstentionism won the day. In that eventuality he, for one, would have little sympathy for them.[96]

The Sinn Féin victory was far from having been 'a foregone conclusion', O'Neill asserted. With speakers from the twenty-six counties the APL could have had a good chance in the election. Sinn Féin 'had few local persons of standing' but roughly seventy men, mainly of the 30-40 age group, came from the south and spent a fortnight speaking 'in every corner of the constituency'. To make matters worse an eve of poll rumour that he had withdrawn was broadcast on Radio Éireann. This, he estimated, cost him 3,000 votes and ensured the loss of his deposit – which 'hurt financially'.[97]

O'Neill had in fact contemplated withdrawing when Forrest entered the lists and the prospect of gaining any unionist votes vanished. He was perhaps influenced in this direction also by the refusal of those TDs he had approached to support him and by the manoeuvring of Gormley and Stewart. However, he was prevailed upon by the Omagh Group to fight the election. The support of the *Ulster Herald* chain, such as it was, was of little consequence beside the strongly pro-Mitchell slant of the *Observer* group. Election workers paid for by McGill failed to turn up.[98] McAteer in Derry, who had long been a critic of the APL for failing to confront Sinn Féin, maintained an attitude of strict neutrality.

O'Neill had no doubt what the result meant. 'It was,' he said, 'the end of the Anti-Partition League.' He doubted that O'Connor would run again and McSparran was reportedly so frightened that he would not go forward either. Lennon, who still maintained it was right to have contests, admitted that the consequences could be disastrous. And on the APL executive, which had progressively grown away from the Parliamentary Party, Traynor was telling Healy in ominous tones that 'something drastic' would have to be done if they were ever 'to recapture a small part of their former popularity'.[99]

Even before the Mid Ulster debacle, their sanguine view that Sinn Féin posed no threat to their Stormont seats had vanished. On 8 February the northern Attorney General reported that 'several of the Nationalist MPs approached him and suggested that all prospective candidates for Stormont be required to take the Oath of Allegiance *at the time of nomination*' (as distinct from the requirement hitherto of taking it *on* election). Their object was to prevent Sinn Féin candidates going forward as abstentionists whose intervention would, they felt, eventually destroy the Nationalist Party and leave no effective opposition. If the government introduced legislation on the matter, the nationalists assured the Attorney General they 'would not criticise it'.[100] Towards the end of the year the Stormont government introduced a ban on Sinn Féin in the six counties, the pretext being a pro-physical force speech by a member of the organisation in Dublin.

PART FIVE

1957-1969

'We are no nearer success than in 1923.'

Iveagh House memorandum,
assessing the effect of Dublin's northern policy,
January 1957.

CHAPTER 13

The End of the APL

The events of the mid 1950s had pushed the Anti-Partition League off centre stage. Most observers date its demise to the period 1953/54 following Liam Kelly's election, with the events of 1955-56 seen as merely a postscript to its existence and a pro-logue to a republican resurgence. In fact, the debacle of Mid Ulster marked a beginning as well as an end.

In late 1956 and early 1957, Eddie McAteer, MP for Foyle, called to the Department of External Affairs in Dublin. He said that he was anxious that some positive gain should be made from the situation. Despite the unfavourable atmosphere which existed since the outbreak of the border campaign, hints were made to his colleague P. J. Gormley, MP for Mid Derry, which suggested that some unionist leaders felt the violence had its origins in what McAteer described as 'the secondary aspects of partition', i.e. the various forms of discrimination endured by the minority population, coupled with the inability of their spokesmen to achieve results at parliamentary or local govern-ment level. In McAteer's view, the failure of constitutionalism was creating despair and turning young men towards violence. 'The present outbreak would be quelled for a time, only to recur again in five or ten years', something certain unionist leaders now recognised, he claimed. The government should capitalise on it by 'making direct high level but off the record' representations to the British government. The Minister for External Affairs con-sidered McAteer's suggestion 'a good one and worthy of the most serious consideration'.[1]

According to a subsequent set of secret memoranda that January, 'the government since it renounced force as a solution to the problem of partition, could undertake one of the few positive lines of action open to it by strengthening the nationalist minority' through measures contributing to more effective representation,

in London, Belfast and at local level and by improving their social and economic situation'. It asserted that the Irish government 'was under a certain moral obligation' to protect, as far as
it could, the nationalists in the six counties, and claimed that the
implementation of McAteer's suggestion was 'very much in the
national interest'. Barring 'totally unforeseen circumstances … it
was useless entering into discussion on the basic facts of partition and the merits of each others' cases'. Emphasis should instead be placed on the discrimination which made violence inevitable, while at the same time no effort would be spared to
prevent violent actions. Other factors besides Mr McAteer's suggestion encouraged them in this view.

Firstly, the cross border raids had concentrated attention on
the partition issue which was usually 'quietly ignored'.
Secondly, it was felt that the Suez and Cyprus questions would
lead Britain to welcome a respite from 'trouble at their back-
door'. In addition, the cost of maintaining an army and paying
compensation must be burdensome to them. Finally, the minister felt that a significant sector of British opinion wanted change.
He was encouraged in this belief by two editorials in December,
one in the *London Times* of the 19th, which described partition as
'an unresolved and explosive political situation', and the other
in the *Manchester Guardian* of the 15th, asserting that 'Britain
must cease pretending the problem does not exist'. Even a blank
refusal by Whitehall to treat Ireland's representations seriously
would not be altogether useless, as the minister would then be
free to announce on a suitable occasion that he had raised the
matter without result. By and large though, it was felt publicity
would be undesirable and terms such as 'economic activity' or
'European co-operation' would be used to throw the press off
the scent.[2]

All of this was taking place within a wider strategy begun by
the Dublin government. Southern Ireland was moving from
isolationism, imposed upon it by the protectionism of the 1930s
and the neutrality of the war years, and was integrating within
the new world order. With multinational capital about to increase its profile in the economies of both states, a convergence
of interest was inevitable. Ironically, the very night Cronin's
columns were to begin the IRAs disastrous 1950s campaign
crossing the border, the person later to play the largest role in
this economic transformation, Sean Lemass, was addressing a
businessmen's meeting in Belfast.[3]

The twin policies on sovereignty and unity were also being modified to fit the process. On the former, the government directive to heads of missions, which in 1951 instructed ambassadors to stress partition as one of the principle obstacles to neutrality, was by 1955 encouraging the omission of this clause.[4] In August 1954 a memo pointedly stressed that the 1951 admission of Greece to NATO did not affect its claim to Cyprus.[5]

In late 1956 the Taoiseach instructed the Department of External Affairs to prepare a detailed memorandum on the economic, social and political impact of the 'peaceful re-integration of national territory' for the twenty-six counties.

The fruits of the Department's labours were presented in February 1957. The document summarised Irish policy on partition as one based on 'an overestimate of our political influence in the United States and of our present day strategic value in the western European Defence System, together with an underestimate of the after effects of our wartime neutrality. It criticised the futility of the anti-partition campaign in Britain revealed most starkly by the House of Commons vote of 1949 'recognising that the policy of external pressure as exemplified by our refusal to join NATO, and the Fogarty resolution in the USA, has similarly got us nowhere ... We are no nearer to success than in 1923', it stated bluntly. It advocated entry into NATO 'prior to actual reunification and suggested the possibility of Commonwealth membership after it. It acknowledged that the 'higher level of social services, particularly in the field of medical care within Northern Ireland, posed a delicate problem' and recognised that 'any attempt at settlement must face the two most original fears' of northern Protestants – domination by Roman Catholicism and economic ruin. With this in mind the memorandum advocated attempts to win over moderate unionist opinion.[6]

In regard to the United Nations as a forum for grievances, it recognised the fine line which Ireland was forced to walk due both to the weakness of its legal position on partition and the Taoiseach's stated policy that Ireland would never 'subtract from the relative power of the west'. This hampered any policy of seeking allies amongst other post-colonial countries who, if asked, 'would support self determination for the penguins of Antarctica'. Overhanging everything was the Irish sensitivity to feelings in the United States. Even though Ireland's anti-colonial past remained a matter of pride for most of nationalist Ireland, and a source of inspiration to struggling and newly independent nations, Irish foreign policy makers have rarely allowed this sentiment to override their perceived self interest as a potential ally of the western powers, particularly the USA. 'As far as American public opinion is concerned', the document stated, 'Ireland stands to gain or lose more than any other country by her actions in the UN ... a favourable resolution, therefore, even if it could be obtained without American support, would be of little use without such backing.

The memo even went so far as to quantify the number of times America's allies had diverged from her in UN votes in an attempt to measure their own freedom of action. Concerning the actual content of the grievances to be raised, it stressed that action should not be taken at the request of local nationalist deputations 'unless they have the support of general six county nationalist opinion', and it advocated a non-political version of the Mansion House Research Committee to supply accurate information on these matters. It continued in this vein.

> While consideration and encouragement has been given in the past to activities in the Council of Europe and by publicity (e.g. the Mansion House Committee's film on the housing in Fintona) with a view to strengthening the position of nationalists, and at the same time there have been sporadic efforts made with a view to increasing social and cultural co-operation between both sides of the border; there has never been a conscious policy. The recent entry of Sinn Féin into six county policy (sic), coupled with the fact that most of the leaders are elderly men, may mean the disappearance of the present Anti-Partition League in the next few years. The minister is of the opinion that there is scope for action on an all-party basis but that any committee that might be set up should include only parties that advocate the solution of partition by peaceful means, and that have forthrightly condemned the use of force.[8]

They acknowledged that, since this was a long term matter, it shsould be deferred to a later meeting. In regard to northern nationalism, it sought to exploit the old east-west of the Bann divide:

> So far as our experience of northern nationalists is concerned, our experience is that the bitter men of the west come to

Dublin. The more levelheaded nationalists of Belfast do not approach us. It is most desirable that the influence of Derry and Omagh (such as it is) should be counterbalanced by the advice of Armagh and Belfast and that the councils of men like Senators Lennon and Donaghy and Mr Frank Hanna be available to the minister.

One can only wonder what McAteer would have thought of this piece of advice deriving from a process which he, the nationalist with the strongest 'republican' profile, had helped to set in motion. The memo was more than just a belated epitaph on the post-war policy of rhetorical anti-partitionism; it marked the genesis of a new policy which, with some relapses, was to continue to the present day.[9]

Throughout 1957, the change of government notwithstanding, the new approach was evident. Cardinal Dalton followed up his 'Commonwealth' proposal with a call to join the Atlantic Alliance, assuring the Irish people that countries were no less independent for having NATO bases. (The unionist *Northern Whig* was to pay him a wry tribute for his remark.) That September Cornelius Cremin was told over lunch by the historian Frank Pakenham that he had been assured by De Valera that, although any link with the Commonwealth 'as a unilateral step' was out of the question until partition ended, there would not be any objection to an association resembling India's 'as a step concomitant with the reunification of the country'.[10]

Up north, while nationalist political utterances on public platforms retained a dreary familiarity, behind the scenes evidence existed that new thinking was not confined to Eddie McAteer. Ernest Blythe had for long been canvassing the idea that northern nationalists should dissolve their identity within the British Labour movement and the sphere of Irish cultural activities, in order to defuse unionist fears that they constituted a 'fifth column' for a foreign state. In the process of doing this, he contended, their grievances – which he felt were overstated anyway – would be eliminated. Late in 1956 he circularised the nationalist MPs with an extensive memorandum setting out his ideas. On 7 July 1957 Healy wrote to him that the unionists might actually prefer the first state to the second as opposition at Stormont would then be solely on social and economic lines. He went on to tell Blythe he agreed with his point 'that the partition problem had best be soft-pedalled for a considerable time', adding that if it were to cease to be a political issue the present tensions would cease and our people would fare far better in housing and employment up here'.[11] However, he entered the *caveat* that such a development would lead to republican growth in the twenty-six counties which would attract disillusioned youth north and south. The 'real opposition to a united Ireland was', he contended, 'in the six counties'. If a majority within the six counties wanted a united Ireland, England would not stand in their way. 'Her liberal grants make partition work.' It was a startlingly frank admission from a man whose political life began as a Sinn Féiner who, as a member of Michael Collins' North East Ulster Advisory Committee, advocated the destruction of property and communication by the IRA if the Craig-Collins Pact broke down. Coming a few months after McAteer's secret proposals in Dublin, it revealed the moderation and pragmatism for which 'the bitter men of the West' have seldom been given credit. Blythe's proposals may well have had some influence on government thinking. Contained alongside it in the file is an unidentified civil servant's typed memorandum expressing approval of its contents.

The collapse of the nationalist organisation after the January 1956 by-election had been startling. At the end of the year Healy told Frank Trainer that 'the public seemingly are not much interested when we meet or indeed as to whether there is any nationalist organisation at all'.[12] It was a situation which made their performance in the March 1958 Stormont elections the more remarkable. In Foyle on this occasion McAteer defeated a Labour opponent by 6,935 to 5,238 votes, a margin of victory almost as great as he enjoyed over his fellow nationalist, the incumbent Patrick Maxwell, five years before. In South Down Joseph Conellan increased his 1953 vote to 6,686 in a contest which saw the unionist vote also increase and the Independent Labour vote stay the same. In the eight other constituencies nationalists were returned without any opposition from their own side. The *Irish News* recorded polls of 100% in parts of East and West Tyrone. Two problem constituencies for the nationalists were Mid Tyrone and South Armagh. In the former, a farmers' candidate, Thomas Gormley, queered the pitch for the nationalist and pushed him to the bottom of the poll. The unionist took the seat. It was a reflection of the agricultural crisis facing northern farmers that Gormley could come a respectable second on such a limited appeal. In South Armagh the difficulties of that maverick anti-partitionist constituency manifested themselves again. Two nationalists ran an Independents while another candidate styled himself as Independent National Labour. It was, in the words of the *Armagh Observer*, 'one of the smallest polls ever … The decision of Mr Charles McGleenan who, in 1953, was returned unopposed as an abstentionist MP to boycott the election, was to all appearances adhered to by the majority of the constituency'.[13] In the final shake-up the nationalists won ten seats, a respectable tally by any standard. Patrick McGill told Healy on 27 March that the election results were very heartening everywhere, considering the gloomy forecasts on all sides. 'It shows the people are with us … West Tyrone did very well, considering the almost total collapse of our agents, etc. following Mid Ulster'.

At the first party meeting held after the elections, on 31 March where Eddie McAteer was to be proposed for party leader, a surprise development occurred. Not only did his proposer, Senator Lennon, fail to turn up but the Belfast block of MPs, Frank Hanna, Harry Diamond and Senators Donaghy and Doctor Stewart, arrived to discuss common policy. They proposed that they should form a united party and become the official opposition. Eddie McAteer and the Omagh group of Roderick O'Connor and Patrick McGill opposed them. Joe Stewart, Cahir Healy, Patrick O'Hare and Tom Gormley joined with the proponents of the motion. James O'Reilly voted against. When the vote was carried eight to four McAteer threatened to withdraw from the party, while O'Connor bullied the aged Stewart – telling him that he would 'go to his grave like T. J. Campbell (who accepted a judgeship), a discredited nationalist, and his children would bear the stigma of his actions to their dying day'. Stewart, visibly shaken, agreed to re-submit the question to the Nationalist Party (i.e. minus Hanna *et al*) the following day. The proposal this time was unanimously abandoned. If any greater example of the 'schizophrenia' affecting the League was needed, it lay in the choice of Stewart as leader in preference to McAteer. The reason subsequently given to the Irish Department of External Affairs õfficials was the latter's opposition to 'collaboration' with Stormont.[14]

The question of the APL's future did not go away. Not least among the factors speeding its demise was the increasing contentment of many Catholics with their lot under a Welfare State denied to their southern counterparts, a fact some APL leaders recognised and were prepared to admit privately. In April 1958 Bishop Cornelius Lucey of Cork said, at a confirmation ceremony, that the primary duty of the Irish State was not the ending of partition or the revival of the language but the preservation of its people's prosperity. The failure of the Irish State to do its duty in this respect was the tragedy of modern Ireland. Following this attack on the twin pillars of Irish nationalism, Cahir Healy wrote to him unprompted a few days later expressing his approval.

> I appreciate your intervention, the more so as I know your views will not be popular with everyone … I never cross the border that I am not appalled at the long lines of poor people on the morning of a big race in England up outside the office of some big bookmaker … so far as we in the six counties are concerned, we lived in a united Ireland prior to 1916, now we live in a divided one. The insistence upon a Republic or nothing but has left us with partition. Passing resolutions or even bombing disused customs huts only hardens public opinion here … There is, indeed, no material lure to northern nationalists to go into a Republic – our land is all de-rated – we get so many subsidies paid indirectly by England, in order to make partition work, that many who used to help the Anti-Partition League now look upon the prospect with different eyes. I know your statement will meet with criticism but you should know they have awakened much approval also. Partition will go in time but the fear is that when the time comes that attraction will only be of a sentimental nature.[15]

Once again the private Healy revealed a pragmatic *persona* to which the public self could only allude. Throughout the year the fissiparous tendencies increased within the League in South Armagh as a caucus, including Malachy Trainor, the Independent Nationalist Labour candidate of the election, attempted to keep the League executive in existence to ensure, Senator Lennon told Healy, their dominance over the Parliamentary Party. By the end of the year they had changed tack and were going for broke, demanding the winding-up of the League.[16] All factions within northern nationalism by now regarded South Armagh as a thorough nuisance. McAteer had reported to the Department of External Affairs in April that 'McGleenan supporters' exercised a disproportionate influence and that the League which was set up to 'weld together all groups opposed to partition has never done such a thing'.[17] He was considering in his mind the question of abolishing it and creating in its stead a Nationalist Party no longer 'hamstrung in plans and policy' by a small group of the anti-partition executive. Stewart, the leader of the party in Stormont, was also well disposed to such a move. McAteer sought and received assurances from the Dublin government that it was not opposed to this type of reorganisation. The minister, however, made it clear that he had no wish to become involved in an inter-nationalist dispute. In reply to his expressed desire that the party be as broad-based and free from clerical dominance as possible, McAteer agreed and stated that it was 'many years since we have had a priest on our platform'. Senator McGill likewise assured him that in his area of Omagh they had been breaking from the previous close identification with the clergy. The Dublin government, the minister told him, found the League objectionable because it had produced an ill-disciplined abstentionist opposition to a well-oiled unionist machine, and because its parish-based structure had given it a sectarian character.

In regard to the money with which it had secretly funded the League, it felt it better to accede to McAteer's request that it be handed over. At the same time Conor Cruise O'Brien felt that by having control over the sum – with the possibility of later forwarding it to the nationalist party – the ministers would at the very least ensure that Dublin would be kept informed of and have a say in the formulation of the new party's constitution.

By January 1959 McAteer was informing O'Brien that a meeting of the Executive of the APL had been held. McAteer desired to abolish it but McSparran opposed its dissolution and argued that if it should disappear, the disappearance should be 'as unnoticed as possible'. McAteer, who respected McSparran – he was the only other nationalist MP besides himself who was not a member of the Knights of Columbanus – abandoned his plan. Agitation continued from Diamond and Hanna for the status of 'Official Opposition'. To McAteer this was a step too far, at a time when the border campaign was fizzling out and more confidence was being shown in the parliamentary party.

Pressure was also coming from other quarters, mainly in the Catholic intelligentsia, for a closer accommodation with the northern State. David Kennedy in *Christus Rex*, Basil Clancy in *Hibernia* and the *Sunday Independent*, Desmond Fennell and Donal Barrington in *The Irish Times* all wrote on the subject of Catholic grievances in a manner which envisaged their solution within greater Catholic participation in the system. Sometimes they seemed to come close to Blythe's suggestion that the plight of Catholics was their own fault.[18] This tendency in Roman Catholic thought reached its apogee in the Catholic Social Study Conference, held in the salubrious surrounds of St McNissis College at Garron Point in August 1958. Some of its speakers, such as Mary McNeill and G. B. Newe, even accused Roman Catholics of 'lack of charity'. The two Nationalist MPs who attended sessions, Healy and Stewart, told the conference that the recognition of partition was 'impossible but that nationalists ought to play a bigger role'. Stewart stated that they could not succeed in a society where two thirds of the population were against them. The contrast between their views and those of the conference mirrored the division between most of the participants and official nationalists' opinion.

The response from the official voices of northern nationalism was an acerbic one. The *Irish News* condemned it as 'a false picture' of the Catholic community in the six counties. Joe Connellan, in the *Sunday Independent* of 21 September, and McAteer, in the *Sunday Independent* of 7 September, denounced it. McAteer was particularly scathing. 1958 saw, in his view, 'an epidemic of superior thinkers ... Monotonous as our complaints may be, but unceasing is the discrimination daily practised upon us ...'. He appealed to the lowest common denominator in the minority community, lacing his argument with inverted snobbery – 'spare a little pity for an uncouth northern nationalist so far removed from the genteel tinkling of intellectual coffee cups in the purified air of Garron Tower' – and pseudo-historical fingerpointing. 'Dermot McMurrough was a co-operator, those who 'took the soup' would be high on the list of co-operators'.[19]

It was a demonstration of the difficulties faced by advocates of any form of new departure that one was himself secretly advocating his own variant of such a course should speak thus. A likely reason was the need to keep 'on side' the more extreme supporters, the consideration Healy had brought to Blythe's attention. McAteer had always been seen as the republican at Stormont and the MP whose views on the IRA were most respected at Iveagh House (see previous chapter). Another may have been his realisation that unionism at grassroots level remained fundamentally intransigent, a fact so graphically illustrated in the Mid Ulster by-election. The mainstream unionist response to Garron Tower did nothing to shake this assessment.

On 25 October at Portrush Brian Faulkner said the 'neo nationalist policy was the policy of the fifth column'. It was, he contended, 'the greatest danger which Northern Ireland has faced'. Referring to Basil Clancy's article in the *Sunday Independent,* he spoke of a siren-song that 'might at last succeed in destroying the Ulster ship of state'. Brookeborough the following December told a meeting of the Grand Orange Lodge of 'a certain confusion caused by those who put forward the idea of accepting the present position in order to change it and those of the minority who have advocated co-operation with the government', advising that 'Loyalists should distinguish clearly between the two and keep the implications of both clearly in mind'.[20] In his view the changed attitude reflected disillusionment with how southern independence had worked in practice as well as being a tribute to the steadfastness of Ulster Protestant resistance. Meanwhile the strategy of the Dublin government was being pursued.

In July 1958 the minister was told by Lord Home at the Commonwealth Relations Office that he had not changed his mind since the previous conversation that the British could do little in regard to discrimination. Home raised the possibility of a Council of Ireland but stated that any advocacy by Britain of a united Ireland would get them into trouble with the unionists in the six counties. He also suggested that Ireland should rejoin the Commonwealth.[21]

This idea was being seriously promoted within foreign affairs circles in Dublin. In December 1959 the Irish Ambassador to Spain, Dr Michael Rynne, wrote to Cremin, communicating his anxiety following a report on 5 November by Mr Biggar of the Department, advocating an 'Indian solution' as having the best chance of acceptance in Ireland, (i.e. an independent republic within the Commonwealth).[22] In reply to his query as to whether or not Ireland was 'contemplating a step back', Cremin reassured him De Valera had in mind the conversation with Cardinal D'Alton in April 1957 and recalled De Valera's speech to the Oxford Union in which he stated that relations between a reunited Ireland and the Commonwealth would be the main item on the agenda.[23]

The change in the policy of the Dublin government was becoming obvious in other areas. Even before the outbreak of the IRA campaign, a deputation from South Armagh, including McGleenan, had complained to Costello that the Garda and Army authorities were vetting applicants through the RUC.[24] Members of the RUC were also giving evidence in southern courts. Costello assured them that co-operation 'in criminal matters' would not extend to the political field. Although Dublin took this line in dealings with Britain on the extradition question, not least because in their own words they recognised that 'any Irish government that tried to put this forward would be out immediately', they felt vulnerable on the issue. When on 2 July 1955 an incident occurred at Goraghwood railway station in which an Irish Army corporal was maltreated in the presence of a witness, the sportsman and writer Ulick O'Connor, McWhite advised the Department to pass over the issue in silence, while acknowledging that the victim, Corporal Mulholland, was obviously wronged by the county police', a complaint would, he warned, invite 'counter complaints raising extradition questions'.[25]

Furthermore, the constraints of international law imposed by the 1925 Agreement restricted their freedom of movement on the partition issue.[26] De Valera assured the 1957 Ard Fheis that the only way to end partition was through getting 'as close a relationship as possible with the people of Northern Ireland, to get them to combine with us on matters of common concern', adding, on the question of international legal arbitration, that were he able to obtain an acceptable judgement he 'would go in the morning'.[27] It was the nearest he ever came to an admission that the 1937 Constitution – which he had claimed in March in a Dáil reply to McQuillan 'repudiated' the 1925 position – was not operable on the plane of international law. In a sign of the development in his own thinking he also counselled against the view that the British presence was the only problem.

Defeat for republicans and Labourites
The republican movement in the meantime had seen its campaign rise and fall. Its decision to launch a campaign in 1956 had by no means been a unanimous one, the matter having been referred to the Military Council for a decision in mid 1956. What

eventually gave the green light was the election victory in the second Mid Ulster by-election.[28] The position of republicanism in the six counties had been improved by the ballot box successes but was still far from ideal, indeed its existence as an indigenous force then is still a matter of some dispute. Both Cronin and Ó Conail have been quite blunt on this point, describing the campaign as a predominantly southern affair.[29] This is a view disputed by Ó Brádaigh who points out that the failure of the four columns which were the spearhead of the offensive – the last one went out of commission by mid 1957 – left the campaign day-to-day activities in the hands of northerners. Though they remained under-represented at the higher levels, only one member of the Army Council, Charlie Doyle, came from the north. The organisational move of the mid 1950s had borne fruit. In the summer before the campaign began, northerners were numerous enough in the organisation to require a training camp to themselves. The hope that the campaign would originate organically in tandem with a growing consciousness and political organisation was cut short by the decision to go ahead when they did.[30]

Despite Cronin's portrait of the struggle as just this form of organic development in his propaganda booklet *Resistance*, it is clear from the 'Operation Harvest' documents, captured with him by the southern police, that this was not the case. The document, which was read out at his trial acknowledged 'a lack of understanding on the part of some of our local volunteers and some our people as to the purpose of the campaign', emphasising the need to 'get our propaganda among the people' and 'build up intelligence in the locality' … The level of training was still very spotty and only in Fermanagh, under the IRA leader Pat McManus, was the strategy of guerrilla warfare envisaged 'beginning to work'.[31] Nonetheless, Ó Brádaigh's adamant contention that northerners were the backbone of the campaign gets some support from an unexpected source, the Dublin government's Department of External Affairs.[32]

Worried about British accusations that the south was the staging post for guerrilla activities, they calculated the origins of those in prison and interned in the north. Of those serving long terms of penal servitude in Belfast prison, 53 came from the six counties and 21 from the south of Ireland. Of those interned, 154 were natives of Northern Ireland, with only five from the southern state. Though, as they acknowledged, twenty-six county men could escape more easily, there can be little doubt that the northern input was far from negligible.[33]

The view put forward that Belfast was avoided in the campaign for anti-sectarian reasons, and that B Specials and RUC personnel were excluded from the target for the same reason, is disputed by republicans and does not stand up to examination.[34] In September 1958 an IRA statement, admitting the bomb blast at Kinawley Orange Hall, declared that the B Specials would in future be regarded as 'legitimate resistance targets', alleging that those involved in the killing of the Sinn Féiner, Crossan, were 'for the most part B Specials'. The Orange Hall attacked in Kinawley had been used a as a drill hall by the Specials – a common practice in Northern Ireland. In regard to Belfast's role, IRA leaders are at pains to point out that the brigade in the city was bedevilled in the early stages by informers.[35] As far back as 1953 an attempt to destroy a transmitter on the Black Mountain had to be abandoned when an RUC party staked out the area. The 1956 internment swoop lifted the key personnel in the city while the reorganisation attempt in late 1958, ordered by GHQ, foundered when the armaments bought in from Scotland went down when the ferry sank. Seán Garland was arrested in the city later that year when he went to reorganise the movement there.[36]

Politically it was obvious to the movement that their 1955-56 election results would not be repeated next time around. In Stormont elections their party, Sinn Féin, (banned in the north) nominated 'shadow candidates' in nationalist constituencies whose names were to be written in on the ballot paper as an act of protest. The results were derisory. In O'Connor's Stormont constituency of West Tyrone, situated within the Westminster constituency of Mid Ulster, scene of the triple win, there were 153 spoiled votes of which a mere three were for J. Doherty, the designated Sinn Féin candidate. Only in South Armagh, with 417 spoiled votes or 5% of the total, was any success recorded. Not least amongst the reasons for the turnabout was the fear of the clergy on the education issue and their realisation of what absenteeism in Stormont might bring, and there was worse on the way for republicanism. In this respect the 1955 analysis of the Sinn Féin Westminster election results by the Dublin Civil Service trio (see pp 200-206) proved superior to both the panic stricken response of the nationalists (see p 313) and the gung-ho triumphalism of republicans.[37] The emotional and symbolic expression provided by the election of abstentionists to London did not translate into a willingness to forego the more practical arena of Stormont politics in support of an increasingly lost cause, and there was worse on the way for republicans. The Westminster election in late 1959 witnessed a collapse of the Sinn Féin vote across the north. Only in Mid Ulster where 30% of the vote went to Mitchell, and in Derry where Manus Canning received 27%, was there any respectable showing. Even then Mitchell was 15,000 votes below his 1955 total, while Canning's had fallen by over 5,000. In some areas, such as Down and Armagh, the vote was lower than in 1924.

Even allowing for their impaired ability to electioneer, owing to the ever-present harassment by the B Specials, the result was an unmitigated disaster, mirroring the failure of the military campaign. Internment had been abandoned earlier in the year in the republic and pressure put on for its abandonment in the north. Volunteers, including Clarke and Mitchell, ignored the leadership and signed themselves out. Faulkner agreed with Harry Diamond in Stormont that the danger had passed.

Diamond, a Labourite with republican sympathies whose election owed much to IRA assistance, could tell the British journalist Paul Ferr of the *Observer* newspaper in 1959 (with some historical inexactitude), 'in the 1918-21 campaign every member of the minority community would have sheltered them'. This was 'entirely missing from the present campaign and for the first time in forty years some of us were able to get up in Parliament and repudiate them. I did'.[38] The statement calling off the campaign in 1962 obliquely acknowledged this, referring to 'the attitude of the general public whose minds have been deliberately distracted from the supreme issue facing the Irish people – the unity and freedom of Ireland'.

The late 1950s had brought problems of identity and efficacy for nationalists and militant republicans. For the Labour tradition within the nationalist community it brought a problem of existence. In the March 1958 Stormont election, candidates styling themselves Independent Labour had performed well in several nationalist constituencies, particularly in Foyle where Stephen McGonagle came within 1,700 votes of Eddie McAteer. In Belfast the three winnable seats of Falls, Central and Dock returned the maverick Labourites Diamond, Hanna and

Morgan respectively. Diamond saw off his traditional rival, McKearney of the Irish Labour Party, with a handsome majority. In Central a more tense situation prevailed. While the official Irish Labour Party had challenged Frank Hanna in 1953, this time they were not willing to do so. A two-sided contest between him and the unionist Craig seemed likely. When Patrick Marrinan, a solicitor rival of Hanna's and a member of Tom Williams defence team in 1942, decided to enter the lists, he found himself abandoned by the traditional party workers.

A Catholic Workers' Association had been formed in the city and Hanna, a leading member of the powerful Clonard Confraternity, was one of its sponsors. Marrinan was an unlikely 'Red' by any standards. The Spanish Consul in Belfast, decorated by Franco for his services, he campaigned under the Falangists' slogan of *Uno, Grande, Libre*. Yet even he failed to get the neutrality much less the support of the clergy. Apart from his family his only backing came from those republicans who remembered him with gratitude from the Tom Williams affair – his cheerleader Harriet Kelly later achieved world publicity for heckling Margaret Thatcher in Belfast in a protest over conditions in the H-Blocks where two of her sons were imprisoned. Marrinan was heavily defeated by a majority of two to one. According to a former speech writer for Hanna, what happened subsequently was Hanna's wounded response to this incursion into his territory.[40]

Labour Party sources dismiss this; after all, challenges to Hanna's seat had occurred before and Marrinan got no party support for his effort. To them it constituted part of a wider pattern which had been forming for some time. Throughout the cold war, anti-communist feeling had been high in Ireland as the Catholic Church in 'Eastern Europe' faced retribution for its clerico-fascist past. In 1946 Archbishop Stepinac of Yugoslavia achieved martyr status throughout the country when he received a prison sentence for his role in the genocidal Ustashi regime. In 1952 a football match against that country had been cancelled due to episcopal pressure. Three years later, when the game went ahead despite opposition from the Archbishop of Dublin John Charles McQuaid, the Army band was withdrawn and Radio Éireann declined to broadcast a commentary.[41]

The November 1956 Soviet suppression of the Hungarian attempt to leave the Warsaw Pact whipped anti-communist frenzy to fever pitch, with mobs attacking the communist party's

Dublin office. This was the background music to the steady attrition of Irish Labour in west Belfast and elsewhere during the decade. Beattie's 33,174 vote win of 1951 and been slashed by half in 1955 when he lost his Westminster seat. His 1953 attempt to take Hanna's Stormont seat had left him bottom of the poll with a lost deposit. Labour, though still holding its own during the 1955 municipal election, was clearly in decline and on the defensive. It was in this context that Hanna played the religious card to oust Labour. He approached the parish priests of Peter's and Paul's and recruited their chapel collector. He roped in Charles Daly, Head of the Vintners Association, and McEntee, leader of the Belfast Knights of Columbanus. Welded together with the membership of the Clonard Confraternity, this constituted a powerful political machine. This 'Independent Labour Group', composed largely of small businessmen from the west of the city with a sprinkling of activists from the Catholic Workers Association, pushed the official Irish Labour candidates to the bottom of the poll in all wards in the municipal election of May 1958. Clerical pressure was so strongly in support of them that the opposition found it difficult to vote, much less campaign. The Falls ward councillor Paddy Devlin's bruising experience when he arrived to cast his vote, prompted him to leave the Roman Catholic Church.[42]

The backlash against official Labour was not confined to Belfast. In Armagh Paddy Agnew, a man of pronounced piety, found himself and his two fellow councillors ousted by a Catholic Ratepayers Association. Agnew could write in his diary, 'How did the Independents win? By a silent canvass accusing Labour members of not voting for things and persons Catholic'. He recalled the treatment of the poor UDC in the 1930s under a nationalist Council, controlled by the late Senator McLaughlin. Hughes, one of the Independents, had been visited by Agnew during the Poor Law troubles, only to be told that he supported the Guardians. The newly elected 'Independents' were invited to a reception at Ara Ceoli, an 'honour' never accorded their predecessors.[43]

Only in Newry was the anti-Labour tide turned back. There the Ratepayers Association, formed by former nationalist MP and *Frontier Sentinel* editor Joe Connellan, which had deprived Labour of all but one of its 11 seats in 1955, was powerless to prevent it from regaining them in the 1958 election. It was very much the exception.

Those Labourites who were elected or performed well in 1958 were forced to do so under the shadow of the clericalist backlash. They were also frequently at pains to stress their Catholicism. Morgan had stated in Dock during the Stormont elections in March that he was a Catholic first and a Labour man second.[44] Neither his nor Diamond's seat was challenged. The organisation in Dock had, in any event, 'gone rogue' as one activist of the period recalled. Campaigns there were fought on a sectarian basis and money collected was frequently misused. They became detached from the official body and were regarded by them with contempt.[45] There was nothing in such a group anymore than in Diamond's clericalism to draw Hanna's ire. The Corporation election for that area in May was most memorable for the emergence, under the banner of Dock Irish Labour, of a flamboyant ex merchant seaman Gerry Fitt. The previous year in a municipal by-election for Falls he had been roundly defeated by the official Labour Party candidate Paddy Devlin. In Derry, McAteer refrained from using the 'Red Scare' against McGonagale – a fact which the latter acknowledged.[46]

This Kafkaesque episode in Irish Labour history raises the question of the role of the Irish hierarchy. The distinguished Churchman Monsignor Arthur Ryan, perceived by Labour as sympathetic to their cause, was deputising for the Bishop of Down and Conor. He was contacted by Jack Beattie who requested he use his influence to curtail the behaviour of the Hannaites. He was forced to acknowledge to Beattie that his efforts in this regard met with opposition from higher up.[47] The anti-Labour campaign ground remorselessly on to its conclusion.

CHAPTER 14

A New Beginning?

As they entered the new decade, northern nationalist MPs were still apparently giving voice to the old varieties. At the St Patrick's Day parade in Dungannon, Joe Stewart rejected the idea that nationalists should acquiesce in the northern state. In Enniskillen, Healy stated that any declaration accepting the 'present constitutional position' would 'render them traitors to their own country'.[1]

A closer look at the speeches reveals the qualifications in the undergrowth of such seemingly absolutist views. Stewart, while rejecting 'talk of a constitutional settlement' and claiming 'every inch of our country', left a door open by proclaiming himself 'in favour of good relations based upon a fair deal for every citizen'. To those who desired such reactions, his advice was, 'Let a start be made in Derry or in Tyrone or in a Fermanagh educational authority'. In a similar view, Cahir Healy, while reasserting the way to change it was 'by persuasion and being friendly', continued with the message to 'our friends over the border' to 'present a better state with good services and low taxation against the giant taxation in the north', so that 'we might eventually find the old Presbyterian republicanism reviving'.

The overall St Patrick's Day message issued by the nationalist MPs stated that 'policies were a product of the moment but principles were unchanging', promising to 'strive unceasingly for the ideal of a united Ireland' and not be deterred 'by seductive suggestions to forget the past, accept the present and embrace a future irreconcilable with the concept of nationality and complete independence'.[2]

The reactive tone of both speeches and statements reflected the degree to which nationalists had been placed on the defensive by such developments as the foundation of 'National Unity' following the Garron Towers conference. As its name implied this organisation sought to win mainstream nationalism to a common policy, not to pose as a rival to it. Their response to Blythe in the second issue of their journal serves to mark out their position:

> We are willing to admit mistakes in our previous attitude towards our unionist fellow countrymen in being too negative, in crying too much over spilt and sour milk of past history, in overstating our case against the northern government as opposed to the behaviour of local authorities, in making too little use of potential goodwill of those on the other side of the fence. Nevertheless, we maintain that while there is room for more co-operation and greater attempts to understand the unionist point of view, it would be fatal to do anything that might appear to betray our ultimate aim and ideal, the unity of Ireland.[3]

It would also be dishonest. Blythe's suggestion was, in their view, 'a form of moral cowardice'. The group's leader, Michael McKeown, in a pamphlet entitled *Unity, new approaches to old problems,* faulted nationalists for failing to form an effective opposition, preferring instead to be 'the guardian of minority rights until such time as some outside force, whether it be Britain, the Republic or the American Congress, forced the Northern Ireland parliament to dissolve itself'. The south, he felt, could best contribute to the situation by curbing IRA activities and fostering cross border co-operation.

Much of this thinking dovetailed with that of Sean Lemass, the south's Taoiseach and helmsman of its new economic course. Questioned in the Dáil by Patrick Giles TD, he confessed himself aware of the anti-Catholic discrimination in the north.[4] Protests, however, he felt did little good. The wisest course lay in the encouragement of the 'large and increasingly influential volume' of enlightened public opinion in the north. He had told a northern Catholic solicitor in private correspondence the previous month that economic progress of the south would have to 'demonstrate in the most practical of ways that unity would mean important economic advantage for the north'.[5] On the subject of northern nationalism, he took the line taken by De Valera and others before him: 'I have considered it to be undesirable for me to attempt to offer advice. Their policy must develop in accord with the circumstances and be based on their understanding of what may be politically practicable'. Ireland's entry into the EEC would, he felt, lead to partition becoming an anachronism. The IRA he saw as 'in character, if not in purpose, similar to Oswald Mosley's Blackshirts'.[6]

The bond with the nationalists had grown weaker since this new policy departure was inaugurated in 1957, and was to become further attenuated after Lemass' accession in 1959. In early 1960 Iveagh House officials were reminding the minister, Frank Aiken, that four and a half years had elapsed since a deputation from the department had gone north and another such visit was long overdue, if only to reassure 'the six county people Dublin had not abandoned them'.[7] The suggestion was not followed up. A year later one southern Cabinet minister was writing to Lemass characterising the nationalist organisation as being in a state of 'breakdown' and expressing support for National Unity as an alternative.[8] In the spring of 1962 Cahir Healy was encouraged by the Taoiseach to proceed with a proposal he had made for the preparation of a detailed dossier on discrimination and other 'secondary aspect of partition' for presentation to the United Nations. Massive quantities of material were duly collected and forwarded to Dublin without any result. In fact, unknown to Healy and his colleagues, the initiative had been stifled at birth. Lemass had sought Aiken's advice and was reminded of the geopolitical caveats[9] underpinning the February 1957 reassessment of the republican northern policy (see pp 318-321). A favourable UN vote could put Ireland in alliance with countries whose support she would rather not have, while alienating others 'whose attitude is in practice of importance to us including the United States.[10] Irish foreign policy moved solidly into the American camp that October during the Cuban missile crisis and, with only one significant relapse in the late 1960s, has largely remained there ever since.

This was the key factor behind Ireland's reluctance to raise the issue of the 'fundamental problem of partition in that forum' he told Lemass. He thought it best to try and get London on board even before raising the question of discrimination and drew hope from the 'present amongst other conjunction' as shown by events, the visit of the British Home Secretary Rob Butler to Belfast the previous week. In this spirit Healy was encouraged to proceed with the project, Aiken assuring Lemass that a document would be produced from it and they 'would consider whether it warranted a formal approach'.[11]

Both the south's economic transformation and the accompanying reordering of its irredentist priorities received a powerful boost in March 1963 when Brookeborough, who had set his face against co-operation, was replaced by the reformist Terence O'Neill. In April after a unionist/Fianna Fáil trade meeting, George Colley assured journalists that 'what might be called our policy of non-recognition' was directed against Westminster, not Stormont. In late July Lemass himself followed up on this with a speech in the republican heartland of Tralee which hinted at *de facto* recognition of partition. Later in the year he told the *Evening Press* Deputy Editor, Tim Pat Coogan, that reuniting people rather than territory was his goal.[12]

Though McAteer was careful at this point not to criticise the Lemass approach, his forbearance did him little good. The following year a proposed pamphlet on discrimination by him was rubbished in Iveagh House on the grounds that 'little if any interest in the problems of the Northern Ireland minority is taken outside Ireland'.[13] A few months previously all Irish embassies had been instructed to take the surplus stock of Mansion House publications, as well as David O'Neill's 1946 publication, *The Partition of Ireland*, off Dublin's hands, deeming them 'somewhat out of date', with *Ireland's right to unity* the only one considered 'adequate as a handout'.[14] The circular concluded that the sooner they were distributed the better. It was the final epitaph on Dublin's failed anti-partition campaign, ended by them as it had begun, for largely opportunistic and selfish reasons.

To summarise where its northern policy stood at this juncture is not, however, as straightforward as it at first appears. Certainly Lemass shared the Childers' view of National Unity as a welcome alternative to the nationalist party, and advised George Colley to approach people likely to obtain financial support for it. (He ignored similar requests from the nationalists.)[15] Yet others within the Civil Service warned against this approach, seeing it as a recognition of Britain's constitutional claim. It seems a paradoxical position to on the one hand abandon traditional anti-partitionism yet on the other to refrain from following through on the logic of this by supporting the increasingly reformist initiatives emanating from within the minority community. Some clarification was provided by Cornelius Cremin to his colleague Hugh McCann in November 1963.[16] He had, he told him, conveyed to the Commonwealth Secretary Duncan Sandys what was 'the essence of the Irish government view': a desire that Britain should state she had no 'interest in maintaining partition' once 'Irishmen wanted to get rid of it'. It was the line taken by ministers meeting with their British counterparts and by the Taoiseach to the Oxford Union. The British, it was emphasised, did not go further than saying they would always 'consider sympathetically' any proposals made. In order to close this largely semantic gap in favour of the Irish position, Iveagh House softpedalled the issue of internal changes.[17]

If this explanation of government policy is the correct one, and there is no reason to doubt it, the implications are staggering. At a time when conciliatory forces were emerging within both northern traditions, when the conscience of British Labour was at last beginning to awaken, a Dublin Cabinet, seen as the most pragmatic in the state's history, played fast and loose with the most auspicious years Northern Ireland had known in a generation, and would not see again for another, in order to establish a point of political theology. Whatever the reason for this, and the need to guard flank against accusations of 'selling out' seems the most plausible, it lays heavy responsibility at Dublin's door for the terrible scenario which was subsequently to unfold.

Up north, the nationalists veered between seeking redress through approaches to prominent personages in Britain and direct dealings with figures in the Orange establishment. In March 1962 eight nationalist MPs and two Senators presented a dossier on discrimination to R. A. Butler, the Home Secretary. This 25-minute meeting, which Butler admitted had been cleared in advance by the northern government, was hailed as the second occasion in forty years when a nationalist delegation met a British minister.[18] On an inter-communal level it seemed new ground had also been broken. Discussions took place throughout the year between Senator Lennon of Armagh and Sir George Clarke, Grand Master of the Orange Order, the contacts originating from a local initiative following a speech by Lennon at an AOH rally, in which he commented on the ability of Europe to unite in the face of communism while Northern Ireland remained divided.

By mid September McAteer had sufficient hope, if not confidence in these Orange-Green talks as they became known, to warn the general secretary of the British-based National Council for Civil Liberties that an inquiry into gerrymandering local government and the Special Powers Act might sabotage them.

Late in December, as the negotiations continued, the nationalists in a statement gave them a cold kiss of approval, wishing them success but saying they were 'best judged by results'.[19] By the following March, Cahir Healy who, along with McAteer, had been invited by Lennon to sit in on the discussions, would write, 'I think you can dismiss from your mind any idea that they can solve any difficulty. Orangemen never surrender any privilege they hold.' He then got to what he saw as the nub of the problem:

Last year we received, by way of grants and subsidiaries from the Westminster Exchequer, almost 45 million and our Imperial contribution was only 8 million. Would Dublin be able to subsidise us to the same extent, and at the same time bring up the social services to a like grade which she must do in a united Ireland? What would the financial position be? I do not want to publicise this too much as it reveals one of the hidden snags inherent in a united Ireland.[20]

By August 1963 the talks had fizzled out. The party was also facing pressure from other quarters. Harry Diamond was pressing them for a united front, while Dr Con McCluskey and his wife Patricia, had begun a mainly middle-class protest group, the Campaign for Homeless Citizens League, in Dungannon. As its name implied the inequitable distribution of houses by the gerrymandered council was the chief plank in the platform. Inevitably the nationalist party's role in confronting the same injustices would come under scrutiny, and in May 1964 four of their councillors were displaced by Mrs McCluskey and her supporters in the local election. Relations between both groups, however, were initially good. In July 1963 Dr McCluskey had congratulated McAteer for his criticism of the failure of the John F. Kennedy visit to raise the grievance of northern nationalists'. He wrote, 'the others are too old and dead to have new ideas'.[21] On the publicity front the McCluskeys were facing an uphill battle. Both of the south's two principal nationalist dailies, the *Irish Press* and the *Irish Independent* newspapers, had failed to reply to his statements. 'They simple do not care,' was Dr McCluskey's despairing conclusion.

Stirrings of activism were taking place within councils also. When the unionists in Derry Corporation rejected a motion condemning the low percentage of Catholics in the workforce, Councillor Seamus Deeny warned them they 'had it in their power to make civic life impossible'.

Early in 1964 the McCluskeys put their work on an organisational footing with the formation of the Campaign for Social
Justice. Among their advisers on the new departure were J. J.
Campbell, principal lecturer in St Mary's College, the Roman
Catholic Teacher Training Institute, and Brian McGuigan, a solicitor. In October 1963 Campbell had welcomed G. B. Newe's
call on Catholics to join public life. The reception would be different this time from 'the Garron Tower days', he claimed, as it
was 'not so fashionable now to oppose Catholic co-operation'.
McGuigan and Campbell had complained to O'Neill the previous August of the failure to appoint Catholics to the Lockwood
Commission. When the Prime Minister did not reply they published the correspondence. The nationalists now faced another
pressure group, this one considerably less green than National
Unity.[22] The Lennon/Clark talks had been a failure and representations to Britain were getting them nowhere. In January
1964 McGill received a rebuff from Harold Wilson who told him
there would be 'no point' in having the meeting he had requested.
What was worse, events on the home front were beginning to
overtake the nationalists.

That February one of their MPs, Patrick Gormley, called in
Enniskillen for a radical left-of-centre organisation and a challenge to unionist bigotry. The dismal performance of James
O'Reilly, MP for Mourne, in a UTV discussion with Brian
Faulkner – he was unable to cite an example of discrimination
when challenged to do so – provided the spark for National
Unity to summon 'all nationalist-minded groups and individuals'
to a convention, eventually held in Macken's Hotel, Maghery,
on 19 April. At the meeting, attended by over 300 people, including nationalist MPs and Senators, 30-year old Michael
McKeown put the motion calling for the creation of a national
political organisation to stimulate the growth of nationalist constituency organisations and urged all nationalist MPs to take immediate steps to create a democratic party with all the machinery of a democratic party. Failing that, the Maghery assembly
'would undertake the creation of such an organisation'. After an
impassioned and at times acrimonious debate, a compromise
was worked out with the parliamentary nationalists, at the urging of Senator Lennon.[23]

A National Political Front was set up under the chairmanship of Joe Connellan. A small provisional council of nationalist

MPs and Senators, together with constituency delegates and co-optees, was also created. Only three members of the nationalist parliamentary party had shown enthusiasm for the idea: Gormley, Healy and Connellan, those last two significantly the oldest MPs, both of whom had entered from the Sinn Féin tradition. Difficulties with their new allies became apparent almost immediately. While no nationalist MP had openly welcomed the Campaign for Social Justice, McAteer the previous August had offered 'to help behind the scenes'. The local elections of May 1964 brought out into the open the differences with the nationalists in the Dungannon area. Supporters of the Campaign for Social Justice chose their own candidates, none of whom except Patricia McCluskey herself were prepared to accept the National Political Front designation. The nationalists who had voted with the unionists in the council chamber to remove the squatters of the Homeless Citizens League, were badly wrongfooted. Correspondence between the leaders of both groups captures the sense of wounded feelings and mutual incomprehension.

McAteer told McCluskey he had taken indirect action to avert a contest but admitted that his powers over councillors were 'extremely limited'. After the meeting held on the subject McCluskey confessed himself 'deeply shocked at the immobility' of the nationalist party and told McAteer that they were 'doomed' unless they shed their '40-year-old ideas and phraseology', urging the latter to free himself of the 'enclave atmosphere of Derry'. McAteer, who deplored this 'self wounding frenzy', rejoindered that 'if you saw immobility on our side we saw on yours a pugnacious eagerness to criticise which is wholly fatal to any hope of harmonious working. I am away down in the depths this morning ... you speak longingly of a wish to get back to your sculpture. Maybe I will follow you back to the books I should never have left.'[24]

The results of the election in Dungannon left the nationalists with only two seats as against four for the CSJ supporters and one for an Independent Labour candidate. But it was to be the impact of republican intervention in the Westminster election which finally burst apart the tenuous unity of the National Political Front.

As early as January 1964 pressure had been placed on the nationalists to contest the Fermanagh-South Tyrone seat. The Bishop of Clogher, Eugene O'Callaghan, had written to Healy twice that month, encouraging him to go forward. To the bishop the republicans were 'the converted fighters of 1956 who disregarded the bishop's directions and brought trouble enough to us on the border by their foolish raids and then escaped across and left our poor people to bear the brunt of the Specials'. Whatever the attitude of his colleagues with whom O'Callaghan raised the matter, no public statement was issued.[25] In the growing climate of conciliation, a reaffirmation of hard-line anti-partitionism struck a discordant note.

Republican candidates increased their 1959 vote from 63,144 votes to 101,428, yet they remained substantially behind their 1955 votes in the winnable constituencies. In Fermanagh South Tyrone, Molloy, a Coalisland man, received only 16,136 votes. Even allowing for the intervention of Labour and Liberal candidates, who between them took over 8,000 votes, it still showed a Catholic abstention rate of roughly 12,000. Likewise, in Mid Ulster, where Mitchell garnered 22,810 votes to the unionist George Forrest's 29,715, the 5,053 votes obtained by the labour candidate were not decisive in denying him the seat. Frankie McGlade, their Director of Elections and himself a candidate in North Belfast, professed himself satisfied that 'some ground lost had been regained'.

When the nationalists' convention in Fermanagh South Tyrone decided not to contest the seat, the executive of the National Political Front passed a motion of condemnation. It was the end of the road. 'The National Political Front has crumbled',[26] said McAteer, not altogether with regret, as he had earlier warned Healy against the danger, as he saw it, of the Front taking over the party. He paid tribute to the sincerity of those in the Front and stated that it would 'require rebuilding from the foundation'. Throughout the 1960s he had been thinking of a new departure. In August the previous year he had, he told Con McCluskey, felt himself in the throes of a personal political ferment for some time past, 'and hoped that his thoughts would soon crystallise out into new though possibly unconventional suggestions as to where our rudderless people might be guided'.[27]

Throughout early 1964 the party had continued its campaign of lobbying British establishment figures. McAteer himself produced a pamphlet entitled, *It Happens in Derry*, outlining the injustices, principally discrimination both in employment and housing, inflicted by the gerrymandered unionist majority on the predominately Catholic city.

Discipline within the party had become a problem and a meeting had been held in May to deal with the issue. Gormley in particular had caused ripples within the party by his advocacy of greater co-operation. In May he had expressed his approval of the Campbell-McGuigan line. Later that month, when the *Irish Press* printed a laudatory profile of him, Joe Connellan wrote a reply which the paper did not see fit to publish. In June McAteer took over the party leadership from Stewart on the latter's retirement from active politics.

By September the collapse of the NPF had cleared the decks for his developing ideas. On 28 September he wrote to Healy, telling him he had called a meeting to decide 'a few things in quietness away from the stream of interruptions which afflict our meetings at Stormont'. He was, he said 'appalled at the public image which we have shown to friends as well as enemies. It may or may not be coincidence', he wrote 'that this has reached a climax since I formally inherited party leadership, but I am resolved that a change must come or I will retreat behind my Derry's walls to pursue the course which to me seems truly nationalist'.[28] He then got to the heart of the matter.

> Despite the antiquated character of the nationalist electoral machinery, severance from the so-called National Political Front each of us is under an urgent obligation to establish or improve constituency organisation. It is becoming harder and harder to defend the traditional congenial get together as the sole source of our authority to speak for our people'.

Regarding the blueprint for the future, he told Healy he did not himself envisage 'a rigid organisational pattern which any schoolboy could dream up (and which he felt was unsuited to northern Catholics) but some form of 'collegiality with interested people in the constituencies and those further afield'. And then he dealt with the issue which had sundered the National Political Front, the question of non-participation in the impending Westminster election

> Twice at least we took unanimous decisions to try to land a man at Westminster. If no effort is made to enforce (or even publicly to amend) this decision we cannot fairly expect that much attention will be paid to our further pronouncements.

On the matter of the Mid Ulster seat he felt the situation was still retrievable since the 'suggested convenors had not acted as the nationalist party had required', and as a compromise he went so far as to propose his own nomination subject to 'the enthusiastic support' of his Stormont colleagues. Confessing himself fully conscious both of the difficulties involved and of the 'possible misunderstanding' of his motives, he left the decision[29] in Healy's hands. McAteer concluded by emphasising the absolute necessity of nationalists either recombining as a fighting force or publicly separating into agreeable groups or even units, as the ongoing 'internal tensions' were damaging to them in every respect.

His suggestion regarding Mid Ulster was not acted upon. A month later he addressed an appeal to the four Labourite and Independent MPs within the nationalist family, Diamond, Hanna, Stewart and Fitt. In it he told them that 'trial borings' had shown approval for the idea of nationalists 'welded into one machine'. They were not divided by any 'weighty doctrinal differences and had mostly played as one team wherever the interests of northern Catholics were threatened. 'United Nationalists' was his 'proposed title'. 'Every consideration of wind and tide was', he felt, 'favourable to the merger.' This idea also proved to be a non-starter. Earlier that month he had received a rejection of his request for a meeting with Sir Alec Douglas Home, the Prime Minister and the Labour leader Harold Wilson. Wilson took the view that such a meeting served little point, as Labour was in opposition.[30] Douglas Home reiterated the line taken earlier by Mr Butler that 'the matter was within the responsibilities of the government at Stormont'. Only Joe Grimmond, leader of the Liberal party, gave a sympathetic response. The letter-writing campaign, McAteer emphasised, was only a 'first step'.[31]

The ideas which had been germinating behind the scenes finally blossomed forth in November with the adoption by the party of a 39-point statement of policy, following a conference in Belfast at which McAteer presided. Though the principal aim remained 'to hasten by positive political action the inevitable reunification of Ireland, and the establishment of a democratic republican form of government', the thrust of the document's emphasis was on better relations between north and south and within the north itself.[32] Under the heading of 'Community Relations in Northern Ireland' (significantly the state was given its full title and without qualification) they advocated 'the creation of an integrated community based on principles of social justice and mutual respect' to be achieved by 'equal opportunity and an end to discrimination'. In the part entitled 'Public Order and Good Government', they advocated the fullest measure of political, civil and religious liberty 'significantly subject to public order'. Law and order was to be maintained by normal judicial process and the Special Powers Act revoked. The B Specials were to be disbanded or reorganised 'into a normal supplementary force of ordinary police work, beneficial to all sections of the community'. An ombudsman was to be appointed to oversee complaints. Two further rubrics, 'Voting Rights' and 'Local Government', covered such matters as the elimination of gerrymandering and plural voting, re-organisation of local government and the creation of an Appointments Commission for the hiring of staff within the council limit. On 'Housing' they proposed a points system and rent reform. On 'Employment', a mixed economy, 'public ownership and democratic control of essential industries and services', training and rehabilitation schemes all balanced by 'recognition of the just rights of the individual to private property'. The section entitled 'Land and Fisheries' recognised the special place of agriculture, not only in the economy but in the social structure of the community itself and advocated a range of measures for greater efficiency with special support for non-viable holdings 'to ensure that the small farmer retains his traditional place'.[33] A listing on workers and trades unions called for general improvements and encouraged 'co-operation with the ICTU on matters of common concern'. Two further headings 'Education, Health and Welfare' and 'Transport and Communications' were unremarkable, except in the former's absence of any reference to voluntary schools. Finally, when they came to consider 'International Organisations' they pledged support for the United Nations Organisation, the Council of Europe and in a return to their starting point 'for the application to Northern Ireland of all Council of Europe conventions'.

The document reflected the result not only of the new thinking within the Nationalist Party, but also, as McAteer later told F. W. S. Craig, the product of a lot of committee work with other nationally minded groups, such as Republican Labour, Independent Labour MP Frank Hanna, and the new National

Democratic Party, an organisation formed by Belfast members of the sundered National Political Front in June 1965. 'The Party is now anxious to step into the twentieth century,' McAteer told the assembled press conference afterwards, expressing the hope that the Unionist Party would follow them in the same direction. 'Up till now we have been content to practice the Ten Commandments rather than write them out in tablets of stone, but these are the tablets of stone.' On what he acknowledged was the 'ticklish question' of becoming the official opposition he said it would be 'examined properly' at a convention. Consultations with Dublin were necessary, particularly after Lemass' support for 'a federal solution as an interim measure' in October 1959. 'It would be essential,' McAteer said, 'to find out how far he would be prepared to go to get us to open our mouths and swallow such a solution', adding that they were 'going to examine all of their sacred cows'.[34]

In Gormley's opinion, the atmosphere in the north had changed a lot. For the first time there was room for positive politics. They could attract a floating vote and 'religious segregation would become less and less'. The next step, as outlined by McAteer, would be the creation of normal political machinery, membership branches and an annual convention. Attempts to achieve nationalist unity continued. In early December nationalists in Tyrone and Fermanagh united with republicans and liberals at a meeting in Dungannon to discuss the loss of the two seats. Later that week McAteer's proposal of a united front received a setback when the Republican Labour Party in Belfast rejected it. The new year saw the issue of official opposition status put to the top of the agenda by the surprise visit of Lemass to meet O'Neill at Stormont at the latter's invitation on 14 January. 'An inevitable happening which has come a little sooner than expected. It is in an accord with the spirit of the times' and he could see much good coming from it, Healy later told the press.[35] Partition had lasted forty-five years and appeals to 'democratic forces at home and abroad' had met 'with little success', he said, noting that 'of late democratic forces in Britain have become worried about happenings here'. The man who was to succeed him as MP for South Fermanagh, John Carron, told him they were 'letting the hare sit' on the official opposition issue until they had heard from Dublin.

After a meeting with Lemass in late January, and following

pressure from the Catholic hierarchy anxious for more concessions on the 'schools issue', the decision was taken to become
the official opposition at Stormont. The decision was a majority
one but was not unanimous.[36] And it came with a *caveat*: 'co-
operation cannot be carried beyond the brink of national principle'
warned McAteer on 2 February, the day he took over from
Thomas Boyd as opposition leader with Roderick O'Connor as
opposition whip. 'We will continue to work for the complete
banishment of all forms of discrimination from this land, though
we trust this kind of activity will become progressively less and
less as real community spirit grows.' The republicans issued a
statement condemning them as having 'forfeited the right to the
title nationalist'.

But this mood of togetherness, most dramatically emphasised
that December when O'Neill and his fellow unionist MP Nat
Minford rushed to the bedside in Drogheda Hospital of Paddy
Gormley MP, injured in a traffic accident, came against a backdrop of reminders that no fundamental change had occurred.

The 'New City', recommended in the Matthew Report designed to curb the outward growth of Belfast, was sited in the
prosperous Lurgan/Portadown district; possible locations in
the unemployment blackspots west of the Bann were ignored.
Sectarian discrimination and not the centre/periphery dichotomy
of capitalism was perceived as the cause among many nationalists, with the naming of the city after Sir James Craig seeming
like salt in the wound. The streamlining of the northern rail system, the most severe closures falling on the western half of the
territory, was viewed in a similar light. Most insultingly of all
from a nationalist point of view, O'Neill went ahead and implemented the report of the already controversial Lockwood
Commission, siting the new university at Protestant Coleraine,
despite the strong case put forward by both the nationalists and
unionists of Derry for an upgrading of the city's Magee College.

And the old sectarian venom had not disappeared from
unionist platforms. William Craig, at an Orange rally at
Letterbreen in March 1964, referrred to 'lack of family planning
among Roman Catholics'. He later clarified this when challenged by the Bishop of Down and Conor by saying he wanted
people 'to plan families intelligently'. The Roman Catholic
church even in the post-conciliar atmosphere did not show itself
much more accommodating. In November Cardinal Conway

said his church tendency would be to prohibit mixed marriages 'rather than to favour them in any way', claiming that 'our separated brethren' were in agreement with them on this point. And O'Neill, with the best will in the world, was hampered in his freedom of movement. The unionist right-wing challenged his rapport with Lemass, some calling for his replacement. Despite his victory on a vote of confidence in April, rumblings continued. Meanwhile, outside parliament, the Reverend Ian Paisley had shown his ability to confront the 'enemy' on the streets, by provoking a riot on the Falls Road during the Westminster election campaign in October 1964 over the flying of a tricolour at the republican candidate's office.

The Lemass/O'Neill/Wilson process continued with negotiations for an Anglo-Irish Free Trade Agreement, signed in December 1965. McAteer, in July at Newtownbutler, welcomed the process as 'a geographical necessity'. Only firm action by the northern government, he felt, would determine whether they stepped 'bravely together into the New Europe or are dragged ingloriously in like a pair of spancelled goats'.[37]

On the question of nationalist organisation, which the young Austin Currie, newly elected successor to Joe Stewart, had described as being 'in an abysmal state', McAteer thought it best for the moment to content themselves with the establishment of 'alert posts in as many areas as possible to pool and exchange ideas'. The organisation drive continued but two general elections in a row – one for Stormont in November 1965 and for Westminster in March 1956 – delayed the first conference until 22 May 1966. The 1965 election saw the contours of future politics become clearer in Belfast. Frank Hanna had withdrawn to be replaced by one of his former followers, Tom Brennan, running on the NDP ticket. Gerry Fitt in Dock received his highest ever vote, while one of the two Andersonstown councillors who deserted his and Harry Diamond's Republican Labour Party, Sean McGivern, ran unsuccessfully in Antrim. The rivalry between Diamond's Republican Labour (which Fitt and his followers joined in 1962) and Hanna's group possessed a cordiality never existing in the battle either of them had with Irish Labour, which continued to fight unsuccessfully to regain Smithfield, Dock and Falls, as well as the corporation seats. In May 1964 the two announced a merger for the purpose of fighting future elections. The marriage of Hanna's son Vincent to Gerry Fitt's daughter epitomised this unity on a personal level.

The *Irish News*, in what may have been a shot across the bows to those unionists inclined to take for granted the new mood of conciliation, trumpeted the old anti-partition tune. On 24 November, the day before polling, an editorial entitled 'For National Unity' urged electors to 'strike a blow for the unity of Ireland', commenting that 'those who sneer at ideas are mentally impoverished, their interests are the bread and butter affairs of men without a country'. On the hustings, nationalist politicians struck a less strident note. Joe Connellan, at an eve of poll meeting in Newry, while reaffirming the 'ultimate aim', stated it was good to know that a great measure of co-operation had already taken place between the six and twenty-six counties in drainage, tourism and electricity. Nationalists were, however, realistic and they knew the day-to-day needs of all people, the unionist no less than the nationalist, the Protestant no less than the Catholic'.[38] This tone continued into the new year.

Lemass, in his St Patrick's Day message of 1966, told his listeners that 'co-operation north and south created a new atmosphere which would hasten reunification'. The *Irish News* of 18 March, in an editorial entitled 'Helping Reunification', picked up on this, stating that Lemass had pointed out how many of the differences were 'contrived not real'. Acknowledging that 'bigotry' and 'mischievous deeds' were 'at work on both sides', they felt reassured that 'the new atmosphere of goodwill showed unmistakable signs that forces were at work for the betterment of the country and for the removal of many long-existing false impressions'.

That same day in Rostrevor McAteer's message to northern nationalists was simple: 'We must open our eyes,' he told them. The *Irish Independent* of 19 March hailed his speech:

In his context this means admitting that the northern legislative and administration has its roots sunk in Irish soil. It means conceding what for many people there represents a security against what is still an unwanted historical development. It means acknowledging enactments which can be made to benefit the entire community to Northern Ireland as some of these laws already do. It does not in any sense mean forswearing the ideal of a united Ireland ... but offers instead in a initial place the aim of making the north a neighbourly place to live in.

In March Westminster elections saw the first serious challenge mounted to the republican candidates on the anti-unionist side. When McAteer's brother Hugh announced he would not be a candidate in Derry, Patrick Gormley felt free to put his name forward. He won 22,167 votes to the republican Neil Gillespie's 2,860. The unionist, of course, won the seat which no nationalist candidate had contested since 1946. Gormley admitted privately that only 66% of nationalists voted as against 84% of unionists, attributing much of the 'slow, low turn out', to republican abstentionism. Derry city was particularly bad, with Creggan not voting in strength. Gormley calculated 3,000-4,000 abstentionists.[39] Many rural areas, however, recorded a 90% poll in his favour. His vote, even in a three-corned contest, marked an increase on that obtained by Hugh McAteer in a straight fight.

In Fermanagh South Tyrone, Donnelly, the Enniskillen shopkeeper who had attempted to go forward two years previously, finally got his wish. Running as a 'unity' candidate, he secured 14,645 votes to 10,370 for the republican Ruairí Ó Brádaigh. The unionist Marquess of Hamilton with 29,352 votes took the seat. Again behind the scenes nationalists were less triumphant than the sidelining of republicans would appear to warrant.

Healy admitted to voting for Donnelly, yet expressed his disapproval of him because of his association with the 'NDP crowd who pushed out Frank Hanna in Belfast'. Healy also noted unfavourably that some of his supporters like Lunney in Enniskillen (later an SDLP councillor) had no previous involvement in nationalist politics.[40] The total anti-unionist vote of 25,015 was a slight increase from the 24,491 of the previous election. Donnelly, it would appear, not only reduced by some 6,000 the republican vote, but garnered the 8,000 odd votes given to them by the Liberals and Labour.

In Mid Ulster, Mitchell was left alone to run against the unionists. As Senator McGill told Healy, he had by then become 'a sort of branded name with unfortunately the aura of having twice won the seat'. Both McGill and Healy discussed the question of organising in Mid Ulster, the latter remarking that 'doing nothing on the issue was fatal'. Yet, Mitchell, they acknowledged had the country 'overrun' and both of them kept before their eyes the experience ten years previously of Michael O'Neill.[41] In the event, Mitchell with 27,169 votes, almost double his 1959 total, still came a respectable second but from Belfast came the most important result of all, when Gerry Fitt, without any republican or NILP opposition as with Diamond in 1964, won the seat with a 2,211 vote majority, the first representative of Catholic Belfast to sit in Westminster since 1955. With the focus on all strands of nationalism increasingly directed on London, the presence of a representative there from outside the mainstream movement increasingly weakened the position of McAteer's party as the voice of the Catholic population.

Whatever ground was lost by republicans in the election, some of it at least was regained the following month with the celebration of the 50th anniversary of the Easter Rising. 1,000 men marched in Derry, 2,000 took part in the Newry parade, the largest since 1949. 5,000 crowded into Lurgan cemetery to hear the oration of veteran republican Kevin Agnew over the grave of Thomas Harte. The presence of the AOH lodges alongside GAA clubs and Catholic Associations at the graveside of an IRA man who died facing a firing squad of the wartime De Valera government, emphasised the degree to which the republican tradition of the past had become the property of all. Even when the Hibernian organiser, worried by the Nelson Pillar explosion in Dublin, appealed to republicans at the Ballygawley St Patrick's Day rally to turn away from violence, he did so by recalling the tricolour's meaning of reconciliation. That this flag and the tradition it represented had consigned their organisation to the margins of Irish politics did not register in the new mood. 'Tradition', as Eric Hobsbawm points out, is 'invented'.[42]

The largest of the parades, a 20,000 strong march along the Falls Road, with 50,000 lining the route, united all strands of non-unionist opinion. McGill expressed the opinion to Healy that the commemorations had 'built in Sinn Féin'. Down south the commemorations were expensive splurges of triumphalism reflecting the complacency of a state still unshaken in its Roman Catholic and nationalist verities and basking in the first glow of material prosperity since its formation. Ritualistic pieties aside, northern nationalists were hardly considered in the new mood. When questioned on the subject, one unnamed cabinet minister was quoted as saying, 'Ah, we don't worry about them – sure the English Catholic MPs at Westminster will look after them'.[43] The increasing coolness was felt north of the border.

Early in November McAteer called at the Department of Foreign Affairs in Dublin and expressed himself 'a little concerned' at the 'growing lack of contact' between northern nationalists and Dublin. The southern government was, he felt 'growing closer to the unionists than to the nationalists'. While not 'for a moment' criticising the north-south reproachment, he urged that nationalists should not be made to feel ignored as a result. They would, he maintained 'feel that they were being forgotten about and begin to despair'. McAteer was told by the Department that nationalist interests were always Dublin's concern but he 'must have regard to the delicate position of Captain O'Neill *vis-à-vis* his extremists', and Dublin could not be seen as 'conspiring with the nationalists against him'.[44]

On McAteer's suggestion that representatives from both sides he invited to the south for non-political purposes, he was told that the Lord Mayors of Derry and Belfast had been invited to the inaugural Aer Lingus flight to Toronto. 'No nationalist had been invited', McAteer reminded them bluntly. Regarding McAteer's final suggestion that the Irish delegation for the United Nations should find some opportunity in discussions of Rhodesia's UDI to point out that 'one man one vote' did not exist in Northern Ireland, he was told that 'such an attack might endanger the present north-south relations'. McAteer pointed out that he was not interested in an attack on partition and even 'private indications' to the British government that Dublin was being 'put in a spot' by him would be helpful. No reply was recorded to this suggestion.[45]

McCluskey had earlier received a rebuff in his attempts to solicit Dublin's backing for the CSJ.[46] A Departmental memorandum prepared for the Lynch/O'Neill meeting in December of the following year asserted that the government supported 'the aims' of McCluskeys' campaign but stressed that the question of open association with it was a 'matter of some delicacy' and had therefore 'been avoided'. Ireland's diplomatic missions overseas had already been advised against involvement with the CSJ, Iveagh House citing as the reason the improved climate in north-south relations.

The conference finally held by nationalists in May added little to the '39 steps' of November 1964, except significantly a demand for increased government aid to the 'voluntary schools. They were, they claimed, 'bled white paying for them'.

The addition may have been prompted by events the previous month, when two nationalists MPs, the Gormley brothers, attended a meeting addressed by the Prime Minister, at which he called for an end to segregated education. Patrick Gormley

defended O'Neill's position on this against the opposition of
Cardinal Conway. The growing threat to the position of the
Nationalist Party within the Catholic community was brought
to the forefront of their minds when the conference was called. It
was, in McGill's words, summoned 'to give our people a base
against the emergence of those labour and liberal elements,'[47]
principally Gerry Fitt and the Liberal MP for the Queen's
University, Sheelagh Murnaghan, whom they feared would succeed where that nationalists had failed in prising open the conscience of the British establishment. Not that the nationalists
were without some successes. Following their 1963 London visit
Fenner Brockway agreed to sponsor a motion supported by 50
other Labour MPs, notably Paul Rose, Stanley Orme and Kevin
McNamara, to hold a Royal commission of enquiry into the situation. Despite repeated attempts to force a discussion on the
subject, they were frustrated by the 'Convention' system whereby all matters relating to Northern Ireland were deemed outside
the remit of Westminster. Any demands that the powers of intervention be exercised were repeatedly brushed aside.

Some light seemed to be breaking through the clouds when,
on 22 May 1966, Harold Wilson expressed his willingness to the
House to 'hold talks' into 'things that go on in Northern Ireland'.
Nationalists expressed themselves pleased 'at the outcome'.
McGill had warned Healy in April of the 'fallacy that British
Labour will do anything for us'. Recalling the Boundary
Commission debacle, he felt it would be 'wrong to expect too
much'. Events were to prove him correct. From 1966 until 1968,
when occurrences at Caledon and Derry moved the northern sit-
uation into a different plane, 'Operation Truth Justice' met with
one rejection after another from leading figures in the two major
British parties.

A request to Quintin Hogg in October 1966 to 'help us bring
the winds of change as far as Derry', by helping the nationalists
promote a conference on the situation in the city, met with the
reply that he 'could not interfere in the re-warding of Derry anymore than he would in Newcastle', but he felt very strongly that
the present policy of the government of Northern Ireland had
been 'very much more progressive' than for many years previously and that O'Neill's recent victory over the extremists was
very encouraging'.[48]

In November 1967 Roy Jenkins told McAteer he would 'not

consider it proper on my part to interfere in the way you suggest in the detailed running of what are transferred services. The most fruitful course, I think, would be for you to seek direct discussion with Captain O'Neill.' Similar replies were received by McAteer from Edward Heath on 8 May 1968 and Lord Shoreham in January of that year.

The memoirs of the McCluskeys contain a postbag of equally dismissive responses to their parallel agitation.

If the strategy of pressurising Britain had run aground, that of improving community relations in the north was not faring much better.

O'Neill dates the failure of his initiative from the attendance of Belfast Catholics at an Easter Rising Commemoration, which left West Belfast 'a forest of flags' for three weeks afterwards. 'It was bound to put the whole future of Northern Ireland into the melting pot', he wrote afterwards.[49]

Certainly, the Easter Commemoration forced O'Neill to take a harder line in his speeches reassuring the extremists. 'We will not yield in loyalty', he warned on 29 April. As far back as December McAteer had expressed disappointment that the Queen's speech made 'no reference to real bridge building' and expressed the view that the absence of plans on the Mater Hospital and voluntary schools showed they had 'not caught up with the times'. But on the surface at least all seemed undisturbed.

In April Joe Connellan, MP for South Down, said that 'nationalists of the future' would have to be 'realistic' and prepared to 'serve the needs of all creeds'. In October Catholics, including the nationalist Chairman of Ballycastle UDC, attended a unionist party dinner at which Captain O'Neill was guest speaker and the toast was 'the Government of Northern Ireland'.[50] The Secretary of the unionist party branch in the area denied the claim that Catholics were debarred from membership. Late in 1966, when O'Neill was recovering from an operation, McAteer visited him in hospital. By April 1967, however, with the Northern Ireland Civil Rights Association three months in existence and the political temperature rising, McAteer was warning on the UTV *Flashback* programme that they had 'no alternative but to reconsider their role on Official Opposition'.

Even though Patrick Gormley attended the garden party at Hillsborough the following month to celebrate the wedding of

Princess Margaret and Lord Snowdon, there was no disguising the increasing polarisation. McAteer made one last attempt at a conciliatory gesture which would place the ball firmly in the unionists' court. He wrote to James Dillon, the Fine Gael TD, and a leading member of the AOH Executive:

> For some considerable time past it has been obvious that the Orange Order grip on politics must be broken or eased before we can begin to hope for anything like normality here in the six counties. If some sort of face-saving pact could be contrived, it would be a great help. We know here that the AOH does not exercise any kind of political power analogous to that exercised by the Orange Order. It is true, however, that the general public can see some common denominators in the two Orders. Though it may have been suggested before, I intend in the very near future to make public a call to the AOH to make the supreme sacrifice of going out of existence if that would encourage the Orangemen to take a step or two along the same road.

The proposal was roundly rejected. Senator J. G. Lennon of Armagh, a leading Hibernian, told him it would be seen simply as a triumph for the Orange Order and an admission of failure on the part of the AOH. Furthermore, it would be totally unacceptable to rank and file members who, as it was a friendly society, would have the final say. If the proposal was made publicly, he (Lennon) would have to disagree publicly with McAteer. He asked him if 'in view of the tremendous publicity it would provoke, he thought such a course advisable'. Senator Patrick McGill, who was never an AOH member, likewise advised McAteer that AOH branches would 'take it very badly'. Moreover, McGill felt McAteer left himself open to the rejoinder 'that logically our party should abolish itself to encourage unionism to do the same'. The equation of Hibernianism with Orangeism would also cause offence. McAteer's suggestion was heard of no more.[57]

In July he sounded his most trenchant warning to O'Neill. Stormont, he told him, must break from the Orange Order. The question of community relations was the real bedrock, he said, advising O'Neill not to misread the 'courteous and welcoming smiles of a couple of Reverend Mothers' as a sign that traditional nationalist aspirations had been abandoned. Continuing, he promised that nationalists were prepared to 'go to any lengths, yes right up to the very brink of principle', to achieve 'an understanding' with those not totally at one with them on the issue of Irish unity and independence. There had been, he felt, 'some snapping of the links with Dublin'. He told the Dublin government that the promotion of friendly relations with unionists was not sufficient. It was equally important, he claimed, to 'maintain friendship with their own kith and kin'. He then advised his own party to refrain from needless provocation and remarked that they had become a 'little too enveloped in our smugness', seeing 'baddies' on one side, 'goodies' on the other.[52]

Following these remarks, the O'Neillite *Belfast Telegraph*, in an editorial entitled 'Freshening Wind', praised McAteer as the 'most pragmatic leader' northern nationalism ever had. It went on to comment that nationalists' increasing tendency to 'look outward to Europe' left only a 'limited function' for a party devoted to 'such a lost cause as a united Ireland'. Nationalists had, it said, received 'little enough encouragement recently from Dublin' which should serve as

> a clear warning to seek their salvation elsewhere, perhaps along the lines suggested by those who would seek a closer alignment with radical and trade union elements.

Whatever the effect, if any, of this editorial on northern nationalists, it was to prompt a minor bout of heart searching in a quarter where the writer had most likely never imagined it would, Dublin's Department of External Affairs. The senior Civil Servant Sean Nolan wrote to the minister and Tánaiste (Deputy leader), Frank Aiken, enclosing a copy of the editorial with the most worrisome parts underlined. The allegation of a loss of context was, he remarked, a 'persistent feature' of speeches by the minority's representatives in recent months. Acknowledging that the 'informal relationship' characterising the 1950 was unlikely since Dublin was 'no longer conducting a propaganda offensive', he went on to warn that a 'general weakening of the link' would be damaging to the long-term interests of Irish unity. A step in the right direction would at least be to strengthen social ties by inviting nationalist representatives more frequently to functions at the Department. Correspondence should also take place avoiding 'cold officialism' in favour of a 'quasi formal language'. He acknowledged that McAteer had a point when he complained that Dublin had more contact with foreigners than with the northern minority. The link with the nationalists had,

Nolan concluded, 'proved invaluable in the past and rather than keep our friends in the cold' their friendship should be cultivated in the 'furtherance of common aims'. Unfortunately for the nationalists, there was no recorded follow-up on this rare spasm of bad conscience.[53]

Nationalists were fighting another battle as well, within their own ranks and against those campaigning on similar issues outside the party. Even though the offshoot from the sundered National Political Front, the National Party and later the NDP, maintained that it was not in competition with the nationalists and desired unity with them, its overtures were rebuffed by the mainstream party. Despite this cold-shouldering they continued to work together for the moment.

A letter to McAteer from McGill in November 1965 captures the fear within the party on this issue.

> I take it that we will not be pressurised by newspaper talk into fusion with these Quigleyites (Gerry Quigley, later Head of the INTO, was Secretary of the NDP) or that a change of name will be considered. Strong against this is Mourne, South Down, West Tyrone and I am sure South Fermanagh and South Armagh ... Fusion merely means a takeover. You are leader of a party, you have not become leader to see your party's name and its structure (capable of improvement thought that may be) assimilated by a crowd of what Lennon rightly calls Johnny-come-latelies. Why don't the Quigley crowd go and ask Diamond? Because they can't and because they are afraid. Similarly with Fitt. We apparently are to be the only frightened ones in the wigwam. Not this time.[54]

An agreement was reached in February 1967 whereby each would eschew organising in a constituency organised by the other. The supporters of each party would work for the other in such areas.

For the nationalists, representation and organisation were the same thing. The question of a tightly knit body was still anthema to many of them in late 1965. As McGill told McAteer

> As for ourselves, we must organise on our own lines a constituency executive springing from local branches in electoral divisions and towns. Each executive to send stated delegates to an annual conference. No cards, no fees, all voluntary ... in a card membership you appear to exclude those who are too shy or unwilling to ask for cards.[55]

In any case the NDP did not abide by the agreement. In the local elections of May 1967 they ran against outgoing nationalists in Strabane, O'Connor's West Tyrone constituency, winning control of the council with seven of the nine seats. Four outgoing members were defeated. They also fought in Downpatrick, Ballycastle and five Belfast wards, some of which had never been contested by candidates from the nationalist community. Overall they won 28 seats and control of two councils. Republican Labour easily beat them in Smithfield. They continued to maintain, however, that their aim was to merge into a 'united nationalist party'.[56]

In April Fitt invited over three Labour MPs from the Campaign for Democracy in Ulster, Paul Rose, Maurice Miller and Stanley Orme. As a result of their tour, Wilson received a report on conditions in the north. This time he confessed to widespread concern and remarked that they felt it right, without departing from the Convention (the ruling of Westminster prohibited discussion of the north), to embark upon a series of talks with Captain O'Neill. The tour put the question of anti-unionist unity back on the agenda and the traditional standard bearers of this cause were worried.

McGill on 19 April wrote to McAteer regarding a newspaper report of the NDP, Rep 'Lab', NILP and nationalists combining to form a single party. Describing it as a 'regurgitation of the Gormley thesis 'all against the unionists', he went on

> It is clear to me that some of our men have been encouraging this latest move and also clear that Fitt's tour was intended to advance it. We have come to a sorry pass when unity can be undertaken on the say so of three British MPs. And what unity.

To McGill the 'disturbing thing' was 'the ordinary man' on the nationalist side would assume there was 'official party backing for this thing'. He sounded a warning to McAteer that if nationalists 'as a party' were seen to give in to this, they were sunk; for others would inherit the mantle leaving them 'discredited'. He outlined his strategy to meet the situation:

> 'On a first thought I incline to the belief that the time is coming when as a leader you must find out who is with you and who not, and if you have only five or six, then take these and stand firm on the bastion. Co-operation yes, even with unionists if it brings practical results; but amalgamation and

eventual engulfment no. You can be sure of all the fellows except the obvious trio. I can foresee that they will elide the odium of any charge of splitting by pointing to the fact that they are going out with Fitt or Diamond.[57]

McAteer seemed to take his advice. At a rally in Newry in support of Michael Keogh, *Frontier Sentinel* editor, who was to replace the recently deceased Joe Connellan as MP for South Down, he stated that 'Nationalists should retain their old clothes until they are sure new ones are delivered.'[58] The 'trio' to which McGill referred were the Gormley brothers and the successor to Joe Stewart in East Tyrone, Austin Currie, the only nationalist MP on the executive of the recently formed Northern Ireland Civil Rights Association.

Currie, despite his PR involvement in London with the CSJ, did not share the Gormley brothers' enthusiasm for the conciliation policy. Before his election he had reached an arrangement with Tyrone republicans not to oppose their Westminster election efforts in return for their support in his bid for Stormont. Interviewed by the *Irish Independent* of 18 September 1964, he confessed himself in favour of the nationalists taking seats in the Dáil 'even without voting rights' and expressed the view that 'if six counties can vote themselves out of the thirty-two, a campaign could be started to enable the two or three nationalist counties to vote themselves out of the six'. He was, he said 'a great believer in the words Sinn Féin'.[59] The border, he felt, had 'economic and religious' reasons for its existence. The policies of Lemass were killing the first, ecumenism was undermining the second. When he joined the squat in a house in Caledon, organised by the Gildernew brothers from the local republican club, whose mother had been passed over for a council house in favour of an unmarried Protestant teenager, nothing was ever to be the same again. In the glare of world publicity northern nationalists' grievances had moved onto a new plane.

As a well-researched study of NICRA shows,[60] the Association and the wider Civil Rights Movement were entirely separate in character. One was merely a Belfast-based directory, the other, the dynamic behind most marches, was organised on the basis of local initiatives outside of the northern capital, only acquiring an indigenous base among the Catholic population there in the aftermath of the 5 October 1968 march in Derry.

Following those events a special conference of the Nationalist

Party was held in Dungannon. The conference reaffirmed the dedication of the party to the ideal of social justice for all and recorded its 'disappointment' with the 'so-called pace of change', reaffirming its previously stated six minimum immediate demands.

They further declared their 'willingness to support the exercise of non-violent civil disobedience at such times and under such circumstances as may be considered expedient to warrant its adoption to wreck a system which has at its base a deliberate policy of denying equal treatment and equal opportunity to all'.

A more militant version of this latter clause, declaring support for civil disobedience, had come from Austin Currie's East Tyrone delegation. He argued for civil disobedience in selected areas, a stance supported by Denis Haughey. Alderman Hegarty of Derry criticised this idea, claiming that non-payment of rents and rates was a policy unacceptable to his branch. After a recommendation by Senator Lennon and South Armagh delegate D. Collins that the wording of the East Tyrone resolution be referred to the executive for consideration, the conference came up with a compromise formula in which the words 'to wreck a system' were replaced by the more innocuous 'to cleanse a system'. This was then unanimously adopted. Nationalists, it seemed, were unwilling even verbally to pander to the more aggressive mood.[61]

James O'Reilly, MP for Mourne, then stressed that the nationalist position on reunification remained unchanged; the final target remaining a thirty-two-county Ireland. The moratorium on demonstration, agreed between NICRA and O'Neill at the end of the year, was welcomed by the party, McAteer personally ringing up O'Neill to congratulate him on it. When the compromise came apart in the fall-out from the attack on the PD marchers at Burntollet, the nationalists, with an election looming, found themselves once more on the defensive. The election called by O'Neill to strengthen his position within his own party sounded the death knell for the nationalists. For the first time in their history only one of their candidates enjoyed an unopposed return.

At the previous election the number had been five. When the votes were counted three MPs – McAteer in Foyle, Richardson in South Armagh and Thomas Gormley in Mid Derry – had lost their seats to John Hume, Paddy O'Hanlon and Ivan Cooper respectively, all of whom were prominently associated with the civil rights movement. In South Down Michael Keogh had seen his 1967 total of 8,598 fall to 4,830, only 200 votes ahead of his PD rival. Even allowing for the possibility that many of the 2,971 unionist votes of 1967 went to Woods, the sole opponent, it still revealed a massive sift in Catholic voting behaviour. Since 1929, the nationalist vote there had never fallen below the five thousand six hundred mark. Keogh, moreover, was editor of the *Frontier Sentinel* newspaper, traditionally a major lever of nationalist power.

In South Fermanagh, Cahir Healy's old seat, his successor John Carron secured a majority of just 2,008 votes over his PD opponent. Only in Mourne did the nationalist James O'Reilly increase his 1965 vote despite an enlarged poll for the unionist candidate. Of the three victories by the Civil Rights Independents, the most spectacular was certainly Mid Derry, where in a four cornered contest the outgoing Nationalist MP came second last. The most predictable was South Armagh where Richardson's vote of 8,049 in a 1962 total poll of 12,400 had by 1965 fallen to 5,223 in a poll of less than 6,000. But most significant by far was the result in Foyle. Though McAteer had never won more than 64.1% of the vote in a constituency not contested by unionists, and though his ailing health had undermined the vigour of his campaign (he had in fact considered retiring),[62] his defeat at the hands of John Hume marked the passing of the last leader who could have salvaged the fortunes of the nationalist party. His moderation in support of the Civil Rights demands, in particular his 'half a loaf is better than no bread' remark, was used against him by Hume. Damaging him also was the conservatism of his own party at local level – the level where power and its abuse was most relevant to people's lives – where the Civil Rights movement launched the spearpoint of its attack.

The minutes of the Derry Nationalist Party for 24 January 1968 record an admission by Alderman Hegarty that 'the nationalist councillors spend hours in the Guildhall agreeing with the unionists and have become known as Green Tories'.[63] It was a complaint re-echoed across the nationalist north and no initiative had come from Dublin to rescue the nationalists.[64]

At the conference the previous June, McAteer acknowledged 'some improvement' in the weakened link he had earlier complained about, but was forced to conclude 'that we are very

much on our own in the North of Ireland.[65] Certainly there was
no shortage of reminders during these years of how painfully
true this was. In early November 1967 McAteer had gone to
Dublin to complain to the Taoiseach Jack Lynch about remarks
his predecessor Lemass had made in Belfast which seemed to
apportion blame for the impasse equally between both traditions. Proposals he made to Lynch's office then and later for
greater involvement in, for example, the Council of State and at
public functions, all with the objective of placing them on a par
with their unionist opponents, were passed over in silence by
the Irish authorities. Even worse, there had not been any nationalist representative included on the committee to review the
constitution set up by the government in late 1966. Now there
was the seismic shift of the election with McAteer himself among
its casualties.

His reply afterwards to a letter of commiseration from fellow
nationalist party member, the playwright Brian Friel, afterwards
summed up his feelings on the situation:

> Your letter is a candle to my darkness. I do not mourn the
> loss of a seat at Stormont but I have a throaty feeling that so
> many of our people seem to have turned their backs on that
> lovely indefinite thing which I mean by nationalism. But I
> think that they will return when they have filled themselves
> with the mess of 'British Rights and Welfare Benefits'.

'There have been other times in Irish history', he assured Brian
Friel, 'when all seemed lost but our faith blossomed again'.[66]

Hume's ability to outflank McAteer on the activism front
was a tribute to his political ability – for many years he had been
beavering away in community politics and single-issue campaigns, such as the controversy over the siting of the university.

An ex-member of the Derry Nationalist Party himself, he had
long been an advocate of new look nationalism, condemning the
nationalist press for 'poisonous attacks' on those like J. J.
Campbell, Basil McGuigan and G. B. Newe, and advocating
greater participation in the system. Recognising the Protestant
tradition as one which was 'strong and legitimate', he attributed
the loss of 'liberal unionist sympathy' to nationalists on the 'constitutional question'. 'If we are to pursue a policy of non-recognition, the only logical policy is that of Sinn Féin,' he concluded.
Despite his refusal to sign the endorsement form for the October
march, both he and Cooper (who had also refused) were elected

to the committee at the meeting called somewhat secretively in its aftermath.[67]

The defeat of Eamon McCann (he received only 1,993 votes and lost his deposit), one of the march's chief organisers, confirmed Hume's ability to marginalise the militants while playing his own militant card against nationalist moderates. It also served to emphasise how tender a plant radicalism was within the nationalist community. Taking the leadership of the movement from the left, McCann later recalled, was like 'taking candy from a baby'.[68]

One consequence of the Civil Rights victory was the growth of an accompanying mythology, according to which an educated Catholic middle class had emerged from the post-war welfare state and redefined the direction of a Catholic community, dominated by Green backwoodsmen obsessed with the partition issue. This view, which gained currency through its acceptance by the Cameron Report, has survived both in folklore and academic work, despite the academic demolition job since done on its shaky premises.[69]

There was, in fact, as Michael Morgan points out, 'little generational change in the occupational backgrounds of Catholic political activists'. In 1945, for example, six of the ten nationalists elected to Stormont had a third-level education. Of 19 nationalist candidates between 1945 and 1969 only one could be described as 'working class'. The view, therefore, of nationalists as a 'pubocracy and shopocracy' clearly does not stand. Likewise the major expansion in Catholic numbers at university occurred only after 1961 and did not swell until the 1970s. As late as 1958 two thirds of Catholic grammar schools had over 40% fee paying pupils, with one third having over 60% in that category.

Veteran nationalists were perplexed at the way events had overtaken them. In probably the last article of his life Cahir Healy, whose career spanned the entire history of Northern Ireland, of nationalist politics within it and more besides, reviewed the history of his party. He disputed the view that nationalists were inactive. 'The principal points of the PD and people's rights groups were exactly those which had been chief planks in the nationalist policy for years,' he stated, recalling the increases in education grants obtained by them 'and increased in the previous twelve months from 65% to 80%'. 'Nor did we ignore the streets,' he reminded his readers, recalling the confrontation in Enniskillen twenty years before. 'In sober fact they went to most of the extremes with which the new party has recently made us familiar.' Nationalists, he acknowledged, were always friendly with 'unionist democracy, more so than they had since become, unfortunately'. The marches had, he felt 'stirred up sectarian feeling to a pitch not seen for years'. While not condemning this as necessarily 'unwise', he commented that many of the changes, such as Mater Hospital concession, were 'coming gradually … owing to the efforts of the nationalists'. He condemned Sinn Féin's 1950s intervention for denying representation at Westminster to Catholics until Fitt's 1966 election victory and the Unity candidates, Bernadette Devlin in 1969 and Frank McManus in 1970.[70] He might have added that the techniques of demanding the rights of British citizens under the terms of the Government of Ireland Act was nothing new, having been tried without success in the late 1920s and early 1930s and again during the late 1950s and the Lemass era.

Only Eddie McAteer essayed an explanation for their demise. In his assessment of the situation in late March, McAteer concluded: 'I do not believe myself that Irish nationalism will die, although its complexion may change. The Civil Rights campaign, of which we hear so much at present, is simply an efficient takeover of the work which has been carried on for many years by us. The takeover was aided by the folly of ex-Minister William Craig, the all-convincing power of television and our own lack of guile in thinking that the Civil Rights Movement was really non-political.' But he took hope from the state of flux in which all parties found themselves, feeling that the 'shake up' of nationalism and unionism might 'force through a more natural political shape.[71]

It would be easy to dismiss this verdict as the sour grapes of a disgruntled election loser, yet as easy as it would be it would also be equally wrong. For McAteer, despite the 'republicanism' both of his image and family connection, had shown signs of possessing a wider vision as his 1956 initiative showed. One could cavil at his subsequent behaviour – his sneering response to 'Garron Tower', his rejection of the idea of an organised party and of official opposition status, both of which he was later forced by events to accept. In all these cases he was acting in the capacity of a tribal leader (worried by potential Orange gains at his people's expense) or simply of a regional chieftain (fearing the dominance of the 'Omagh group') rather than the statesman manqué future historians may yet see him as having been. To fault him too strongly for these seeming lapses is to forget the fine line northern Catholics have had to walk between an obdurate unionism and a self-regarding south. One only had to look at the perversion by Dublin of his 1956 initiative and the subsequent disillusionment with Lemass to see the dangers any new departure posed. Therefore it is only fair to assess on its merits this post mortem on his defeat.

He was correct, as was Healy, in pointing out that the Civil Rights agenda had featured in nationalist demands down through the years, having taken priority over the simple anti-partition message in the period 1928-34 under Devlin's leadership, and again from the late 50s onwards under McAteer himself. He was also correct (and many historians would support this interpretation) to see the paranoid over-reaction of the Stormont Home Affairs Minister, William Craig, as crucial in tipping the scales towards disaster. For the Civil Rights movement in its initial stages did not reflect a groundswell among northern Catholics. The initial Coalisland to Dungannon march attracted under 3,000 people. The attendance on the watershed march of 5 October 1958 in Derry was measured in three figures, only two hundred of whom came from Derry city itself. (To put this in perspective, 5,000 Derry Catholics attended a football match held at the same time in the Brandywell.) There was little reason therefore why the movement could not have gone the way of other such organisations in the community's history – the IUA in the 30s, for instance, vanishing into the footnotes of academic dissertations – had it not been for Craig's heavy-handedness and the other factor identified by McAteer – that of television.

For the power of the visual image, being demonstrated at that time so effectively in conflicts from Biafra to Vietnam, made it impossible for Catholics to remain apathetic when the brutalisation of their co-religionists confronted them in their living-rooms. In the parlance of the 1960s, their consciousness was raised. Contemporary opinion poll data collected by Professor Richard Rose bears this out. Catholics surveyed in the spring and summer of 1968 were asked if republicans should be permitted to hold parades or meetings banned by the government. 43% disapproved, with 40% agreeing. A year later the percentage disapproving had plummeted to 26%, those approving increasing to 47%, and the number of don't knows expanding from lowly 3% to a substantial 26%.[72] McAteer and most of his colleagues had laid themselves open to criticism by their reluctance to expose the confrontational style of street politics the Civil Rights entailed, a caginess that was to cost them dearly in electoral support, yet they were not alone in their caution. Other supporters of the Civil Rights agenda, members of the NILP, the Liberal party, even the veteran communist Betty Sinclair, who sat on the NICRA executive, all were reluctant to move politics onto the streets, understanding as they did from a lifetime's experience how easily the Pandora's box of tribalism could thereby be opened. After thirty years of conflict and over 3,600 deaths, it is a viewpoint which cannot be lightly dismissed.

CHAPTER 15

Flashpoint

O'Neill has warned his cabinet in January that in 'resisting this molehill of reform we are allowing a mountain to fall on us'. In late April he was gone from office, his election victory having proved a pyrrhic one. His replacement by his cousin, Major James Chichester Clark, who had resigned in protest at O'Neill's belated concession of 'one man one vote', showed the hardliners to be once more in control of the government.

Before Northern Ireland descended into the abyss, one final act remained to be played out. It was to come on Tuesday 12 August in Derry city with the Apprentice Boys demonstration, and to end that weekend with the dispatch of British troops to Belfast after the worst sectarian assaults on Catholic districts there since the 1920s. Tension had remained high in the Bogside and Creggan areas of Derry city since the the previous October, owing to RUC onslaughts in January and April, the latter leaving Samuel Devenney, a father of five, so badly battered in his living room that he died the following July. Not surprisingly, attempted incursions by the police and Orange mobs in the wake of the Apprentice Boys march met with fierce resistance and were repulsed, pitched battles raging on the streets between rioters and the state forces. To relieve the police pressure on the Bogsiders, Civil Rights protests were organised in towns across the north, resulting in serious violence in Dungiven, Dungannon and Armagh, a fatality caused by the B Specials occurring in the latter town. Then the contagion spread to Belfast. Hundreds of Catholic homes were burned in interface areas and thousands of refugees fled before rampaging Orange mobs, while the RUC, abandoning all pretence of impartiality, strafed defenceless Catholic districts with gunfire.

The nationalist leadership, both new and old, turned in despair to Dublin. On 14 August McAteer, on behalf of the beleaguered Bogsiders contacted Neil Blaney, the south's agriculture minis-

ter, following a mob attack on the Roman Catholic cathedral.
Blaney then telephoned the Department of the Taoiseach urging
a response, citing an army source who had confirmed for him
the gravity of the situation.[1] Others adopted a more direct approach. On Friday 15 August, the nationalist MP for East Tyrone
Austin Currie, accompanied by the member for Mourne James
O'Reilly, arrived in Dublin and met the Taoiseach Jack Lynch.
Currie told Lynch that the situation in Coalisland and
Dungannon was 'explosive' and that any announcement Dublin
would make and any course of action adopted 'should highlight
the word 'protection' for the Catholic population'.[2] Lynch had
already gone on television on the night of 13 August to declare,
in words that were to embolden the embattled Bogside as much
as they inflamed Loyalist Belfast, that the Republic would not
stand by and allow innocent people 'be injured or even worse'.
This was accompanied by the establishment of field hospitals
along the border. Clearly Currie had something more substantial in mind when he made his request two days later. Others
were prepared to do more than use ambiguous language in their
approach. On Saturday 16th three MPs arrived in the
Department of External Affairs requesting a meeting with the
Taoiseach. After being told he was unavailable, they were met in
the waiting room by the First Secretary, Hugh McCann. The
three, all newly elected to Stormont that February, were Paddy
Devlin (who had defeated Diamond in Falls on an NILP ticket),
Paddy Kennedy Republican Labour (victorious in Central over
Hanna's successor Brennan running under NDP colours), and
Paddy O Hanlon Independent (the winner in South Armagh).
With Paddy Kennedy as their spokesman they came straight to
the point. The B Specials were running amok in Belfast there was
'continuous sniping' and people were being killed and injured.
Catholics were increasingly being driven deeper into the Falls
Road area and worse seemed in prospect. 'Soon the whole
Catholic population of Belfast' would 'be concentrated' there
and 'would be massacred'. Derry's Bogside was 'mild' by com-
parison. The Catholics of Belfast 'would have to defend themselves and their homes' and it was imperative that the Taoiseach
be seen in connection with this matter. If it were not possible to
send Irish troops across the border, then 'they wanted guns and
would not leave without a definite answer to their request as the
position of the Catholics was increasingly untenable. Nothing,

they stressed, by way of reassurance needed to be done 'openly or politically' – a few hundred rifles could easily be 'lost' and would not be missed.[3]

McCann told them he would have to go through the motions of conveying their message to the proper quarter, assuring them that it would be delivered immediately. The high drama of this meeting, unique in the history of north-south relations, was soon to degenerate into Gilbertian farce.[4] As they had insisted on returning for answers in less than an hour, hurried consultations took place behind the scenes with the 'unavailable' Jack Lynch on an agreed reply. At 11.30 am the three MPs re-entered the department and once more sought a meeting with Lynch. This time they were informed that he could not be found and might even have left the capital for the weekend. They were told that the government had taken 'all the action open to them', that British troops had entered the beleagured Ardoyne enclave in North Belfast, and the situation had calmed down. A request for troops or arms was a matter for the government or even the Dáil and could not be acceded to in this manner, the Secretary stated, though he assured them this did not indicate a lack of concern by the south.

The three MPs reacted angrily to this, accusing the government of fobbing them off. The mercurial Paddy Devlin, 'more angry and emotional than the others, made for the door', insisting that he would see Jack Lynch before leaving for Belfast. He then returned, McCann recalled, 'and muttered something abusive about the government being responsible for death' before leading the others out of the building. Despite assurances before leaving that no lack of concern should be inferred, or that action open to the Irish side would not be taken, they returned empty handed to Belfast.[5]

All three addressed an agitation meeting in O'Connell Street demanding arms for northern Catholics, in company which included the poet John Montague and the historian Liam De Paor.

Behind the scenes, the Irish government had not been idle. On 1 August, at a meeting in the Foreign Office in London, the issue of the likely situation in Derry headed an agenda which included the Nigerian Civil War and Ireland's prospects of EEC membership.[6] In the interests of making matters easier for both the British and Stormont governments, Dr Hillery, the Irish Minister for External Affairs, stressed that the visit was not to be publicised. The minister foresaw trouble at the forthcoming Apprentice Boys march and asked that it be banned or at least rerouted. Neither of these suggestions met with British approval. The head of the British team Michael Stewart, Secretary of State for Foreign and Commonwealth Affairs, waxed lyrical on the 'hopeful signs' that the northern government was pressing ahead with its reforms, denied that these lacked credibility and then added 'very deliberately' that responsibility for the area rested with Stormont and London 'and not with your government'. Dr Hillery accepted that control was in their hands but emphasised the 'very serious repercussion' for Ireland if the situation were to explode. The Secretary of State went on to assure him that Britain was in close touch with Stormont on the issue of reforms that they 'must be the judges of what was best in the circumstances' and matters would not 'get out of hand'. Hugh McCann, Secretary of the Department, among those accompanying Hillery on the Irish side, then pointed to 'gaps' even in the promised reforms 'including some aspects of the discrimination' in housing allocation and employment. North, the Assistant Secretary, countered by pointing to legislation introduced by Stormont for the creation of an Ombudsman at central government level and its stated intention of introducing one at local government level also.[7] The Irish minister then realised he had hit a brick wall. Britain was determined to treat as a purely domestic issue the affairs of Northern Ireland, trusting in the bona fides of the Stormont government to put any irregularities to rights. The exchange between himself and Stewart said it all:

Dr Hillery: You want to handle this yourself. Is the position that we cannot discuss it further?

Rt Hon Michael Stewart: Yes

Hillery: You realise our concern.

Stewart: Yes but I must say to you that there is a limit to which we can discuss with outsiders, even our nearest neighbour, this internal matter. Even if violence erupted engulfing the south, as Hillery feared it might, this would, Stewart reminded him, remain the British line. It was an accurate statement of a position which was to remain without modification until the Anglo Irish Agreement of 1985. An equally unfruitful meeting at the Foreign Office on the 15th,[8] when the predicted violence was an undeniable and ongoing reality, led the Irish government to direct its attentions towards the one supranational authority it believed could help, the United Nations.

Despite the high standing which this organisation enjoyed in Ireland, it was the state's policy since its admission in 1955 not to raise the subject of partition formally therein on the grounds that it would not lead to an effective international mobilisation against the border and would destroy the prospects for a co-operative north-south solution. It now had to consider whether the events since the previous October justified an approach based not on the grounds of self determination but on the threat to peace and human rights.[9] An External Affair memorandum of the following day (16 August) considered these options and the five possible organs of the United Nations to which they might be referred: the General Assembly, the Security Council, the Secretary General, the International Court of Justice and the Economic and Social Council. The final three were ruled out immediately, two of them on largely technical grounds. As far as the International Court of Justice was concerned the memorandum was quite explicit. The 'main difficulty' lay in the 'probability' that the British would take their stance on the Agreement of 1925 and Ireland 'could not afford in any circumstances to have the validity of this Agreement made the determining factor in the UN approach to the question'.[10] It was a reiteration of the departmental conclusion of some years previously that this agreement, so bitterly resented by northern nationalists then and since, had left the southern state with 'little basis' for a legal case against partition.[11] Of the two remaining options the General Assembly offered the better prospect as Ireland would have an opportunity of participating in debates throughout, the procedural requirements of the Security Council making it unlikely that an affirmative quota of nine out of its fifteen members could be obtained. Yet the question of appealing to this body for a peace keeping force was not ruled out although the advice was that the British veto, as a permanent member, meant 'such action' had 'practically no prospect of success'. The earlier calling up of army reserves and creation of field hospitals had been undertaken, Hillery admitted, in the belief that Britain would agree to such a request.[12] The 'main value' of such an approach to this forum would, in the view of his civil servants, simply be the ventilation of the question and the accompanying publicity it would bring.[13] In this spirit, Hillery made his appeal to the Security Council for a UN force. Behind the scenes Hugh McCann lobbied the American Ambassador, John Moore, for help in the matter, to be told that 'United States alliances' made a negative response likely. Confidential trans-Atlantic phone calls made by Moore from his London embassy to Washington (to avoid a British tap on the Irish line) elicited only the prospect of a hearing for the Irish case without any formal placement on the agenda.[14] As events turned out the Irish efforts were unnecessary. Britain waived its right to oppose 'inscription' and the matter went ahead. Zambia, perhaps under British direction, pressed for an adjournment and the issue vanished. The British Home Secretary, James Callaghan, later explained that Britain understood the Irish action as one which lay within the realm of gesture politics intended largely for home consumption.[15]

With the Security Council a non-starter, Irish efforts then turned towards the General Assembly. In its preparation of the case, the Department of External Affairs stressed that its explanatory memorandum 'should be couched in general and restrained language', emphasising the human rights issues involved and eschewing any references to 'the right of self determination or similar political concepts'. This, they were careful to point out, did not preclude 'in the course of the debate, relating the present crisis ... to the root cause' of partition.[16] An intensive canvass to secure 'inscription' was called for, and was undertaken with mixed results. The debate in the Assembly went ahead, revealing confusion about the situation among many of the countries involved. Significantly Nigeria (the beneficiary of British military backing in its ongoing two year war against the Biafran secession) successfully terminated matters by calling for an adjournment to allow a vote be taken. Certain that it lacked the number required to carry the day, the Irish side tactfully withdrew,[17] the second and final phase of its UN diplomatic offensive having proved as much a damp squib as the first.

Yet the initiative was the first undertaken internationally by the government since the 1950s on the partition issue. In its reactive, moderate, even tentative nature, it spoke eloquently of the inherent limitations within the republic's northern policy. It also served to show how the international community was no more receptive to this muted message than it had been to the strident border-bashing of a decade and a half earlier.[18] And it reaffirmed the obstacles placed by international law in Ireland's path, not only those deriving from the UN's founding charter regarding the integrity of states (which Dublin was at that time reasserting in support of Nigeria's struggle against its break-away region),[19] but also those bequeathed by an earlier Irish government through the 1925 Agreement.[20]

Even before the final rejection had been received, the Irish government was reassessing the situation. On 29 August every member of the Cabinet was circulated with a memorandum on the question, drafted by the Tánaiste, Erskine Childers himself, three days earlier.[21] Partition, it stressed, had had 'divergent effects at different periods since 1921': thirty years earlier 'less' developed educational and investment benefits existed north of the border and the Nationalist Party was 'more active but still not effectual'. Within the previous twenty years growth had taken place in the north's social services, its capital investment, industrial employment and GNP which placed it ahead of the republic. These benefits were, however, unequally distributed; discrimination had continued 'even if diminished in certain fields' and by the standards of western society was 'now accentuated', a point which could be used with 'elaboration and reorientation' by the government's PR team. But the memorandum was explicit from the start that its objective was not the furtherance of a public relations campaign on what had taken place in the north, but the future outlines of Dublin's policy on unity. This policy, according to the document, had been inaugurated through the Lemass/O'Neill initiative with a view to the demolition of inter communal prejudices, making both communities 'more mutually dependent', with a view to better trade relations and EEC entry. Hopeful pointers in this regard 'were the tariff reductions, the tourism, railway, road transport' and electricity agreements and the inter-governmental Foyle fisheries commission. The parallel process of ecumenism within the Catholic Church since Vatican II had, it was stressed, contributed to this climate of reapproachment, with 'middle class groups meeting socially on a basis unheard of ten years previously'. In this context a section of the Protestant population, the more prosperous and better educated, had become champions of the deprived and victimised among the Catholic community and to a lesser extent among their own. The 40-50% of Protestants expressing the opinion that 'partition would end some day' was seen as reflective of this new mood. In his assessment of the nationalist group, the writer was scathing, criticing the absence since 1921 of a 'Fianna Fáil type movement' among them. 'On the basis of the Fianna Fáil evolutionary policy of 1932-47, the nationalist party's policies had, he asserted, been 'weak, contradictory' and 'unrealistic'. The document acknowledged, in the course of its appraisal of the north's better social services, that a new type of Catholic was being produced who queried the feasibility of unity unless the republic could match the British subvention, a fact reflected in opinion polls. If Dublin was to engage in a campaign of trying to 'revive nationalism in the north' the economic argument was therefore inescapable and a thirty-two-county finance policy a necessity. Southern policy had, consequently, to be viewed in 'two phases', of an 'ad hoc policy' in response to the immediate crisis and a 'permanent policy' which would emerge were peace to continue with the British army maintaining public order and the promised reforms implemented. The key factor determining which policy would gain the ascendant was the question of whether or not the bulk of the minority population would adopt 'a strong nationalist political organisation', non-sectarian and non-abstentionist in character, 'taking the Fianna Fáil party as an example in not rushing fences too quickly', an organisation prepared to have cordial relations privately or otherwise with Dublin. The writer was pessimistic of the chances of this policy succeeding, and not simply because of hardline unionist opposition. There was the problem of left wing elements within the Civil Rights movement 'plus the old nationalist element and extreme Marxist republicans'. There were the hundreds of thousands on both sides, who wished 'above all for peace' and whose consequent lack of direction could delay a nationalist revival, and there were what the report sniffily described as 'the Bogsider type of people' from the last named category.

In order that the policy should succeed many problems had to be addressed not least the abovementioned economic one. A sympathetic international press had to be cultivated, unionist majority consent had to be obtained, a clear formula for ending partition had to be created *ex nihilo,* considering amongst other matters constitutional change and the removal of denominational legislation.[22] The author recalled how Fianna Fáil's own accession to power in 1932 'compromised' its '1916 position as political realists' and asked if the success of a 'gradualist policy' in the twenty-six counties since partition might not predispose the electorate there to accept a similar one north of the border. The

'official policy' would look 'extremely rigid' on entering the
EEC and could be counter-productive from a public relations
point of view if a northern peace settlement was reached.[23]

The document marked another milestone on the road first
mapped out by the Department of External Affairs in early 1957,
a road already signposted by the Lemass/O'Neill meeting, the
Anglo Irish Free Trade Agreement and the changes recommended
by the government's committee on the constitution. Coming at a
time when Catholic homes in Belfast had barely stopped smoul-
dering, with the south having passed through one of its biggest
emotional spasms since the 1950s, and the government PR agen-
cies abroad still peddling the 'official line', its significance cannot
be overstated.[24] It contained in outline the elements which
would inform government policy for the foreseeable future: a
strategy of conciliation towards unionism, a parallel fostering of
an alternative to the nationalist party within the minority community (the use of the term 'our people' was to be deprecated), a
trust that a process of incrementalism would chime with the
reformism of the British government to produce a new dispensation.[25] One clause of the memorandum deserves to be quoted in
full, as it pointed to a cloud on the horizon:

> Everything I have said presumes a tough control of the new
> IRA. Their incursion will spell disaster. The IRA can only de-
> stroy any reputation we have and discourage unity in the six
> counties'.[26]

On the surface, this seemed a reasonable assertion by a state
over those acting without a 'mandate' from within its jurisdiction. Yet what if Britain's reform policy was to fail, if 'the
Bogsider type of people' proved more numerous than expected,
if the 'new IRA' was to become not a southern shock minority
but the striking force of a large alienated section of the northern
Catholic working class? The continuation of this policy would
then be possible only by ignoring the grievances and even the
existence of this constituency. It was to be part of the tragedy of
Northern Ireland that this approach of wilful blindness was persisted in for most of the next twenty years.

The ten months following the arrival of British troops gave
the co-operation policy a new lease of life. The British government had been forced at last to sit up and take notice. In one
sweep all the *desiderata* of the Civil Rights Movement and the
nationalist party before them had been granted. Catholics sat on

the Advisory Committee of the UDR. Some Nationalist MPs encouraged Catholics to join the new regiment. Likewise the RUC, in the process of being disarmed and restructured under the terms of the Hunt Report, was slowly regaining lost ground. Eddie McAteer, in October 1969, recommended that Catholics should 'accept' the 'new unarmed' force.[27]

Events were overtaking the policy, however. The inquiry into the savage beating of Samuel Devenney in April 1969 (he died three months later) foundered on what Chichester Clark called a 'conspiracy of silence'. A Criminal Justice Act, directed against rioters, hit hardest at the youth in disturbed nationalist areas. Incitement to Hatred legislation proved farcical when the sole prosecution brought against a loyalist extremist collapsed on a technicality. The Derry Bogside exploded in rioting when Bernadette Devlin received a six month jail sentence for her part in the defence of the area the previous August, in what the inhabitants saw as an official commemtary on the morality of the resistance. Then early in July the British army carried out a savage house-to-house search for arms in the Lower Falls, deluging the area with CS gas and imposing a thirty-five-hour curfew.[28]

With the Catholic community so sensitised by the events, it was to be a fatal milestone on the road towards their outright alienation from the state. And there was an extra parliamentary pole for this alienation. The emergence of a separate northern command within the IRA the previous September was the forerunner of the major split within the entire movement which resulted in the formation of a 'Provisional Army Council'. The development was a reflection not merely of resentment at the movement's impotence in the face of loyalist attacks upon the Catholic community in Belfast the previous August, but also of hostility at the leftward drift it had been taking under the McGiolla-Garland leadership. In their statement outlining the reasons for the split, the caretaker executive of the Provisionals' political wing listed only as number four the 'failure to give maximum possible defence in Belfast and other areas in August 1969', behind such factors as 'internal methods in the movement', 'extreme socialism leading to dictatorship' and, above all, the recognition by the mainstream movement of the Dublin, Stormont and Westminster parliaments'.[29]

While the involvement in the split of the Dublin government was certainly greater than IRA Chief of Staff MacStiofáin admits,[30] though probably less than his erstwhile comrades allege,[31] there is clear evidence from the diaries of Peter Berry, Secretary of the Department of Justice, that a redirection of the movement from its preoccupation with social agitation in the south was desired by them.[32] Under the pressure of events in August 1969, a northern sub-committee had been conceded to hardliners in the Cabinet who then proceeded to liaise with members of the Defence Committees formed in Catholic areas of the north in the wake of that month's events, promising relief which included weaponry.[33] The Dublin Arms Trial of 1970 rang down the curtain on this aberrant episode in the republic's policy but left unanswered the question of Cabinet complicity in the affair.

McAteer's worry that nationalism had passed into history was premature, though the reality was to do his party little good. Faced with the apparent failure of reforms and an ever-increasing level at state repression, the one tradition of resistance with roots in Irish soil, the republican one, acquired a new significance extending far wider than the north's pockets of traditional republicanism, encompassing the most deprived and put upon sections of the Catholic population and, most importantly, including for the first time in its history, Belfast. In Derry city, for example, where the Easter Commemoration of 1969 had attracted only a derisory attendance, by 1971 with military repression a daily occurrence, one writer could recall how 'the guiltily discarded tradition on which the community was formed was after all meaningful and immediately relevant'.[34] This new development in northern nationalism uncovered an extra division cross cutting the more established cleavages of region and tradition within that community's politics, one of social class, as well as producing the most successful guerrilla war against the British state in Ireland since the 1920s. Caught between the upper and nether millstones of long-standing injustice and pro-state repression – Dom Helder Camara's first and third tier of violence – this constituency continued to provide a support base for the 'middle tier', the violence of the oppressed, despite the unanimous and unrelenting hostility of 'respectable' Ireland.[35]

The Nationalist Party, which met in convention in November 1969, did so in an atmosphere of gloom and uncertainty made worse by the defection of two of its representatives, Thomas Gormley and Austin Currie, shortly beforehand. Even the presence of the young Fianna Fáil TD, Ray McSharry, as a fraternal delegate from the republic's government and the welcome the conference gave to Jack Lynch's recent speech in Trale, Co Kerry (in which he pledged Dublin as the 'second guarantor' of the northern minority's position, Britain being the first), could not disguise the feeling that events had overtaken them. One delegate summed up the mood vividly when he remarked, 'even on a grave flowers can grow and life begin again'. In this spirit, the party gave McAteer the consolation prize of party president, approved the British-imposed northern reforms, supported the Tyrone MP, Roderick O'Connor, in his new role as parliamentary leader, and looked, with more hope than confidence, to the future.

Though the Nationalist Party had effectively been written out of the script by the Dublin government, it did not seem aware of the fact. On 2 December, replying to a supplementary question in Dáil Éireann, Jack Lynch explicitly stated that it would be wrong ... and rather divisive to have consultation 'only with them' yet they persisted in their approaches to Dublin as if nothing had changed. On 14 February 1970 their Executive Secretary wrote to the Taoiseach's office stating that it would be of 'very considerable advantage' if a 'combined committee' could be established consisting of members of the republic's government and of the party itself 'to keep the situation in the six counties under constant review'. The reply drafted by the Dublin civil servants for the Taoiseach's approval said it even more clearly than Lynch himself had. Not only was the suggestion unacceptable for 'reasons of principle' which existed in the past against the idea of a 'formal connection' between the government and a northern political party, but there was the 'additional consideration that the Nationalist Party itself' was in a disorganised condition and might even vanish as a serious force within 'a foreseeable time'. The writer went on to explain:

> The main reason for this loss of influence is connected with the ideas and techniques developed in the Civil Rights Movement which proved to be far more successful in changing the situation in the north than the traditional approach of the nationalist party. This is recognised even among nationalist MPs such as Austin Currie who has shown a public tendency to disassociate himself from the nationalist party.[36]

But there was another reason for Dublin's wariness. Secret information had reached them that there was 'a move on foot in the north to create a new political party which would be entitled something like 'Social Democratic and Labour Party', the founding members of which were likely to include John Hume, Ivan Cooper and Paddy O'Hanlon (Independent), Paddy Devlin (Northern Ireland Labour Party), Austin Currie (Nationalist) and probably Thomas Gormley (ex-Nationalist). There was still considerable doubt as to whether Gerry Fitt (Republican Labour) would participate but the information was that the others intended to go ahead without him in that eventuality, with a decision due on the subject the following day (February 24th). The new party, if it took wing, would be likely to attract other members if the opposition and, though the four remaining nationalists were tied to a pledge at their last party conference not to enter any new party, it was thought probable that they would in due course form at least a relationship with it. It was further likely that Paddy Kennedy, the Republican Labour MP for Belfast Central, would follow Fitt into the party (he didn't) were the latter to take the plunge (he did and was elected the party's leader). The sole remaining member of the Stormont opposition, Vivian Simpson, was deemed unlikely to leave the NILP.

In conclusion, therefore, the advice was that the creation of this new organisation and its 'probable consequences for the future' meant it was 'not the time to form a liason with the nationalist party, even if there were not other objections of principle'.[37]

The new party's choice of title, when it held its inaugural meeting on 21 August 1970, was the one the government had anticipated, the SDLP, a reflection of the need to encompass the labourites from Belfast.[38] The choice of Gerry Fitt as leader also served a similar purpose (Hume became his deputy and Devlin ran the new Belfast office). In addition it provided the party not only with an entré to British Labour circles, where Fitt's stock stood high since his election in 1966, but also through his good offices, with an affiliation to the Socialist International and its (considerable) financial support.

Eddie McAteer was among those welcoming the new arrival, recalling correctly that his thinking had long been moving along similar lines. In fact two months beforehand, when Hume had supported McAteer's unsuccessful candidacy for Westminster, managing his campaign and writing his manifesto, (to the chagrin of some within the nascent party) he allegedly received a promise that a merger would occur.[39] Ideologically, in its forthright acceptance of change only with the consent of a majority within Northern Ireland, the SDLP reflected the influence of the NDP which was absorbed into its ranks *en masse*. Given the ease with which the creation and character of the new organisation fitted Dublin's overall strategy, there was little doubt what the response would be from that quarter. 'They were running after us – whatever he wanted we got', one of the founding members recalled.[40] Those who predicted that the new party would wrest the initiative from the Provisionals and move politics off the streets were to be disappointed. Like so much else before it, the SDLP found itself dragged along by the momentum events.

In July 1971, after giving a qualified welcome to the proposals of the new Prime Minister, Brian Faulkner, offering a role to the minority on Stormont committees, they found themselves forced into the old nationalist tactic of withdrawal from parliament when an inquiry into two killings of Catholic youths by the British Army was refused.[41] By that stage, the Provisionals' defensive role had given way to an all-out war on the state. With the introduction of internment, Catholic alienation from the state reached a climax, demonstrated by withdrawals from all public boards, resignations from the UDC and RUC (now included within the IRA's range of targets) and the inauguration of a civil disobedience campaign. This and the maelstrom of violence which followed swept away the Stormont regime and paved the way for a new British initiative.

One group who failed to benefit from it was the nationalist party. Caught between the Provisionals on one side and the SDLP on the other, they found themselves without a role. When the elections were called for the 1973 Assembly, (part of Britain's new policy of inter communal powersharing with an 'Irish dimension', i.e. a role for Dublin) Eddie McAteer went to meet Ruairí Ó Brádaigh, President of Sinn Féin, in Bundoran to request that the Provisionals lift their election boycott and enable his party to mount a serious opposition to the SDLP.[42] When the request was turned down McAteer went back to Derry to face electoral eclipse. With only 8,270 first preference votes in a contest where the SDLP obtained 159,773 and the Republican Clubs 13,064, the Nationalists had reached the end of the road as the representative voice of northern Catholics.

The SDLP, like Sinn Féin in 1955, had maximised its vote by the number of constituencies in which it ran. A closer look at the figures reveals that their poll was under half that of eligible Catholic voters in the north (47.3%). Even in the constituency where the percentage of the poll was highest, 71.7% in Fermanagh South Tyrone, there was resentment by the party towards the Unity MP at Westminster, Frank McManus, for supporting the boycott which they felt lost them a seat.

The continued existence of another type of nationalism from the one they represented had been emphasised as early as the May local elections when four Unity candidates were elected to Fermanagh County Council. A similar number were elected to Dungannon UDC and two more to Omagh. Republicans were represented among them; one councillor in the Dungannon area, Patsy Kelly, held an officership in the Provisional IRA (he was later murdered by loyalists).

The existence of two Catholic norths was re-emphasised with a vigour in the Westminster general election in February 1974 (during the reign of the short lived Executive) when the SDLP opposed the two Unity candidates, McManus and McAliskey, who had both been critical of the Sunningdale package. The total SDLP vote of 34,782 was only slightly larger than the non-SDLP one of 32,401. Significantly neither of the newspaper chains, the North West Publishing Company nor the Observer group, ever swung their weight totally behind the party.[43] In the West Belfast seat, while Gerry Fitt romped home with a comfortable 19,554, it was still far behind his 1966 and 1970 election totals though his sole opponent from within the Catholic community, Albert Price, received only 5,662 votes.

The powersharing executive marked the apogee of Dublin's masterplan formulated in that wicked month of August 1969. Its collapse clearly demonstrated that there were limits to its potential. Not only the most obvious one, its failure to win over the bulk of loyalist opinion whose protest action toppled the executive, but also the refusal to recognise, much less understand, this other nationalist north. With the downfall of the Sunningdale Agreement the attempt to relate to the former group achieved a new urgency often reaching heights which worried even moderate sections of northern Catholic opinion. The prospects of getting a hearing for this latter group, declined in inverse proportion.

Epilogue

As the decade wore on this policy of self-delusion continued within the Irish establishment, aided by a stifling climate of censorship and state repression. Though elections north of the border in 1975, '77 and '79 brought slippages in the votes of leading SDLP figures and revealed the electoral potential of an organised alternative,[1] any recognition of this failed to register in a mood dominated by the need to bolster Gerry Fitt's party and deny legitimacy to the ongoing IRA campaign. Not even the unprecedented mobilisations in support of the H Block prisoners were able to make an impact. The August 1978 condemnation by Cardinal Tomás Ó Fiaich of conditions prevailing in the jail drew criticism even from the traditionalist *Irish News*. Questioned in the Dáil on the issue by the veteran socialist Dr Noel Browne, the Foreign Affairs Minister Michael O'Kennedy wondered aloud if the deputy understood the implications of what was being asked. After the crisis escalated into a hunger strike in 1980 a prominent journalist, sympathetic to the protestors, could conclude from the largely northern composition of the massive demonstrations held in the capital that the nationalist minority was doomed to go its own way, ignored and despised by the rest of Ireland.[2] When the issue reignited the following spring with the hunger strike of the prisoners' leader, Bobby Sands, so confident was RTÉ of the latter's defeat in the Fermanagh South Tyrone by-election that it refrained from sending a camera crew to Enniskillen to cover the result. This attitude of denial remained a *leit motif* throughout the saga despite the undeniable groundswell of support for the protest among northern Catholics (Sands' funeral was the largest accorded to any Irishman since Parnell) and electoral successes for hunger strikers and their allies north and south of the border. Only with the Sinn Féin vote in the northern assembly elections of 1982 and the Westminster contest of 1983 did change finally occur.

278

Faced with the shortcomings of its own propaganda, the Dublin government reacted with panic. The complacency of 1955/56 was not to be repeated. Garret Fitzgerald later acknowledged in his autobiography that this fear of a Sinn Féin resurgence was the principal reason behind the Forum process and the subsequent Anglo-Irish Agreement.[3] The intended beneficiary, the SDLP, happily adapted to the new greener political landscape.

Thatcher's rejection of the Forum report produced an outraged restatement by Hume of the old case against the border, in a southern Sunday newspaper.[4] The eventual November 1985 Anglo-Irish Agreement, for all the fanfarade surrounding it, simply formalised what had been accepted practice since the foundation of the state – Dublin's role as 'second guarantor' (in Jack Lynch's 1969 phrase) of the rights of the Catholic minority. This had been demonstrated many times before, never more successfully than during the conscription crisis of 1939 and 1941 and the Williams affair of 1942. On issues like the funding of the Mater Hospital, it had continued through the 1960s. What was significant now, apart from the optics, was the inability thereafter of the British to tell their Irish counterparts publicly or privately to mind their own business.

While the symbolism of the new accord pushed the north to the brink of civil war, its lack of substantive accomplishments was grist to the republican propaganda mill. London, moreover, showed every sign of seeing the agreement in a different light than did Dublin. The Catholics, on whose behalf the whole exercise was supposedly being conducted, remained singularly unimpressed. An opinion poll published almost three years after the agreement showed 64% of Catholics disagreeing with the proposition that it had ameliorated in the position of nationalists. 54% disagreed with the view that it had produced an improvement in the fair allocation of jobs. Only in the area of co-operation between the Gardaí and RUC did a majority of Catholics, 54%, feel that any change had taken place.[5] Significantly, while 60.4% of Catholics 'would find it acceptable' that Dublin should be given a voice under the Anglo-Irish Agreement, 30.5% stated the opposite. On the 'alienation' which the accord was designed to reverse, a Price Waterhouse survey published nine months before it was signed, showed 47% of Catholics agreeing with the view that 'the RUC was doing the job fairly' as against 53% who felt the opposite.[6] However, only 4% felt they were 'very fair' – the corresponding figure for Protestants was 37%.

With this new approach by mainstream nationalism came an increased willingness to condemn actions of the northern state which had previously been allowed to pass uncensored. Not that the behaviour of the south's own security forces gave it room for comment. The year 1984, which marked the tactical change about to the northern question, was characterised by several scandals involving the Garda Síochána including the acquittal of policemen charged with the death of a man in custody and the extraction of confessions from a County Kerry family in an infanticide case. Condemnations made of the northern authorities on the strip-searching issue overlooked the fact that the practice remained a routine one in southern prisons. Likewise the controversy over the use of 'plastic bullets' revealed that the more lethal rubber bullets which they replaced were still stocked by the Irish army. The northern minority itself was not of course immune to the same form of doublethink.[8]

Moxon-Browne's 1979 survey found that 61% of Catholics felt a 'tougher line' on the IRA was required from the southern government with 64% approving of extradition in the cases of political offences. It is this mentality which explains the 'gut reaction' of 'absolute delight' voiced by a prominent SDLP member when members of the Irish army and Gardaí staged an ambush on two republican fugitives in 1987, killing one of them.

As the Anglo-Irish process unfolded Sinn Féin drew sustenance from the hard line taken by constitutional nationalism. A booklet entitled *The Good Old IRA* (documenting the atrocities of the early movement as a riposte to those who contrast it favourably with its successor) stated in the foreword (written by Sinn Féin publicist Danny Morrison)[9] that Peter Barry's definition of the northern state as 'a nationalist nightmare, the SDLP's 'own complaints about the system' and Cardinal Ó Fiaich's December 1984 statement on the subject of 'alienation' (the vogue word of political discourse since Sinn Féin emerged) 'lend credence to the republican case for armed struggle'. It was this seeming convergence of mainstream and militant nationalism which elicited the first signs from the republican movement of a willingness to move towards the centre. This is a fact constantly forgotten by those who see in the genesis of the peace process simply Sinn Féin's response to such phenomena as the changed international climate, the exigencies of Pax Americana, the increased attrition by both loyalist death squads and the security forces, the party's failure to overtake the SDLP or even, as one northern professor has suggested, a mid life crisis among republicans. While all of these factors have their place in any overall explanation, none of them can be considered decisive. Many were encountered and surmounted in the past. Others, like the loyalist threat, can be overstated. Down to the ceasefire the IRA possessed a military capacity which enabled it to strike hard at the upper echelons of Protestant paramilitarism and to continue offensive operations reaching even into London's financial heartland.

What was significant was that for the first time a section of constitutional nationalism, principally within the SDLP (with some help from elements of Fianna Fáil) chose to approach republicans with a view to achieving an accommodation. Northern republicans, whose heart had always been in some form of pan nationalism, responded with a will. As far back as 1986 Gerry Adams publicly regretted that the class differences between Sinn Féin and the SDLP leaders had been 'unnecessarily brought out' by the emergence of his party. Though he acknowledged that these differences could not be disguised it might have been better, he felt, 'in this phase of the independence struggle if there could have been some kind of general unity'.[10]

The modification or even the abandonment of radicalism in the interests of this objective was, of course, no cause for amazement. The history of Irish republicanism provides many such examples. But no matter how great the pressures, 'armed struggle' remained a central tenet of faith, suspended only under force of circumstances with the intention of being resumed at the first available opportunity. Considerations of feasibility came a poor second to the perpetuation of a tradition within what was mostly a closely knit family based organisation. The seeming illogicality and casuistry of Patrick Pearse's Court Martial Speech, with its assertion that 'to fight is to win', would have made perfect sense to such people. But, as this history has attempted to show, for most of the twentieth century that tradition remained a heavily marginalised one in the nationalist north, its practitioners seen largely as southern interlopers.

It was not, however, an alien tradition. Peripheral though it was, it remained the extreme expression of the national culture within which most northern Catholics were reared. Down the years it had functioned as a psychological comfort blanket for many, gaining an occasional, transient, emotional and largely symbolic electoral endorsement. Then came 1969 and its aftermath. In the sensitised, inflamed and emotional circumstances, a dialectic of oppression and ethnic consciousness made the extreme seem reasonable.

It was the absence of any other meaning system as an explanatory framework for those forced into rebellion by the injustices of the northern state which gave the republican movement its relevance. As far back as the late 1970s, long before Sinn Féin established itself as a political force, a participant observation study conducted in the Ardoyne area of North Belfast (a stronghold of the Provisionals, surrounded on all sides by loyalist territory) noted the undeniable but widely suppressed fact that this IRA campaign was the first since the 1920s to win mass support. It concluded by way of explanation:

> Volunteers in the IRA to the 1960s were fighting much more of a national liberation war while those today are fighting in a civil rights war expressed in national liberation terms. Support in the north did not originally emanate from the desires of national aspiration but from the drive for civil equality. Without the civil rights consciousness there would be little support for the IRA's traditional goal of a united Ireland to be obtained by force; with civil equality there would be nothing like the allegiance to a united Ireland there is in the Catholic communities. The irony in the unionist jibe that CRA (Civil Rights Association) was just another way of writing 'IRA' was not that it was true, because the IRA never totally dominated that movement, but that civil rights were later to become expressed in terms of republicanism.[11]

Despite appearances to the contrary, northern republicans brought a practical cast of mind to bear on the hidebound sacrosanctities of the tradition within which they operated. Theory sat uneasily on them and held a perfunctory and pro forma character. Asked in 1978 what mandate the IRA campaign had, an Army Council spokesman replied that though he 'could return' to the one obtained in the 1918 election, his movement preferred to see theirs as deriving from the injustices of the system they were opposing.[12] Similarly Sinn Féin's 1986 abandonment of ab-

stentionism from Dáil Éireann, a cornerstone principle of traditional republicanism, produced major repercussions only among
its southern supporters.[13] Theologians and pragmatists came to
a parting of the ways as a largely northern component, originating in the Civil Rights Movement, diverged from a minuscule
southern one, deriving from that state's civil war, a conflict in
which few northern Catholics had taken the republican side.
While the influence of republicanism on northern Catholics
brought a restraining hand on the sectarian impulses which
many times in the subsequent decades had threatened to engulf
the province by repaying militant loyalism in kind, the non-
ideological character of northern nationalism, its concern with
status and identity rather than territorial expansionism, worked
its spell in the opposite direction. Republicanism never matched
in depth what successive elections showed it was capable of
achieving in extent. As the late Professor J. H. Whyte pointed
out shortly before his untimely death, only one opinion poll out
of twenty five conducted between 1973 and 1985 showed as
many as 50% of Northern Catholics citing a united Ireland as
their preferred option.[14] Although Irish reunification remained
for most a 'distant objective sometime in the future', this figure
(77% in 1974, 82% in the early 1980s) did not translate into a
positive political choice or even prove incompatible with continued support for the union (consistently rating in repeated
surveys as roughly a quarter). Even among Sinn Féin's followers
support for a united Ireland (79%) is not absolute. Likewise the
twin axioms of republican thinking, that 'British Rule' and 'the
Border' are the biggest problems, received a rating of 44% and
11% among the party's faithful, dropping to a lowly 4% endorsement from those of the SDLP. Overall in the nationalist community a mere 9% and 5% viewed them in this light. Similarly the
view that the presence of British troops constituted the biggest
problem received a 4% ranking (13% among Sinn Féin supporters, 3% among the followers of the SDLP). Topping the list of
changes necessary to end the troubles was the creation of equal
opportunity, clocking up a total of 33%.[15]

The absence of a split or even a significant splinter following
the republican movement's decision to move from armed conflict to participation in a devolved administration is not, therefore, to be wondered at given the cultural and historical background within which it operated. In what is perhaps a further

reflection of the northerners' disregard for dogma, those among them who actually departed – principally the so called 'Real IRA' – stayed separate from Ó Brádaigh and his southern doctrinaires. Significantly such discontent as was recorded north of the border came largely from the puddles of traditionalist thinking, principally South Armagh.

The IRA campaign had begun in an era of one party rule, unfulfilled civil rights demands, and growing military repression. It ended at a time when an enlarged Catholic middle class, the beneficiaries of British Fair Employment Legislation, had diverged even further from their working class co-religionists. Its conclusion opened the way for a Sinn Féin resurgence north and south of the border as the party widened its appeal, giving it for the first time the serious prospect of both leadership of the nationalist community and participation in the Republic's government. The unmistakable nationalist endorsement of the 1998 Good Friday Agreement (most opinion polls put Catholic support for it in the upper 90% range) reflected hope as well as complacency. The injustices which sustained support for guerrilla warfare across two and a half decades had not suddenly disappeared. A survey compiled three years before the ceasefire demonstrated clearly that a world still remained to be won. Entitled the *Directory of Discrimination*, it confirmed Catholic under-representation across eight major sectors of the economy, including the 'politically correct' academic institutions. Other studies have shown Catholic male unemployed to be three times the UK average, with Catholic areas and West Belfast exceeding by a similar multiple the worst affected area of Britain. On top of this social deprivation, itself an inextricable part of the legacy of historical injustice, these areas have endured the majority of sectarian assassinations and the bulk of military repression. How successfully their needs are catered for in any final settlement will determine not only the quality of the peace which is to come but also the contours of northern nationalist politics in the future.

Overview and Conclusion

The 1918 general election in Ulster emphasised a division within northern nationalism as clearly as it emphasised the one between Ulster and the other three provinces.[1] Though an overall trend towards Sinn Féin was reflected in nationalist Ulster outside of Belfast, Devlin's Falls constituency remained loyal to the IPP.

The municipal elections of 1920, conducted on the older franchise, confirmed by the success of the IPP over Sinn Féin across the north that their earlier success in that province, if nowhere else, derived from the enlargement of the electorate.

In May 1921 the election, conducted on the new franchise and under PR, highlighted even more clearly the existence of two Catholic norths, the more so since both parties professed unity in a common cause. Despite the transfer arrangement between the parties, of Sinn Féin's 34,654 transferable votes only 7,016 went to the IPP (a figure heavily weighted by the vote of Fermanagh Sinn Féin candidate, Sean O'Mahony which transferred in its entirety). Once again the east-west division was emphasised with Sinn Féin, despite an increased vote, still trailing Devlin in his stronghold and the latter admitting privately that only an arrangement with Sinn Féin enabled him to win votes elsewhere.[2] He had in fact been reluctant to commit his party to the election at all, only being persuaded by Dillon and others. Nonetheless the ability of the IPP to scrape home there, despite a manifest lack of cooperation from its uneasy allies, bore witness to the continued existence of the Home Rule constituency largely impervious to the changed patterns of the Irish political scene.

The IRA, as John McCoy recalled from his Armagh experience,[3] developed in the leeway of Sinn Féin, never matching it in extent. The lack of a significant IRB tradition (crucial in those areas of Ireland where rebellion was strongest), coupled with the loyalist presence, the Hibernian opposition and apathy within their own ranks, all left the northern IRA a derisory contrast with the 'war zone' counties. Out of more than 500 IRA casualties in 1920-1921 only 25 were from the six counties.[4] And it was mainly rural. In both Belfast and Derry it remained a marginal force, realising itself only in a defensive capacity. The presence of National Volunteers alongside them in that role, and the constant supervision of the Catholic Church, ensured that no long term benefit would accrue. The Catholic Church, despite its dalliance with Sinn Féin, deprecated IRA activity. The 1919 Lenten Pastorals of even the pro-Sinn Féin bishops, McHugh and Mulhern, remained at one with that of the Home Ruler Logue in their condemnation of secret societies. Faced with the possibility of success at the Peace Conference, the increase in military repression and, above all else, a threat to their control of education, it was important to counsel unity on a divided flock.

In class terms Sinn Féin differed from the Home Rule Party in the greater preponderance both of the *petit bourgeoisie* and of intellectual occupations within its ranks. For the alternative social force, that of organised Labour, which outpolled Sinn Féin and the IPP in the province in the January 1920 municipal elections, these were to be significant years. By 1919, Derry city alone had 12,000 unionised workers. The movement, however, tacked to the prevailing wind of pan-nationalism in the elections of June 1920 and May 1921 as much as in 1918. With all allowances made for personal pique, as he himself had played the Labour card, there was some point in the jibe of the Tyrone Home Ruler, Skeffington, at his party's conference in Killymoon Castle, that Labour had deserted Protestant workers by 'running the movement at the tail end of Sinn Féin'.[5] Had Labour not done so, conflict such as later resulted with the Catholic Church would have been inevitable. Throughout this period the northern bishops muttered darkly about 'class warfare', 'the greatest evil of the present day' as Bishop McKenna told a St Vincent de Paul function in December 1919.[6]

Much and all as the electoral results revealed the cleavage between Belfast and the west in terms of willingness to reach an accommodation with the system, the hard line of many Home Rulers in the city must not be lost sight of. Even though fracture lines had appeared by autumn with the nationalist party's April 1921 rejection of the northern parliament, none more eager for a refusal of the policy than Devlin himself, a proposal by a nationalist councillor in the city to this end in early 1922 was roundly condemned at a subsequent branch meeting.[7] The presence of 9,000 expelled workers in their midst stiffened their rejectionist attitude. By June, with widespread demoralisation set in, the Devlinite electorate reverted to type. That Devlin's own attitude at this stage remained one of non-recognition, even with the bishops in a state of near paranoia on the educational question, reflected his new found loyalty to the strategy of the Dublin government.

Dublin throughout these eventful years had remained a distant presence, its wartime exhortations to the northern IRA unfulfilled, unfulfillable and unsupported by practical aid from GHQ. Southerners like Charlie Daly, sent north to command the 2nd Northern Division, had been met with local suspicion and the mistrust was mutual.[8] A southern fear of 'sectarianism' lay behind De Valera's rejection of a pan-Catholic front proposed by a Cookstown doctor after the Truce.[9]

The outmanoeuvring of the Irish delegation to the Treaty negotiations meant the acceptance of a Boundary Commission and the inevitable exclusion from the Free State of the AOH stronghold east of the Bann. The 'will o' the wisp of sovereignty had been pursued at the expense of unity and in the end neither had been served', was one writer's accurate summary.[10] In the Treaty debates it occurred to only one deputy, Sean McEntee, that the Boundary Commission might interpret its brief in a manner which would not grant Dublin even a sizeable portion of the nationalist north. In all only nine of the 338 pages of the debate were on the subject of partition at all.[11] At best, if the anticipated new partition proved temporary, Devlin would emerge strengthened in his role as the representative of the new minority; if not then Devlin still had built up substantial credit with the Dublin government through his support for its strategy.

* * *

It was ironic that within months of the Home Ruler, T. P. O'Connor, complaining to Dillon that he had been sidelined by the Dublin government as the representative of northern Catholics, government strategy was to bring him to centre stage again.[12] A measure of Dublin's changed approach was their disregard of their adviser O'Shiel's request in April 1923 not to meet with a delegation which included Devlin and, still more clearly, an offer to Devlin of a safe seat in Dáil Éireann which he refused.[13]

Northern nationalist resistance to the northern State had been broken by the autumn of 1922. That September a report to the Cabinet Secretary could hail the 'hopeful signs' of Catholic magistrates sitting on benches and of 'priests sympathetic to Sinn Féin co-operating with the constabulary not only in asking for assistance but also in denouncing unruly Sinn Féin elements'. In Belfast matters were even better for the government, with Roman Catholic leaders 'most anxious to co-operate in every way possible in maintaining order'.[14] It was a state of affairs which further strengthened Devlin's hand in his dealings with Dáil Éireann and he understood the realpolitik of the situation. Far from being in pursuit of a secret deal involving the release of the *Argenta* prisoners, as Dublin feared, the Northern Ireland Cabinet Secretary could assure the Colonial Office that in the view of the 'Roman Catholic leaders' the 'release of the majority of the interned persons would have a most deplorable effect on the situation'. Devlin's standing by late 1923 was such that a majority of the city's Catholics, including Free State supporters, were 'prepared to follow his leadership', the Dublin government was told. Despite the widespread 'apathy and cynicism of the Catholic population in the city towards the Boundary Commission', Devlin's approach helped maintain a semblance of unity, blurring the east/west division, a cleavage reflected in the creation of separate rural (Clones) and urban (Belfast) based secretaries to the North Eastern Advisory Committee, and so obvious also in the attitude to the Craig/Collins Pact, divisions, as O'Higgins put it, between 'the man who has and the man who has not a dog's chance of getting out of the Boundary area'.[15]

For the former, the abolition of PR, coming as it did before the north had even opted out under the treaty, augured ill for their future. Harbinson, the Home Ruler, on a deputation with his former Sinn Féin opponents to the Dublin government, conveyed their anguish.

'I join here with my friends from the north who come to you as the only party we have in this country now to defend our rights. They have been taken from us. We have been robbed. On the day that the treaty was published first I formed one of a deputation who came to the then President as to the position of Catholics all over the six counties. I then ventured to prophecy that one of the very first things they would do would be to take from us our franchise, gerrymandering our

Courtesy of The National Library of Ireland (R 25491)

Joe Devlin MP, 1871-1934. Leader of the rump Home Rule movement in Ulster following the countrywide annihilation of the Irish Parliamentary Party in the 1918 election. He later came to head a united nationalist movement in the north, which included many of his erstwhile Sinn Féin opponents.

Who are They who want to help the English Government to Conscript You?

HERE THEY ARE!

This is a List of the Parliamentarians who on the 17th of January, last, in the English House of Commons, **would not** Vote against Conscription for Ireland:—

Boyle, Daniel, North Mayo
Byrne, A., Dublin Harbour
Clancy, J. J., Dublin, North
Cosgrove, James, Galway East
Crumley, P., Fermanagh South
Devlin, Joseph, Belfast West
Dillon, John, Mayo West
Donelan, Captain, Wicklow East
Donovan, J. T., Wicklow West
Doris, W , Mayo West
Duffy, W. J., Galway South
Esmonde, Captain, Tipperary North
Esmonde, Sir Thomas, Wexford North
Farrell, J. P., Longford North
French, P., Wexford South
Field, William, Dublin St. Patrick's
Fitzpatrick, J. C., Ossory
Fitzgibbon, John, Mayo South
Flavin, M., Kerry North
Gwynn, Stephen, Galway South
Hackett, J., Tipperary Mid.
Hazleton, Richard, Galway North
Hearn, Michael, Dublin South
Joyce, Alderman, Limerick City
Kelly, E., Donegal East
Kennedy, Vincent, Cavan West
Kilbride, A., Kildare South
Lundon, Thomas, Limerick East

McGhee, Richard, Tyrone Mid.
MacNeill, Swift, Donegal South
Meagher, Michael, Kilkenny North
Meehan, Francis, Leitrim North
Meehan, P. J., Leix
Molloy, M., Carlow
Mooney, John J., Newry
Muldoon, John, Cork East
Murphy, M. J., Waterford East
Nolan, Joseph, Louth South
Nugent, J. D., Dublin College Green
Nugent, Sir Walter, Westmeath, South
O'Connor, T. P., Liverpool
O'Doherty, Philip, Donegal North
O'Donnell, Thomas, Kerry West
O'Dowd, John, Sligo South
O'Shaughnessy, P. J., Limerick West
O'Shee, J. J., Waterford West
O'Sullivan, T., Kerry East
Reddy, Michael, Birr
Redmond, J. E., Waterford
Redmond, W. A., Tyrone East
Sheehy, David, Meath South
Smyth, T. P., Leitrim South
White, Patrick, Meath North
Whitty, P. J., Louth North
Young, Samuel, Cavan East

Vote for McCARTAN and Down with the Consciptionists.

Reproduced by kind permission of Newry Museum

Sinn Féin poster for the South Armagh by-election of January 1918. The introduction of conscription in Britain in 1916 raised fears of its extension to Ireland. Sinn Féin played on this issue, unsuccessfully in this instance as the Home Ruler won, but very successfully three months later when the threat became a reality. Its resurrection during the second world war proved equally electrifying in the nationalist north.

Courtesy of The National Library of Ireland (Hogan/Lennan B21)

Members of the Boundary Commission on their 1924 visit to Ireland. Eoin McNeill, the Irish representative, is on the left. Beside him is Joseph R. Fisher, his Northern Ireland counterpart. On the extreme right of the picture is Judge Richard Feetham, the South African born chairman. The revelation that the Commission intended merely a rectification of the original 1920 frontier caused consternation in majority nationalist areas which had confidently expected transfer to the Free State.

Reproduced by kind permission of Newry Museum

The Northern Ireland Prime Minister, Sir James Craig (front row, fourth from left) meets with members of Newry Urban District Council on 8 February 1927, during a tour of south Down. Hugh McConville (front row, far left) had been a member of the council which was suspended for recognising the authority of Dáil Éireann during the war of independence, the only northern council to do so. The photograph typified the spirit of conciliation within northern nationalism which found expression in the National League of the North, formed the following year.

SOUTH ARMAGH ELECTION.

POLLING DAY, THURSDAY, 30th NOVEMBER
Between 8 a.m. and 8 p.m.

Your Number is *279.*   You Vote at *College Sq. P.E. School*

MARK YOUR BALLOT PAPER THUS :—

I	L E N N O N	**X**
2	M c L O G A N	
3	O ' N E I L L	

Do not put any other mark or you will spoil your Vote.

Do not put any figure on the Ballot Paper.

Do not vote for more than one Candidate.

Vote Early. Call at Lennon's Tally Room before Voting.

Printed and Published by PATRICK MALLON at the "Observer" Office, Dungannon.

Reproduced by kind permission of Armagh County Museum

Leaflet from the campaign of James G. (Gerry) Lennon in the November 1933 election for the Stormont Parliament. His solo intervention against the official nationalist candidate, Daniel O'Neill, ensured a triangular contest. The republican Paddy McLogan, a native of County Laois, won the seat in what was to be that movement's greatest victory in a contest most memorable for De Valera's election in nearby South Down, following an invitation from local nationalists.

GENERAL ELECTION TO BRITISH PARLIAMENT.

CONSTITUENCY OF COUNTY ARMAGH.

Republican Election Campaign

IN THE SIX-COUNTY AREA.

MANIFESTO.

In the elections of 1918 the Irish people, by an overwhelming majority, repudiated the claims of England and her parliament to rule them, and they established the Republic of Ireland which was proclaimed in arms in 1916.

The Republican Government and State then established were later overthrown by treason backed by England, and the Nation was forcibly partitioned into two British statelets. The cardinal objective of the Irish people is the restoration of the Republican regime thus unlawfully subverted.

Notwithstanding the decisive repudiation of English Rule and of the English parliament in 1918, disloyal sections of our people have continued to send representatives to this alien legislature. By doing so they are attempting to give it a semblance of authority to legislate for the people of North East Ulster.

It is particularly deplorable that citizens styling themselves Irish Nationalists should sit in defiance of the wishes of the Irish Nation, in the Parliament of the conqueror. Representation in this Parliament is a symbol of Ireland's slavery and subjection.

I ASK YOU AGAIN IN THESE ELECTIONS TO REPUDIATE THE CLAIMS OF AN ALIEN PEOPLE AND PARLIAMENT TO RULE AND DOMINATE THE IRISH NATION AND TO LEGISLATE FOR THE IRISH PEOPLE.

My National faith is based on the Proclamation of the Republic 1916, which declared Ireland to be a sovereign and independent State, the right of the Irish people to the unfettered control of Irish destinies, to be sovereign and indefeasible, and which guaranteed civil and religious liberty and equal rights and equal opportunities to all its citizens.

I ask you to declare your allegiance to the Sovereign Republic and the principles enshrined in that Proclamation, and to elect me to a Parliament of the Republic of Ireland.

In an effort to obtain a semblance of democratic sanction for British rule in North East Ulster and to give an artificial majority to avowed Imperialists, the electoral areas have been flagrantly gerrymandered. This, however, does not deter us from our duty of challenging and exposing the evils it is sought to sustain and conceal.

These elections must be regarded as a plebiscite against British rule and domination, against the claims of the English Parliament to legislate for the Irish people, against the subjection and partition of the Nation and against any attempt by England and her agents to conscript Irishmen for service in her Imperial Wars, and to use Ireland as a war base.

The dangers of an Imperialist war are imminent and menacing. The British are feverishly arming and preparing for war. Their agents in Ireland are forwarding their plans and designs. Already Lord Craigavon has publicly declared that he is ready to enforce Conscription in the Six-County area in the event of an Imperialist war, and so to sacrifice Irishmen on the battlefields of rival Imperialisms. This menace to the lives and liberty of Irish citizens must be frustrated and defeated. A blow against this policy of the Imperialists can be struck in these elections.

The Proclamation of the Republic guarantees religious liberty to all citizens. Republicans uphold that principle and we plead for religious toleration and for the ending of sectarian strife. We condemn religious persecution and pogroms incited by the Imperial leaders to serve the Imperial object of keeping Irishmen at enmity. England and her agents foment sectarianism to keep the mass of the people divided, so that they may be a more easy prey for economic exploitation. We appeal to the people to come together and to work and plan for their common good.

The material interests of the people of the Six Counties are inseparable from those of the rest of Ireland, and therefore only as one political and economic unit can Ireland achieve prosperity or greatness. The mass of the people of the entire country, united by their common interests in a free Nation, could end the present social order which is impoverishing and degrading them and robbing a large section of the dignity of human beings. Within Ireland, with the industrial and agricultural resources of the Nation organised and controlled to serve the needs of the people, the opportunities for a full and free life for all the people would be boundless.

People of North-East Ulster, regardless of religious creeds, which in the past have kept you apart, you have now an opportunity to declare for National Freedom and Unity; to register your protest against the unnatural barriers of partition which separate you from your fellow-citizens in the rest of Ireland to their detriment and yours; to assert that you will not submit to being dragged off to serve England in her Imperial wars.

The Republican Movement calls for the support of the people everywhere in making this plebiscite a success.

NOV., 1935.   CHARLES McGLENNAN.

VOTE FOR McGLENNAN.

Issued on behalf of the Candidate by his Election Agent—JAMES TRODDEN, Irish Street, ARMAGH.

Printed and Published by Gerard McGouran, 27 Bank Street, Belfast.

Reproduced by kind permission of Armagh County Museum

Election manifesto of the republican Charles McGleenan (spelt here McGlennan) in the Armagh constituency in the Westminster election of 1935. The intervention of a largely southern republican movement in all the northern constituencies forced the adoption of compromise candidates in Tyrone and Fermanagh. McGleenan, a native of south Armagh, was returned to Stormont in a 1950 by-election for that area, re-affirming its unique character within the northern nationalist culture.

An illustration by the Dublin artist, Harry Kernoff, for the *Capuchin Annual* of 1943, which featured *Ultach*'s case against partition. It conveys the Catholic sense of powerlessness within a seeming Orange monolith which denied equality before the law, had flogging within its judicial armoury (as had the south and Britain) and made religion the basis for full citizenship. *Ultach* (J. J. Campbell) later moderated his views and became an advocate of greater Catholic participation within the state.

Eddie McAteer addresses an early meeting of the Anti-Partition League. Begun with enthusiasm in 1945, the APL soon foundered on grassroots indifference and an unpropitious political climate both nationally and overseas.

St Patrick's Day anti-partition demonstration in 1951. Two uniformed RUC men run to the aid of a plainclothes colleague who had attempted to seize the tricolour under the provisions of the Special Powers Act. Eddie McAteer, third from the left, was among those who resisted. Two councillors were arrested and detained.

Photographs courtesy of the McAteer family, Derry

De Valera on his way into Derry to open a sports festival in 1951. Eddie McAteer MP, third from the left, and members of Derry Corporation walk behind.

'When he came up Rossville Street in an open car the crowds surged forward and almost swamped him … Women craned precariously from upstairs windows waving handkerchiefs, frantically screaming Dev! Dev! Dev! Everybody said afterwards that it was the greatest day there had ever been in Derry. That was the measure of our Bogside innocence that the old Fagin of the political pickpockets could, by his mere presence, excite such uncensorious fervour.'
— Eamonn McCann, *War and an Irish Town*, p 26, Penguin 1974.

Eddie McAteer meets Eamon De Valera. The Fianna Fáil Party, founded by the latter in 1926, became the focus of the hopes and aspirations of many border nationalists on the rebound from the 1925 agreement. Despite bitter disappointments, this belief never entirely vanished.

Photographs courtesy of the McAteer family, Derry

Eddie McAteer MP, 1914-1986. His attempt to map a new course in the late 1950s foundered on the attitudes of the Dublin, Belfast and London governments. By the time he became party leader in 1964 events were beginning to overtake him.

Hugh McAteer, brother of Eddie. He was IRA Chief of Staff in the 1940s, an adviser to the south's Inter-Party Government in the period 1948-51 and, towards the end of his life, a founder of the Provisional IRA in Derry City.

Photographs courtesy of the McAteer family, Derry

Jack Beattie of the Irish Labour Party in a bid to regain the Westminster seat he occupied from 1943-1950. Beattie had also represented a Stormont constituency in the east of the city until 1949. A Protestant, his battles were not only with unionism but also with the sectarian and reactionary forces inside the nationalist community. Although he was successful on this occasion, the tide of right-wing church-backed workerism, in keeping with the mood of the time, eventually overwhelmed his party in the Catholic ghettos.

Electors of West Belfast

I have accepted the invitation of the Irish Labour Party to contest West Belfast.

For thirty years I have advocated the principles on which it is based. The Party founded by Connolly embodies the democratic tradition that has sought for 150 years to combine the national and social aspirations of our people.

The fight is against the Unionists, the enemies of the people. This political arm of the landlords and industrialists has, by the exploitation of sectarian prejudices, divided the people and maintains power in the Six Counties; that power has been used in the interests of privilege to the detriment of the people. The recent amending of the Rent Restrictions Act which will result in increases in working-class rents is an example of the way in which political power is used by the Tories.

If elected I shall attend Westminster to focus attention on the unnatural division of the country, the undemocratic practices of the Tories and to express the working-class view on social and economic problems.

In particular I shall demand the immediate restoration of price control and the limitation of profits and dividends. I shall oppose any attempt to cut or curtail the social services and where practicable advocate their extension. I am opposed to the recent charges in respect of benefits under the Health Service.

The return to power of the British Tories and their Six-County allies would be detrimental, not only to the Irish people but would be a potential threat to the peace of the world. I appeal to the workers of West Belfast, irrespective of creed, to support the cause of Labour on 25th October, 1951.

Yours sincerely,

JOHN BEATTIE

Reproduction courtesy of The Linenhall Library, Belfast

The Anti-Partition League's parliamentary group assemble outside Stormont for the 1956-57 session.

Left to right, Front Row: Senator Patrick McGill, Senator James G. (Gerry) Lennon, Cahir Healy MP South Fermanagh, Joseph F. Stewart MP East Tyrone, Patrick J. Gormley MP Mid Derry, Senator Cathal Bradley.
Back Row: Senator Patrick J. O'Hare, Eddie McAteer MP Foyle, Roderick H. O'Connor MP West Tyrone, James McSparran QC MP Mourne, Senator Louis D. Lynch.

Photograph courtesy of the McAteer family, Derry

Members of the Nationalist Party outside the Pro-Cathedral in Dublin after a Mass to celebrate the inauguration of De Valera as President of Ireland on 25 June 1959.

Left to right, Front Row: Senator James G. (Gerry) Lennon, Joseph Connellan MP South Down, Cahir Healy MP South Fermanagh, Joseph F. Stewart MP East Tyrone, Patrick J. Gormley MP Mid Derry, Senator Patrick J. O'Hare.

Back Row: Eddie McAteer MP Foyle, Senator Patrick McGill, James O'Reilly MP Mourne, Edward G. Richardson MP South Armagh, Senator John F. Donaghy, Roderick H. O'Connor MP West Tyrone, Senator John A. McGlade.

The term 'Nationalist Party', long used colloquially, had now come to be employed in a semi-official manner, despite reservations by some who remembered and resented its Home Rule connotations. In 1958 the party had accepted and immediately reversed a decision to become the official opposition at Stormont.

Photograph courtesy of the McAteer family, Derry

Reproduced by kind permission of Newry Museum

On the first weekend of July 1970 the British Army imposed a curfew on the lower Falls area of West Belfast, after deluging the area in CS gas during a massive search for arms. The operation, which resulted in four deaths, hundreds of arrests, and the widespread wrecking of houses, marked a turning point in the changing Catholic perception of the army as being a pillar of the discredited Stormont regime rather than an impartial buffer force. Republicans, as in the above poster, capitalised on this feeling of vulnerability.

BOBBY SANDS
Election Manifesto

"My name is BOBBY SANDS. I am 27 years old. I am an Irish political prisoner, a blanketman and a republican.

"I was born in Rathcoole, a predominantly Protestant area of Belfast. I was keen on sports and won a lot of medals and ran for Protestant clubs. In 1972 my family was intimidated out of our home and we moved to Twinbrook on the outskirts of Belfast. Soon after this I was intimidated from my work place at gun point. Shortly after this I joined the Republican Movement – I had seen too many homes wrecked, Fathers and sons arrested, neighbours hurt, friends murdered, too much gas, shootings and blood, most of it our own peoples".
—BOBBY SANDS.

The election of the hunger striker, Bobby Sands, as MP for Fermanagh South Tyrone in a by-election in April 1981 confounded the predictions of the Irish political class and marked a watershed in the northern troubles. It energised the republican movement into electoral participation, producing the dynamics which lead ultimately to a peace process and a settlement.

HIS LIFE IS IN YOUR HANDS
Vote – SANDS

THE BLANKETMEN AND THE WOMEN PRISONERS IN ARMAGH ARE BORROWING THIS ELECTION IN AN ATTEMPT TO ILLUSTRATE YOUR SUPPORT FOR THE PRISONERS AND YOUR OPPOSITION TO THE BRITISH GOVERNMENT.

USE YOUR VOTE TO SAVE THE SEAT

Published by Election Agent OWEN CARRON, Florencecourt, Fermanagh and printed by CUCHULAINN PRESS, COALISLAND.

Published in 1973, this booklet was immediately banned by the Dublin government. Possession of it helped secure convictions for IRA membership in the Republic's courts. The escalating IRA campaign led to a culture of censorship south of the border in which all manifestations of opposition to the injustices of the northern state became suspect.

seats, and drive us into political oblivion. They have now done it.'[16]

Dublin threw the ball back into their court, insisting they formulate their own strategy. By 1924 through a combination of a nationalist poll boycott and the Leech Commission's electoral alterations, the nationalists had lost the County Councils and all the Rural District Councils in the majority Catholic counties of Tyrone and Fermanagh. Dublin's attitude to the Boundary Commission had never been more than a tactical one. Telling the truth on this, O'Higgins remarked in a memorandum, before the Commission began its work, 'would be tantamount to showing your trump before you play your hand'. He predicted only 'minor ratifications' which would leave 'probably a majority of nationalists still under the northern government'.[17] When this forecast proved correct and the agreements of 1925 and 1926 consolidated partition as a fact of International Law, northern nationalists were left with the consequences. As the aftershocks of the betrayal were felt they looked increasingly towards Fianna Fáil, and when the proposed union with this party fell through in 1928, moved down a reformist road, the divisions within them now increasingly blurred by the enforced co-operation since 1921 and the attendance of all but the two republicans at the Belfast parliamant.

The evolution of Cahir Healy from a Sinn Féiner to an admirer of Devlin, from participation in the post-1916 resurgence to an attitude of regret that the Home Rule strategy on partition had been swamped, epitomised the mood in which the term nationalist had come to refer to both groups. The period from 1926-32 was the first 'window of opportunity' for the integration of the Catholic population into the running of the state since the Craig/Collins Pact and the last until the late 1950s. The failure of the unionists to avail of it was consequently a major miscalculation. By the opening of the new parliament at Stormont in November 1932 the increasing emphasis on partition in the National League manifesto, following on their withdrawal from parliament in frustration that summer, showed which way the wind was blowing. While the treaty had split southern nationalist politics, its 1925 sequel had produced a new unity amongst northern anti-unionists.

One group remained more alienated than every before from this camp – the Labour movement. From December 1923 when nationalist leaders in Belfast, Alderman Oswald Jameson and Irish National Forester Society organiser Martin Hopkins, approached parish priests and asked that they use their influence in favour of the unionist candidate and against the BLP contender, Harry Midgley, it was clear what the future held.[18] The exigencies of anti-unionist co-operation masked the animosity between nationalists and labour throughout the mid 1920s, as did the social reformism of the National League. Devlin's electorate had after all showed by its second preferences in 1925 that it favoured a Protestant Labourite McMullan over a republican. By 1929, with the abolition of PR in Stormont elections, the honeymoon was over and a bitter conflict was to recur through the years, pitting Catholic corporatist workerism against 'revolutionary socialism'. Great though this divide was to be, it was only one of several fault lines which were to re-emerge within northern nationalism once the unifying figure of Joe Devlin disappeared from the scene.

The years following Devlin's death left the mainstream nationalist movement without direction until De Valera's 1937 constitution emerged to give them one. But what appeared to be a new dispensation proved illusory. Their exclusion from the Anglo-Irish Agreement of 1938 reminded them that they were a people apart, a lesson most starkly brought home to northern Catholics by the closure of the Irish army to them on the outbreak of World War II. And this was happening at a time when unionism was increasing its sectarian viciousness and tightening the screws of discrimination. The stage was set for the most sinister chapter in their history, an approach to the Third Reich as France fell to its advancing legions. It is in this context of frustration and abandonment that this action must be seen, placed within the contemporary right-wing cultural milieu which encompassed not only Irish nationalists but also their British and unionist opponents.

* * *

The foundation of the Anti-Partition League had represented the continuation of the pre-war movement spurred into life by the post-war mood. Its lack of impact on the political scene in both southern Ireland and Britain for its first two years revealed how public opinion in both states had other things on its mind. With the League's sympathisers in the British Labour party more opposed to the injustices of the northern state than its existence, both groups soon found themselves arguing from different premises. Neither argument was in any event likely to find much favour with a British establishment which remembered with bitterness the south's wartime role. Comparisons of the northern state with fascist occupied territories were sure to ring hollow in this context, the more so given the northern Catholics' flirtation with the Germans. At a time when the post-war 'Butskellite' consensus was widening the living standard gap between north and south, the British public had even less reason to feel sympathy with the League's objectives.

The British Welfare State met with the hostility of northern nationalist politicians, not only because of their innate conservatism but also due to its potentially destructive effect on anti-partition sentiment. Harry Diamond's provocative reference to 'Beveridge bribes', coming from a representative of the labourism which replaced the nationalists in Belfast, reveals not only how this worry was shared in that city but also how the western 'green Tory' conservatism was not totally rejected there either.

This essential conservatism explains how they could both later unite in a clergy-backed project to oust a more radical alternative. The other older division between erstwhile Home Rulers and former republicans had all but vanished by this time, though the idea of adopting the colloquial term 'nationalist' as an official one still caused concern in some quarters. South of the border the Clann na Poblachta promise to open the Oireachtas to northerners had so little impact that McAteer, on a speaking tour, could complain bitterly of abandonment by the south. Not until the fall-out from the Republic of Ireland Act did the issue move centre stage in Dublin, uniting both government and opposition in a common anti-partitionism. But the southern intervention, opportunistic and in some respects cynical, soon faded leaving the northern nationalists to fight alone. Their hope of some form of Dáil role – equally opportunistic for most of them and increasingly frantic as the republican threat mounted – foundered on the limits of the very Constitution which claimed them as citizens (a forerunner of the 1990s debate on the extension of voting rights to Irish emigrants) and on the lack of agreement among nationalists themselves on the issue. Healy's 1926 summary of Dublin politicians, 'out of power they will use us, in power they will find a hundred reasons for letting us paddle our own canoe', was to re-echo many times during this period.

The republican electoral intervention reaffirmed the traditional east-west pattern with regional variations: strongest in Mid Ulster and Fermanagh South Tyrone, drawing on the vote which Kelly had garnered in Mid Tyrone; strong also in South Armagh, as *sui generis* under McGleenan as it was under McLogan in the 1930s, an area where whole Anti-Partition League branches had gone over to the republicans; weakest as always in Belfast. But their lack of indigenous roots in northern soil meant that the republicans were even more likely to suffer the fate which had already befallen the APL, mass apathy from the very people on whose support they depended. And even before the 1959 debacle, at the height of their 1955 glory it was clear in the decrease from the 1951 nationalist vote in the constituencies which they won that, even with Hibernianism increasingly a thing of the past and no opposition on the Catholic side, there were limits to their potential.

The lack of any sense of crisis in Dublin's response to the Sinn Féin challenge, inexplicable when compared with their panic-stricken response of 27 years later, even when confronted as in 1956 with nationalists fighting on a platform of support for their authority, becomes more understandable when the number of facts are taken into consideration. Militant republicanism had been co-opted into the political system, through Clann na Poblachta. Fianna Uladh had been given a degree of respectability as Kelly's appointment to the Senate showed. The clergy on the ground in the north were in many cases sympathetic to the republican intervention. Above all else, the movement lacked any 1930s style subversive social content allied to a proven ability to sustain a guerrilla campaign.

For the mainstream nationalists, the period after the republican intervention was characterised by a regional factionalism reminiscent of that which followed the death of Devlin in the 1930s. Throughout, they had been characterised by the same ideological features that marked them in earlier periods: social conservatism, ambivalence towards the south, an ambiguous attitude to Protestants and a clericalism facilitated by the loose *ad hoc* regional nature of their organisation which had long been refined into a more subtle form in the rest of Ireland.

It remained to be seen whether or not the new era ushered in by the collapse of anti-partitionism in all its forms would bring a change.

* * *

The collapse of the IRA's 1950s campaign, the stirrings of a new approach within the ranks of mainstream nationalism and outside it, all combined with the economically driven north-south rapproachment to make the 1960s a time of potential change.

By 1962 nationalists on both sides of the border were basking in a feeling that changes for the better were taking place. Lemass privately enthused that his policies of goodwill were winning over the younger generation of unionists[20] while McAteer acknowledged a belief among 'all sections of northern opinion' that the European Economic Community would lead to a 'lowering of the border'.[21] Among six county nationalists the pace of the new thinking was proceeding slower than envisaged at Garron Tower, but faster than anyone could have predicted in the strident anti-partitionist atmosphere of the previous decade.

The role of official opposition at Stormont had been accepted in 1958 and then withdrawn within 24 hours on a vote which revealed the east-west divide once again. Yet McAteer, who was among its opponents, had plotted his own 'new course', focusing on the 'secondary aspects of partition' almost simultaneously with the crystallisation of a new approach in Dublin's Iveagh House. Neither group saw eye to eye with the other, though it was to be the mid 1960s before this became evident. Before this Dublin tried unsuccessfully to push nationalists into greater public involvement in the north,[22] the south's Minister for External Affairs, Frank Aiken, already having rebuffed an attempt to have their grievances raised at the United Nations. Instead, Aiken pledged 'all efforts' would be directed to 'getting London to do something'.[23] Aiken had been considerably encouraged by the meeting earlier that week between the nationalists and R. A. Butler, the British Home Secretary, and asked his department to begin drafting a new booklet on partition to which Healy, who had requested the United Nations approach, was asked to provide data 'proving conclusively the existence of such disadvantages'. But British willingness to listen proved illusory. On unionist advice Butler proceeded no further with the dossier supplied to him. Dublin's initiative was heard of no more and the southern state enveloped itself in 'self congratulation' as the anniversary of the Easter Rising approached. In the absence of British pressure, unionist concessions were not forthcoming at this most critical juncture, the first time in thirty years when an opportunity existed for the integration of northern

Catholics into the political life of the state. Under Brookeborough the mere suggestion of Catholic membership of the unionist party had thrown that party into convulsions. His successor, Terence O'Neill, remained a hostage to the role which discrimination had played in consolidating unionist power, however well-meaning his attempts to reform.

Faced with the impotence of their leaders, the imperviousness of their rulers and the indifference of the government which posed as the protector of their interests, northern Catholics turned on their own resources. In the Zeitgeist of the 1960s, a movement from below, inspired by TV images of similar protests elsewhere, and feeding off TV images of itself, took the initiative.[24]

The regional pattern, demonstrated as far back as 1918, showed itself as clearly as before. Commenting on the grievances of northern Catholics, one writer later remarked:

> A group of local authorities in the west of the province provide a startlingly high proportion of the total number of complaints. All the accusations of gerrymandering, practically all the complaints about housing and regional policy, and a disproportionate amount of the charges about private and public employment come from this area.[25]

Defence of Catholic areas was to be the primary impulse in moving the focus to Belfast. In the process, the republican subculture in the city found itself acquiring a relevance it had not enjoyed since the early 1920s and even then only sporadically.

The 1969 election proved to be the last kick of the new nationalist party. To those Catholics who felt they knew what it represented – and 35% said they did not know[26] – it continued to be seen, however unfairly, as a party obsessed with a border which Catholics felt should be talked about less. Concentrated in selected constituencies, without a parliamentary presence in Belfast since 1946, and now challenged successfully in its strongholds, its position was crumbling as a new configuration in northern Catholic politics began to take shape.

The frustration on the ground of the Civil Rights demand, conceded on paper, and increased military repression, converted into support for a secessionist rebellion, the most successful in half a century and the longest in Ireland's troubled history. Yet its basis in justice denied in the lived experience of the most underprivileged members of the Catholic community, rather than in any deepseated ideological substratum, meant that the eventual reversion to a peace strategy proved a relatively seamless one. The common denominator remained the pursuit of first class citizenship.

This preoccupation with fair play, rather than with any grand ideal or project, has arguably been the chief dynamic of northern nationalism throughout its history. During the period of home rule agitation, support in Ulster for the IPP was framed in terms of a desire to end unionist domination. Northern opposition to partition, which led them belatedly towards Sinn Féin, derived not from any abstract allegiance to a united Ireland but from a well-founded fear that any division would entrench and increase the existing injustices.

Even with the boundary provisionally established, many of the representatives from areas contiguous to it were prepared to accept it within the framework of an all-Ireland jurisdiction.[27] Southern nationalists of various hues have seen in this qualified and highly reactive nationalism evidence of both sectarianism and supineness. The former accusation, which constituted the sum of De Valera's 1921 objection to a proposed united northern nationalist front, ignores the degree to which Irish nationalism, notwithstanding its ecumenical pretensions, almost inevitably gives rise to polarisation in view of the religio-political geographical realities. The 1919-1921 war of independence often assumed a highly sectarian character in those parts of southern Ireland where the Protestant population was thickest on the ground.[28] Unionism, it must not be forgotten, was a thirty-two-county force for most of its existence.

Likewise, the related criticism of northern nationalist clericalism (excessive though it was even by Irish standards) runs the risk of forgetting the minority's beleaguered position, its sense of abandonment by Dublin, and its lack of unity in the face of a common enemy. Inevitably in that situation the mantle of leadership fell on those whom the peculiarities of Irish Catholic culture fitted for such a role. The other allegation against northern Catholics, that of national apostasy, made for instance by *An Phoblacht* in 1934 (and muttered once more in the 1990s by republican ultras in the aftermath of the ceasefires), ignores what one writer terms the 'variegated and highly contradictory' nature of Irish nationalism,[29] never more clearly demonstrated than when under British rule. An essentialist view of the phenomenon is misleading, fluctuating as it does over time and region. In

Ireland, the move from Hobsbawm's first stage of nationalism, protonationalism (ie. the common culture of nationality), through the second stage of minority activism, to the final stage of mass participation, was contingent on a variety of variables, most notably the religious and land questions of the nineteenth century. Nationalism, there as elsewhere, has always been a 'process addiction'.[30] Missing this same point in a different way are those like Christopher Hewitt who have lambasted northern Catholics as motivated by 'nationalism' pure and simple, rather than by the genuine experience of injustice.

As Denis O'Hearn comments in the last installment of his long-running debate with Hewitt in the *British Journal of Sociology*,

> The identification of nationalism and inequality as mutually exclusive variables is a false dichotomy … Nationalism is not a somehow inferior and morally indefensible position. In the face of a sectarian loyalist state, a refusal to share power and opportunity, it is indeed a quite logical response.[31]

Measured on Max Hyndman's classifications of nationalism into 'oppression, irredentist, precautionary and prestige' varieties, that of northern Catholics belongs clearly in the first category as a reaction to the historical experience of being the bottom dog, and the inability of ameliorative measures to benefit the most deprived section of their community.[32]

The attempt to present it as irredentist ignores not only those periods post 1925 and 1956 when northern Catholics attempted unsuccessfully to find a role within the state, but also those periods when, forced back on outright anti-partitionism by the intransigence of that state, they came up against other limitations – those placed by independent Ireland on its acceptance of them. This view, like its mirror image – the republican one which sees loyalism as unsustainable without British patronage – underestimates the importance of indigenous dynamics.

And for as long as those indigenous dynamics – a well-founded sense of victimhood allied to an Irish identity, an obdurate and non-inclusive unionism, an arms-length approach by both London and Dublin – remain in place as components of the problem, so too will northern nationalism.

Sources Consulted

National Archive, Dublin
   'S' files : Dept. of Taoiseach
   'DFA': Dept. Foreign Affairs – including all 'P' files
   'DE' files - Dáil Éireann files

PRONI: Public Records Office of Northern Ireland, Belfast
   'Cab' files: Cabinet Conclusions and Cabinet Secretariat
   'HA': Home Affairs Office

PRO London
   'Cab': Cabinet Office
   'Co': Colonial Office
   'DO': Dominions Office

PRIVATE PAPERS

Public Records Office of Northern Ireland, Belfast
   Patrick Agnew Papers
   J. H. Collins Papers
   Fred Crawford Papers
   Joe Devlin Papers
   Cahir Healy Papers
   George Leeke Papers
   James G Lennon Papers
   Seamus MacCall Papers
   J. J. McCarroll Papers
   Patrick McGill Papers
   Jack Macgougan Papers
   Anthony Mulvey Papers
   Patrick O'Neill Papers
   Wilfred Spender Papers
   Wilfred Spender Diaries
   Joe Stewart Papers
   Prime Ministerial Correspondence of Lord Brookeborough
   Lord Charlemont / Viscount Montgomery Correspondence

UCD Archive
   Frank Aiken Papers
   Ernest Blythe Papers
   Dan Bryan Papers

Desmond Fitzgerald Papers
Hugh Kennedy Papers
Sean McEntee Papers
Patrick McGilligan Papers
Eoin McNeill Papers (also in National Library)
Mary McSweeney Papers
Richard Mulcahy Papers
Ernie O'Malley Papers
Ernie O'Malley Notebooks

National Library of Ireland
Frank Gallagher Papers
Thomas Johnston Papers
Patrick McCartan Papers
Joseph McGarrity Papers
Maurice Moore Papers
William O'Brien Papers
John Redmond Papers

TCD Archive
Erskine Childers Papers
John Dillon Papers
E. M. Stephens Papers

Ara Coeli, Armagh
Cardinal Logue Papers
Cardinal O'Donnell Papers

Archbishop's House, Drumcondra, Dublin
Archbishop Byrne Papers
Archbishop Walsh Papers

Franciscan Archive, Killiney, Dublin
Eamon De Valera Papers
Sean McKeown Papers

Department of Defence Archive, Cathal Brugha Barracks
Michael Collins Papers

PARLIAMENTARY PAPERS

Northern Ireland
Parliamentary Debates Official Report 1921-1972
House of Commons Senate

Republic of Ireland
Dáil Éireann Private Sessions of Second Dáil
Dáil Éireann Official Report on the Treaty between Great Britain &
Ireland, signed in London on 6 December 1921
Dáil Éireann, Official Report 1922-72
All-Party Anti-Partition Conference material, including pamphlets

GOVERNMENT REPORTS

Cameron Report: Disturbances in Northern Ireland: Report of the
Commission Appointed by the Governer of Northern Ireland,
HMSO 1969, Command 532
Hunt Report: Report of the Advisory Committee on Police in Northern
Ireland
Lockwood Report: Higher Education in Northern Ireland, HMSO 1965,
Command 475
Scarman Report: Violence and Civil Disturbances in Northern Ireland in
1969. Report of a Tribunal of Enquiry, HMSO 1972, Command 565
(2 vols)

NEWSPAPERS AND JOURNALS

Andersonstown News
Belfast Morning News
Belfast Newsletter
Belfast Telegraph
British Journal of Political Science
British Journal of Sociology
Bullán
Capuchin Annual
Catholic Bulletin
Catholic Historical Review
Christus Rex
Clogher Record
Coleraine Chronicle
Crane Bag
Creggan Journal
Derry Journal
Derry People
Donegal Annual
Dungannon Democrat
Economic & Social Review
Éire
Éire/Irel and
Fortnight
Guardian (Manchester Guardian)

Hibernia
Historical Studies
History Ireland
History of Education
Hot Press
Labour Progress
Ireland Today
Iris
Irish Echo
Irish Historical Studies
Irish Independent
Irish Jurist
Irish Monthly
Irish News
Irish Political Studies
Irish Press
Irish Review
Irish Statesman
Irish Studies in International Affairs
Irish Times
Irish University Review
Irish Weekly
L'Irlande Revue Politique et Sociale
Journal of Contemporary History
Magill
Moirae
Mourne Observer
The Nation
National Unity
New Hibernia
New Left Review
Newman Review
Newry Reporter
Newry Telegraph
New Statesman
Northern Whig
Obair
The Observer
The People
An Phoblacht
The Proletarian
Republican Progress
Republican News
Review of Politics
The Round Table
Saothar

The Scotsman
Seanchas Ardmhacha
The Separatist
Social Review
Studia Hibernica
Studies
Sunday Independent
Sunday Press
Sunday Times
Sunday Tribune
Time Magazine
Ulster
The Watchword and the Voice of Labour
This Week
The Dungannon centred *Observer* chain of newspapers, in particular the *Dungannon Observer* and *Armagh Observer*.
The North West Publishing Company chain, in particular the *Ulster Herald* and *Frontier Sentinel*.

INTERVIEWS

Noel Browne, 21 February 1991
Andrew Boyd, 19 March 1991
Paddy Devlin, 17 April 1991
'Sean Fox', 12 May 1991
Joe Cahill, 27 April 1991
Jack Myers, 7 May 1991
Jimmy Kelly, 8 April 1991
Ruairí Ó Brádaigh, 16 August 1991
Jack Mulvenna, 6 September 1991
Patrick Marrinan, 8 April 1991
Micheál Ó Cuinneagáin, 19 August 1991
Jack Macgougan (correspondence), 1991 / 1992

Bibliography

As this work is based largely on primary source material, some of it obtained through privileged access and much of it available only since the January 1991 release of the documents, I did not feel it necessary to insert a complete bibliography.

From the plethora of books and other secondary sources consulted on the northern question therefore it lists only those which have had a direct input or a significant background influence.

Adams, G., *Falls Memories*, Brandon Press, 1982.

Adams, G., *The Politics of Freedom*, Brandon Press, 1986.

Adams, G., *Before the Dawn*, Brandon Press, 1996.

Akenson, D. H., *Education and Enmity*, Harper and Row, 1973.

Akenson, D. H., *Conor: A Biography of Conor Cruise O'Brien*, Magill and Queen's University Press, 1994.

Arthur, Paul, *The Peoples Democracy 1968-73*, Blackstaff Press, 1974.

Arthur, Paul, *Governments and Politics of Northern Ireland*, Longman, 1980.

Augusteun, Joost, *From Public Defiance to Guerilla Warfare*, Irish Academic Press, 1996.

Barritt, D. P. & Carter, C. F., *The Northern Ireland Problem: A Study in Group Relations*, OUP, 1962.

Bardon, Jonathan, *A History of Ulster*, Blackstaff Press, 1992.

Barton, Brian, *Brookeborough: The Making of a Prime Minister*, Institute of Irish Studies, 1982.

Barton, Brian, *The Blitz*, Blackstaff Press, 1989.

Bell, Geoffrey, *British Labour and Ireland 1969-79*, Pluto.

Bell, J. Bowyer, *The Secret Army: A History of the IRA*, Anthony Blond, 1970.

Bew, Paul, *Conflict and Conciliation in Ireland: Parnellites and Radical Agrarians*, Clarendon, 1988.

Bew, P. & Patterson, N., *Sean Lemass and the Making of a Modern Ireland*, Gill and Macmillan, 1982.

Bew, P., Gibbon, P., and Patterson, H., *The State in Northern Ireland*, Manchester University Press, 1979.

Bew, P. & Patterson, H., *The British State and the Ulster Crisis*, Verso, 1988.

Biggs-Davidson, J., *Catholics and the Union*, Belfast, Unionist Party, 1972.

Bing, Geoffrey, *John Bull's Other Island*, Tribune Publications, 1950.

Bishop, P. and Mallie, E., *The Provisional IRA*, Corgi, 1987.

Blake, J. W., *Northern Ireland in the Second World War*, HMSO, 1950.

Bythe, Ernest, *A New Departure in Northern Politics*, Basil Clancy, 1958.

Boal and Douglas, *Northern Ireland: Integration and Division*, London & New York, 1983.

Boland, Kevin, *We Won't Stand (Idly) By*, Kelly Lane (nd).

Boland, Kevin, *Up Dev*, Dublin 1977.

Bolster, Evelyn, *The Knights of Columbanus*, Dublin, 1979.

Bowen, Kurt, *Protestants & Catholics in a Catholic State: Ireland's Privileged Minority*, Gill and Macmillan, 1983.

Bowman, John, *De Valera and the Ulster Question, 1917-73*, OUP, 1982.

Boyce, D. G., *Englishmen and Irish Troubles 1918-22*, Cambridge, 1972, revised edition, Routledge, 1991.

Boyce, D. G., *Nationalism in Ireland*, CUP, 1982, revised edition, Routledge, 1991.

Boyle & Hillyard, *Law and State: The Case of Northern Ireland*, Martin Robinson, London, 1980.

Brett, C. E. B., *Long Shadows Cast Before Midnight*, Edinburgh, 1978.

Buckland, Patrick, *The Factory of Grievances: Government in Northern Ireland 1921-39*, Gill & Macmillan, 1978.

Budge, I. & O'Leary, C., *Belfast: Approach to Crisis*, Macmillan, 1972.

Burton, Frank, *The Politics of Legtimacy: Struggles in a Belfast Community*, Routledge & Kegan Paul, 1978.

Butler, D., *The Electoral System in Britain Since 1918*.

Butler, Hubert, *Escape from the Anthill*, Lilliput Press, 1985.

Campbell, T. J., *50 Years of Ulster*, Irish News, 1941.

Campbell, J. J., *Catholic Schools: A Survey of a Northern Ireland Problem*, Fallons, 1964.

Campaign for Social Justice in Northern Ireland: *One Man No Vote*.

Campaign for Social Justice in Northern Ireland, *Why Justice Cannot be Done*.

Campaign for Social Justice in Northern Ireland: *The Plain Truth*.

Canavan, Tony, *Frontier Town: An Illustrated History of Newry*, Blackstaff Press, 1989.

Canning, Paul, *British Policy Towards Ireland*, OUP, 1990.

Clark, W., *Guns in Ulster*, Constabulary Gazette, 1967.

Collins, Eamonn, *Killing Rage*, Granta, 1997.

Coughlan, A., *Fooled Again: The Anglo-Irish Agreement and After*, Mercier Press, 1987.

Coogan, T. P., *The IRA*, Fontana, 1980.

Coogan, T. P., *Ireland Since the Rising*, London, 1966.

Coogan, T. P., *Michael Collins: A Biography*, Hutchinson, 1990.

Cormack & Osborne (eds), *Religion, Education & Employment Aspects of Equal Opportunity in Northern Ireland*, Appletree Press, 1983.

Cradden, Terry, *Trade Unionism, Socialism and Partition*, December Publications, 1993.

Cronin, Sean, *Irish Nationalism*, Academy Press, 1980.

Cronin, Sean, *The McGarrity Papers*, Anvil 1972.

Cronin, Sean, *Resistance: The Story of the Struggle in British Occupied Ireland*, (Joe McGarrity).

Cronin, Sean, *Washington's Irish Policy 1916-1986*, Anvil, 1987.

Curran, F., *Derry: Countdown to Disaster*, Gill and Macmillan, 1986.

Darby, John, *Conflict in Northern Ireland*, Gill and Macmillan, 1976.

Darby, J. & Williams, A. (eds), *Violence and the Social Services in Northern Ireland*.

D'Arcy, Marguerite, *Tell Them Everything*, Pluto Press, 1980.

De Baróid, Criostóir, *Ballymurphy and the Irish War*, Dublin 1989.

De Blaghd, Earnán, *Briseadh na Teorann*, Basil Clancy Publishers, 1957.

De Paor, L., *Divided Ulster*, Penguin, 1970.

Deustch, R. and Magowan, V., *Northern Ireland: A Chronology of Events 1968-1974*, (3 vols) Blackstaff 1968-1974.

Devlin, Paddy, *The Fall of the NI Executive*, Belfast, 1975.

Devlin, Paddy, *Yes, We Have No Bananas*, Blackstaff Press, 1982.

Devlin, Paddy, *Straight Left: An Autobiography*, Belfast 1993.

Devlin, Polly, *All of us There*, London, 1984.

Donoghue, Denis, *Warrenpoint*, Jonathan Cape, 1991.

Edwards, Owen Dudley, *The Sins of our Fathers*, Gill and Macmillan, 1970.

Elliott, Marianne, *Catholics in Ulster*, Penguin, 2000.

Elliott, S. and Smith F. J., *The District Council Elections of 1985, A Computer Analysis*, Queen's University, Belfast.

Elliott, S. and Smith F. J., *The District Council Elections of 1989, A Computer Analysis*, Queen's University, Belfast.

Equality Working Group, *Directory of Discrimination*, Belfast, 1991.

Farrell, Michael, *The Orange State*, Pluto, 1976.

Farrell, Michael, *Arming the Protestants*, Pluto, 1983.

Farren, Sean, *The Politics of Irish Education*, Belfast, 1995.

Faul, Denis and Murray, Raymond, *The Alienation of Northern Ireland Catholics*, Belfast, 1984.

Faulkner, Brian, *Memoirs of a Statesman*, Weidenfield & Nicholson, 1976.

Fennell, Desmond, *The Northern Catholic*, Tower Publishers, 1958.

Fisk, Robert, *In time of War. Ireland Ulster and the Price of Neutrality, 1939-45*, Paladin, 1984.

Fisk, Robert, *The Point of No Return*, Times Books, 1974.

Fitzpatrick, David (ed), *Ireland and the First World War*, Trinity History Workshop, 1986.

Flackes, W. D, and Elliott, Sydney, *Northern Ireland A Political Directory, 1968-88*, Blackstaff Press, 1989.

Foot, M. L. R., *Fighting for Ireland*, Routledge, 1995.

Gallagher, Frank, *The Indivisible Island*, Gollancz, 1957.

Garvin, Tom, *The Evolution of Irish Nationalist Politics*, Gill and Macmillan, 1981.

Gellner, Ernest, *Nations and Nationalism*, Oxford, 1983.

Gilbert, Martin, *Winston Churchill 1916-1922*, Minerva Publications, Vol IV, 1975.

Gilmore, George, *Republican Congress 1934*, Dóchas Publishers, 1968.

Griffith, R., *Fellow Travellers of the Right*, OUP, 1983.

Gwynn, D., *The Life of John Redmond*, London, 1932.

Hand, Geoffrey (ed), *The Report of the Irish Boundary Commission 1925*, IUP, 1969.

Harkness, D., *Northern Ireland Since 1920*, Helicon, Dublin, 1983.

Harnden, Toby, *Bandit Country: The IRA and South Armagh*, Hodder & Stoughton, 1999.

Harris, Mary, *The Catholic Church and the Foundation of the Northern State*, Belfast, 1994.

Harris, Rosemary, *Prejudice and Tolerance in Ulster*, Manchester University Press, 1972.

Healy, Cahir, *The Mutilation of a Nation, The Story of the Partition of Ireland*, Derry Journal, 1945.

Heatley, Fred, *The Story of St Patrick's, Belfast*, Portylemore.

Heskin, Ken, *Northern Ireland: A Psychological Analysis*, Gill and Macmillan, 1980.

Heslinga, M. W., *The Irish Border as a Cultural Divide*, Van Gorcum, Netherlands, 1962.

Hezlet, Sir Arthur, *The B-Specials*, Tom Stacy, 1970.

Hindley, Reg, *The Death of the Irish Language*, Routledge, 1991.

Hobsbawn, Eric, *Nations and Nationalism since 1780: Programme, Myth and Reality*, CUP, 1983.

Holland, Jack,

MacDonald, Henry, *INLA Deadly Divisions*, TORC, 1994.

Hobsbawn, E. & Renger, T. (eds), *The Invention of Tradition*, CUP, 1983.

Hogan, Patrick, *Could Ireland Become Communist?* Fine Gael, 1933.

Hopkinson, M, *Green Against Green*, Gill & Macmillan, 1988.

Horgan, John, *Sean Lemass: The Enigmatic Patriot*, Gill & Macmillan, 1997.

Jones, Tom, *Whitehall Diary III*, K Middlemas (ed), OUP.

Keenan, Joe, *An Argument on Behalf of the Catholics of Northern Ireland*, Athol Press, 1987.

Kelly, Henry, *How Stormont Fell*, Gill and Macmillan, 1972.

Kelly, James (Capt.), *Orders for the Captain*, Jas Kelly, 1971.

Kelly, J, *Bonfires on the Hillsides*, Belfast, 1995.

Kelley, Kevin, *The Longest War: Northern Ireland and the IRA*, Brandon, 1989. (Revised Edition).

Kenna, G. B. (Rev John Hassen), *Facts & Figures of the Belfast Pogrom*, Dublin 1922.

Kennedy, Dennis, *The Widening Gulf: Northern Attitudes to the Independent Irish State*, Belfast, 1988.

Kiely, Benedict, *Counties of Contention*, Dublin, 1950.

Kirby, Peadar, *Is Irish Catholicism Dying?*, Mercier, 1984.

Laffan, Michael, *The Partition of Ireland*, Dublin Historical Association, 1983.

Limpkin, C., *The Battle of the Bogside*, Harmondsworth, 1971.

Livingstone, Peadar, *The Fermanagh Story*, Enniskillen, 1969.

Lord Longford, *Peace by Ordeal*, New English Library, 1935.

Lynn, Brendan, *Holding The Ground*, Aldershot, 1997.

McAllister, Ian, *The Social Democratic and Labour Party*, Macmillan Publishers, 1977.

McAteer, Eddie, *Irish Action*, Derry Journal, 1945.

McAteer, Eddie, *It Happens in Derry*, Derry Journal, 1964.

McArdle, Dorothy, *The Irish Republic*, Gollancz, 1937.

McCann, Eamonn, *War and an Irish Town*, Penguin, 1974.

McCauley, Ambrose, *The Life of Bishop Patrick Dorrian*, Manchester University Press, 1989.

McClean, Raymond, *The Road to Bloody Sunday*, Ward River Press, 1983.

McGrath, M., *The Catholic Church and Catholic Schools in Northern Ireland*, IAP, 2000.

McCluskey, Conn, *Up off our Knees*, Conn McCluskey and Associates Publishers, 1988.

McEoin, Uinseann, *Harry: The Story of Harry White*, Argenta Publications, 1986.

McEoin, Uinseann, *Survivors*, Argenta Publications, 1980.

McEoin, Uinseann, *The IRA in the Twilight Years 1923-1948*, Argenta Publications, Dublin, 1997.

McGarry, Fearghal, *Irish Politics and the Spanish Civil War*, Cork University Press, 1999.

MacGoilla Choille, Breandán, *Intelligence Notes*, Dublin, 1966.

McGuffin, John, *Internment*, Anvil, 1973.

McIlroy, G, *The Catholic Church and Northern Ireland Conflict*, Gill and Macmillan, 1991.

McKeown, Michael, *The Greening of a Nationalist*, Murlough Press, 1986.

MacMahon, Deirdre, *Republicans and Imperialists: Anglo Irish Relations in the 1930s*, Yale, 1984.

MacManus, Francis (ed), *The Years of the Great Test*, Mercier, 1967.

MacNally, Jack, *Morally Good, Politically Bad*, Belfast 1989.

MacStiofáin, Seán, *Memoirs of a Revolutionary*, Gordon Creminosi, 1975.

Maloney, Ed & Pollak, Andy, *Paisley*, Poolbeg, 1996.

Martin, F. & Byrne, F. J., (eds), *The Scholar Revolutionary: Eoin McNeill*,

Miller, David W., *Church, State and Nation in Ireland 1898-1921*, Dublin, 1973.

Mitchell, Arthur, *Revolutionary Government in Ireland 1919-22*.

Moody, T. W. & Beckett, J. C., *Ulster Since 1800*, BBC, 1954.

Morgan, Austin, *Labour and Partition The Belfast Working Class 1905-23*, Pluto Press, 1991.

Morgan, Kenneth, *Labour in Power 1945-51*, OUP, 1984.

Morrisey, Hazel, *Betty Sinclair*, Belfast, 1983.

Munck, R. & Rolston B., *Belfast in the 1930s: An Oral History*, Blackstaff Press, 1988.

Murphy, Dervla, *A Place Apart*, John Murray, London, 1978.

Murphy, Desmond, *Derry, Donegal and Modern Ulster 1790-1921*, Aileach Press, 1981.

Murray, Gerard, *John Hume & The SDLP*, Irish Academic Press, 1998.

National Graves Association, *The Last Post: Details and Stories of Republican Dead*, 1976.

Northern Council for Unity, *The Partition of Ireland, the Root of Discontent, Disorder and Distress*, Omagh, 1938.

North Eastern Boundary Bureau, *The Handbook of the Ulster Question*, Dublin, 1923.

O'Callaghan, Sean, *The Informer*, Bantam Press, London, 1998.

O'Connor, Emmet, *A Labour History of Ireland 1824-1960*, Gill and Macmillan, 1994.

O'Connor, Finnuala, *In Search of a State: Catholics in Northern Ireland*, Blackstaff 1993.

Ó Cuinneagáin, Micheál, *Partition from Michael Collins to Bobby Sands*, NPD, 1986.

Ó Dochartaigh, Neill, *From Civil Rights to Armalites*, Cork University Press, 1997.

O'Dowd, L. & Rolson, B., *Northern Ireland: Between Civil Rights and Civil War*, CSE Books, 1980.

Ó Fearghail, Seán, *Law and Whose Orders: The Story of the Belfast Curfew*, Central Citizens' Defence Committee, 1970.

Ó Glaisne, Risteárd, *Conchúir Cruise Ó Briain agus an Liobrálachas*, Clódhanna Teo, 1974.

O'Halloran, Clare, *Partition and the Limits of Irish Nationalism: An Ideology Under Strain*, Atlantic Highlands, 1987.

Ó hUid, Tárlach, *Ar Thóir mo Shealbha*, FNT, 1960.

Ó hUid, Tárlach, *Fá Ghlais*, FNT, 1989.

Ollerenshaw, D. and Kennedy, L., *An Economic History of Ulster*, Blackstaff Press, 1988.

O'Malley, Mary, *Don't Shake Hands with the Devil*, Belfast, 1989.

O'Malley, Pádraig, *The Uncivil Wars*, Blackstaff Press, 1983.

O'Malley, Pádraig, *Questions of Nuance*, Blackstaff Press, 1991.

O'Neill, Terence, *Ulster at the Crossroads*, Faber and Faber, 1969.

O'Neill, Terence, *The Autobiography of Terence O'Neill*, Hart Davis, 1972.

O'Nualiain L., *Finances of Partition*, Dublin 1949.

Oliver, John, *Working at Stormont*, Institute of Public Administration, 1978.

Oppenheimer, Martin, *Urban Guerilla*, Penguin, 1970.

Patterson, Henry, *The Politics of Illusion*, Radius, 1989.

Patterson, Henry, *Class Consciousness and Sectarianism*, Blackstaff Press, Belfast, 1980.

Phoenix, Eamon, *Northern Nationalism, Nationalist Politics, Partition and the Catholic Minority in NI, 1890-1940,* UHF, 1994.

Purdie, Bob, *Politics in the Street,* Blackstaff Press, 1990.

Rafferty, Oliver P., *Catholicism in Ulster, 1603-1983: An Interpretative History,* Gill & Macmillan, 1994.

Rea, Desmond (ed), *Political Co-operation in Divided Societies,* Gill & Macmillan, 1982.

Rose, Paul, *Backbencher's Dilemma,* London. 1981.

Rose, Peter, *How the Troubles came to Northern Ireland,* Macmillan, 2000

Rose, Richard, *Northern Ireland, A Time of Choice,* London, 1976.

Rose, Richard, *Governing without Consensus,* Faber and Faber, 1971.

Quinn, Raymond, *A Rebel Voice, A History of Belfast Republicanism 1925-1972,* Belfast, 1999.

Rowthorn, B and Wayne, *Northern Ireland: The Political Economy of the Conflict,* Cambridge, 1988.

Rumpf & Hepburn, *Nationalism and Socialism in Ireland,* Liverpool University Press, 1977.

Shannon, Elizabeth, *I am of Ireland: Women of the North Speak Out,* Little Brown & Company, Boston, Tokyo, Ireland, 1989.

Skinner, Liam C., *Politicians by Accident,* Metropolitan, 1948.

Smith, David, & Chambers, Gerald, *Inequality in Northern Ireland,* Clarendon Press, 1991.

Shafer, Boyd T., *Nationalism, Myth & Reality,* 1955.

Sluka, Jeffrey, *Hearts and Minds, Water and Fish, Support for the IRA and INLA in a Northern Irish Ghetto,* Greenwich JAI Press, 1990.

Snyder, Louis L., *The Dynamics of Nationalism, Readings in its Meaning and Development,* Princeton, 1964.

Shea, Patrick, *Voices and the Sound of Drums,* Belfast 1981.

Stewart, A. T. Q., *The Ulster Crisis, London,* 1967.

Street, Major C. J., *The Administration of Ireland 1920,* Phillip Allen, 1921.

Sunday Times Insight Team, *Ulster,* Penguin, 1971.

Sweetman, Rosita, *On our Knees,* Pan, 1972.

Townshead, Charles, *Political Violence in Ireland,* Oxford, 1983.

Van Voris, W. H., *Violence in Ulster, An Oral Documentary,* University of Massachussets, Amherst Press, 1975.

Walker, B. M., *Ulster Politics. The Formative Years,* Ulster Historical Foundation, 1989.

Walker, G., *The Politics of Frustration, H Midgley and the failure of Labour in Northern Ireland,* Manchester University, 1986.

Walsh, Dick, *Géarchéim in Éirinn,* FNT (no date given).

Walsh, Dick, *The Party: Inside Fianna Fáil,* Gill & Macmillan, 1986.

Walsh, Patrick, *Republicanism and Socialism in Modern Ireland,* Athol Press, 1994.

Watson, Raymond, *Newry's Struggle,* (no date and no publisher given).

Watt, D. (ed), *The Constitution of Northern Ireland,* London, 1981.

West, Trevor, *The Downfall of the Liberal Party,* London, 1963.

Williams, T. D. (ed), *The Irish Struggle*, Dublin, 1967.

Whyte, Barry, *John Hume, Portrait of a Statesman*, Blackstaff Press, 1984.

Whyte, J. H., *Church and State in Modern Ireland 1923-1979*, 2nd edition, Dublin, 1980.

Whyte, J. H., *Interpreting Northern Ireland*, Oxford, 1990.

Whyte, Robert W., *Provisional Irish Republicanism, An Oral and Interpretative History*, Greenwood, 1993.

Wilson, Des, *An End to Silence*, Mercier, 1989.

Wilson, D. & Kearney, O., *West Belfast: The Way Forward*, Belfast, 1986.

Wilson, T. R., *Urban Elections in Ulster*, Methuen, 1965.

Wilson, Thomas (ed), *Ulster Under Home Rule, A Study of the Political and Economic Problems of Northern Ireland*, London, 1955.

Wilson, Tom, *Ulster: Conflict and Consent*, Oxford, 1989.

Wright, Frank, *Northern Ireland, A Comparative Analysis*, Gill and Macmillan 1988.

Wright, Frank, *Two Lands on one Soil, Ulster Politics Before Home Rule*, Gill & Macmillan, Dublin, 1996.

Younger, Calton, *Ireland's Civil War*, Collins & Sons, 1979.

Younger, Calton, *A State of Disunion*, London, 1972.

UNPUBLISHED THESES

Carroll, Terence M., 'Political Activists in Disaffected Communities', PhD, University of Carleton, 1974.

Chauvin, Guy, 'The Parliamentary Party and the Revolutionary Movement in Ireland', PhD, Trinity College, Dublin, 1977.

Dooher, J. B., 'Tyrone Nationalism and the Border Question 1910-1925', D.Phil, University of Ulster, 1986.

Elliott, Sydney, 'Parliamentary Election Results in Northern Ireland', PhD, Queen's University, Belfast, 1971.

Fitzsimmons Harbinson, John, 'A History of the Northern Ireland Labour Party 1181-1949', MA, Queen's University, Belfast, 1966.

Foy, Michael, 'The AOH: A Political Religious Pressure Group', MA, Queen's University, Belfast, 1976.

Johnston, Patricia, 'Anthony Mulvey and Nationalist Politics in Northern Ireland 1945-51', B Ed, St Mary's College, Belfast.

McDonnell, Arthur, 'The 1918 Election in Ulster and the career of Denis Henry MP', PhD, Queen's University, Belfast, 1986.

Martin, John, 'The Anti-Partition League 1945-54', MS Sc, Queen's University Belfast, 1985.

Millotte, Mike, 'Communism in Modern Ireland', PhD, Queen's University, Belfast, 1977.

Morgan, Michael, 'The Civil Rights Movement: A Reassessment', MS Sc, Queen's University, Belfast, 1984.

Sheehan, K, 'The Northern Policy of the Provisional and Irish Free State Government 1922-24', MA, University College, Dublin 1982.

Whitford, F. J., 'Joe Devlin: Ulsterman and Irishman', MA, London University, September 1959.

ARTICLES

Birrell, Derek, 'Relative Deprivation as a Factor in Conflict in Northern Ireland', *Social Review*, 20 March 1972, pp 317-43.

Farren, Sean, 'Nationalist Catholic Reaction to Educational Reform in N. Ireland 1920-30', *History of Education*, 1985, Vol 14, no 3, pp 227-36.

Birrell, Derek, 'Relative Deprivation as a Factor in Conflict in Northern Ireland', *Social Review*, 20 March 1972, pp 317-43.

Feeney, Vincent E, 'The Civil Rights Movement in Northern Ireland', *Éire Ireland*, 9 February 1974, pp 30-40.

Gannon P. J., 'In the Catacombs of Belfast', *Studies*, Vol V, No XI, 1922.

Gallagher, M., 'The Struggle for the Belleek Triangle', *Donegal Annual*, 1982.

Harris, Mary N., 'Catholicism, Nationalism and the Labour Question in Belfast. 1925-38', *Bullán*, Vol 3, No 1, 1997, pp 15-33.

Hepburn, A. C., 'Catholics in the North of Ireland 1850-1921. The Urbanization of a Minority', *Minorities in History*, London, 1978.

Hepburn, A. C., 'The AOH in Irish Politics 1905-1914', *Cithara*, Vol X, 1971, pp 5-18.

Hewitt, C., 'Explaining Violence in Northern Ireland', *British Journal of Scientology*, no 38, 1987, pp 88-93.

Hewitt, C., 'Catholic Grievances, Catholic Nationalism and the Demand for Civil Rights: A Reconsideration', *British Journal of Sociology*, no 32, 1981, pp 362-380.

Hewitt, C., 'Catholic Grievances and Catholic Nationalism in Northern Ireland', *British Journal of Sociology*, no 36, 1985, pp 102-105.

Hopkinson, M., 'The Craig-Collins Pacts of 1922', *Irish Historical Studies*, Vol 27, no 106, November 1990.

Johnson, D. S., 'The Belfast Boycott, 1920-22', *Irish Population Economy and Society, essays in honour of the late K. H. O'Connell*, (eds) J. M. Goldstrom and L. A. Clarkson, Oxford, 1981.

Kennedy, David, 'Whither Northern Nationalism?', *Christus Rex*, 13 April 1959.

Kennedy, David, 'Catholics in Northern Ireland', *The Years of the Great Test*, (ed) Francis McManus, Thomas Davis Lecture Series, pp 138-150.

Kovalcheck, K. A., 'Catholic Grievances in Northern Ireland: Appraisal and Judgement', British Journal of Sociology, 38, 1987.

McAllister, Ian, 'Political Opposition in Northern Ireland: The National Democratic Party 1965-70', *Economic and Social Review*, 6 March 1975, pp 353-66

McAllister, Ian, 'The 1975 Northern Ireland Convention Election', *Glasgow Survey Research Centre Occasional Paper*, 14 November 1975.

McAuley, Ambrose, 'Catholics in the North 1870-1970', *Newman Review*, 2:1, 1970, pp 21 -32.

McAuley, Ambrose. 'Britain's New Irish State', *Capuchin Annual* 1972.

Moxon-Browne, E., 'The Water and the Fish: Public Opinion and the IRA', *British Perspectives on Terrorism*, (ed) Paul Wilkinson, Allan and Unwin, London, 1981.

Norton, Christopher, 'The Irish Labour Party in the Northern Ireland 1949-58', *Saothar*, no 21.

Newe, G. B., 'The Catholic in the Northern Ireland Community', *Christus Rex*, 18.1, 1964, pp 21-32.

O'Hearn, D., 'Catholic Grievances, Comments', *British Journal of Sociology*, no 38, 1987, pp. 94-100. Again on discrimination, 'A Reply to the Rejoinder', *British Journal of Sociology*, no 36, 1985, pp 94-101.

Purdie, Bob, 'The Friends of Ireland, British Labour and Irish Nationalism 1945-49', *Contemporary Irish Studies*, (eds) Tom Gallagher and James O'Connell, Manchester University Press, 1983.

Purdie, Bob, 'The Irish Anti-Partition League. South Armagh and the Abstentionist Tactic 1945-58', *Irish Political Studies*, 1986, pp 67-77.

Staunton, Enda, 'Michael Collins' Northern Policy: A Reassessment', *Irish Stadies Review*, Autumn 1997.

Staunton, Enda, 'The 1925 Agreement: Aftermath and Implications', *History Ireland*, Summer, 1996.

Walker, Graham, 'The Northern Ireland Labour Party in the 1920s', *Saothar*, 1984.

Walker, Graham, 'Jack Beattie', *Obair*, 1985.

Whyte, J. H., 'How Much Discrimination was there under the Unionist Regime 1921-68?', *Contemporary Irish Studies, op. cit.*

Glossary

Agnew, Patrick

Armagh City Labour politician. Resided Railway Street, Armagh. Had his greatest success in 1930 with his election to Armagh Board of Guardians County Council and, as a result of nationalist boycott, unopposed to Stormont as MP for South Armagh. Ousted 1945 in a bitter contest. Lost his council seat in 1958 in equally controversial circumstances. Died 1960.

Aiken, Frank

Born Camlough in South Armagh, 1898, son of a local farmer. He was prominent in IRA during war of independence, rising to command in the 4th Northern Division. Responsible for numerous successful operations including the Newtownhamilton Barracks attack in May 1920 and the Adavoyle Embankment explosion the following year which devastated a British troop train. Fought a savage sectarian war in the period to Summer 1922. When south's Civil War broke out he was forced to take Republican side. Later active in Fianna Fáil. Rose to become Minister for External Affairs and Tánaiste (Deputy Leader), under Éamon de Valera, Sean Lemass and Jack Lynch. Died 1983.

Beattie, Jack

Born 1886. Protestant shipyard worker and blacksmith. Served in British army, first as boy batman and later in King's Royal Hussars. Northern Ireland Labour representative for East Belfast 1925-29. Expelled from (NI) Labour Party 1934, readmitted 1942. Expelled again 1944. Set up Federation of Labour with J. H. Collins and others. Elected MP Pottinger 1929-49. Lost his Pottinger seat in the envenomed atmosphere caused by the 'Chapel Gate' collection funded anti-partition campaign. Won West Belfast Westminster seat 1943, lost it in 1950, regained it in 1951 but Sinn Féin intervention in 1955 reduced his vote leading to unionist victory. Anti-Partitionist and a founder of the Irish Labour Party following the 1949 split. Died 1960.

Blythe, Ernest

Born 1889, County Antrim, of Presbyterian stock. Heavily involved in Sinn Féin movement. Minister of Trade and Commerce and later Finance in first Free State government. Detested in some Northern nationalist circles after 1925 Agreement in which he played a prominent part. Following his 1933 electoral defeat and his subsequent retirement from politics, he continued to advocate a policy of northern nationalist acceptance of the state as a first step towards ultimate unity.

Browne, Noël
Born in Mayo. Elected to Dáil as Clann na Poblachta TD 1948. Received Health portfolio in the State's first inter-party government which ended 16 years of Fianna Fáil rule. Involved in speechmaking for the party in Westminster Election of February 1950 when he crossed the border to support an anti-partitionist panel which included IRA prison inmates. In 1951 his proposals for a free health system for mothers and their children brought down the government due to medical and episcopal opposition.

Byrne, Richard
Nationalist MP for Falls, came to Belfast in 1890. Publican and slum landlord. Member of AOH. Died 1942.

Cahill, Joe
Born 1920. Joined IRA in 1930s as a teenager. In 1942 he was sentenced to death along with five comrades for the killing of an RUC man. Was reprieved with four others of those condemned, the sixth, Tom Williams, going to the gallows in September of that year. Released in the late 1940s with other sentenced republican prisoners. Interned in the 1950s, was active in the formation of the Provisional IRA and later became its Belfast Commander.

Campbell, T. J.
1871-1946. Kings Counsel and *Irish News* editor. Winner of June 1934 by-election for Joe Devlin's Belfast Central seat. His acceptance of a Belfast County Court judgeship in 1945 earned him the opprobrious sobriquet 'Judas' Campbell in nationalist circles.

Collins, J. H.
From old Newry family. Qualified as a solicitor 1910. Sinn Féin MP Armagh 1921-25, 25-29, South Down 1929.

Conlon, Malachy
Former IRA member elected South Armagh 1945. Toured America with McBride 1950. Died in that year.

Connellan, Joe
Editor *Frontier Sentinel* for 59 years. Entered Stormont as MP for South Armagh 1929. Had been a Sinn Féiner on the Board of Guardians 1920-27. Retired in 1933. Returned to politics in 1949 to succeed Peter Murney in South Down on the latter's death. Remained on as MP until his death in April 1967.

Devlin, Paddy
Born 1925. Became Minister for Health and Social Services in the North's short lived power sharing Executive until it was toppled by Loyalist Action in May 1974. One time IRA member. Interned during second World War. Was floorman in Andrew's Flour Mill. Elected as Irish Labour Party Councillor for Falls on Belfast Corporation, defeated Gerry Fitt of Dock Irish Labour. Rejoined NILP after Irish Labour, was routed by Frank Hanna's independent Labour Group in 1958. Defeated Harry Diamond for parliamentary seat in Falls Constituency 1969. Joined SDLP on its formation. Expelled 1977. Ran unsuccessfully in later elections. Headed taxi firm until his death in 1999.

Devlin, Joe
Born to working class family in Belfast, 1871, of Tyrone ancestry. Elected Home Rule MP for North Kilkenny in 1902. Following the defeat of Bishop Henry's Catholic Association the way was open for his victory in West Belfast in 1906. Defeated Éamon De Valera, Falls 1918. His revitalisation of the AOH and his popularity among workers ensured a solid base of support. With the creation of a new West Belfast constituency in 1922 he ceased to represent the area at Westminster 1929 as MP for Fermanagh and Tyrone. The respect in which he was held by his unionist opponents was demonstrated after his death in January 1934, when Craigavon and his audience at the Uster Hall heard the news they rose in silent tribute.

Dillon, John
1851-1927. Home Rule MP for East Mayo, 1885-1918. A veteran of the Land War and the anti-Parnellite cause, he became leader of the party on the death of John Redmond in March 1918 and led the party into the disastrous election at the end of that year in which he, along with most of his colleagues, lost their seats.

Donnelly, Alexander (A. E.)
Omagh Solicitor. Elected to Tyrone County Council 1914-24, first as Home Ruler, later turned to Sinn Féin 1927-29 as nationalist representative. Elected for West Tyrone 1929. Left Stormont in April 1934. Elected 1945. Retired from politics in 1949. Died 1958.

Donnelly, Eamonn
Born in County Armagh. Ulster organiser for Sinn Féin 1921. Anti-Treatyite Sinn Féin MP for Armagh 1925-29. Elected as Fianna Fáil TD for Offaly 1933-37. Defeated in his bid for seat in southern Senate. Elected in Falls by-election 1942. Died December 1944.

Dulanty, J. W.
Irish High Commissioner in London 1930-1949.

Diamond, Harry
Born 1908. Began his career as nationalist Poor Law Guardian member. Formed his own Anti-Partition League which unsuccessfully contested the Belfast Central Seat left vacant on Devlin's death. Elected as Socialist Republican for Falls 1945, he held the seat until 1969. Joined Irish Labour 1949. Expelled 1951. Lived in retirement at Waterfoot, Co Antrim. Died 1996.

Hanna, Frank
Born 1915. Elected as Councillor for Nationalist Party. Left in 1942 with Councillor James Collins as part of nationalist decline in Belfast. Joined NILP, elected on that party's ticket as MP for Belfast Central 1947 by-election defeating Victor Halley (an Independent Labourite and Presbyterian, later associated with Diamond's party). Resigned from NILP, joined Irish Labour when that party expanded into north. Resigned shortly afterwards. Defended his Belfast Central seat against challenges, annihilated Irish Labour in the Corporation elections of 1958 with a small clericalist Independent Labour Group. Succeeded in the seat by Tom Brennan, member of this group who later joined the National Democratic Party.

Harbinson, T. J. S.
1864-1930. First elected as UIL MP for East Tyrone, one of the survivors of the 1918 election in Ulster. Continued as representative for Fermanagh and Tyrone at Westminster until his death. Did not contest the 1929 election for his Stormont seat.

Healy, Cahir
Born Donegal 1877. Trained as a national school teacher. Became involved in the pre-1916 Sinn Féin movement. Worked for Sean McDermott in the 1907 Leitrim by-election. Member of Collins' North East Ulster Advisory Committee. Arrested in the swoop of May 1922 and interned on the *Argenta*. Elected MP for Fermanagh and Tyrone in 1922. Kept in confinement until 1924 despite his re-election in December 1923 and a controversy in the House of Commons over his custody. Elected MP for South Fermanagh 1925 and retained seat mostly unopposed until 1965 when he retired. Interned in 1941 in Brixton Prison. A writer, insurance officer and journalist. Died 1970.

Leeke, George
MP for Mid Derry 1925-39. First elected Derry city and county in 1921. Succeeded his father as a Home Rule councillor on Limavady Rural District Council. A prosperous hotelier and member of the AOH. Died March 1939.

Lennon, J. G.
A prominent member of the AOH, he is best remembered for his role in the 1962-63 talks with Sir George Clark, Grand Master of the Orange Order, the Orange-Green Talks as they came to be known.

McAleer, Hubert (H. K.)
President of Tyrone AOH. Former national school teacher, retired 1899. Became auctioneer and merchant at Sixmilecross. Active in GAA, County President, elected MP for Mid Tyrone in 1929, left Stormont October 1935. Died 1941.

McAteer, Eddie
Born in Scotland in 1914. Father was a docker in Derry. Charged as a young man, along with his family, with IRA offences but acquitted. First elected in 1945 in Mid Derry. Published pamphlet, *Irish Action,* advocating an approach of 'dumb insolence' towards the northern government. Ran against Patrick Maxwell, outgoing MP for Foyle, in 1953 and defeated him. Held seat until his defeat by John Hume in 1969. A civil servant and later a self-employed accountant. Died 1986.

McAteer, Hugh
Older brother of Eddie MacAteer. Joined the IRA as a sixteen year old. First sentenced for republican activity in 1936. Released 1941. The following year was promoted from O/C of the movement's Northern Command to Chief and Staff. Rearrested in September 1942 in RUC 'Sting' Operation. Made a daring escape in early 1943 but recaptured later that year. Left the movement after the war but remained on good terms with it, acting as link man between it and inter-party government of Sean McBride and John A Costello for which he acted in a consultative role. Rejoined movement when issue of defending Catholics led to the formation of the Provisional IRA.

McCall, Seamus
Born in Dublin, 1892, of northern Protestant stock, he spent an adventurous youth in Latin America. Captain in British army during World War I. Colonel, Western Command, IRA during south's civil war. Served as observer for League of Nations in Spanish Civil War. Appointed Liaison Office by the All-Party Anti-Partition Mansion House Committee and sent north in 1949 to provide periodic appraisals of the situation. A literary man, his books include *And So Began the Irish Nation,* 1931, *A Life of John Mitchell,* 1938, *A Biography of Thomas Moore,* 1935, as well as radio plays and at least one novel, *Gods in Motley.* Chairman of PEN and editor of *Garda Review,* he died in 1964.

McCarroll, Frank
Born 1889 in Augher, County Tyrone, son of a farmer. Began working life as journalist with *Derry People*, later became editor of *Derry Journal*. Presented nationalist case for the Boundary Commission. Elected for Foyle in 1929. Died 1937.

McGill, Patrick
Nationalist Senator and editor of *Ulster Herald*. The most prominent member of the 'Omagh Group' in northern nationalist politics of the 1950s.

McHugh, J.
Nationalist Senator in 1930s. Began political life as a Home Ruler. Unsuccessfully contested Stormont general election of 1925. An hotelier by profession.

McLaughlin, Thomas
Nationalist Senator. Prominent Armagh businessman. Heavily involved in the AOH and Knights of Columbanus.

McMullen, William
Veteran Belfast Protestant trade unionist, active in the Irish Labour Party from its foundation. Elected for West Belfast 1925-1929 with the help of Joe Devlin's transfers. Lost seat due to abolition of PR. Later lived in Dublin and became a member of the senate.

McSparran, James
Queen's Counsel and MP for Mourne from 1945 until his retirement in 1958. Came from long-established County Aritrim family which had held controlling interests in the *Irish News* and Belfast Celtic Football Club. Prominent in AOH.

Mulvey, Anthony
Journalist and editor of *Ulster Herald* newspaper. Had republican past in Co Wexford before moving north. Accepted as compromise candidate for Fermanagh and Tyrone when republicans intervened in 1935 Westminster Election along with Michael Cunningham, a progressive farmer from the Omagh District. Held the seat until 1951. Became a strong opponent of abstentionism from Westminster and stayed apart from Anti-Partition League though he worked closely with it.

Murnaghan, George
Omagh solicitor and supporter of Healy within the Home Rule Party, expelled as a result. Became leading figure in Bishop McHugh's Irish Nation League known as League of Seven Attorneys because of the prominence of lawyers in it, including Murnaghan's partner, O'Shiel. Joined Sinn Féin, supported Treaty. Appointed judge in south.

Murney, Peter
County Down republican. Took republican side in the southern Civil War. Interned by Free State. Successfully contested South Down in 1945 Died 1949.

Ó Brádaigh, Ruairí
Born Longford, son of an IRA veteran. Active in 1950s campaign as IRA commander in the west of Ireland and later as Chief of Staff. Elected for Longford Westmeath constituency as abstentionist in 1957, one of four Sinn Féiners to win seats in the emotional aftermath of the Brookeborough raid that January. A founder member of the Provisional IRA and Sinn Féin President, he broke with the republican movement in the 1980s on the decision to accept seats in the southern parliament and has since led his own militant micro-group, 'Republican Sinn Féin'.

O'Connor, Roderick
MP for West Tyrone in succession to Alexander Donnelly. Held seat in 1969 election unopposed. Omagh solicitor and proprietor of the *Ulster Herald*. He is now retired.

O'Connor, T. P. (Timothy Power)
1848-1929. Irish Parliamentary Party MP for Liverpool, the only Home Rule MP to sit for an English constituency. Re-elected in 1918.

O'Neill, Patrick
A native of County Tyrone. First elected in 1921 on Home Rule ticket for Down seat, the only Home Ruler in the race. Held Mourne seat until his death in 1938. Warrenpoint hotelier.

O'Shiel, Kevin R.
Law partner of George Murnaghan. Involved with him in the INL and later Sinn Féin. Appointed legal adviser to provisional government on north. Pursued a career in southern Civil Service until his death.

Redmond, John
1856-1918. Became leader of the re-united Home Rule Party after heading the Parnellite faction following the split in 1890. Held the leadership until his death in March 1918.

Stewart, Joe
Born 1889. Prominent member of the AOH and Licensed Vintners' Association. Member of Tyrone County Council and Stormont MP from 1929-64. Led Nationalist Party after McSparran's retirement. On his death in 1964 he was succeeded in his leadership of the party by Eddie McAteer and in his Tyrone seat by Austin Currie.

ORGANISATIONS AND TERMS

(AOH) Ancient Order of Hibernians
Originally a Roman Catholic Welfare Society with roots in the
Sectarianism of the 17th and the 18th centuries, it was remodelled by its
National President Joseph Devlin, the Belfast MP, in 1905 to become a
powerful organisation often equated with the Orange Order. Linked to
the Home Rule Party, it was clericalist, conservative and strongly opposed to both republicanism and social radicalism.

All-Party Anti-Partition Committee
Formed from an initiative undertaken by the southern parties in
January 1949 in the climate of recrimination with Britain following a decision to declare Ireland a Republic, its inaugural conference at the
Mansion House pledged aid to APL, Anti-Partition League, candidates
in the 1949 northern election. These collections taken up at churches in
the south became known as 'the chapel gate collections'.

(APA) Anti-Partition Association
Southern support group for the north's Anti-Partition League formed
in 1948. Its publications included a newsletter, *Fírinne* (Truth) and some
pamphlets, e.g. *East is East but North meets South*, Dublin 1951.

(APL) Anti-Partition League
The Nationalist Party as it reconstituted itself in late 1945.

Ard Fheis
Annual party conference

Belfast Boycott
A boycott on Belfast goods imposed by insurgent Dáil Éireann in 1920
in response to the expulsion of Catholics in the city.

B Specials, see USC (Ulster Special Constabulary)

Chapel Gate Collections, see All Party Anti-Partition Committee

Cameron Report
A 1969 report prepared by a commission chaired by Lord Cameron to
enquire into the disturbances since October 1968.

Civic guards. Garda Síochána. Gardaí.
26 county police force formed in 1922.

(CDU) Campaign for Democracy in Ulster
Founded June 1965 in London by a group of British Labour MPs, con-

cerned about the anti-Catholic discrimination in Northern Ireland. Its chairman, Paul Rose, was a Labour MP for Manchester.

(CSJ) Campaign for Social Justice

A pressure group formed in Dungannon by a local GP, Conn McCluskey and his wife Patricia, to highlight sectarian discrimination.

Clann na Poblachta

'Family of the Republic' party formed in 1946 by ex-IRA Chief of Staff, Sean McBride, which entered the government in the south after the 1948 general election.

Cumann na nGael

Party formed in 1923 from main pro-Treaty faction in the south.

Dáil Éireann

Parliament of southern Ireland. Its upper house is known as the *Seanad*. Both houses of the legislature are termed the *Oireachtas*.

Fianna (Na Fianna)

Youth wing of the republican movement.

Fianna Fáil

Southern political party founded by Éamon de Valera.

Fianna Uladh see Saor Uladh.

Fine Gael

Party formed in 1933 from merger of Cumann na Gaedhal with two other parties.

Friends of Ireland

Pressure group formed in British Labour Party after World War II to relieve the disabilities on northern Catholics,

(ICA) Irish Citizens' Association

Title of group formed in Newry area by Joe Connellan, MP for South Down and *Frontier Sentinel* editor, who sat on the APL executive. It came to dominate Newry Corporation, losing to Irish Labour in 1958.

(IrLP) Irish Labour Party

Founded 1912 by James Connolly. Has been both in opposition and in government south of the border since partition. In 1948 it took a decision to establish in the north, drawing nationalist elements from the Northern Ireland Labour Party. In 1949 local elections it made a clean sweep of two Belfast wards and won control in Newry and Warrenpoint. Throughout the 1950s its strength was gradually whittled down by splits and clericalist opposition. By the start of the troubles it had largely vanished north of the border. In 1973 it was wound up in the north.

Iveagh House
Dublin Department of Foreign Affairs (formerly External Affairs).
(IPP) Irish Parliamentary Party
The Home Rule Party which lost to Sinn Féin in 1918.

(IRA) Irish Republican Army
Guerrilla army founded after the 1916 Rising to end British rule in Ireland. It split in 1922 over the Treaty, leading to the south's civil war, in which those who continued to retain the title IRA were defeated. Illegal in the south since 1936, the cataclysmic events in Northern Ireland in 1969 led to a further split into 'Official' and 'Provisional' factions.

(IRB) Irish Republican Brotherhood
Secret revolutionary organisation which served as the nucleus of the 1916 rising.

(IUA) Irish Union Association
Short-lived anti-partitionist organisation formed in July 1936. Was largely confined to portions of nationalist areas in Tyrone, Fermanagh and Derry.

(NDP) National Democratic Party
A party which grew from the National Unity movement formed in 1959 to promote the modernisation of the Nationalist Party. When the National Political Front, which comprised both them and the Nationalists collapsed, the NDP was created.

National League of the North
Title used by constitutional nationalist opposition from 1928 to mid 1930s.

National Political Front (NPF)
Formed in 1964 after National Unity movement pressed for changes in the Nationalist Party.

National Unity
Movement established in 1959 to accelerate progress within the Nationalist Party.

(NEBB) North East Boundary Bureau
A unit formed by the Dublin government to promote the Irish case before the Boundary Commission.

(NILP) Northern Ireland Labour Party
Left wing party formed in 1924 with cross community support. Initially it refused to commit itself on the partition issue. In 1948, when the Irish Labour Party expanded into the north, its anti-partitionist membership was siphoned off and the party moved to an explicitly pro-union position.

Northern Council of Unity (Also: Ulster Council)
A strongly anti-partitionist organisation set up in the aftermath of De Valera's 1937 Consitution. It leaned towards Fianna Fáil but included some more hardline republican elements.

Republican Congress
A left wing republican group formed in 1934 from a split with the IRA. It split later on that year and was dissolved the following year.

Republican Labour
A group formed by Harry Diamond, Victor Halley and others who had been expelled from the Labour Party in 1951. It was led first by Diamond and from 1962 by Gerry Fitt. It succeeded in recovering the three winnable seats of Falls (Harry Diamond) Central (Paddy Kennedy) and Dock (Gerry Fitt) and in rolling back much of the ground lost by Irish Labour on Belfast Corporation. It fell apart after Diamond lost to Paddy Devlin in 1969 and Fitt left to join the SDLP the following year.

Saor Éire (Free Ireland)
A left wing breakaway from the IRA in the 1930s which became the subject of a Red Scare and the precursor to the Republican Congress.

Saor Uladh (Free Ulster)
A republican splinter group founded in County Tyrone as the military wing of Fianna Uladh in 1954. Its founder, Liam Kelly, had been elected to Stormont on an abstentionist ticket the previous year. It accepted the south's 1937 Constitution. Kelly, its leader, was appointed to the Senate by Sean McBride.

Sinn Féin (We Ourselves)
Originated in 1905 as dual monarchy movement under Arthur Griffith. After 1916 Rising became a mass movement based on republican abstentionism and later supported the IRA's independence struggle. Was the foundation organisation from which the precursors of the two main Treatyite southern parties split: the pro-Treatyites in 1922 and De Valera's faction, later Fianna Fáil, in 1926. A minor IRA supporting party in the 30s and 40s, it became that organisation's political wing in the early 1950s, enjoying some electoral success north and south. It divided again in 1970 following the split within the IRA between

Provisional and Official factions. The Sinn Féin section aligned with the Provisionals later became a serious electoral force in the north.

(SDLP) Social Democratic and Labour Party
The principal party of the northern minority since the early 1970s. Founded in August 1970, it incorporated diverse elements from the NDP, Republican Labour, the Nationalists and the NILP, the most common feature uniting them being an involvement with the Civil Rights Movement.

Tánaiste
Deputy Prime Minister of the Republic.

Taoiseach
Prime Minister of the Republic.

(TD) Teachta Dála
Member of parliament in the Republic.

(UPA) Ulster Protestant Association
An extreme loyalist organisation which maintained a reign of terror with likely official connivance in East Belfast in the period 1920-23. Their victims included not only Catholics but also many Protestants who fell foul of their racketeering and corruption.

(UPL) Ulster Protestant League
An organisation formed in 1931 with the ostensible purpose of protecting Protestant employment. Its message of loyalist supremacy acted as a catalyst for much of the trouble in the city during the 1930s. Men like Alexander Robinson, 'Buck Alex', a former B Special in the Docks area, were among its leaders.

Notes

Introduction

1. In support of this point on the economically disadvantaged position of northern Catholics, see S. J. Connolly, 'Catholics in Ulster, 1800-1850' in P. Roebuck (ed), *Plantation to Partition: Essays in Ulster History in honour of J. L. McCracken*, p 158. Connoly's sources include Wakenfield's *Account of Ireland*, London 1812 and Mason's *Parochial Survey of Ireland*, Dublin 1814-19, as well as Ordnance and Estate Surveys, all of which confirmed Catholics as the owners of inferior land.

2. S. J. Connolly, *ibid*, p 166.

3. B. M. Walker, *Ulster Politics: The formative years*, U.H.F. 1989.

4. Belfast had 349,000 inhabitants in 1901. The Catholic population of the city had reached a peak of 34% in 1861 before a Protestant influx diluted the percentage. On the growth of Belfast, see E. R. R. Green's 'The Beginning of Industrial Revolution' in J. C. Beckett and R. E. Glassock (eds), *Belfast: The origin and growth of an industrial city*, BBC 1967. On the above and also on Catholic politics in the city, see I. Budge and C. O'Leary, *Belfast: Approach to Crisis*, Macmillan 1923, *passim*. For a general survey of Catholic politics in the period, see A. C. Hepburn, 'Catholics in the North of Ireland, 1850-1921' in A. C. Hepburn, *Minorities in History*, pp 84-85. Also Walker, *op. cit.*, pp 176-215 gives a good account of the collapse of the liberal alliance as in smaller scale does David Kennedy, 'Ulster and the Antecedents of Home Rule, 1850-1886' in *Ulster since 1800*, pp 79-92. Ambrose MacCauley, *The Life of Bishop Patrick Dorrian*, Manchester University Press 1989, and Eamonn McCann, 'Shepherds in the Ghetto: The Catholic Church in West Belfast', part I, *Magill* magazine, August 1988, provide between them a vivid and comprehensive account of how the alliance fractured within Belfast.

5. Crime Branch Survey, National Archive, Dublin, 4861/S CBS.

6. F. J. Whitford, 'Joseph Devlin and the Catholic Representation Association of Belfast, 1895-1909' in *Threshold*, Vol 1, No 2, Summer 1957. F. J. Whitford, 'Joe Devlin: Ulsterman and Irishman', unpublished MA thesis, University of London, 1959.

7. John Gray, *City in Revolt: James Larkin and the Belfast Dock Strike of 1907*, Blackstaff Press 1985, pp 52-55, 151-153, 162-163, 169, 189, 190, 214.

8. M. Foy, 'The AOH: A politico-religious pressure group', unpublished MA thesis, Queen's University Belfast 1976.

9. Foy, *ibid*,

10. 4861/S CBS, *op. cit., loc. cit.*

11. F. Martin, 'McCullough, Hobson and Republican Ulster', in F. Martin (ed), *Leaders and Men of the Easter Rising*, Methuen 1965.

12. Devlin to Dillon, 20 December 1907. 6729, No 120, Dillon Papers, TCD Archives.

13. Michael Laffan, *The Partition of Ireland*, DHA 1983, pp 24-56.

14. Nora Connolly O'Brien, *Portrait of a Rebel Father*, p 201. On the lack of response in west Ulster, see N. Marlowe, 'The Mood of Ireland', *The British Review*, 11/1 1915.

15. F. Martin, *op. cit.*.

16. O'Connor to Dillon, 31 October 1916, O'Connor to Redmond, ms 15,215/2, Redmond Papers, NLI.

17. *ibid.*

18. Devlin to Horgan, 3 July 1916, ms 18271, NLI. Devlin letter, Dillon Papers 740, no 313, loc. cit..

19. Dillon to O'Connor, 8 July 1916, Dillon Papers. Dillon to O'Connor, 20 June 1916, op. cit. Devlin to Redmond, 19 June 1916, Redmond Papers, ms 15, 181 (2), NLI. The east-west divide was firmly emphasised in the St Mary's Hall vote:

Region	For	Against
Antrim	130	8
Down	116	7
Armagh	67	35
Derry County	58	59
Fermanagh	28	51
Tyrone	52	102
Derry City	7	30

(*IN*, 24 June 1916). The groundwork for the Sinn Féin advance in Ulster had already been laid. The anti-exclusion ptotests strengthened the feeling.

20. D. McArdle, *The Irish Republic*, Corgi 1937, p 187.

21. *FS*, 26 January 1916.

22. In 1892 the unionist vote was 2242. In 1895 it was 1995. In 1909 this fell to 1628. A district by district beakdown of the figures in the *Armagh Guardian*, 8 February 1918 was as follows:

	On Register	Voted
Ballybot	1700	917
Crossmaglen	1038	772
Clady/Middletown	870	475
Forkhill	1261	836
Newtownhamilton	1014	650
Poyntzpass	466	189

23. For the nature of the alliance with the unionists, the 'coupon' from which the election took its name, see Trevor West, *The Downfall of the Liberal Party*, pp 157-161.

24. Quoted in P. Bew, *Conflict and Conciliation in Ireland, Parnellites and Radical Agrarians*, Clarendon, 1988, p 217-218.

25. CO/904, July 1918, NLI.

26. See letter from Bishop McHugh to J. Murrin, 15 September 1918 and 12 October 1918. McHugh felt that it would be a 'very uncatholic thing' if McNeill's selection resulted in the loss of the seat. McNeill Papers, No 10880, NLI.

Chapter 1
The 1918 election and its aftermath

1. *FJ*, 24 October 1918.
2. *Ibid*, 15 November 1928.
3. *Ibid*, 21 November 1918.
4. *Ibid*, 21 November 1928.
5. *Ibid*, 25 November 1918.
6. Sinn Féin Standing Committee Minutes, 28 November 1918, no. 3641, p. 3269, NLI.
7. Bishop McRory, of Down and Connor; Bishop McKenna of Clogher; Bishop McHugh of Derry; and Bishop Mulhearn of Dromore.
8. Devlin to Dillon, 29 November 1918, Dillon Papers, 6730, 201, *loc. cit.*
9. CO/904, January 1917, CO/904, February 1918 and December 1918. NLI.
10. CO/904, *op. cit.* (see also John McCoy, OMN P17/B/116).
11. Donnelly to Dillon, 29 November 1918, Dillon Papers 6730, no 197, *loc. cit.*
12. Logue telegram, Archbishop Walsh Papers, Archbishop's House, Dublin.
13. Alleged in C/904, January 1919.
14. Dillon to O'Donnell, 9 December 1918, Dillon Papers 67641, 114.
15. *FT*, 12 December 1918.
16. Devlin in his appeal admitted it was one of the constituencies 'with which I am least familiar' (*IN* 11th December). For the fullest accounts of the East Down election see article by Anita Gallagher in David Fitzpatrick (ed), *Ireland and the First World War*, pp 90-108, and A. McDonnell, 'The 1918 General Election in Ulster and the Career of Sir Denis Henry MP', PhD thesis, Queen's University of Belfast, 1983. There has never been any evidence offered to substantiate T. M. Healy's claim (*Letters and Leaders of my Day*, vol ll, p 611) that Home Rulers were acting in cahoots with unionists in return for a unionist decision not to contest West Belfast. Devlin had a conference 'with some men' from East Down on 28 November, he told Dillon. 'There is a split in the ranks over the man O'Neill Doherty from Glasgow', he stated, remarking that if he could not 'fix things up' the seat would go to the unionists. Dillon Papers 6730, no 201. See also O'Donnell, PhD thesis, Queen's University of Belfast, 1983.
17. *IN*, 10 December 1918.
18. *II*, 16 December 1918.
19. Sinn Féin Standing Committee, minues, 28 November 1918, *op. cit.*, NLI.
20. *Ibid.*
21. *Ibid*, 20.CO/904, January 1919.

The IPP after the election
22. Donnelly to Dillon, Dillon Papers 6763, TCD Archive.

23. Dillon to T. P. O'Connor, *op. cit.* McCoy deposition OMN, *op. cit.*
24. *IN*, 24 December 1918.
25. F. S. L. Lyons, *John Dillon: A Biography*, Chicago 1968, pp 446-450. The hope of a solution through the peace conference surfaced in several pastoral letters from the northern bishops in February 1919. Little came of the Irish approach when it was finally made. As one writer put it (President) 'Wilson's first thought upon receiving the Irish deputation had been to tell them to go to hell.' A. Cobdan, 'The national state and self betrayal', quoted in Guy Chauvin, 'The Parliamentary Party and the Revolutionary Movement in Ireland', unpublished PhD, TCD. For a detailed account of the Wilson rebuff to the Irish American delegation see Arthur Mitchell, *Revolutionary Government in Ireland: Dáil Éireann 1919-22*, Gill and MacMillan 1995, pp 38-42.
26. Devlin to O'Donnell, 22 January 1919, O'Donnell Papers, Armagh Archdiocesan Archives, Ara Coeli Armagh.
27. Devlin to Dillon, November 10 1919, Dillon Papers, *loc. cit.*
28. Dillon to Devlin, *op. cit.*, Devlin to O'Donnell 13 February 1920, *ODP, loc. cit.*
29. *Ibid.*
30. Devlin to O'Donnell, 2 April 1920, *op. cit.*
31. *Ibid.*
32. Devlin to O'Donnell, 13 February 1920, O'Donnell Papers, Ara Coeli Armagh.
33. *Ibid.*
34. Devlin to O'Donnell, *ibid.*
35. Devlin to T. J. Hanna. 'The *Freeman* has been treating us scandalously', Dillon Papers, 27 March 1919. Devlin to Dillon, 'I had letters saying the *Belfast Evening Telegraph* is giving much better reporting than *The Freeman* or the *Irish News*', Dillon Papers, no 261.

Chapter 2
The War of Independence in the six counties

1. Memorandum to Divisions, UCD Archive, Mulcahy Papers, P7/A/172, 24 March 1921.
2. P7/A/220, *ibid.*
3. *Ibid.*
4. CO/904, February 1918-October 1920, NLI.
5. *Ibid*, December 1920-January 1921.
6. CO/904, *Dungannon Democrat*, September 1920.
7. CO/904, April 1921, *loc. cit.*
8. O'Duffy, 4 March 1922, P17A/184, O'Malley Papers, UCD Archive.
9. Daly reply, 8 March 1922, *Ibid.*
10. CO/904, January 1918 – August 1920, NLI.
11. Michael Collins Papers, A/0460, Department of Defence Archives, Cathal Brugha Barracks.

12. *Ibid.*
13. *Ibid.*
14. *Ibid.*
15. *Ibid.*
16. CO/904, 1 November 1920, *loc. cit.*
17. CO/904, April 1921, *loc. cit.*
18. MP, p 7/A/18/322, 20 June 1921, *loc. cit.*
19. MP, p 7/A/18/270, *loc. cit.*
20. P 7/A/18/272.
21. CO/904, August 1920. In fact two contingents of the best (and most wanted) men were sent to join flying columns in the safer territory of Donegal. See Joost Augustiein, *From Public Defiance to Guerilla Warfare*, IAP 1996, p 115 .
22. CO/904, September 1920.
23. McCoy OMN, p 17/B/116, UCD Archive.
24. *Ibid.*
25. CI Report, 26 November 1920, FIN/1/173, PRONI.
26. P 7/A/17, *op. cit.*
27. McCoy OMN, *op. cit.*
28. CO/904, July 1920, *loc. cit.*
29. Skinner, profile of Frank Aiken, *Politicians by Accident*, pp 151-180.
30. CO/904, March-July 1921, NLI.
31. Livingstone, *The Fermanagh Story*, pp 288-289.
32. S 11208, O'Shiel's memo recommending Sean Carty as Rural Secretary to Advisory Sub-Committee, 25 September 1922.
33. M. Gallagher, 'The Struggle for the Belleek Triangle', in *Donegal Annual*, 1982.
34. P 7A/26, Mulcahy Papers, *loc. cit.*. FH, March-April 1921, CO/904, NLI.
35. Healy to Joe Slevin, 28 January 1956, Box 7, Healy Papers D 2991, *loc. cit.*
36. McCorley, OMN, P.176/98, *loc. cit.*
37. Woods MP, 12 July 1921, *loc. cit.* The GHQ memo did, however, allow for 'some' (activity) by way of reprisal. After a further outburst of sectarian violence in September, secret consultation took place between government representatives and those of both communities, including Sinn Féiners. They resulted in the imposition of Martial Law by the British authorities, a decision welcomed by the Catholic side. This measure had been sought at an earlier set of meetings in July. FIN 18/1, PRONI.
38. CO/904, October 1920, NLI.
39. Interview Jack Mulvenna, 6 September 1991.
40. Woods to GHQ, MP 7//77, *loc. cit.*
41. GHQ memo 7/A/5, 7 April 1921. When one member of the ASU was killed in Cavan the Brigade had to pay his funeral expenses. Mulcahy Paperrs, *loc. cit.* McEntee was also well aware of the ability

of other elements in the Catholic community to mobilise behind a sectarian objective and warned GHQ of 'a sinister movement'. MP p 7/39/346, *op. cit.*

Chapter 3
The elections of 1920 and 1921

1. 'PR Society of Ireland', pamphlet no 7, (1920 urban election). The Watchword and the Voice of Labour, June 1920.
2. *IN*, 10 June 1920.
3. *Ibid.*
4. Logue Papers, folder no 3(203), Ara Coeli Armagh.
5. *Ibid.*
6. Dillon Papers, *loc. cit.* Devlin may have, in fact, favoured giving Sinn Féin a clear field but Dillon felt otherwise. See Devlin to Dillon, 1 February 1921, Devlin to Dillon, 11 February 1921.
7. De Valera to Collins, De Valera Papers, no 140, Franciscan Killiney Archive.
8. *Ibid.*
9. *Ibid.*
10. O'Connor to Dillon, 12 March 1921, Dillon Papers, 6743, no 821, TCD.
11. *FJ*, 29 March 1921. From the unionist side of the fence the Sinn Féin decision to participate was welcomed as a legitimisation of the northern parliament. See Craig's remarks, *Irish News*, 19 July 1921.
12. De Valera Papers, no. 140.
13. *Ibid.*
14. Devlin to Dillon, 22 April 1921, Dillon Papers, 6730, no 294, TCD.
15. *Ibid.*
16. De Valera Papers, no 140, *loc. cit.*

Chapter 4
Truce, Treaty and Aftermath

1. P 7/B/77, UCD Archive.
2. Sinn Féin Standing Committee, minutes, *loc. cit.*
3. *Ibid.*
4. ll, DE 11/159, 23 August 1921, PRONI.
5. Sinn Féin Standing Committee, minutes, *loc. cit.*
6. De Valera Papers, 1 December 1921, p 178
7. *Ibid.*
8. *Ibid.*
9. Gillespie letter, T16/31, 23 November 1921, p 178. De Valera reply, 29 November 1921, De Valera Papers, *loc. cit.*
10. *IN*, 7 September 1921.
11. O'Higgins, 5 December 1921, De Valera Papers, *loc. cit.*
12. Recollections of conference of representatives of six county area, 7 December, Bonner File, Box 7, Healy Papers, D 2991, PRONI.

13. Minutes of conference, 8 December 1921, De Valera Papers, Killiney.
14. *Ibid.*
15. *Ibid.*
16. *FS*, 10 December 1921.
17. *IN*, 5 January 1922.

Sinn Féin and IRA – Post-Treaty
18. S 1011, National Archive.
19. *Ibid.*
20. S 1801 (J), Box 2, National Archive.
21. DE 4/14/22, received 12 January 1922, National Archive. The idea of the provisional government supporting Catholic secondary schools in the north came from McRory who wanted a guarantee for the Catholic Teacher Training College, St Mary's, on the Falls Road (PG minutes, 10 February 1922). Roughly one-third of Catholic schools participated in the initiative at its height. This disquiet at the lifting of the Belfast Boycott (PG 30 January 1922) reflected that of some Belfast Sinn Féiners, e.g. Crummie who wanted it reimposed thought others like Father Hassan and Dr McNabb were against such a move (PG 21 March 1922). It was in the search for an alternative that the 'burning' policy was first discussed by the government in March (PG 21 March 1922).
22. *Ibid.*
23. Woods, P 7/B/77, UCD Archive.
24. P 7/A/18-136, *loc. cit.*
25. *Ibid.*
26. McKelvey, P 7/A/18/322, 16 August 1921. MP, *loc. cit.*
27. Woods, P 7/B/77, MP, UCD Archive.
28. P 7/A/26, OMP, *loc. cit.*
29. Blythe Papers, p 24/559, *loc. cit.*
30. *Ibid.*
31. P 7/A/26, OMP, *loc. cit.*
32. McCartan to Maloney, McGarrity Papers, MS 17645, 31 March 1922, NLI.
33. *IN*, 28 April 1922.
34. Aiken on O'Duffy, Childers Papers 7844, TCD, 18 September 1924, general correpondence, pp 1-58. See for example *Ulster* magazine, March 1992.
35. Blythe Papers, P 24/559. P 7/B/77, UCD Archive. S 1011, National Archive.
36. For Wood's calculation see MP p 7/B/77. Quoted Martin Gilbert, 'Winston Churchill 1916-1922'', in *World in Torment*, vol IV p 729.
37. The Galway murders of convalescent policemen and an alleged informer was one of many such freelance operations carried out in the south during the truce, severely embarrassing Collins and the Provisional Government.

38. For a good general account of the pacts see M. Hopkinson, *The Craig-Collins Pacts of 1922 and the Attempted Reform of the Northern Government*, vol 27, no 106. Also M. Farrell, *Arming the Protestants*, pp 90-92, 104-124, 147-152.
39. Craig-Collins correspondence, PM 11/1, PRONI. Includes an account of their meeting.
40. S 1011, National Archive.
41. *Ibid.*
42. *Ibid.*
43. *Ibid.*
44. *Ibid.*
45. *Ibid.*

The IPP since the Truce
46. O'Connor to Dillon, 17 October 1921, Dillon Papers, no. 5743, TCD Archive.
47. Dillon to O'Connor, 22 January 1922,. Dillon to O'Connor, 7 February 1922, 6744, *loc. cit.*
48. *Ibid*, 7 February 1922.
49. Devlin to Dillon, 24 March 1922, Dillon Papers, 6744.
50. S 1011, National Archive.
51. *Ibid.*
52. O'Connor to Dillon, 11 April 1922, Dillon Papers, no. 6744, *loc. cit.*
53. PM 9/1, PRONI.
54. Dillon to O'Connor, 11 April 1922, Dillon Papers, no. 6744, *loc. cit.*
55. S 1801, National Archive.
56. McRory to Collins, 7 May 1922, S 1801(A), National Archive. O'Connor to Dillon, 27 June 1922. O'Connor to Dillon, 7 July 1922, Dillon Papers, *loc. cit.*
57. LA/1/H/94, McNeill Papers, UCD Archive.

Chapter 5
The collapse of the northern IRA

1. S 1011, minutes of the Sub-Committee meeting, National Archive
2. *Ibid.* The Catholic Church through its prominence in the White Cross Committee was, in fact, to become a major landlord in the rebuilt Catholic Belfast. The most visible evidence today of the rebuilding process is Amcomri Street in the Beechmount area, its name deriving from the acronym of the Committee's full title 'American Committee for Relief in Ireland'. Between Sinn Féin, the Catholic Church and the Devlinites, the representatives of the expelled workers themselves were to be the main losers. In January 1923 their representatives came at the bottom of a poll in the elections. Unemployable as a result of his record, James 'Dungaree' Baird, one of their two councillors, migrated to Dublin to take up a trade union position.

3. *Ibid.*
4. *Ibid.* The second Craig-Collins pact faded into oblivion. The arrest of two Catholic members of the Police Committee on their way back from its second meeting epitomised the contradictions. Tallents, in his report on the pact's failure, cited a missive from the most belligerent of the Northern Divisions, Aiken's 4th Northern, relating to the objective of bringing down the northern State. McCorley, *OMN,* records this as the objective behind the damp squib May offensive. See also Hopkinson, *Green against Green,* 1987, p 85.
5. Blythe Papers, p 24-554, UCD Archive.

   The northern government had some difficulty in getting a man to inflict the floggings, Healy records, 'for a Belfast Orangeman will shoot the supposed enemy on sight without scruple but would not volunteer to flog him'. In the event, an ex-naval member (a Catholic) was enticed from Scotland to carry out the sentences. The veteran journalist, James Kelly, remembers the man being pointed out to him once in the Belfast High Court. He recalls a man of vicious and frightening countenance, an appearance well in keeping with the legend which had grown around him. Healy papers, Box 15. Also Kelly interview.
6. *Ibid,* P 7/B/77.
7. Aiken, *op. cit.,* TCD Archive.
8. McCorley, *OMN, loc. cit.*
9. P 7/B/77, *loc. cit.*
10. McCorley, *OMN, loc. cit.*
11. P 7/B/77, MP, UCD, 14 July 1922.
12. *Ibid,* 1 June 1922.
13. Woods, P 7/B/77, *loc. cit.*
14. *Ibid.*
15. S 1011, *op. cit.*
16. Woods, P/7/B/77, *loc. cit.*
17. Dillon to O'Connor, 11 August 1922, Dillon Papers, TCD Archive.
18. Woods, *op. cit.*
19. Memo from 2nd Northern Division, MP Papers, P7/B/77, *loc. cit.*
20. *Ibid,* remarks on morale of Catholic population.
21. O'Shiel-McCarthy report on County Down visit, Kennedy Papers, UCD Archive.
22. DE 4/6/7, National Archive. See also published PG minutes. Collins' pact with De Valera may have been the factor precipitating the introduction of internment by the Belfast government, See Barton, *Brookeborough,* p 51. A Free State intelligence agent based in Belfast reported in December 1923 that 95 officers and men of the 3rd Northern Division, serving in the southern army, were 'wanted on warrant' by the northern government. Among those named by him were Free State Army Colonels McDonnell and McCorley and Commandants McNally, Devlin and O'Neill. An extensive search

had been made in County Antrim for McDonnell and the McCorley brothers who came home in late December. (Report dated 30 December 1923, 12A 177, O'Malley Papers, UCD Archive.)

23. MP P7/B/77, Woods to Collins, 24 July 1922, *loc. cit.*

24. S 11,208, National Archive.

25. Affairs in Southern Ireland, 24/7605, 16 April 1923, Cab 86/14.

26. Position of 2nd Northern Division, Thomas Johnston Papers, ms 17, 145, NLI. McCorley, OMN P7/76/98, *loc. cit.*

27. *The Separatist*, 8 April 1922. E. Staunton, 'Michael Collins' Northern Policy: A Reassessment', in *Irish Studies Review*, Autumn 1977.

Chapter 6
Collins' Northern Initiative

1. S 8998, National Archive, Bishop Street, Dublin.

2. *Ibid.*

3. *Ibid.* It helps to put in perspective the Catholic response when one considers the swathe of destruction cut through their areas by the violence of the previous three years. A Dublin Government representative was told in late 1923 that out of the 430 mainly Catholic spirit groceries 149 were wrecked and only 32 had been rebuilt. In the Willowfield district a Catholic population of over 1,000 had been reduced to a dozen families. No Catholic expelled from the Queen's Island had been reinstated. St. Joseph's parish near the Docks had lost 250 families in all. The organisation responsible for the terror in the East of the city, the Ulster Protestant Association, was not proceeded against in earnest by the government until late 1922. A private initiative by local clergy from both denominations had been taken after the assault on the spirit grocers in summer 1921. Those responsible for the terror campaign in the West of the city conducted from Brown Square Barracks never faced any legal sanction. D. I. Nixon, believed responsible for the McMahon atrocity, later became a Unionist MP for Woodvale.

4. *Ibid.*

5. *Ibid.*

6. *Ibid.*

7. *Ibid.*

8. Blythe memo, Kennedy Papers, P 4/387, UCD Archive, 11 August 1922.

9. M. Cunningham, *Partition, Michael Collins to Bobby Sands*, J. Feehan, *The Shooting of Michael Collins: Murder or Accident, passim.* T. P. Coogan, *Michael Collins: A Biography*, Hutchinson, 1990, p 385. See also E. Staunton, 'Michael Collins' Northern Policy a Reassessment', *Irish Studies Review*, Autumn 1997.

10. DE 4/6/7, National Archive.

11. Woods, S 1801, National Archive.

12. Healy, S 5751/16, National Archive.

Chapter 7
In the Shadow of the Boundary Commission

1. Dillon to O'Connor, 29 September 1922, Dillon Papers, no 6744, *loc. cit.*
2. Grants from Special Dáil Funds, S 8289, National Archive.
3. S 11209, National Archive.
4. *IN*, 23 September 1922.
5. J. H. Collins Papers, D 921/3, PRONI. J. H. Collins hoped also to win over northern republicans to what he termed an 'all hands on the rope' policy in support of the Boundary Commission. He wrote to Peadar Murney, then an internee in Newbridge, Co Kildare, asking him to 'give Mr Principle a rest' until the Commission had completed its findings.
6. Kennedy Papers, P 4/388, UCD.
7. Dillon to T. P. O'Connor, 11 August 1922, Dillon Papers, *loc. cit.*
8. *IN*, 14 June 1923.
9. McNeill Papers, LA/1/H/96/1, UCD.
10. *UH*, 6 June 1923.
11. *IN*, 3 April 1923.
12. *DD*, 18 April 1923.
13. *FS*, 16 May 1923.
14. *FH*, 19 May 1923.
15. *DD*, 23 May 1923.
16. HA, 5/1854, PRONI.
17. *Ibid.*
18. Farrell, *Orange State,* 1976, p 101. Healy to Bishop McKenna of Clogher that 'it would be unwise to enter the Belfast House of Commons until the Boundary Commission had reported'. *IN,* 10 February 1923. In October of that year the bishops declared that the time had come 'for our people to organise on constitutional lines'.
19. HA/5/577, PRONI.
20. HA/5/1854, PRONI.
21. 'Argenta Memories', Healy Papers, D 2991, Box 15, PRONI.
22. *Ibid.*
23. *Ibid.*
24. *Ibid.*
25. *Ibid.*
26. *Ibid.*
27. S/5750, National Archive.
28. S/5750/16, National Archive.
29. *Ibid.*
30. Kennedy Papers, P 4/391, UCD Archive.
31. P 4/391/44 *op. cit.*
32. P 4/391/89, *op. cit.* On the alleged reasons for Cosgrave's choice of MacNeill, see Geoffrey J. Hand, 'MacNeill and the Boundary Commission' in F. X. Martin and F. J. Byrne (eds), *The Scholar Revolutionary,* IUP 1973, pp 210, 211.

33. McNeill Papers, LA/1/H/99, UCD Archive. In various memos O'Shiel acknowledged that nationalists felt betrayed that they would advise the government to convene the Commission without delay, that in his view the government should do anything which 'would detract from its rights under the Treaty', that 'inherent divisions' within northern nationalists 'prevented them from carrying out a scheme of organisation, that it was unwise to have the views of border nationalists only and that northern nationalists would be the only chief losers in any attempt to enforce a Boundary Commission against the unionists' will'. They were also, he felt, ignorant of the functions of a Commission believing it could be made to function 'like an ordinary Law Court'.

34. LA/1/96/1, *loc. cit.*

35. *Ibid.*

36. Kennedy Papers, P 4/390/1, *op. cit.*

37. *DJ*, 11 February 1924.

38. *The People,* 23 March 1924.

39. Healy Diary, Box 18, Healy Papers, D 2991, PRONI.

40. O'Malley Papers, Intelligence Report, P 17/A/178, UCD.

41. 17/A/179, *loc. cit.*

42. *Ibid.*

43. *IN*, 13 October 1924.

44. *Ibid,* 15 October 1924.

45. *Ibid,* 21 October 1924.

46. J. McNally, *Morally Good and Bad: The Memoirs of a Belfast IRA Veteran,* Andersonstown News, 1985, p. 20-21.

47. Stephens' visit to Armagh and Newry, Fitzgerald Papers, NEBB, P80/924, UCD, 22 December 1924. Se also Stephen's Papers, TCD and NEBB Papers SPO, National Archive.

48. *Ibid.*

49. *Ibid,* 16 January 1925.

50. *Ibid.*

51. Report from Stephens in Fermanagh, *op. cit.,* 16 February 1925.

52. Report from Stephens in Derry city, *op. cit.,* 25 May 1925.

53. *Ibid.*

54. Report from Stephens in Tyrone, *op. cit.,* 22 June 1925.

55. *Ibid.*

56. *IN*, 17 September 1925.

57. *IT*, 2 May 1924, Birkenhead speech, 1 May 1924, on his appeal to Craig to appoint Commisioner.

58. HC Debates, 3 October 1925.

59. *Ibid.*

60. *Ibid.*

61. Fitzgerald Papers, P 80/947, *loc. cit.* It has since been revealed through research by Professor A. Guelke that Feetham had been a member of a pro-imperial South African Unionist Party, a fact

which, if known at the time, would have seriously compromised his impartiality in the eyes of Irish nationalists.

62. G. Hand (ed), *Report of the Irish Boundary Commission*, Shannon, 1969.
63. Hugh McCartan visit, *loc. cit.*, 24 March 1925.
64. *Ibid.*
65. *Ibid.*
66. North East Boundary Bureau Papers, National Archive.
67. Healy Diary, Box 18, Healy Papers, D 2991, PRONI.
68. For O'Shiel's fear of a Republican-Labour alliance in the south see S 600, National Archive.
69. S/8289, National Archive.
70. Fitzgerald Papers, *loc. cit.*, P 80/947.
71. *Ibid.*
72. O'Connor to Dillon, Dillon Papers, 6743, 1 December 1924.
73. Sinn Fein Advisory Committee, minutes, 2B/82/117, PRONI, 12 March 1925.
74. Dillon to O'Connor, 12 April 1925, Dillon Papers, 6748, *loc. cit.*
75. *FJ*, 7 May 1985.
76. *II*, 27 October 1925.
77. S 1801/0, Healy, 10 October, National Archive. Bonner, the Derry Alderman, told Murnaghan on 5 June that the trend of questions to Customs Officials suggested a desire to bring all of Inishowen into the six county area. NEBB, Box 6.
78. Healy to O'Higgins, S 1801/0, National Archive.
79. S 4720/A, National Archive.
80. *Ibid.* O'Higgins admitted that the charge of having sold the northern nationalists was 'no more than a half truth'. Concessions may have been promised on disbandment of the Specials which were never implemented, e.g. Farrell, *Arming the Protestants*, pp 249-252.
81. *Ibid.* See also E. Staunton, 'The 1925 Agreement aftermath and Implications', *History Ireland*, Summer 1996,
82. 94 S/4720 I G.
83. *DJ*, 4 December 1925.
84. *IN*, 4 December 1925.
85. *II*, 7 December 1925.
86. *FS*, 8 December 1925.
87. *II*, 5 December 1925.
88. *DJ*, December 1933.
89. *IN*, 30 December 1925.
90. *FS*, 13 March 1926.

Chapter 8
Nationalists after the Agreement

1. S 4782, National Archive. Also CAB/9/B/182, 9J/24, for Cosgrave's pressure on Devlin. Devlin to Healy, Healy Papers, Box 1, PRONI, November 1926.

2. *IN*, 16 August 1927.
3. *Ibid*, 18 August 1927.
4. McHugh to Healy, McHugh-Healy correspondence, 27 August 1927, Healy Papers, Box 7, D 2991.
5. Donnelly to Healy, 4 October 1927, Box 1. *Ibid*, 10 September 1927.
6. Healy to Donnelly, 20 October 1927, D 2991, Box 1, *loc. cit.*
7. Healy to Coyle, 24 December 1927. Correspondence with Father Eugene Coyle, D 21991, Box 7, *loc. cit*, 30 January 1928.
8. Healy to Devlin, 8 February 1928, Box 8, *loc. cit.*
9. Harbinson to Healy, *loc. cit*, 10 February 1928.
10. *IN*, 29 May 1928.
11. *Ibid*, 15 September 1928.
12. McAllister to Healy, 27 August 1928, McAllister correspondence, Healy Papers, D 2991, Box 1, *loc. cit.*
13. *IN*, 15 September 1928.
14. *FS*, 19 January 1928.
15. *IN*, 29 May 1929.
16. Calculated from *IN*.
17. Dillon Papers, O'Connor correspondence, no 6744, passim, TCD Archive. Throughout the latter half of 1923 Dillon and O'Connor discussed the idea of Devlin's return to Westminster for 'Tyrone and Fermanagh'. They felt he was needed there. On 28 November 1923 Dillon told O'Connor that 'young Murnaghan' told a friend that Harbinson was 'no good' but he was the only man to keep Devlin out. Dillon to O'Connor, *op. cit.*
18. These facts came to light in June 1956 when F. J. Whitford was researching his MA thesis on Joe Devlin's life and work for the University of London. From his base in Queen's University Belfast Whitford contacted De Valera and Seán T. O'Kelly and a correspondence with Healy ensued both on this topic and on the 1921 election campaign. Healy, in a letter of 10 June, confirmed the facts relating to the meeting of early 1933. De Valera to Healy, 8 June 1956; Healy reply, 10 June 1956; De Valera response, 27 June 1956. De Valera Correspondence, Box 9, Healy Papers, D 2991, PRONI.
19. References to Devlin's attempt at a rapproachment with republicans can be found in F. J. Whitford, 'Joe Devlin: Ulsterman and Irishman', final chapter, MA thesis, London University, 1987. R. Munck and B. Rolston, *Belfast in the 30s: an Oral Documentary*, Blackstaff, 1988. J. McNally, *Morally Good, Politically Bad*. Also my own interviews with Jack Mulvenna and James Kelly, *op. cit.*
20. Healy Papers, *loc. cit.*
21. *IN*, 23 December 1930.
22. D. H. Akenson, *Education and Enmity: The Control of Schooling in Northern Ireland, 1920-1950*, p.106.
23. J. J. Campbell, *Catholic Schools*.
24. Akenson, *op. cit.*, pp 107-111.

25. *IN*, 10 January 1930.
26. *Ibid*, 17 January 1930.
27. *Ibid*.
28. *FS*, 19 March 1932.
29. *IP*, 15 January 1932.
30. *FS*, 28 January 1932.
31. Twomey to McGarrity, MS 17/490, 23 June 1931. 'The starting of a party a few years back by Devlin and company was a crime. It knit the Orangemen together and brought things back to sectarian lines. Labour and the farmers could have thrown out Craigavon by this time and as in the Free State anything could arise out of the new situation'.
32. *DJ*, 20 November 1933. McCarroll file, D 2991. Healy Papers, Box 7, *loc. cit.* McCarroll to Healy, 4 December 1933.
33. *AP*, 2 December 1933.
34. McGarrity Paper, MS 17490, NLI.
35. *AP*, 27 October 1933.
36. *Ibid*, 9 April 1934.
37. *Ibid*, 10 May 1934.
38. *Ibid*, 30 May 1934.
39. *Ibid*, 1 June 1934.
40. *Ibid*, 30 May 1934.
41. Interview with Jack Mulveena, 6 September 1991.
42. *Ibid*. For the 'tying to railing' and kidnap allegations see Republican Congress, 17 November 1934.
43. *IN*, 21 September 1936.
44. Midgley had, in fact, been present for the first stages of the riots. Jack Macgougan, who also defended the Spanish Republic, and was supported by Catholics in his candidature in Oldpark, disputes that Spain was the reason for Midgley's downfall (correspondence with author). Anyone opposing the Catholic Church in Belfast faced a formidable power block. It was in the diocese of Down and Connor that many of the leading Catholic organisations, including the Knights of Columbanus and the Catholic Truth Society, had their origins. The Clonard Confraternity, the most important Catholic lay body in the city, had 6,000 members by January of 1940. It had begun with 60 in 1897.
45. *IN*, 3 January 1938.
46. McLoughlin to Healy, 1 June 1939, McLoughlin File, Box 7, Healy Papers, D 2991, *loc. cit.*
47. Mulvenna interview, *op. cit.*
48. See McNally for a personal testament, Ch 23, pp 112-115. Coogan for a general account, *The IRA*, Fontana, 1980, p 228.
49. Mulvenna interview, *op. cit.*

Chapter 9
The 1935 Westminster Election and after

1. *IN*, 29 October 1935.
2. *Ibid*, 4 November 1935.
3. Healy/Stewart to De Valera, 23 October, De Valera reply, 27 October, De Valera correspondence, Box 8, Healy Papers, D 2991, PRONI.
4. *II*, 1 November 1935.
5. *IN*, 4 November 1935.
6. Interview with his son Michael Cunningham, Tantallon, Co Donegal, 19 August 1991.
7. *IN*, 5 November 1935.
8. Gilmore to Healy, 27 October 1935. 'The IRA are heading for the old Sinn Féin wilderness and are aiming at using the northern elections to give an artificial backing to a policy of sheer negative abstentionism,' Healy told him he had not the authority to call the proposed Dungannon conference, Gilmore file, Box 8, Healy Papers, *loc. cit.* *Republican Congress*, no 23, 1935, 29 October 1935, for evidence of Congress support to republicans.
9. *II*, 1 November 1935.
10. *IN*, 9 November 1935.
11. Nethercott to Healy, Box 1, D 2991, *loc. cit.*
12. *IP*, December 1935.
13. *AP*, 21 March 1936.
14. PM/4/20/2, PRONI.
15. Andrews to Montgomery 6 November 1935. Montgomery Charlemont correspondence, PRONI.
16. See F. Gallagher, *The Indivisible Island*, Ch XV, Victor Golancz 1957. The Derry gerrymander review was never intended to last for more than five years. This fact was revealed by one of its architects, Edmond Warnock who became Minister for Home Affairs in the 1940s and the State's Attorney General in the 1950s. At the cabinet meeting after the events of October 1968 the 82 year old Warnock, by then far less a rightwinger than he had been three decades earlier, told his colleagues that the Prime Minister James Craig and others had acknowledged this at the time.
17. *IN*, 14 April 1936.
18. *Ibid.*
19. *Ibid.*
20. *Ibid.*

Nationalists after the Election
21. Andrews to Montgomery, *op. cit.*
22. *IN*, 4 January 1936. Increasingly the Hibernian heritage was being accepted by both of the south's main parties. Devlin's anniversary Mass was attended by Fianna Fáil and Fine Gael representatives.
23. *IN*, 16 June 1936. *AP*, 22 June 1936.

24. J. Bonner to Healy, 20 July 1936, Bonner File, Box 7, Healy Papers, D 2991, *loc. cit.*

25. *IN*, 23 October 1936.

26. O'Connor, Donnelly speeches, *IN*, 31 October 1936.

27. *IN*, 24 April 1937.

Nationalists and De Valera's Constitution

28. McShane to Healy, 10 December 1937, McShane File, Box 7, D 2991, Healy Papers, PRONI.

29. *FS*, 8 May 1937, 19 June 1937, 26 June 1937, 3 July 1937.

30. Correspondence Donnelly File, Box 7, D 2991, *loc. cit.*

31. Stewart to Healy, 7 January 1938, Stewart File, Box 7, *ibid, loc. cit.*

32. *Ibid.*

33. Healy to Mulvey, 10 October 1936, Mulvey File, Box 7, Healy Papers, D 2991, *loc. cit..*

34. Healy to Maxwell, 15 October 1937, Maxwell correspondence, Box 7, Healy Papers, D 2991, *loc. cit.*

35. *IN*, 29 October 1937.

36. *IN*, 24 November 1937.

37. *IN*, 10 November 1937.

38. O Neill to Healy, 6 December 1937, Neill File, Healy Papers, D 2991, *loc. cit.*

39. 'Agnew does not represent South Armagh. His occupancy of the seat is a usurpation' proclaimed the *Frontier Sentinel. FS* 22 January 1938.

40. McLaughlin to Healy, 29 January 1938, McLoughlin, File Box 8, Healy Papers, D 2991, *loc. cit.*

41. E. Phoenix, *Northern Nationalism*, p 384; Healy to *Irish Press, IP* 14 January 1938.

42. Stewart to Healy, 13 February 1938, Box 7, Healy Papers, D 2991, *loc. cit.*

43. Walsh to Healy, 29 November 1938, Louis Walsh correspondence, Box 7, D 2991, *loc. cit.*

44. *IN*, 14 January 1938.

45. *Ibid*, 18 January 1938.

46. *Ibid*, 14 January 1938.

47. *Ibid.*

48. Stewart to Healy, 13 February 1938, Box 7, Healy Papers, D 2991, *loc. cit.*

49. *DJ*, 4 April 1938.

50. *IN*, 28 April 1938.

51. *Ibid.*

52. *FS*, 28 April 1938.

53. S 15, 585, Department of Taoiseach, National Archive, Dublin.

54. *FS*, 30 April 1938.

55. Healy to Murray, Box 7, Healy Papers, D 2991, *loc. cit.*

56. *IN*, 12 October 1938

57. *Ibid*, 28 April 1939

58. Maxwell, *IN*, 21 October 1938.

59. *Ibid*, 28 April 1939.

60. S 15 585 D/T, National Archive Dublin.

61. *Ibid*.

62. *Ibid*.

63. *Ibid*. The strength of the British army tradition within northern Catholicism is generally forgotten. After the First World War subscriptions from the minority community helped towards the erection of war memorials in many northern towns, and organisations like the AOH were represented at the unveiling. Advertisements for the Armistice Day Poppy Appeals continued to appear in the *Irish News* throughout the inter-war years. The only Victoria Cross awarded to a native of Northern Ireland went to a Falls Road Catholic. Up to the start of the recent troubles, the Catholic Ex-servicemen's Association was to the fore in collating data on the discrimination which its members also experienced, despite their proven loyalty.

64. They had already received word from across the Irish sea of how badly matters were going there. In March 1939 Hugh Delargy, the Labour MP for Manchester, had written to Cahir Healy complaining of the inertia within the movement in England – the Anti-Partition League as it had become known. The first edition of its pamphlet had not yet been sold out and the initiative was in danger of losing its way. Significantly, unlike later historians and some of his political contemporaries, he placed the blame for this on the apathy of the Irish in Britain, not on the resumed campaign of the IRA.

65. Delargey to Healy, 21 March 1939, Box 1, D 2991, *loc. cit.*; S 15 585, National Archive.

Chapter 10
The Second World War

1. Murney to Healy, 29 November 1939, Box 7, Murney File, Healy Papers, D 2991 *loc. cit.*

2. Phoenix, *op. cit.*, p 389.

3. Maxwell to Healy, 5 June 1940, Box 7, Maxwell correspondence, D 2991, *loc. cit.*

4. McLaughlin to Healy, 31 May 1940, Box 9, McLaughlin correspondence, D 2991, *loc. cit.* Inter factional rivalry between nationalists characterised this process as it did so many others. McLaughlin noted what Healy had said about James McSparran's desire to be 'top dog' in the affair. The east/west divide had already been emphasised by the ousting of Healy in June 1938 by McSparran from the *IN* Board of Directors. D 2991, Box 9, *IN* file. He had been on it since 1929.

5. Confidential Garda correspondence, GFA / A / 23, National Archive.
6. Stewart to Healy, 19 June 1940, *loc. cit.*
7. The illusions in the Dublin government, even when shattered by events, proved hard to abandon. When the 'more virile' organisation desired by Donnelly finally came into being in November 1940 and held its inaugural meeting in the Mansion House, the message was that they were 100% behind the Taoiseach. When Donnelly, who described as 'murder' the death of the Derryman Sean Dolan from tuberculosis on the 'Al Riydah' prison ship, was challenged to apply the same description to the death before a southern firing squad of Lurgan IRA man Thomas Harte, he refused to answer. From the platform Patrick Maxwell MP restated what he had said earlier in Glasgow, that he 'was prepared for whatever force they drive us to' and that no neutrality could exist between England and Ireland as long as partition also lasted. When Maxwell was challenged by republicans in the audience to subscribe to *War News* he replied that he had written some of it. Maxwell was later made a Resident Magistrate in Derry. The Mansion House meting was chaired by Kathleen Clarke. Sean McBride, Peadar O'Donnell and Joe Stewart MP were on the platform with Eoin O'Duffy. Karl Petersen of the German Embassy was in the audience. The new organisation was titled 'The Six County News Association'. *DJ*, S 1104/40, National Archive. Corvin, Donnelly, Senator Maguire, Healy, Quinn from Newry, T J Campbell and Patrick Cunningham, along with General Eoin O'Duffy, were all trustees of Green Cross, the organisation which collected for republican prisoners in the north. A Department of Justice memorandum expressed concern over this because of the IRA's activity in the south. They need not have worried. DJ S 1069/40, National Archive.
8. J. Lee, *Ireland Politics and Society 1912-1985*, pp 267-268. Fisk, p. 437, reports how British intelligence heard of a meeting between McRory and the Italian consul in Dundalk. They believed he was attempting to ensure Ireland would not be invaded. Though McRory who maintained close links with the IRA turned down a request from the movement, made through Cathal Brugha's widow, for a meeting with a member of the Nazi General Staff illegally present in Ireland, this may have had much to do with the timing of the offer, 20 October 1941, when German fortunes were inextricably bound up with operation Barbarossa and the invasion of Britain was no longer an option, than with any more elevated consideration. (Rafferty, *op. cit.*, p 241)
9. *Time* Magazine, 12 October 1942.
   Spender diary, 22 February 1944, D 715/15, PRONI.
10. Healy File, 22 August 1941, DFA / 1244 / 80, National Archive.
11. *Ibid*, See also Fisk, *In Time of War*, pp 344, 397.
12. *IN*, 16 January 1939. Brian Moore's 1965 novel, *The Emperor of Ice*

Cream, provides a good insight into this mentality which was common in the Catholic community. See pp 28, 29, Mayflower edition 1970.

13. *Ibid*, 3 November 1938. On the admiration of British Catholics for Mediterranean as distinct from German fascism, see R. Griffith, *Fellow Travellers of the Right*, OUP 1983, pp 261-262.

14. Interview with Joe Cahill, 27 April 1991.

15. Interview with 'Sean Fox', 12 May 1991. For a view of 'the Buck Alex' from the 'other side' as a rough diamond folk hero of the loyalist working class in the area, see the memoirs of two of Protestant Belfast's most illustrious sons, James Galway, *An Autobiography*, Elm Tree Books 1975, p. 15, and Kenneth Brannagh, *Beginnings*, Chatto and Windus, London 1989, p. 12.

16. *DFA*, p 70, National Archive.

17. *IN*, 23 May 1941.

18. *DFA*, p 70.

19. *Ibid*.

20. *IN*, 27 May 1941.

21. *Harry: The Story of Harry White*, chs 10, 12, 15, Argenta Publications. See pp 101, 102 and 103 on the ambivalent attitude of Cardinal McRory and Bishop Mageean to the movement in the aftermath of the Williams case. McRory's infamous 1931 repudiation of the Protestant churches as not forming 'part of the true Church of Christ' found an echo in the 1943 Lenten pastoral on mixed marriages in which Protestantism was described as a 'schismatic and heretical sect'. *IN*, 3 March 1943.

22. Interview with Paddy Devlin, 17 April 1991.

23. Williams case, *DFA*, p 80, National Archive.

24. *Ibid*.

25. *Ibid*.

26. *Ibid*.

27. Information from James Kelly interview, Belfast, 8 April 1991. Beattie said in Stormont on 20 May 1947 that 'recently' a 'big change' had taken place in the RUC. He was not prepared to say it 'was the finest or best in the world' but 'it had been very badly led for 25 years' so much so that 'revolts had taken place'. On Beattie's attitude to Spain see Walker's biography of Midgley, p 101.

28. James Kelly interview, *op. cit.*

29. *IN*, 10 February 1943.

30. *Ibid*, 3 February 1943.

31. Uinseann McEoin (ed), *Harry, the Story of Harry White*, pp 101-103.

32. Devlin interview, *op. cit.*

33. *SI*, 6 and 13 July 1941.

34. Donnelly to Healy, 24 November 1944, Donnelly correspondence, Box 7, D 2991, *loc. cit.* On 30 November he told Healy there were 'contacts which should be renewed in Moscow'.

35. *IN*, 16 November 1944.
36. *Ibid*, 30 March 1944.
37. *Ibid*.
38. Healy to press, 29 September 1944, McEntee File, Box 7, D 2991, *loc. cit.*
39. *IN*, 9 May 1945.

Chapter 11
The Foundation of the Anti-Partition League

1. *IN*, 25 June 1945, editorial entitled 'The New Charter and Ireland'.
2. *IN*, 27 May 1946.
3. Bob Purdie, 'Friends of Ireland, British Labour and Irish Nationalism' in Gallagher and Connell (eds), *Contemporary Irish Studies*, Manchester University Press, 1983, pp 81-84.
4. *IN*, 6 June 1945.
5. De Valera, Dáil Debates, Vol 96.
6. *IP*, 7 November 1945. De Valera told the Ard Fheis that Irish unity was 'our one remaining task'. The title Anti-Partition League had of course, originated in the Diamond-Corvin camp who had contested Belfast Central in 1934. It had been used by the English based nationalists in the pre-war anti-partition drive. The first use of the name can be traced to the time before partition had become a reality. Bishop McHugh's group in Derry, founded in the autumn of 1916 and later absorbed into the Irish Nation League, used the title.
7. *IN*, 2 July 1945.
8. Campbell, *IN* 13 June 1945. Also McSparran in House of Commons. For evidence of Healy's apparent approval of De Valera's policy see his letter to McBride, 13 January 1948, McBride correspondence, Healy Papers, D 2991, *loc. cit.* For the Harry White affair see McAteer Papers, Derry.
9. *DFA* 305/14/65, Seamus McCall report to Department.
10. For the best content analysis of APL statements and speeches see John Martin, 'The Irish Anti-Partition League', unpublished minor thesis, Queen's University Belfast 1985.
11. *IN*, 5 August 1946.
12. *IN*, 13 December 1945. Contrast the claim by John Bowman, *De Valera and the Ulster Question*, OUP 1982, p 258, that nationalists were disillusioned with De Valera and the formation of the league was an implied criticism of him.
13. *IN*, 17 March 1947.
14. *Ibid*, 24 September 1947.
15. *Ibid*, 10 December 1947.
16. McBride to Healy, McBride/Healy correspondence, Healy Papers, Box 8, D 2991, PRONI, 13 January 1948. Healy on the 20th told him that the idea of seats in the Dáil had been urged without success by the late Eamonn Donnelly. As the election in the south had been fought on issues unconnected with them, they would not involve

themselves. They would go to the Dáil if invited and expect cross party support on the issue.

17. Interview with Dr Noel Browne, Galway city, 21 February 1991.
18. *Connaught Tribune*, 23 June 1948.
19. N. Browne, *Against the Tide*, Gill & MacMillan 1986, pp 129-34.
20. Kevin Boland, *Up Dev*, Dublin 1977. Also Kevin Boland, *Rise and Decline of Fianna Fáil*, Mercier Press, 1983, pp 10-11.
21. For Mulvey's remarks see *IN*, 25 April 1949. Mulvey may also have been the unnamed Nationalist MP who described as 'misjudged, mistimed and misdirected' the decision to raise the Anti-Partition 'chapel gate' collection. Given that the failure of southern parties to address their plight in the post-election atmosphere had led the APL to move its campaign southwards in the summer of 1948, this sudden departure caused by the internal politics of the south would like the 1937 constitution be seized on by most nationalists as a life-line yet greeted by others with scepticism.
22. S 6390/A, National Archive.
23. *IN*, 4 February 1950.
24. *UI*, November 1948.
25. McCall Report, *DFA*, National Archive, 21 March 1951. Hugh McAteer had told him that 'among the IRA in general there was an inclination towards now acknowledging the status quo in the 26 counties'.

The Armagh by-election and the issue of Dáil seats
26. *IN*, 18 February 1950.
27. S 6390 A, National Archive.
28. Report on visit of nationalist deputation, National Archive.
29. *IN*, 7 August 1950.
30. McCall's November report to Mansion House Committee, *DFA* 305/14/65, National Archive.
31. McCall's December report to Mansion House Committee, *DFA* 305/14/66, *loc. cit.*
32. *Ibid.*
33. *Ibid.*
34. Report on visit to An Taoiseach, S 6390 C, National Archive.
35. *Ibid.*
36. *Ibid.*
37. *Ibid.*
38. S 6390 C, National Archive.
39. McCall's May 1950 report, *DFA* 305/14/63, National Archive.
40. McCall's January 1950 report, S 6390, *loc. cit.*
41. *Ibid.*
42. *Ibid.*
43. *Ibid.*
44. S 6390 B, National Archive.
45. *IN*, 29 May 1950.

46. *IP*, 4 April 1950.

The APL and Labour
47. Martin, *op. cit.*, p 68.
48. NIHOC., Senate debates, 20 May 1958.
49. *IN*, 13 January 1950.
50. *Ibid*, 17 January 1950.
51. *Ibid*, 12 April 1951.
52. *Irish Workers' Voice*, May 1956.
53. McCall's May 1951 report, *DFA*, National Archive.
54. *IN*, 11 May 1950.
55. McCall's May 1951 report, *loc. cit.*
56. *DFA*, P/203.
57. McCall's January 1951 report, *loc. cit.*
58. *DFA*, P/203/2, National Archive.
59. Connellan to Healy, D 2991, PRONI, 15 September 1954. McGill to Healy, *op. cit.*, 27 March 1958. McCall's report, *loc. cit.*, April 1951, Jack Macgougan correspondence with author 1990-1991. The information on the pro-unionist APL votes comes from McCall via the leader of the League in Warrenpoint who claimed he voted for Macgougan.
60. Interview with James Kelly, 8 April 1991. Beattie became increasingly isolated from many of the Labour activists in Belfast, particularly after his marriage to a wealthy woman, the daughter of McMaster the builder. Jack Macgougan recalls how he went to live in her Newtownards Road mansion and became a gentleman of leisure. In a report, Cruise O'Brien described him as an 'inordinately vain, lazy and stupid MP'.
61. Macgougan Papers, D 3699/7, PRONI.
62. McCall's 'Report from the North', 3 July 1951, 24 July 1951. Additional note on the Labour Party crisis in the North, P 104/4577 (11-31), Aiken Papers, UCD Archive. On Beattie see Terry Cradden, *Trade Unionism, Socialism and Partition*, December 1993.
63. *IN*, 18 April 1951. 'The power and spirit behind practically all social legislation is, as the Bishop of Derry remarked, taken from the worst principles of Nazi and Soviet materialism', the editorial entitled 'A necessary warning' asserted. 'Thus in England the findings of the Royal Commission on population have been the occasion of solemn protests of the hierarchy. So, too, in the 26 counties we see the bishops intervening to prevent a possible similar error', it remarked in conclusion.

McSparran referred to the number of clerics in Stormont and the '20-30 Bishops' in the House of Lords and used the argument that Catholics comprised 93% of the Republic's population. NIHOC Debates, 21 June 1951.
64. *IN*, 6 December 1951.

65. McCall's May 1951 report, *DFA*, National Archive.
66. Healy to Maguire, Maguire File, Box 10, D 2991, PRONI.

Chapter 12
The APL Adrift

1. DE Debates, July 1951.
2. *Ibid.*
3.   S 6390, National Archive.
4. McCall's report on advisability of admission of Northern Representation, S 6390 C, National Archive.
5. *Ibid.*
6. *Ibid.*
7. *Ibid.*
8. *Ibid.*
9. *Ibid.*
10. *IN*, 28 March 1951.
11. McCall report, S 6390, National Archive. Healy to Maguire, 12 November 1950, *op. cit.*
12. Account of the visit of nationalist respresentatives, *loc. cit.*
13. Minutes of All Party Anti-Partition Committee, S 9361, National Archive.
14. DFA, 305/14/96, *loc. cit.*
15. DFA, 305/13/172, *loc. cit.*
16. DFA, 305/14/64, *loc. cit.*
17. McCall's March 1951 report, DFA, National Archive.
18. O'Brien report, *op. cit.*
19. *Ibid.* The film depicted the situation in Fintona, Co Tyrone, a village of 1200 inhabitants. Over two thirds nationalist in composition, only one in four of the houses built went to that community, although Catholics comprised four fifths of those in need of housing. In one new estate, Craigavon Park, over 48 new houses were built, none of them going to a Catholic family. The overcrowded slums in Brunswick Row and Mill Street were, by contrast, almost entirely Catholic. The film was 'not a success', the Irish Ambassador in London admitted, when it was first shown at a Fleet Street restaurant in April 1954. By August 1955 Cruise O'Brien was considering pressing ahead with McAteer's original idea of a film on the more flagrant case of Derry City. DFA 305/14/31/2.
20. February 1953, McGill File, Box 7, Healy Papers, D 2991, *loc. cit.*
21. McBride correspondence, Box 8, *ibid*, 26 February 1953.
22. O'Neill to Healy, 4 August 1953, O'Neill File, Box 8, *ibid, loc. cit.*
23. Healy to Maguire, 26 March 1953 and 19 March 1953, Maguire File, Box 10, *ibid, loc. cit.* Healy had, since 1925, been moving to the view that 1916 marked a wrong turning in Irish political life, its net effect being to have consolidated partition. In the *SP*, 5 July 1968, he marked the extent of his political odyssey in a correspondence entitled 'Was Pearse Justified?' when he praised Joe Devlin and com-

mented that the idea of 1916 which had woven a 'strange magic' was 'wearing thin'. 'I only knew Joe Devlin in the closing years of his life and recall him saying without bitterness that, although he had borne a blame for tolerating partition for a limited period of five years, the new party which succeeded him had accepted it for much longer.' In 1954 Healy told a correspondent that 'partition was really the offspring of the rebellion of 1916' and that the Council's Bill of 1911 accepted by Pearse would have 'led by now to a united and free Ireland'. Healy to Martin Nyoul, 4 May 1954, Box 8, D 2991, PRONI.

24. Diamond's remarks, *SP*, 6 November 1953. Maguire to De Valera, 30 November 1953, S 6391, *loc. cit.*
25. *IN*, 8 February 1954.
26. McAteer speech, *ibid*, 31 March 1953.
27. Healy Papers, 17 February 1954 and 13 February 1954, Maguire File, Box 10, D 2991, PRONI.
28. Maguire to Healy, *ibid, loc. cit.*
29. Report on visit of Dr O'Brien to Anti-Partition centres, 21-22 July 1954, DFA 305/14/2/3.
30. *Ibid.*
31. *Ibid.*
32. *Ibid.*
33. *Ibid.*
34. DE Debates, Vol 147, October 1954, pp 159-250.
35. *Ibid.*
36. Healy to Costello, John A. Costello File, Box 8, D 2991, PRONI.
37. McAteer to Costello, S 6390 C, National Archive.
38. *FH*, 13 November 1954.
39. S 6390 C, National Archive.
40. O'Mahony, 11 March 1954, *loc. cit.*
41. *Ibid.*
42. *Ibid.*
43. *Ibid*, 21 March 1954.
44. Healy to O'Reilly, APA File, *loc. cit.*
45. Healy to Maire Comerford, 25 March 1954, APA file.
46. *Ibid.*
47. *II*, 'Taoiseach meets Nationalists', 18 January 1955.
48. Confidential report on situation in nationalist constituencies, DFA 305/14/92, *loc. cit.*
49. *Ibid.*
50. *Ibid.*
51. O'Brien to Moynihan, 23 November 1954, S 6390, National Archive.
52. Interview with author, 16 August 1991.
53. Many mainstream nationalists viewed the republican resurgence with despair. Healy noted to Bishop O'Callaghan, 'We must have got many farms in the county in recent years and secured hundreds of new houses, both here and elsewhere, though not all to which we

are entitled.' Intrusion and physical force only consolidate unionist opinion and result in injury to Catholics as a whole. Healy to O'Callaghan, correspondence with bishops, 5 August 1955, Box 10, D 2991, *loc. cit.*

54. S 9351 E SC 7/86, National Archive.
55. DFA/14/281, *loc. cit.*
56. *Ibid.*
57. *Ibid.*
58. *Ibid.*
59. Deputation from South Armagh constituency of APL, S 9361 E, National Archive.

Sinn Féin emerges
60. Interview with Ó Brádaigh, Roscommon, 16 August 1991.
61. Maguire File, Box 7, Healy Papers, D 2991, PRONI.
62. *FH*, 21 May 1955.
63. Interview with Ó Brádaigh, *op. cit.*
64. *FH*, 21 May 1955.
65. *Ibid.*
66. *Ibid*, 14 May 1955. On the vetting of the Sinn Féin constitution by clergy, see Coogan, p 330. The campaign's best known martyr epitomised this right wing clericalist character. Seán South (Seán Sabhat) of Garryown, a member of the ultra-Catholic Maria Duce movement, held anti-Semitic views, was an opponent of trade unions and an admirer of Senator Joseph McCarthy. It is a significant indicator of how much his actions were a product of the Irish government's anti-partitionism than of traditional republican thinking that he had served with distinction in the Defence Forces reserve unit, the FCA. On South, see Mainchín Seoighe, *Maraíodh Seán Sabhat Aréir*, FNT 1963, Patrick Walsh, *Republicanism and Socialism in Modern Ireland*, Athol Books 1994.
67. Belton, O'Brien, McWhite report of visits to Anti-Partition centres, 28-30 July 1955, DFA 305/14/265, National Archive.
68. *FH*, 7 May 1955. *Ibid*, 14 May 1955.
69. *DO*, 11 June 1955.
70. *IN*, 17 May 1955. Beattie's defeat left the seat occupied by the unionist Patricia McLaughlin, one of the few women to hold public office in Northern Ireland. Successive attempts by Labourites to regain the West Belfast seat came to nothing. In 1959 Brennan, a member of the Hanna group, failed to improve on Beattie's 1955 total, despite a halving of the Sinn Féin vote. In 1964 Harry Diamond, Republican Labour, and William Boyd (NILP) both tried their luck against Mrs McLaughlin's successor, Jim Kilfedder, and failed again. Their combined vote of 26,000 was, however, more than 5,000 higher than Kilfedder's. The republican vote slipped even further to 3,256. At the next Westminster election, Gerry Fitt, Republican Labour, re-took the seat with a margin of 2,000 votes in a two-horse race.

71. Belton, O'Brien, McWhite report, visit 28-30 July 1955, *loc. cit.*
72. *Ibid.*
73. Republicans received an extra boost in July when Canon Maguire of Newtownbutler invited Thomas McCurtain from Cork, Sinn Féin candidate in Armagh, in May to appear on the platform at the Fermanagh Aeridheacht in the village. The gathering, banned under the Special Powers Act, was stormed by the RUC with water cannons. Much publicity ensued when Maguire was hit by a blast from one of them. Both Healy and the Bishop of Clogher were outraged by McCurtain's presence as he had been sentenced to death in the south for killing a garda but was reprieved by De Valera.
74. *Ibid.*
75. *Ibid.*
76. Joe Horan to Conor Cruise O'Brien, 2 February 1954, DFA 305/M/246, National Archive. Interview with Ruairí Ó Brádaigh, *loc. cit.*
77. DFA report on visit to Anti-Partition centres in six counties, 20-23 September 1955, DFA 305/14/270, *loc. cit.*
78. *Ibid.*
79. *Ibid.*
80. *Ibid.*
81. DFA report 20-23 September 1955, *op. cit.*
82. *Ibid.*
83. *Ibid.*
84. *Ibid.*
85. *Ibid.*
86. *Ibid.*
87. *Ibid.*
88. *Ibid.*
89. *Ibid.*

The 1956 Mid Ulster by-election
90. PM 4/20/18, PRONI.
91. *Ibid.*
92. *MUM,* 11 February 1956.
93. *IN,* 7 May 1956.
94. *MUO,* 14 April 1956. Unlike the pseudo-humanitarianism characterising the opposition of the Irish establishment to the campaign begun in the 1970s, its response to that of the 1950s, in tune with the spirit of the age, was authoritarian in character. The Taoiseach, John A. Costello, in his radio broadcast following the deaths of South and O'Hanlon on the Brookeborough raid in January 1957, used the words 'authority' and 'legitimacy' three and four times respectively. The bishops' Pastoral of the previous January similarly stressed the 'supreme authority of the State' as alone possessing the right to wage war. Cahir Healy, in emphasising that the existence of overwhelming British power made rebellion futile and therefore unjusti-

fiable, was expressing an attitude commonplace among Home Rulers in the pre-independence era – another reflection of how his tradition and theirs had converged within northern nationalism.

95. Healy Papers, O'Neill File, Box 8, D 2991, PRONI. Prominent people were willing to be identified with the campaign in a manner unthinkable twenty years later. And when they argued the case, they did so in an unabashedly right-wing fashion. Professor Liam Ó Briain of the Romance Languages Department of University College Galway debated with Cahir Healy the moral right of rebellion as asserted by George Washington, the Tyrolese patriot, Andreas Hofer – and General Franco!

96. Quoted in J. McGarrity (ie. Sean Cronin), *Resistance – The Story of the Stuggle in British Occupied Ireland,* 1957, p 72.

97. DFA 305/14/2, National Archive.

98. *Ibid.*

99. McGill and Healy correspondence, Healy Papers, McGill File, Box 8, see especially letter of 22 April 1966.

100. 8 February 1956, CAB 4/994/7, PRONI.

Chapter 13
The End of the APL

1. S 9361G, National Archive.

2. *Ibid.*

3. For the fullest analysis of this economic convergence see Paul Bew and Henry Patterson, *Sean Lemass and the Making of Modern Ireland,* especially chapter 5, 1982. In tandem with this process came an eventual decline in the role of British capital in the southern economy and an increased presence of US, German and Japanese firms.

4. DFA 305/14/192 C, National Archive.

5. *Ibid,* 24 August 1954.

6. S 9361, *loc. cit.*

7. *Ibid.* The accession of John F. Kennedy to the presidency in 1960 made little difference to the prospects of northern nationalists. Despite the mythology wrapped around his name by Catholic Ireland the Boston Brahman proved unreceptive to appeals from his ancestral country. 'He is by education British inclined,' wrote the Irish Ambassador to Washington, T. J. Kiernan, after a meeting with him, 'and made no secret of his attachment to Britain.' When Kiernan expressed the widely held optimism of the period that the border would gradually crumble as both countries entered the Common Market, Kennedy had replied coolly, 'Yes, that is the best way'.

8. *Ibid.*

9. *Ibid.*

10. Discussion on Partition, DFA P 203/2, National Archive, 18 September 1957.

11. Blythe memo, S 9361 G. Also Healy Papers, D 2991. Healy to Blythe, Blythe File. In the introduction to his booklet on this topic, *A New Departure in Northern Politics*, published by Basil Clancy, Blythe claimed the support of two nationalist MPs for his ideas.

12. Healy to Frank Traynor, Traynor File, Box 7, Healy Papers, *loc. cit.* See also McGill file for discussion of the threat from the Smythe-McKeown-Traynor faction. McGill to Healy, 27 March 1958, 11 June 1958, 16 November 1958; Traynor to McGill, 1 June 1958, *ibid.*

13. *AO*, 29 March 1958. The seat was run by the independent nationalist Eddie Richardson, a former all Ireland cycling champion.

14. Department of Foreign Affairs, 305/14/2/4. National Archive.

15. For Lucey's remarks in Cork see *IN*, 15 April 1958. Healy/Lucey letters, Healy to Lucey, 18 April 1958, Lucey to Healy, 23 April 1958, Correspondence with bishops, Box 10, Healy Papers, D 2991, *loc. cit.*

16. Lennon/Healy correspondence, *ibid*, Box 7.

17. DFA 305/14/2/4, National Archive.

18. *Ibid.* The League did, in fact, disappear as quietly as McAteer had wished. From the start of the new decade the term ceased to be used. 'Nationalist Party', despite what McWhite reported were its worrying Redmonite connotations to some members, replaced it. Rumpf and Hepburn relate how a branch of the APL in South Down was still unaware in the 1960s of its demise and wrote to headquarters for clarification. *Nationalism and Socialism in Ireland*, p 185.

    For an example of this new thinking see Desmond Fennell, *The Northern Catholic: An Inquiry*, Tower 1958, pamphlet based on his *IT* articles on the subject in May of that year.

19. *IN*, 18 August 1956, *SI*, 21 September 1958, *SP*, 7 September 1958.

20. *IP*, 25 October 1958 and 11 December 1958.

21. DFA P 203/2, *loc. cit.* One proposal which, had it become known, would have left the conciliation policy dead in the water came in October 1959. The Papal Nuncio, De Riberi, suggested to the Department that the best way of creating a United Ireland was by helping Catholics acquire land and encouraging the birth rate amongst them, which as he helpfully pointed out was higher in country areas than in towns.

22. *Ibid.*

23. *Ibid.* Rynne need not have worried. It was an approach which met with little sympathy from the British side. In 1957 the Cabinet in Whitehall advised its ministers attending the United Nations to avoid making any concessions to Frank Aiken who had, it noted, indicated that he time was ripe for a conciliatory response from Britain. The onus to make the first move rested in its view with the Republic. The British side poured cold water on the idea of Ireland rejoining the Commonwealth firstly by questioning De Valera's sincerity and then by recalling the disruptive effect Ireland's presence had during the years of its membership.

24. S 9361 E, deputation, 19 May 1955, National Archive.

25. S 9361, *op. cit.*

26. DFA 305/14/263 II, *loc. cit.*

27. De Valera, 1957 Ard Fheis, *IP*, 20 December 1957.

28. Interview with Ruairí Ó Brádaigh, Roscommon, 16 August 1991.

29. Cronin, *Irish Nationalism*, p. 171. Interview with Ó Conail, *Hibernia*, 24 August 1973.

30. Interview with Ó Brádaigh, *op. cit.*

31. *II*, 19 January 1957.

32. DFA/12/1/A.

33. *Ibid.*

34. *Ulster*, Sunday Times Insight Team, p 16-17. Patterson, *Politics of Illusion*, p 82.

35. Interview with Cahill, *op. cit.*

36. DFA 305/14/9/3, O'Connor information to McWhite. On 5 April 1957 Lennon told De Valera that the Cardinal was 'anxious to see him' and that 'we should do our utmost to prevent the cutting down of grants'. DFA P 273/1.

37. Ó Brádaigh boasted to this writer, 'But for the oath we would have driven right through them.' Ó Brádaigh interview, *op. cit.*

38. Diamond, *Observer*, 21 June 1959. For a republican verdict on Diamond delivered in 1985 by IRA veteran Harry White see *Harry*, Agenta Publications Dublin 1985, p 151-152. 'The only sound Irishman was Harry Diamond ... he was at our beck and call ready always to do what he could. Even in London in 1939 he allowed a select few of us to make use of his house. Diamond was a man of the people ...'

39. Interview with Patrick Marrinan, Belfast, 8 April 1991. Hanna certainly was outraged by Marrinan's intervention. 'The campaign against me was the worst I had to encounter,' he told Healy, 'Imagine the effrontery of anyone with this man's background appealing to the republican voters.' Hanna to Healy 24 March 1958, Frank Hanna Correspondence, Box 7, Healy Papers, D2991, *loc. cit.*

40. Interview with Andrew Boyd, Belfast, 19 March 1991. Hanna's own private correspondence would seem to suggest that the Labour Party's interpretation is the correct one. After seeing off Beattie's challenge in the Stormont general election of October 1953, using both the sectarian card and the anti-communist one, Hanna wrote to Healy admitting his campaign 'was somewhat rough', but delighting that he 'was able to account for Mr Beattie and those hiding behind him'. He went on to state that it really was time 'the people had their eyes opened', a remark which may indicate his intention of undermining the Labour position in West Belfast. Hanna to Healy, 27 October 1953, *ibid.*

41. Hubert Butler, *Escape from the Anthill*, Lilliput Press, 1985. For the role of the Irish church in lionising and sheltering Ustashi war crim-

inals see 'The Artukovich File', chapter in above. See *IN*, 12 October 1946, front page, on Stepinac case. A 'saintly prelate symbol of the church militant in a war against Atheistic Communism. For information on Stepinac (beatified in 1998) see Carlo Falconi, *The Silence of Piux XII*, Faber and Faber 1970, part III. Also Richard West, *Tito and the Rise and Fall of Yugoslavia*, Carroll and Graff 1994, *passim*.

42. Interview with Paddy Devlin.
43. Agnew Diary, D 1676/2, PRONI.
44. Murtagh Morgan speech, *IN*, 4 March 1958.
45. Source confidential.
46. Fergus McAteer information, 3 May 1992. Though the veteran socialist Eamon McCann recalls McAteer's canvassers booming out the sectarian message 'The Protestants are voting for McGonagle'. Information to author.
47. Interview with Devlin, *op. cit.*

Chapter 14
A New Beginning?

1. *IN*, 18 March.
2. *Ibid.*
3. *National Unity*, no 2, October 1963.
4. DE debates, 22 February 1961.
5. Lemass to Donaghy, 16 January 1961, S 9361K/61, National Archive.
6. *The Scotsman*, 12 February 1961.
7. DFA p 338/1, *loc. cit.*
8. D/T 516272, Childers to Lemass 1 March 1961, loc. cit.
9. DFA 305/14/341, Aiken to Lemass 27 March 1962, in reply to Lemass query 3 March 1962, Lemass to Healy 31 March 62, *loc. cit.*
10. *Ibid.*
11. *Ibid.*
12. In January Cremin had told the Taoiseach that north-south co-operation was not as good as it should be because of Stormont's insistence on recognition of the constitutional position. D/T S 9361 IC 63, Cremin to Lemass 19-1-63 , National Archive. Lemass' Tralee speech IT 30-6-63, Colley remarks, *IP*, 17 April 1963, Lemass to Coogan 7 September 1963, S 9361 K 63, *loc. cit.*
13. DFA 305/14/303. Gallagher to Department, August 1964.
14. Circular marked to all embassies, DFA 305/14/170/3, *loc. cit.*
15. See John Horgan, *Sean Lemass the Enigmatic Patriot*, Gill and MacMillan, p 270. Also DFA 305/14/325, *loc. cit.*
16. D/T S 9361 K 63, Cremin to McCann, 15 November 1963, *loc. cit.*.
17. *Ibid.*
18. *IN*, March 1962.
19. McAteer Papers, in possession of McAteer family, Derry.
20. Healy to McCool (McCuile), 15 March 1963, Box 8 D 2991, *loc. cit.*
21. C. McCluskey to E. McAteer, 1 July 1963, McAteer Papers, *loc. cit.*

22. *IP*, 18 December 1963.
23. *IN*, 3 January 1964.
25. McCluskey to McAteer, 1 July 1963, McAteer to McCluskey, 19 August 1963, McCluskey to McAteer, 8 May 1964, McAteer Papers, *loc. cit.*
26. McAteer, *IN*, 9 September 1964.
27. McAteer to McCluskey, 19 August 1963, in possession of McAteer family, Derry.
28. McAteer to Healy, 28 September 1964, McAteer File, Box 7, Healy Papers, *loc. cit.* McAteer wrote to republicans in November asking them to join a united political party, see *IN*, 3 November 1964.
29. Healy Papers, 29 October 1964, McAteer File, Box 7, PRONI.
30. Replies contained in McAteer Papers (uncatalogued), loc. cit. Wilson rebuff to McGill, *DJ*, 17 January 1964.
31. McAteer, 'Letters First Step', *BT*, 17 November 1964. McAteer File, Box 7, Healy Papers, D 2991, *loc. cit.*
32. *IN*, 21 November 1964. Also McAteer Papers, *loc. cit.*
33 *Ibid.*
34. *Ibid.*
35. *IN*, 16 January 1965.
36. Carron to Healy, 23 January 1965, Carron File, Healy Papers, D 2991, Box 7, *loc. cit.* See Carron's admission on the decision to become the official opposition in Micheál Ó Cuinneagáin, *Partition from Michael Collins to Bobby Sands*, pp 36, 37 (NP) 1986.
37. Newtownbutler speech, *IP*, 30 July 1965.
38. *IN*, 24 November 1965. *IN*, 29 March 1965.
39. *IN*, 18 March 1966, *II*, 19 March 1966. McGill to Healy, 22 April 1966, Healy Papers, D 2991, Box 7, *loc. cit.*
40. Healy to McGill, *op. cit.*
41. McGill/Healy correspondence.
42. The political significance of the AOH had by this stage almost to vanishing point. A 1971 survey (Rose, p 260) showed 69% of Catholics unaware what the organisation represented. It remained insignificant within the SDLP. Only one 1973 SDLP. assembly representatives, Hugh News, was a member. The Rose survey also showed widespread acceptance of the Easter Rising. 60% of Catholics believed it 'was right' for people in the south to take up arms and fight in order to make the Republic. *Governing Without Consensus: An Irish Perspective*, Appendix, 1971, p 483.
43. Kevin O'Connor's *The Irish in Britain*, Torc Books, 1974, p 76. Two years earlier, in January 1964, the senior Dublin's civil servant Cornelius Cremin told his colleague Hugh McCann that he was 'particularly interested' in the new approach of northern nationalists (focusing on injustice rather than partition) as it seemed close to a policy which an internal minute circulated within the department two years previously had suggested was 'worth examining'. DFA

p 338/2., Cremin to McCann, 13 January 1964. A letter on this subject by Patrick Gormley MP to the new statesman three days previously may have inspired the above comment.

44. DFA P/338, 3 November 1966, *loc. cit.*

45. *Ibid.*

46. Interview with McCluskey, 22 November 1989, Pat Kenny Show, RTÉ Radio 1. DFA 305/14/340, 8 December 1967. It also emphasised that Dublin had stood aloof from the efforts of the CDU and Gerry Fitt at Westminster to break through the convention system and resurrect section 75 of the Government of Ireland Act. The issue of discrimination was in Dublin's view an extremely emotive one with a high political content and therefore 'outside the scope' of north-south discussions. McCluskey had hoped amongst other things to obtain Irish government support for the taking of a case to the Court of Human Rights on the issue. As an acceptable solution the memorandum proposed De Valera's compromise pre-Treaty 'Cuban solution' of a united Ireland with safeguards for the interests of the western powers. On the advice to overseas missions, see Rohan to Dept, 17 Feb 1965, DFA 2001/43/304, *loc. cit.*

47. McGill to Healy, *op. cit.*

48. Hogg to McAteer, McAteer Papers, 6 October 1966; Jenkins to McAteer, McAteer Papers, 28 November 1967, *loc. cit.* Jenkins had simply acknowledged the letter in October 1966. For the response to McCluskey see *Up off our Knees*, 1989, p 32. The kindest interpretation to place on Britain's behaviour is that the government wished (and Labour occasionally pushed) to improve matters in the north but trusted in the *bona fides* of O'Neill and those around him. Certainly Harold Wilson's professed concern on the issue was taken at face value by Patricia McCluskey and not seen merely as a bid for the Irish vote. Peter Rose, *How the troubles came to Northern Ireland,* MacMillan 2000, offers the best exposition of this benign interpretation. On the other hand sceptics can point to the *Sunday Times* Insight Team's revelation that Wilson said regarding Alec Douglas Home in the 1964 election campaign, 'Any politician who wants to get involved with Ulster ought to have his head examined.' In five years, the Insight Team pointed out, the Home Secretary Sir Frank Soskice only visited the province once – for an afternoon. *Ulster,* pp 80-81, Penguin 1972.

49. *Autobiography of Terence O'Neill,* Rupert Hart Davis, 1972, p 78-79, 87.

50. *CC,* 22 October 1966.

51. McAteer to Dillon, 17 June 1967; Lennon to McAteer, 26 June 1967; McGill letter, 21 June 1967, McAteer Papers, *loc. cit.*

52. *IN,* 5 July 1967.

53. DFA, 305/14/359.

54. McGill to McAteer, 30 November 1965, McAteer Papers.

55. *Ibid.*

56. *Ibid.*
57. McGill to McAteer, 19 April 1967, McAteer Papers, *loc. cit.* For a vivid account of the CDU's Northern tour by one of the MPs involved see Paul Rose, *Backbencher's Dilemma*, London 1981, pp 179-196.
58. McAteer speech, *IN*, 20 April 1967.
59. *II*, 16 September 1964.
60. M. Morgan, 'The Northern Ireland Civil Rights Movement: A Reassessment', unpublished MSSc thesis, Queen's University of Belfast, 1983.
61. Minutes of special conference, 27 November 1968, McAteer Papers, *loc. cit.*
62. McAteer had hoped for a suitable replacement from within the ranks of the Derry Nationalist Party. John Hume, on a visit to his house, had allegedly denied any intention of contesting the seat. Only when McAteer heard of Hume's nomination did he decide, on the urging of his organisation, to enter the lists. (Information to author.)
63. Minutes of Derry Nationalist Party, McAteer Papers, *loc. cit.*
64. McSparran was to write to Healy regretting the latter's departure from Stormont where he could expose 'the cynical attitude of the Dublin government', 18 October 1968, Box 10, D 2991, PRONI.
65. McAteer remarks, *IN*, 23 June 1968.
66. McAteer to Friel, 27 February 1969, McAteer Papers, *loc. cit.*
67. Hume's remarks, 19 May 1964. Michael Viney articles, *Irish Times*, 14-20 May 1964. On the takeover of the Civil Rights campaign in Derry see McCann, *War and an Irish Town*, especially pp 43-49.
68. Article by McCann, *IT*, 6 October 1971.
69. Article by Michael Morgan, 'The Catholic Middle Class: Myth or Reality', in *L'Irlande Revue Politique et Sociale*, vol 1, no 3, New Sorbonne University publication. For a restatement of the Education Act mythology see Humbert School speech by Father Denis Faul, *Western People*, 8 September 1992.
70. 'Nationalist Approach Since 1920', draft of article by Healy, D 2991, Box II, PRONI. It is also worth bearing in mind that most of the data regarding discrimination and gerrymandering which figured in CSJ and civil rights publications had been compiled over the decades by nationalists and presented repeatedly to deaf ears. It was not researched *de novo*.
71. McAteer to Corinne Philpott, 24 March 1969, McAteer Papers, *loc. cit.*
72. As a cult book of the period pointed out, the educational effect of watching Police State tactics on television seems to vary with the attitude the watcher brings with him; if he is already pro 'law and order' or anti-demonstration he will see only confirmation of his attitude. Martin Oppenheimer, *Urban Guerrilla*, Penguin 1970 (Quadrangle 1969, USA) p 124. Members of the northern minority

through their acculturation were predisposed to see the spectacle of their co-religionists being beaten by policemen drawn from the 'other side' in only one way. Opinion poll data in Rose, *Governing Without Consensus, op. cit.*, pp 194, 195 and 530 note 22.

Chapter 15
Flashpoint

1. S 9361 M, National Archive, Dublin.
2. Report of Currie, O'Reilly visit, 16 August 1969, S 9361 M, National Archive.
3. Report marked 'secret' visit of Northern Ireland MPs to Department, S 9361 N, National Archive.
4. *Ibid.*
5. *Ibid.*
   Note of discussion at the Foreign Office at 12.50 p.m. on Friday 1 August 1969, S 9361, *loc. cit.* Aiken had in April ruled out UN involvement after a meeting with U Thant, the Secretary General. His wish was he said to 'line up Britain to end the discrimination as a first step'. As far back as March 1962 he had advised Lemass against it on the grounds that it might, by winning Soviet support, alienate the United States and other countries 'of importance to us'. See also N 157.
6. *Ibid.*
7. *Ibid.*
8. Discussion at Foreign and Commonwealth Office London on 15 August concerning Northern Ireland. S 9361 N, *loc. cit.*
9. Memorandum for the information of the government re bringing the situation in the north before the UN, 16 August 1969, *loc. cit.*
10. *Ibid.*
11. E. Staunton, 'The 1925 Agreement Aftermath and Implications' *History Ireland*, summer 1996.
12. Discussion at Foreign and Commonwealth Office, *op. cit.*
13. S 9361, *op. cit.*
14. McCann to Department, 20 August 1969, report marked secret, S 9361 N, *loc. cit.*
15. Report of UN meeting, S 9361 O, *loc. cit.* Sean Cronin, *Washington's Irish Policy 1916-1986*, Anvil 1987, p 300. James Callaghan, *A House Divided*, Collins 1973, pp 51-53.
16. Memorandum re bringing the situation in north before UN, *op. cit.*
17. Report on General Assembly debate, S 9361. Report to Department on probable voting pattern of general assembly executive, 23 September 1969, stated that China, Equador, Poland, Mongolia, Panama and the USSR were the 'not more than six countries' likely to support Ireland's case. The 8-10 likely to oppose it included Britain, France, Ghana and the United States. The rest were likely to abstain.

18. Ireland's canvass produced some interesting results. The government of General Franco appeared sympathetic as did the Indian government. Though both promised help they were not numbered among the likely supporters. In Holland the Catholic press proved surprisingly hostile with most support from the socialists and liberals. The French Ambassador, Bernard, told the Irish on 8 September that he wished to help 'behind the scenes' but had to make an outward show of opposition given (a) Article 2.7 of the UN charter and its general policy on secession, (b) France's own attitude to the recent Algerian crisis, (c) France's inability to give open support to Biafra for the above reasons despite her deep sympathy for the secessionists.

19. E. Staunton, 'The Case of Biafra: Ireland and the Nigerian Civil War', *Irish Historical Studies*, Vol XXX1, No 134, pp 513-534.

20. Staunton, 'The 1925 Agreement', *History Ireland, op. cit.*

21. Notes on the present situation, S 9361 P, *loc. cit.*

22. *Ibid.*

23. *Ibid.*

24. For all the emotion the events of August 1969 evoked, the south's cabinet ministers seemed happy to allow Britain get on with the job. For a vivid pen picture of this see the account by the only member of government to resign his seat in protest at Dublin's northern policy, Kevin Boland, *We Won't Stand (Idly) by*, Kelly Lane Ltd (nd), chapter 5. Some of his colleagues were apparently annoyed at being recalled from their summer holidays to discuss the crisis.

25. Though various events north of the border were to produce temporary reversions to the 'ad hoc' policy, the 'permanent policy' lived up to its title becoming the cornerstone of the government approach to the question. In the late Autumn and Winter of 1969, Iveagh House officials perfected this policy in consultation with Irish diplomatic missions worldwide. Co-operation with the north was encouraged, the 'use of force, emotionalism and opportunism' abjured, the advocacy of unity to become a 'soft sell', and southern public opinion to be educated in these new attitudes. Later, on 28 May 1970, an interdepartmental unit was established by the Department of the Taoiseach which held its first meeting, under the chairmanship of S. J. Ronan, on 18 June. It considered the question of Irish reunification as one which was likely to last a generation and involve three stages. The first stage, lasting perhaps a year, entailed reforms within the north. An intermediate stage would require greater cooperation between both parts of Ireland to break down prejudices. The final stage would move from this to a united Ireland. D/T S 18576, 2001/6/SG.

26. The first stirrings of a policy of repression, censorship and exclusion were to be see that autumn with some dismissals from the Irish army and with a controversy over the 'subversive' content of a

school textbook. As the IRA campaign escalated in the north, censorship was tightened (the RTÉ authority was sacked in 1972) and a climate of detachment from traditional nationalist pieties was fostered, e.g. the official Easter commemorative marches were abandoned in 1971.

27. *IN*, October 1969. It is important to remember that throughout the O'Neillite period the RUC had benefited from the decrease in communal tension. To Senator O'Hare as far back as 1963 they were 'a fine body of men who are doing a good job'. Early in 1968 McAteer at Stormont supported 'without qualification' a proposal to grant a supplementary estimate of £29,000 for the B Specials. See Bew, Gibbon and Patterson, *The State in Northern Ireland 1921-1972*, p 169. The events of October 1968 came as a shock to the collective psyche of Catholics, an indication that traditional prejudices might have been right after all. The Hunt Report and other reforms helped restore the balance once more. By April 1970, Catholics accounted for 20% of the membership of the UDR (Ulster Defence Regiment) and 40% of applicants to join the reconstituted RUC.

28. Sean Óg Ó Fearghall (i.e. Michael Dolly), *Law and Whose Orders?: The Story of the Falls Road Curfew*. The culture of censorship (frequently of the self-censorship variety) had taken off unprompted from an early stage in some quarters that were later to become notorious for it. In November 1970 when 'Seán Óg Ó Fearghall' (i.e. Michael Dolly) published his pamphlet on the Falls Road curfew, the Irish government, despite reservations, was prepared to purchase 500 copies and help cover the cost. The distribution arm of Independent Newspapers, however, refused point blank to handle the booklet.

29. The Provisional IRA, *Freedom Struggle*, 1973.

30. Seán MacStiofáin, *Memoirs of a Revolutionary*, Gordon Cremonisi, 1975, p 139-140.

31. *Fianna Fáil and the IRA*, Official Sinn Féin publication.

32. Berry Diary, *Magill* Magazine, July 1980. It is also the case that a Department of Justice memorandum of that time urged an 'active political campaign' to split 'the IRA organisation' and discredit 'the communist element', within it. The marginalisation of Republican Congress in the 1930s; a result of a church and state supported Red Scare, was the example it wished the Irish establishment to follow.

33. The archive releases for 2001 go some way towards confirming the view that the militant policy had government sanction; the view taken by the jury in the arms trial cleared all the defendants of *illegal* arms importation. It has, for instance, been shown that on 6 February 1970 the Cabinet considered the question of incursions into Northern Ireland in the event of a doomsday situation. It has also been revealed that evidence to the first arms trial was doctored within official circles in order to exculpate the Defence Minister, Jim Gibbons, of involvement. See Justin O'Brien, *The Arms Crisis*, Gill &

MacMillan, Dublin 2000. Also Kevin Boland, *Up Dev*, Dublin 1977, and James Kelly, *Orders for the Captain* (publ. Kelly nd.). Also Dick Walsh, *The Party, Inside Fianna Fáil*. McAteer gave support to both tracks of Irish government policy. On May 8 1970 while reaffirming his support for the Lynch line he called for an 'end to Blaney bashing', reminding people of the latter's service to the Bogsiders and pledging the previous August that the minority would not submit 'like sheep to the slaughter' in any future crisis scenario.

34. E. McCann, *War and an Irish Town*, Penguin 1974, p 82-83. Unlike Dixieland African Americans, the Northern Catholics had an explanatory anti-state meaning system, that of nationalism, to refer to if the goal of reforming the system was seen to fail.

35. Despite this carefully fostered official culture of hostility to all things and persons perceived as sympathetic to the Provisional IRA much of southern public opinion remained stubbornly intractable. At the end of the 1970s a government sponsored survey concluded, on the basis of empirical data collected, that 'opposition to IRA activities is not overwhelming and certainly does not match the strong opposition so often articulated by public figures'. E. E. Davis and Richard Sinott, 'Attitudes in the Republic of Ireland relevant to the Northern Ireland problem', Economic and Social Research Institute Paper No 97, September 1979, Dublin Government publication.

36. Secretary to Taoiseach, 14 February 1970. Reply to Mr Holmes, 23 February 1970, DFA 305/14/360, National Archive.

37. *Ibid.*

38. It was not likely to do it too much harm west of the Bann either. McAteer had successfully adopted the 'left of centre' tag despite McGill's objections. To veteran socialists this sudden adoption of a left-wing nomenclature was galling. Eamon McCann, ever ready with a picturesque phrase, remarked that it was 'the greatest mass conversion since General Kim Li Tsu baptised a regiment of Chinese soldiers into Christianity with a fire-hose'. Given both the SDLP's later willingness to use the Red Scare tactic against Sinn Féin and to accept funding from the CIA-backed National Endowment for Democracy, recent revelations about the origins of the party have a ring of truth about them. These suggest that the primary impulse behind its foundation was the fear of NICRA becoming contaminated by 'extreme republicans and extreme left wingers'. Hume expressed this view privately to Iveagh House officials. See Justin O'Brien, *The Arms Trial*, Gill and Macmillan 2000, p 162. Hume also went on record to the German press claiming that the British Labour Party was 'too socialist'. Paul Routledge, *John Hume: A Biography*, Harper Collins 2001, p 91.

On the April 1984 meeting of the SDLP with the National Endowment for Democracy, see Kevin Kelley, *The Longest War: Northern Ireland and the IRA*, revised ed., Brandon Books 1989, p 363.

39. See Barry White, *John Hume: Statesman of the Troubles,* Blackstaff 1984, p 100. In fact, leading members of the SDLP were extremely worried that certain nationalists would join the new party. Both Eddie McAteer and Roderick O'Connor were *personae non grata* in this regard. Devlin and Hume confirmed this independently to Eamon Gallagher of the Department of External Affairs. The visit of Devlin and Fitt to the Irish Labour Party in Dublin in September 1970 was related to this question of keeping out undesirables. The SDLP made overtures to both the Unity MPs, Bernadette Devlin (Mid Ulster) and Frank McManus (Fermanagh South Tyrone), but were rebuffed. D/T 2001/6/57.

40. Paddy Devlin interview with author, *op. cit.*

41. Some nationalists and ex-nationalists stood aloof from the 'Assembly of the Northern Irish People' formed by the MPs who withdrew. Senator Patrick McGill described it as a serious error. Thomas Gormley declared he had no intention of attending. The decision to withdraw from Stormont caused consternation in Dublin's Department of Foreign Affairs (the term External Affairs had been scrapped earlier in the year). Officials saw in it an attempt by Hume to outflank the Nationalist Party and to elicit southern support for a condominium strategy which they feared as too extreme. Dublin deliberated as to whether they should (a) endorse Hume's decision, (b) temporise, or (c) reveal that they had privately protested about the deaths to Britain. Characteristically they opted for (b).

42. Information from Ruairí Ó Brádaigh.

43. SDLP Front Bench member, 1970s, P. A. McLoughlin. Information to author.

The computation of the nationalist electorate as 337,716 (McAllister) gave the SDLP 47.3% and 46.2% of the Catholic vote in the 1973 assembly and 1975 Convention elections respectively. In November 1949 Frank Gallagher, of the Mansion House anti-Partition conference, commented in a letter that the 1921 vote of 165,293 with 12 seats was 'the minimum they should get' as it represented 23% of the seats 'whereas they probably are 34% of the electorate'. In fact it was their maximum. He attributed this failure during the PR period to the 'aftermath of the pogroms' and the Treaty split with consequent three cornered contests.

Epilogue

1. One party which provided a focus for a stronger nationalism than provided by the SDLP was the Irish Independence Party (IIP) founded in 1977. Headed by former unity MP for Fermanagh South Tyrone Frank McManus (brother of the 1950s IRA leader Pat McManus) and Eddie McAteer's son Fergus, it secured representation on councils in Antrim, Derry, Down, Fermanagh and Tyrone. Its biggest success came in the Westminster election of 1979 when

Pat Fahy, an Omagh solicitor, secured over 12,000 votes to the 19,000 plus obtain by the SDLP (the seat was won by the official unionist). In many ways both in personnel and policies the IPP was a reprise of the Nationalist Party. Eddie McAteer himself joined its Derry branch. It vanished for want of space when Sinn Féin entered the electoral.

2. The *Irish News* editorial remarked a propos of the Cardinal's visit: 'on the face of it this is not the time to bring up this lingering issue. To do so is to be labelled a provisional sympathiser or to act as their propagandist.' Quoted in Liam Clarke, *Broadening the Battlefield: The H Blocks and the Rise of Sinn Féin*, p 95, Gill and MacMillan, 1987.

3. See Fitzgerald's autobiography, *All in a Life*, 1991, p 462. The opportunism of the reversion to more traditional rhetoric was acknowledged by Iveagh House officials. 'It is a side road for a year or so to pick up a problem. Once we have dealt with the repairs, we will be back on the main road again.' 'The Greening of Foreign Affairs', *Magill* Magazine, November 1984. Within the SDLP Seamus Mallon told the 1985 conference that any attempt to place Irish unity on the back burner hands the 'initiative to the boys in the balaclavas, as had happened,' he stated, in South Armagh.

4. 'These are also out', John Hume, *SP*, 6 November 1984.

5. *BT*, 5 October 1988.

6. Ibid, 6 February 1985.

7. David E. Schmitt, *The Irony of Irish Democracy*, Lexington Publications, 1973, provides an interesting theoretical analysis of how the authoritarian content of Irish culture co-exists with the absence of any major departure from the democratic form of government since the state was established..

8. A willingness to measure human rights violations, north and south, by different yardsticks has always been a characteristic of northern nationalism as several examples from this work demonstrate. As far back as November 1923 Harbinson, the Tyrone MP, could compare northern prison conditions to the 'black hole of Calcutta' and in the next sentence deny any analogy with prison conditions in the south. See HA/5/1804.

9. *The Good Old IRA: Tan War Operations*, introduction, November 1965.

10. Gerry Adams, *The Politics of Irish Freedom*, p 154. In an attempt to achieve just this his party had periodically and unsuccessfully sought a pre-election agreement with the SDLP. During the 1988 talks between the two parties, Belfast Sinn Féin Councillor, Mairtin Ó Muilleoir, defined their position as being merely 'a few degrees to the left of the SDLP', a considerable backpedalling on the radicalism of earlier years and one re-echoed by other voices.

A Sinn Féin position paper described the southern state as a 'Social Democracy'. One prominent Belfast activist in the *Irish News* regretted that they had 'in the past' tended to view the SDLP as 'a class enemy' while Adams, in what sounded suspiciously like a proposal to revive the 1949 Mansion House All-Party Committee, hinted at a possible suspension of the IRA campaign based on a union of anti-partitionist forces (*IT*, June 1988).

IRA Volunteers facing extradition have argued and argued successfully to the southern Supreme Court that their campaign was designed merely to extend the limits of the 1937 Constitution.

11. Frank Burton, *The Politics of Legitimacy, Struggles in a Belfast Community*, p 121, Routledge and Kegan Paul 1978. Of the 45 Belfast IRA volunteers killed on active service in the period 1969-75 only 10 came from a republican background, Robert W. White, *Provisional Irish Republicanism, an Oral and Interpretive History*, p 85, Greenwood 1983. In White's view it signified the progression from 'a kin based conspiratorial clan to a mass movement'.

12. Interview with IRA Army Council representative, *Magill*, August 1978.

13. Of the original 20 on the caretaker executive of Sinn Féin in 1970 10 of them from 26 counties remained in November 1986 at the time of the second split. 9 of these ten joined the breakaway group 'Republican Sinn Féin'. Of the 21 members of this organisation's first executive only 2 came from Northern Ireland, White, *op. cit.*, p 157.

14. John H. Whyte, *Interpreting Northern Ireland*, Oxford 1990. For a discussion of this topic following on the publication of the yearly British Social Attitude Survey, see Garret Fitzgerald, 'Vision of Northern Ireland Catholics outbreeding Protestants is a dangerous myth', *Irish Times*, 26 July 1997. Niall O'Dowd reply 30 July, Daltún Ó Ceallaigh, rejoinder, 31 July. See also *Is there a concurring majority about Northern Ireland?* R. Rose, I. McAllister, main Opinion Research Centre, Strathclyde University, 1991.

15. For an analysis of this data see David Smith and Gerald Chambers, *Inequality in Northern Ireland*, Chapter 3, Clarendon Press, 1991.

Overview and Conclusion

1. DP 6734/197, TCD Archive. Even in those constituencies where the Logue agreement was observed, mass abstentionism took place by the other Catholic side. Dillon calculated a shortfall of over 5,000 in the Sinn Féin vote for Harbinson in North-East Tyrone.

2. Calculated election percentages from Knight and Baxter-Moore, *Northern Ireland: The Elections of the 20s*, and J. R. Wilson, *PR Urban Elections in Ulster*. That Sinn Féin's Ulster vote was predominantly rural, young and non-owner/occupier is shown by the greater Home Rule vote in the January 1920 election, conducted on the old franchise.

3. John McCoy recollection, *OMN*, P 17/B/116, UCD Archive.

4. Calculation from *The Last Post: Details and Stories of Republican Dead*, National Graves Association, 1975.

5. *DD*, 20 August 1919.
6. *Ibid*, 16 December 1919.
7. *IN*, 13, 14, 15 March 1922, on reaction of Smithfield branch to Councillor O'Kane's proposal.
8. Daly himself complained of this to GHQ: 'The principal characteristic of most northerners is the suspicion of all strangers.' OMP, UCD Archive, P 17/A.184.
9. Reply of De Valera to Dr Gillespie, Cookstown. De Valera Papers, T/16/31, 29 November 1921, p 178.
10. Lord Longford, *Peace by Ordeal*, NEL 1935.
11. Maureen Wall, 'The Ulster Struggle 1916-1926' in T. D. Williams, *The Irish Struggle*, p 87.
12. O'Connor to Dillon, 8 April 1922, Dillon Papers, 6744, 884, TCD Archive.
13. The offer was made by Cosgrave in August 1923. R. F. Whitford, 'Joe Devlin: Ulsterman and Irishman', MA thesis, final chapter, University of London, 1957.
14. Report to Colonial Office from Northern Ireland Secretary and Cabinet, CAB 6/18, PRONI. John McGuffin, *Internment*, note 6, p 175, Anvil 1973, speculates Devlin expressed more indignation over a search of Cardinal Logue's car than over internment because the minority was inured to coercion bills. There is, as can be seen, another explanation.
15. S 11209.
16. *Ibid*.
17. O'Higgins memo, Stephens Papers, 4328, TCD Archive.
18. Intelligence Report dated 7 December 1923, O'Malley Papers, P 17/A/178, UCD Archive. Catholic abstention in West Belfast was considerable. The *IN*, 8 December 1923, estimated it at 12,000. Midgley got 22,255 votes in all but failed to secure the seat.
19. Fascism was essentially a militarised attempt to destroy the labour movement, which ended up being itself destroyed by what was arguably that movement's greatest achievement, the Soviet Union. The Second World War did not have the character of a morality play which has been conferred on it after the fact. Western powers, including Britain, attempted unsuccessfully to divert Germany's attention eastwards through the Munich Pact of 1938. When that strategy collapsed with the attack on Poland (a fascist anti-Semitic state involved in the Munich carve up), a series of alliances drew those powers into war with Germany. Down to the summer of 1940 Britain tried to bring Italy, the cradle of fascism, into the war on her side.

    Prominent British and unionist pre-war collaborators included Lord Londonderry who made no secret of his anti-Jewish views (He even published a book, *Ourselves and Germany*, 1938.) and enjoyed a close relationship with Hitler's Foreign Minister, Von Ribbentrop.

Even before the war's end, Britain recruited right-wing collaborators into a Greek puppet government to Undercut ELAS, the left-
wing resistance. The defeat of Germany and the fear of Soviet advance saw the western allies collude in sheltering war criminals and
making the promise of denazification a non-starter. When set beside
all of the above, the actions of the northern nationalists seem almost
innocent.

On western intentions at Munich, see Paul Schmidt, *Hitler's
Interpreter*, London 1950. On Lord Londonderry and the other UK
collaborators, see Richard Griffiths, *Fellow Travellers of the Right:
British Enthusiasts for Nazi Germany, 1933-39*, OUP 1980. On Greece,
see Richard Gott, 'A Greek Tragedy to haunt the Old Guard', in *The
Guardian*, 6 July 1986 (An article related to the broadcast of a contro-
versial documentary.) Also Constantine Tsoucalas, *The Greek
Tragedy*, Penguin 1969. On the failure to denazify Germany, see
Tom Bower, *Blind Eye to Murder: Britain, America and the purging of
Nazi Germany – a pledge betrayed*, Paladin 1983.

20. Roisin McAonghusa, Lemass's private secretary, replying to AOH
    in America, S 9361/K/62, 5th March 1962.
21. McAteer, IP, 10th July 1962.
22. For a somewhat coloured account of the nationalist response, see
    Conor Cruise O'Brien, *States of Ireland*, 1972, p 141.
23. For the Dublin response to the Nationalist overtures see S 9361/
    K/62, National Archive. See also note 5 on U.N. proposal and
    Aiken's response.
24. The degree to which the Civil Rights movement raised a Catholic
    consciousness of discrimination can be seen in Rose's 1969 survey.
    Of the 74% of Northern Catholics who believed that their community
    was 'treated unfairly' 36% knew of discrimination from 'personal
    knowledge', 38% were in the 'only heard' read about it' category.
    Governing Without Consensus: An Irish Perspective, Rose, p 497.
25. J. H. White, 'How Much Discrimination was there under the
    Unionist Regime 19221-1968?' in Contemporary Irish Studies, 1983,
    p 30-31.
26. Rose, *op. cit.*, p 228.

Index